Introduction to E-business

To Debbie and Richard

Introduction
to
E-business
Management and
strategy

PARK LEARNING CENTRE
UNIVERSITY OF GLOUCESTERSHIRE
PO Box 220, The Park
Cheltenham GL50 2RH
Tel: 01242 714333

Colin Combe

AMSTERDAM • BOSTON • HEIDELBERG • LONDON • NEW YORK • OXFORD
PARIS • SAN DIEGO • SAN FRANCISCO • SINGAPORE • SYDNEY • TOKYO
Butterworth-Heinemann is an imprint of Elsevier

ELSEVIER

Butterworth-Heinemann is an imprint of Elsevier
Linacre House, Jordan Hill, Oxford OX2 8DP
30 Corporate Drive, Suite 400, Burlington, MA 01803

First edition 2006

British Library Cataloguing in Publication Data
A catalogue record for this book is available from the British Library

Library of Congress Cataloguing in Publication Data Control Number: 2005938727

ISBN−13: 978-0-7506-6731-9
ISBN−10: 0-7506-6731-1

For information on all Butterworth-Heinemann publications
visit our website at http://books.elsevier.com

Printed and bound in The Netherlands
06 07 08 09 10   10 9 8 7 6 5 4 3 2 1

Contents

Preface

The twentieth century will be remembered for the rapid changes in technology every bit as much as the social and political upheavals that changed the lives of so many people. In fact, such has been the speed of development of new products, devices and gadgets that it is often easy to become ambivalent about technological advance. However, some inventions are of such life-changing significance that they make everyone sit up and take notice. Few technologies can be considered revolutionary in the impact they have had on society. Certainly, the telephone, television, air travel and some medical advances can be considered revolutionary in this context.

To this list can be added the internet as a means of communication. Although there are some sections of society for whom the internet remains an alien device, the majority of people in countries with internet access have made use of this technology for a myriad of reasons, including education, entertainment, information, business and communication. The internet has been a catalyst for change in the way people communicate and has drawn the attention of diverse bodies including government, police and security agencies, the legal profession, public sector organisations, educational establishments and many, many more.

The business community has been fundamentally changed by the advent of the internet as a means of communication and trading. The development of the World Wide Web in the mid 1990s opened up the commercial viability of the internet as, for the first time, ordinary citizens were able to access the resources that it held. Soon, the number of websites increased from tens of thousands to millions. The internet has become an integral part of many organisations' means of undertaking business. It can be used as an additional channel through which businesses communicate with and trade with customers (business-to-consumer, B2C) and suppliers and partners (business-to-business, B2B).

The internet and related technologies, such as intranets and extranets, also help organisations to increase efficiency in their internal processes. From a business perspective, the internet has had a profound effect on the way firms operate, how they communicate with others, what products they produce, how they deliver products and services, and how they seek competitive advantage. The internet has changed the 'rules' of trading by presenting new challenges and opportunities and altering the way firms engage and build relationships with customers.

This book is designed to highlight the key issues that affect businesses who have adopted the internet as a means of trading or improving internal processes. Electronic business (e-business) is the use of the internet for these purposes. Consequently, e-business has implications for a range of issues affecting an organisation, including the adoption of technology, choice of business models, economics, marketing, legal and security issues, management and the strategies for gaining a competitive advantage. This book highlights and explains the nature and characteristics of e-business in the context of each of these key issues. Examples of e-business applications are a feature of the book and these help the process of comprehending how the internet has been used to different effects in different business settings.

Following on from the discussions of the key issues, the book then focuses on the management of e-business and the formulation, implementation and evaluation of e-business strategies. These chapters bring together elements of the key issues to articulate how organisations manage their resources and create strategies for gaining competitive advantage through undertaking e-business. Gaining and sustaining competitive advantage is a theme that runs throughout the book, but its importance to the viability of internet-based firms (or firms that use the internet for some aspects of their business) is such that it is afforded its own chapter. The book chapters close with analysis of the stages of evolution that e-business has traversed since the commercialisation of the internet in the mid 1990s as well as some informed speculation as to the future prospects of e-business. The book also contains five case studies of well-known organisations that have successfully (or not in the case of boo.com) harnessed the attributes of the internet to create such compelling value propositions that they have been able to build global businesses through their online activities.

The structure and content of this book has been compiled to help undergraduate and postgraduate students new to the subject of e-business understand the key issues from both theoretical and practical perspectives. The book is also a valuable source of guidance and information for practitioners seeking an insight into the key issues affecting an e-business venture. There are many books covering different aspects of the internet, some focus on the technology, others on marketing or economics. There has, in recent years, been a proliferation of books on the security and legal aspects of the internet. Many business and management books incorporate elements of online trading into the narrative or as featured case studies.

This book uses rigorous academic theories and practical examples to bring together the business, management and strategic issues relating to e-business in a coherent and lucid manner to help the process of learning for students and practitioners seeking an introduction to e-business. In particular, the book offers readers an insight into how organisations can build an effective e-business venture using a mix of resources and capabilities. There are practical issues relating to security, law, economics and human resources that provide the basis for creating an effective e-business. This is complemented by an outline of the main business models that can be adopted as a means of competing in the e-business environment. The chapters on formulating and implementing a strategy for e-business provide a guide to the stages involved in developing a coherent strategy that is geared towards leveraging a competitive advantage by engaging in e-business activities.

Acknowledgements

The author would like to thank the editorial team at Butterworth-Heinemann in Oxford for their help in producing this book. In particular, thanks go to commissioning editor Maggie Smith and editorial assistant Francesca Ford. I would also like to express my gratitude to the reviewers of the book proposal for invaluable advice and guidance in determining the content and structure of the book: Andrew Slade, Sunderland University; Linda Macaulay, UMIST; and Maurice Mulvenna, Ulster University. I am also grateful to Caledonian Business School for providing me with the time and resources needed to commit to this challenge. Finally, thanks to Debbie and Richard for their patience and encouragement during the writing of this book.

CHAPTER 1

Introduction

Key issues:

- Defining e-business;
- The development of the new economy;
- Types of e-business and related industries;
- The growth of e-business;
- Use of the internet;
- Key people;
- Scope of the book;
- Structure of the book.

Defining e-business

Electronic business (e-business) can be defined as the use of the internet to network and empower business processes, electronic commerce, organizational communication and collaboration within a company and with its customers, suppliers, and other stakeholders. E-businesses utilise the internet, intranets, extranets and other networks to support their commercial processes. Electronic commerce (e-commerce) is the buying and selling, marketing and servicing of products and services via computer networks. Since e-business includes the process of transacting with suppliers and customers there is an overlap in activities with e-commerce.

Although the terms 'e-business' and 'e-commerce' are often used synonymously, the distinction between them lies in the broader range of processes in e-business that incorporates internal transactions within an organisation. These include transactions relating to procurement, logistics, supply chain management, payments, stock control and order tracking. As Chaffey (2004) notes, e-commerce can best be conceived as a subset of e-business. Where the two concepts overlap is in the buying and selling of products and services.

E-business	E-commerce
← →	
Buying and selling electronically	Sell-side e-commerce
Electronic procurement	Buy-side e-commerce
Electronic distribution	
Online customer service	
Electronic marketing	
Secure transactions	
Automation of processes	
Electronic collaboration	

Figure 1.1
The relationship between e-business and e-commerce

Buy-side e-commerce refers to electronic transactions between a purchasing organisation and its suppliers and sell-side e-commerce refers to electronic transactions between a supplier organisation and its customers. Figure 1.1 illustrates the relationship between e-business and e-commerce.

The development of the new economy

Throughout the book references will be made to 'the internet economy', 'the information economy' or 'the digital economy'. These terms are used to define the distinct contributions to the economy through use of the internet, digital technology, or information and communications technology (ICT). Together these types of technologies have created the so-called 'new economy', one that is based on entrepreneurship in knowledge creation and sharing, innovation and creativity, and utilising information technology for developing and selling new products and services. The new economy defined the industrial landscape of the late twentieth century and will be the dominant driver of economies well into the new millennium.

The new economy has been boosted by the development of the infrastructure that supports the internet, ICT and digital technology. The rollout of high-speed broadband internet access means more people can connect to the internet at higher speed and with greater flexibility and scope of activities. Digital exchanges and fibre-optic networks mean that the convergence of technologies further boosts the new economy. Where once the internet, television broadcasting and telecommunications were separate and distinct industries, convergence means that these sectors have increasingly merged, thereby offering consumers greater scope for accessing services via one technology. For example, the new economy is boosted by the development of internet access on mobile phones because it means knowledge workers can access information and communicate with others from almost any location. The convergence of the internet and television means that interactive television provides an additional media for facilitating online sales of products and services.

At the business level, organisations are no longer viewed as individual entities but as part of an integrated network of organisations where information and communications technologies play a key role in smoothing transactions and collaborative ventures between partners. The internet has opened up the possibility of exchanging information, products and services around the globe without any restraints of time or distance. This has given rise to the concept of the 'boundaryless' organisation. Indeed, the new economy is characterised by changes to the boundaries of whole economies as well as industries and firms. In the last few decades these changes have led to a marked acceleration in globalisation.

The diffusion of information technologies has played a key role in knowledge sharing, encouraging innovation and creativity, integrating global supply chains, facilitating global trade and creating wealth. There is also a local characteristic to the new economy as organisations utilise information technologies to serve local or regional demand. The scope of the new economy encompasses the spectrum from localisation through to globalisation and lends meaning to the concept of the 'boundaryless' organisation, industry or economy.

Information technology has also enabled new forms of management and control, both within organisations and between organisations. Information technology makes it possible to simultaneously co-ordinate economic activity in many different locations and beyond traditional organisational boundaries. This has enabled organisations to create new structures, such as the network organisation or the virtual organisation, that are more flexible and efficient, harness the best skills and experience of workers and eliminate many of the costs associated with running traditional hierarchical and rigid organisations.

The new economy is also characterised by changes in the competitive structure of industries. The traditional model, based on mass production where competitive advantage was gained through decreasing production costs or increasing productivity, has given way to a need for organisations to adapt to changes in market conditions, seek new opportunities, enhance learning, embrace change and innovation, and create and share knowledge. Managers in organisations

Issues	Old economy	New economy
Economy factors		
Markets	Stable	Dynamic and complex
Competition	National	International and global
Structure	Manufacturing	Service
Value driver	Physical capital	Human capital
Business factors		
Organisation	Hierarchy	Network or virtual
Production	Mass	Flexible, customised
Growth driver	Capital and labour	Innovation and knowledge
Technology driver	Machines	Digital and electronic
Competitive advantage	Low cost/high production	Innovation, speed, quality
Relationships	Independent	Collaborative
Consumer factors		
Tastes	Stable	Dynamic, segmented
Skills	Specialised	Multiple and flexible
Educational needs	Trade orientated	Lifelong learning
Workplace relations	Confrontational	Collaborative
Nature of employment	Stable	Insecure, opportunistic

Figure 1.2
Key differences
between the old
and new economy

have to co-ordinate and control the use of information technologies such as the internet, intranet, extranet and applications software to help meet these challenges and take advantage of the opportunities associated with operating within the new economy. Figure 1.2 summarises the key differences between the old and new economy from the perspectives of the overall economy, businesses and consumers.

Types of e-business and related industries

E-business varies in scope and type of activities undertaken. The entire supply chain of many industries has been radically transformed by the development of the internet and related technologies. Some organisations specialise in business-to-business (B2B) activities by providing e-business services across the supply chain or in parts of the supply chain such as e-procurement, logistics, stock control, ordering, payments and distribution. E-business also includes the organisation of collaboration platforms that allows different organisations to share information and knowledge for mutual benefit, i.e. the organisation of e-marketplaces that bring organisations together for buying and selling products and services or providing an online business support service.

The most high profile types of e-business involve those that sell products or services to customers. The business-to-consumer (B2C) sector has attracted the highest number of entrants as well as some of the most successful e-business ventures such as Amazon.com, e-Bay and FriendsReunited. The latter two also incorporate a consumer-to-consumer (C2C) element to their service by bringing consumers together for specific purposes. Most organisations now have a website that is used for promoting the activities of the business or marketing their products and services. More and more traditional firms are creating their own e-business and e-commerce websites to offer an additional sales channel for their customers (Tesco.com, marksandspencer.com).

There is a large industry sector that supports e-business, including Internet Service Providers (ISPs) such as Yahoo!, Google and AOL. These organisations run a number of services including internet access and search engines and have built up enormous databases of websites that form the basis of their search engine. Organisations who want to have their websites on the search engine pay an amount relative to the prominence on the list. Other organisations specialise in providing applications software for facilitating e-business or sell hardware such as computers and modems (Dell, Compaq, IBM). There are many thousands of businesses that specialise in maintaining and supporting e-businesses, including computer analysts, IT specialists, software consultants, applications consultants, computer trainers, security consultants and so on. The development and maintenance of the network infrastructure is a vital industry for ensuring high quality access to internet services and includes some of the world's biggest and most complex organisations such as BT and Cisco.

The growth of e-business

The most significant factor that transformed the internet into a global communications phenomenon was the development of the World Wide Web (WWW) in the early 1990s. This extended the functionality of the internet by introducing hypertext that linked documents held on the internet servers. This facilitated access to particular parts of documents or even to other relevant documents held on other servers. This was called the hypertext transfer protocol (HTTP) and derived from a mark-up language called hypertext markup language (HTML). Within the servers, each document, or pages within documents, are given a unique address. The addresses are termed universal resource locators (URL's). The ability to access pages, documents and servers from many different websites created a network of interconnectivity and gave rise to the term the World Wide Web.

The Web was the catalyst for huge changes in the business environment as more and more firms sought to integrate their traditional business models with those online. By the mid 1990s firms 'born on the net' emerged, whose function was to exploit the opportunities in the marketplace by using the internet. However, the key driver of the phenomenal rise of the internet was the rapid increase in the use of computers with access to the internet and the Web by the public. From 1993 to 1996 the number of computer users with access to the internet and the Web rose from zero to 10 million. In 2004 the figure stood at around half a billion. Also, the number of websites appearing on the Web has increased exponentially from 1993 onwards. In the months following the release of HTTP and HTML there were less than 50 websites in existence. By the end of the decade there were countless millions available.

Since the commercialisation of the internet in the mid 1990s demand for its use has increased hugely each year. In fact, the growth of the internet has been such that there are fears that the existing infrastructure may be unable to sustain demand into the future. The internet has had a profound effect at so many different levels including individuals, society, business, governments, education, health, security services, entertainment, news services, financial markets and many others. To comprehend the staggering growth of the internet many analysts turn to the prediction of the founder of Intel and inventor of the chip, Gordon Moore. In the mid 1960s Moore predicted that the number of components that could be located on a single chip would double every twenty-four months. In the twenty years between 1974 and 1994 the Intel 8080 chip increased the number of transistors from 5000 to over 5 million. This exponential growth phenomenon became known as Moore's law and can easily be related to the growth witnessed in demand for access to information technology in general, and the internet in particular.

The internet has created a new communications channel and provides an ideal medium for bringing people together cheaply, efficiently and for a wide range of different reasons. It has also presented opportunities and challenges for the business community. As consumers become more knowledgeable about using the internet to service their needs and wants so the business community has been boosted by the potential the internet presents for extending markets, developing new products and services and achieving a competitive advantage and profitability. New markets quickly emerged based on applications of the internet, most prominently the business-to-consumer (B2C) and business-to-business (B2B) sectors.

One of the key characteristics of e-commerce is the ease of entry for firms. The cost of entry and exit is low relative to traditional industries, as firms do not require large sales teams, costly investment in infrastructure or high sunk costs in order to compete effectively. Rising connectivity rates among potential customers ensures increasing competition among e-commerce firms as more are attracted to the source of potential revenue. Importantly, the internet does away with geographical boundaries thereby increasing yet further the extent of competitive rivalry. Intense competition is a characteristic of the internet economy and has spread across all e-business and e-commerce sectors. Figure 1.3 outlines the main benefits that firms and consumers gain from using the internet.

Advantages of using the internet

Firms	Consumers
Ease of access	Ease of access
Ease of use	Ease of use
Access to wider market	Access to market information
Potential economies of scale	Convenience
Marketing economies	Lower prices
Improved logistics	Personalisation
Automated processes	Customisation
Network externalities	Network externalities
Improved customer knowledge	One-to-one customer service
Lower costs	Access to internet community
Increased efficiency	Empowerment

Figure 1.3
Advantages of using the internet for firms and consumers

Use of the internet

Demand for internet services has been growing year on year since it became generally available to the public in the mid 1990s. The internet has had an impact on the economic and social fabric of many societies and has been the catalyst for changes in the way people interact, do business, gain information and seek entertainment. The internet has provided a whole new economy with its own rules and terms of engagement. Businesses and customers have been through a period of learning about how they can best leverage advantage from using the internet and many users are now adept at utilising the technology in a versatile and effective way to enhance their lifestyle.

In the UK around 60% of adults actively use the internet (Oxis). Of those, seven out of ten regard the internet as important or very important to their lives. The average time spent on computers by the 2200 people surveyed by the Oxford Internet Institute (OII) in 2005 was one and a half hours. The time spent using the internet has been at the expense of other activities such as reading, watching television and family life. There are many types of activities available on the internet but searching for information or communicating via e-mail are the two most popular. Figure 1.4 lists the percentage of internet users undertaking a sample of activities.

Not everyone enjoys the benefits of the internet. There is, in each country, a section of society that remains marginalised or excluded from the digital revolution. The digital divide has implications for government, social services and society as a whole. In particular, children from poorer homes are more likely to find themselves excluded from the benefits of internet use because their parents lack the skills to help them use the internet as effectively as their middle-class counterparts (LSE, 2005). A study of 1500 young people conducted by the London School of Economics found that children from middle-class backgrounds had greater access to the internet at home (88%) compared to working-class children (61%). Children from middle-class backgrounds are more likely to gain benefits from exploiting the resources available on the internet to enhance their education and, eventually, their job prospects.

There are, of course, some people who deliberately exclude themselves from the digital revolution and shun the internet. In the UK, internet diffusion stands at 60% compared to 75% in the USA. After taking into account the 8% of internet users who have lapsed, that leaves around 32% of the UK population as non-users of the

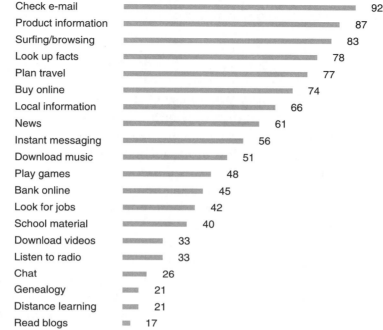

Figure 1.4
UK internet users'
online activities (%).
Source: Oxis
(Sample of 2200)

internet (Oxis). There is also around 15% of the UK population who do not possess a mobile phone.

A number of reasons have been put forward to explain the rationale of people who wish to exclude themselves from engaging with advances in information technology. Some have interests they see as incompatible with the internet, such as hillwalking or other outdoor activities (although mobile internet access could be useful for determining geographical positioning or a mobile phone could be useful should one require rescue services). Some people do not wish to be continuously accessible to communicating with others and view use of information technology as an invasion of privacy. The risk of being victims of fraud or other security breaches are other reasons put forward by those who do not participate in the digital revolution.

However, perhaps the most important reason is that many people feel daunted by the prospect of learning how to use new technology to their benefit. The challenge is for manufacturers to make computers more user-friendly so that more people can access the resources of the internet. The internet is a technology that has to be used and experienced before the benefits become apparent. Persuading non-users to engage with the internet requires better learning facilities, tailored marketing for all segments of society, availability of free advice, easier navigation of computers, increased security and cheaper access.

Key people

The development and use of the internet has been made possible by the foresight, ingenuity and innovative prowess of a number of key people. The development of the internet stems from the work of a long line of inventors, technologists and engineers. Although the driving force behind its development stemmed from military needs, the commercialisation of the internet required a concerted effort to create the necessary communications infrastructure that supports internet-based activities.

The creation of the World Wide Web enabled many millions to access the resources held within the internet. The navigation of the internet became easier thanks largely to the development of web browsers and search engines. The commercialisation of the internet presented opportunities for entrepreneurs and computer buffs to create business models that attracted many millions of customers. The development of the internet and its use for business purposes is the result of the combined effort of a large number of people. This section of the book gives a brief profile of just some of the key people involved in bringing e-business and e-commerce to online consumers.

Tim Berners Lee

In 1984 physicist and computer buff Tim Berners Lee was working at CERN, the European particle physics laboratory in Switzerland, when he developed the idea of linking all the information stored on computers to other computers on a global scale. Berners Lee's ambition was to create a single, global information space that would be freely available to anyone with access to a computer. By 1990 enough progress had been made to name the project the World Wide Web (WWW).

The WWW was located on the internet and consisted of a computer language for formatting hypertext files (Hypertext Markup Language − HTML); a method for moving between files (Hypertext Transfer Protocol − HTTP) and a web address for each file (Universal Resource Locator − URL). The WWW was one of the most significant developments leading to the globalisation and commercialisation of the internet because it allowed free access to huge amounts of information, facilitated communications between people and provided a mechanism for different activities to take place, including e-business.

Marc Andreeson

In the early 1990s Marc Andreeson was a young programmer at the National Center for Supercomputing Applications in the USA. In 1993 he released the first Web browser called Mosaic. The browser was easy to install, easy to use and could be operated on numerous systems including Microsoft Windows and Apple Mackintosh. The popularity of Mosaic grew quickly with around half a million users in the first year of its rollout. The most important contribution that Mosaic made was to transform Web browsing on the World Wide Web from being a slow, laborious and inefficient process to one that made navigation of websites quick and easy. It also allowed users to design their own websites.

Andreeson later teamed up with Jim Clark, an associate professor at Stanford University and founder of personal computer company Silicon Graphics. Between them they commercialised Mosaic and later called the browser Mosaic Netscape. After a legal wrangle with the University of Illinois over licensing fees Andreeson and Clark changed the name to Netscape. The Netscape Navigator browser was launched in December 1994 and by the end of the first quarter in 1995 had amassed three million users. Netscape was to become the world's most popular Web browser.

Bill Gates

In 1975 Bill Gates and business partner Paul Allen began writing software for computers and created a company called Microsoft. The company is now one of the world's most recognised brands and is a multi-billion dollar enterprise with interests in many hundreds of multimedia products. The basis for the success of Microsoft was the vision that Gates and Allen had in recognising the huge potential that personal computers would have as technology developed and demand grew. Today Microsoft enjoys a huge market share in computer software and related products and is fully established in the firmament of global corporations. The influence of Microsoft on the internet, and computers generally, cannot be underestimated, with the vision and leadership skills of Bill Gates still very much a driving force behind the company's success.

Michael Dell

Michael Dell started his computer business when still an under-graduate at the University of Texas. Dell is now the world's leading direct-sale personal computer company. Dell built the success of the company around the concept of direct ordering through mail order, telephone and online by using the internet. The competitive advantage gained by the company lay in the ability to take large volume orders, transform those orders into products configured around customer specifications and, finally, assemble, package and deliver the product to the customer quickly, efficiently and in good condition. Dell takes orders amounting to around £20 million per day and is valued at around £20 billion.

Jerry Yang

Jerry Yang and business partner David Filo created internet search engine Yahoo!. The concept began when the two Stanford University PhD students started compiling lists of their favourite websites. This so-called 'hotlist' formed a database that web users could access to quickly find web pages. Yang and Filo recruited specialist managers Tim Koogle and Jeff Mallet to grow the business. By the late 1990s Yahoo! had grown into one of the world's leading search engines. However, it has not all been plain sailing for Yahoo!. Although Yahoo! had a market capitalisation of over $100 million the company suffered the same fate as so many other dot-com firms in 2000. As the valuation of the company plummeted the attention of managers turned to survival. The rollercoaster story of Yahoo! is one of the case studies featured in this book.

Pierre Omidyar

Pierre Omidyar is the son of French-Iranian immigrants to America and is famous for creating the world's biggest and most well-known internet firm, e-Bay. Omidyar was a computer fanatic and spent a great deal of his student years programming on Apple. His move to

Silicon Valley was a natural progression for the self-confessed computer nerd. Omidyar had a vision for the internet that centred on
providing the perfect market for trading. He decided that an online
auction website would be the nearest thing to perfect competition as
it would bring buyers and sellers together to negotiate transactions
in the quickest and most efficient way possible. The phenomenal
success of e-Bay is worthy of greater scrutiny and forms part of the
case study series for this book.

Jeff Bezos

Jeff Bezos left his job on Wall Street to start a new business from his
garage in Seattle. His idea was to use the internet to take orders for
books and deliver them to customers quickly. His company, which he
called Amazon.com, quickly built up a reputation and customer base
that ensured growth. The Amazon strategy has remained consistent
since its inception, to grow the business as quickly as possible and
diversify the online retailing concept. The Amazon.com website now
caters for a wide range of different products and services including toys, garden implements, healthcare products, media products,
business services and so on.

In the first decade of its existence Amazon.com failed to make a
profit but was able to survive through the goodwill of investors and
lenders based around the huge market share the company had built
up. Eventually, in 2003, Bezos was able to announce that Amazon
was profitable and that the company would be extending its products
and services further. The Amazon.com story features in the case
studies series in this book.

Scope of the book

The main foci of this book are e-business from two perspectives:

- The use of the internet by organisations to improve internal
  communications and efficiency, speed administration and
  transactions, market products and services, communicate
  with supply chain partners, add value to customers and
  create a competitive advantage;
- The application of the internet as a basis for creating
  business models for selling products and services and

providing secure payment systems for transactions. It is concerned with using the internet as a mechanism for facilitating the exchange of value. This is commonly known as e-commerce, which is a function of e-business.

The book is designed to give a valuable insight into the key factors that organisations have to understand when undertaking e-business. The internet changes the way businesses operate and alters the marketing and economics of providing and selling products and services. There are distinct legal implications associated with selling products and services online and managers have to understand the complexities of incorporating new technologies into their organisations to improve internal efficiency and/or serve customers better. The scope of the book also includes ways in which competitive advantage can be gained through the effective management of e-business and the formulation, implementation and evaluation of strategies for e-business. The book concludes by giving an overview of the three distinct phases of e-business development and the performance of the e-business industry up to 2005. The final section offers some judgements based on current knowledge regarding the future for e-business and the key changes that are likely to impact the future prospects of the internet economy.

Structure of the book

Following the introduction the book proceeds to focus on technology as one of the most important drivers of e-business. Chapter 2 (*E-business technology*) charts the development of the internet and the World Wide Web. It also gives an overview of the information infrastructure that is necessary to allow e-business and other internet-based activities to take place. The chapter then goes on to explain the key issues relating to the technical aspects of electronic communications such as Electronic Data Interchange (EDI), the development and use of program languages, the pros and cons of creating industry standards and the development of wireless technology and interactive television. The characteristics of new and emerging technologies are also highlighted. The chapter concludes with an overview of the types of technologies that are used to effect secure payments for e-business and e-commerce.

The key markets that exist for e-business and types of internet-based business models form the basis of the discussion in Chapter 3

(*E-business markets and models*). The chapter begins by identifying the types of businesses that use the internet as a means of communications and transactions. There then follows an overview of the e-business competitive environment before going on to highlight the advantages associated with e-marketplaces and the characteristics of the key e-business markets that have emerged. The main part of the chapter includes definitions and examples of the main e-business models used by internet-based organisations. The chapter concludes with a framework for analysing the effectiveness of e-business models.

Another important driver of e-business concerns the economics of undertaking trade online and the cost savings and efficiencies that organisations can gain by using the internet and related information technologies. Chapter 4 (*E-business economics*) starts with a discussion on how the internet pushes markets towards perfect competition. This is followed by a wider discussion of how the internet affects the competitive environment. There are a number of key economic factors that contribute to the formation of a distinct e-business competitive environment. The main ones form the basis for the rest of this chapter and include cost factors; disintermediation and reintermediation of organisations along the supply chain; the economics of information-based products and services, levels of connectivity and interactivity; economies of scale and scope; the effects of low transaction costs; the role of switching costs in creating a competitive advantage and building a critical mass of customers. The chapter concludes with an examination of the effects of online trading on prices.

The internet provides an additional communications channel for organisations and provides a mechanism through which marketing and promotional activities can be undertaken. Chapter 5 (*E-marketing*) focuses on the key aspects of marketing using the internet, including the creation of a marketing plan; the marketing mix; the way the internet can be used to underpin the strength of branding; the targeting of online customers; the effect of the internet on advertising; the emergence of interactive television and its impact on e-marketing; and the development of customer relationship management (CRM) systems as a means of building knowledge of customers' online browsing and buying habits and as an aid to marketing products and services to key customer segments.

The development of the internet has raised a number of new and pressing problems relating to issues of law and security.

One of the strengths of the internet is the freedom of individuals to access and use it largely as they see fit. However, this strength can also be a weakness since it offers the opportunity for individuals, groups or organisations to abuse the freedom it offers. The internet has raised a number of issues that require the intervention of legislators, public policy makers and law enforcement agencies. There are ethical (pornography), legal (contracts for electronic transactions), trust (sharing sensitive information), privacy (securing information) and security (cyber-terrorism, fraud, spam) issues to be addressed. Chapter 6 (*The internet: law, privacy, trust and security*) highlights and discusses these key issues and analyses the impact that they have on the development and growth of e-business.

Creating a competitive advantage begins with effective management of e-business. Chapter 7 (*The management of e-business*) begins with a discussion of managing knowledge. For many modern organisations competitive advantage stems from the ability of managers to communicate a vision and build a positive organisational culture based around knowledge and learning. The discussion of knowledge management links into the section on managing applications for e-business where the advantages of implementing some of the main types of applications are highlighted. Technology itself cannot create a competitive advantage and this is recognised in the section dealing with management skills for e-business. The development of the internet and other information technologies has placed extra demands on managers who are charged with the task of deciding what technology is appropriate for their organisation, linking it to the skills of workers, and bringing it all together to help achieve stated aims. There are a number of risks associated with undertaking e-business and the final section of this chapter focuses on identifying the key risks and their related problems as well as suggesting some solutions.

To gain a competitive advantage organisations have to formulate and implement a strategy. A strategy is a formal set of activities that have been identified as the means through which stated aims and objectives are to be achieved. There are three parts to the strategic process – formulation, implementation and evaluation. Chapter 8 (*E-business strategy: formulation*) sets out the key elements that comprise objective setting for organisations. An explanation of the strategic process is the precursor to identifying and explaining some key elements of an internal and external analysis. This section uses theoretical models such as the value chain and the five forces model as frameworks for analysis and discussion. The chapter concludes by highlighting competitive strategies for gaining a competitive advantage by using Porter's (1985) generic strategy model.

Chapter 9 (*E-business strategy: implementation*) features the second element of the strategic process. The chapter starts by identifying and explaining the key elements that comprise strategic control. Control functions are necessary in order to link the chosen strategy with outcomes so that performance can be evaluated. This is followed by discussion and evaluation of three main ways of implementing strategy: organisational learning, organisational culture and organisational structure. These three elements are linked and come together to help organisations achieve their stated aims and objectives. The chapter concludes with a discussion on change management as part of an implementation strategy. In particular, this section focuses on the practicalities and tactics for implementing change and highlights some of the problems and solutions to resistance to change.

Chapter 10 (*E-business strategy: evaluation*) forms the third part of the strategic process. All organisations have to undertake some form of evaluation of strategy in order to determine whether or not progress has been made towards achieving stated aims and objectives. The chapter begins with an overview of the evaluation process before outlining the role that evaluation plays in the control function within organisations. This is followed by discussions centred around the key elements of the organisation that have to be evaluated, including finance, technology, human resources, the website and the business model adopted for achieving competitive advantage.

The main reason why organisations undertake a strategic process is to ensure that their resources are being utilised in a way that maximises returns and helps achieve a competitive advantage. Once competitive advantage has been achieved managers need to turn their attention to ways in which the competitive advantage can be sustained into the future. The issues relating to the ultimate aim of developing a strategy are discussed in Chapter 11 (*Gaining and sustaining a competitive advantage*). The key issues addressed in this chapter include the importance of first-mover advantages; the factors that determine the choice of generic strategy; the integration of generic strategies; expanding product lines; the lock-in and switching costs of customers; the mix of traditional and online business (bricks and clicks); and the winner-takes-all characteristic of many e-business models. The chapter concludes by highlighting some of the problems of sustaining competitive advantage.

The final part of the book is Chapter 12 (*E-business: the future*). This chapter starts by giving an overview of the three distinct phases that the evolution of e-business has passed through since the commercialisation of the internet in the mid 1990s. This is followed by analysis and discussion of the performance of e-business in the UK and the USA in the decade since e-business and e-commerce started to emerge on to the industrial landscape. The knowledge gained through analysing past performance and experiences alongside understanding of emerging technologies and business models forms the basis for making value judgements about the future prospects for e-business. This final section of the book looks to the future of e-business from the perspective of key parts of the internet economy.

Case studies

The book includes five case studies. These are:

Amazon.com:	one of the first-movers in e-business and e-commerce.
e-Bay:	the world's most successful online auction site.
Tesco.com:	the online service of the UK's leading supermarket.
Yahoo!:	the rise, fall and rise again of the Internet Service Provider (ISP).
boo.com:	the failed online fashion e-tailer.

The cases have been chosen based on four main criteria:

- They are widely recognised brands with distinct business models based wholly, or in part, on the use of the internet or associated technologies;
- They clearly illustrate some of the key issues featured in chapters in the book;
- They cover the most prominent internet-based business models (e-tailing, auction, ISP and as an additional service provided by an established bricks and mortar organisation). The cases also cover the main e-business markets of business-to-consumer (B2C), business-to-business (B2B) and consumer-to-consumer (C2C);
- They provide an insight into the success and failure, risks and benefits, and opportunities and threats that trading online or providing internet-based services can bring to organisations.

References

Bober, M. and Livingstone, S. (2005). UK Children-Go-Online (UKCGO). LSE Research: London. www.children-go-online.net

Chaffey, D. (2004). *E-Business and E-Commerce Management* (2nd edition). Prentice-Hall: Harlow.

Oxford Internet Survey (Oxis), June 2005. Oxford Internet Institute, Oxford. www.oii.ox.ac.uk

Porter, M. E. (1985). *Competitive Strategy*. Free Press: New York, NY.

E-business technology

Key issues:

- The development of the internet;
- The World Wide Web (WWW);
- Information infrastructure;
- Electronic Data Interchange (EDI);
- Program languages;
- Industry standards;
- Wireless technology;
- Interactive television;
- Payment systems.

Introduction

Chapter 2 focuses on the key technological factors relevant to e-business. The chapter starts with an historical overview of the development of the internet and the World Wide Web. An outline of the information infrastructure that supports electronic communication is featured, using issues of connectivity and interactivity as a basis for highlighting the growth of electronic communications on a global scale. The rollout of broadband internet services is also discussed in this section. The history of electronic communications in business is further explored by discussing the role of Electronic Data Interchange (EDI) in the development of e-business.

There then follows a discussion of the key program languages that underpin e-business communications via the internet. The chapter then features analysis of the issue of standardisation of technology in e-business. Examples of attempts at standardisation and the advantages and disadvantages of each are discussed. The analysis offers an understanding of how the evolving e-business environment may benefit from universal standards whilst articulating the reasons for the continuing lack of an accepted universal standard. The chapter also highlights emerging technologies and discusses the key developments in mobile wireless technology, interactive television and payment systems.

The development of the internet

The development of the internet stems from innovations in computer technology. The first attempts at constructing a computer date back to the early twentieth century. In 1913 Vannevar Bush invented the Prolific Tracer, a device comprising a bicycle wheel, a rotating drum, gears and a pen. The device could measure distances over uneven ground. By 1919, Bush had created the first computer that could solve mathematical equations, called the 'differential analyser'. The onset of two World Wars meant that greater investment was poured into developing technology for military purposes. Computers became bigger and more sophisticated.

In the UK, the invention of the Enigma code-breaking computer by Alan Turing played a crucial role in turning the tide in favour of the Allies against Nazi Germany. In the USA, the momentum for developing the computer was enhanced by the setting up of the National Science Foundation (NSF) in 1944 to support scientific research. Microphotography was invented in 1945. This was the first system that could store large amounts of information in small storage units – the same principle as digital technology in the modern era. The immediate post-war period also saw the development of the cathode ray tube that could display text on a screen. The proposed system that combined data storage and visual text that could be linked by files was called the 'memex'. Although it was never built the idea was the forerunner of the World Wide Web.

The application of business activities via the internet has been a feature of the business environment since the late 1980s, but the roots of its development stems from scientific research dating back to the Cold War era of the 1950s. In an effort to co-ordinate the activities of the US military, President Eisenhower set up the Advanced Research Project Agency (ARPA) in 1958. A decade later ARPA had successfully introduced a system called ARPANET that facilitated the sharing of information electronically between its headquarters and selected universities across the USA.

By the mid 1970s the National Science Foundation (NSF) of the USA was commissioned to further the activities of ARPANET across the university sector. The development of electronic mail (e-mail) was one feature of the burgeoning interest in electronic communications. In 1980 the NSF formally introduced an academic network system called CSNET that connected US university computer science depart-ments. With the NSF supplying the support network called 'NSFNET', the number of computers supplying information through the network more than doubled each year throughout the 1980s. Simultaneously, other networks connecting communities emerged across the USA and Europe. The use of NSFNET became diluted by the emergence of independent network companies who set up international links for the electronic transfer of information. However, all networks used the same protocol (TCP/IP) and the same open operating system (Unix). This network of networks formed the birth of the internet as we know it today.

By the early 1990s the use of the internet had expanded beyond university departments and government bodies to incorporate the business world. However, the use of the internet for business purposes got off to a slow start because no infrastructure existed that could connect users to the network from any location around the globe. Only those with a good knowledge of the technology could find their way around the large number of databases. Even then the whole process was time-consuming and frustrating. For the internet to be adopted by the business community, and the general public, there was a need for a system that made navigation of the network simple and narrowed down the number of documents that users had to search through before accessing the information they needed. Early search facilities included Gopher, a system that used menus as a means of searching for documents.

The World Wide Web (WWW)

Perhaps the most significant development in bringing forward the application of business via the internet was the emergence of the World Wide Web (WWW). The usability of the internet was greatly enhanced after researcher Tim Berners Lee developed the hypertext transfer protocol (HTTP) at the CERN atomic research centre in Switzerland in 1993. Through HTTP it is possible to use a hypertext markup language (HTML) to design web pages with text, graphics and a range of other formatting techniques to create a visually appealing layout, as well as linking documents electronically to other documents. The links in each document are connected to links in other documents thereby creating a network of information sources on a worldwide scale. The technology underpinning the WWW is relatively simple. A computer acting as an internet server is turned into a site on the WWW by activating software on the server that enables it to talk the language of HTTP. The language facilitates access to documents marked up with HTML codes and allows users to link from other servers to the documents or to use the documents as jumping off points to other sites on the WWW.

Crucially, the WWW brought together information on a common topic to ease the process and speed of searching. However, there was still work to be done before the internet could become the global phenomenon that it is today. In the months following the release of Berners Lee's HTTP there were only 50 websites in existence compared to the millions there are today. Hyperlinks alone could not attract a global level of usage because the internet still ran on the open operating system Unix. The problem of usability remained. To overcome this, researchers had to find a way of moving the internet beyond the confines of the academic world to one that would be readily available to anyone with access to a computer.

Thus, very soon after the development of the WWW in 1993 a team of researchers at the National Center for Supercomputing Applications (NCSA) at the University of Illinois developed a windows-based graphical user interface for the internet. The window is a specialised form of software which is run on client computers to provide an instant interface for the Web. The generic name for the software is a Web browser.

The web browser developed by Marc Andreeson and his team of researchers at the NCSA was called 'Mosaic' and represented the first truly worldwide web. In 1994 the same group of researchers developed Netscape, a browser with a 'search engine' that enables searches using keywords. Netscape briefly enjoyed a near monopoly of the market for web browsers. However, the market domination of Netscape has subsequently been eroded by competition, most notably from Microsoft's Internet Explorer. The market for web browsers is also competitive, with Google, Lycos, Yahoo! and AltaVista being among the more prominent websites specialising in facilitating keyword searches. By 1995 the NCSA team had been tempted into the commercial arena by Jim Clark, Chief Executive Officer of computer hardware company Silicon Graphics. Between them they created one of the world's best-known browsers – Netscape Navigator.

Prior to the development of the WWW and Netscape, businesses had mostly used the internet for publishing information online relating to products, prices and other marketing material. However, by the mid 1990s businesses across the globe began using the internet for conducting online transactions (e-commerce) and a host of other business activities such as communicating with suppliers, distributors, partners, manufacturers and government bodies (e-business). The need for quick and efficient access to information became the key to gaining a competitive advantage in the web browser industry. A keyword search results in a long list of sites offering a large amount of information on a common topic. What firms wanted was for web users to be channelled towards their particular website. This could be arranged by advertising on a portal. A portal is a website that acts as a gateway to the information on the internet by providing search engines, directories and other services such as personalized news or free e-mail.

Information infrastructure

The information infrastructure is the support system that allows the internet to work. The main infrastructure support facilities exist in developed nations where access to the internet has moved beyond fixed location computers to incorporate mobile wireless computers and mobile phones. Even in developing nations such as India and China the connectivity rates for internet access are rising exponentially year on year. Most developed nations have been constructing their own national information infrastructure (NII) to facilitate connectivity in homes, educational institutions, businesses and public organisations.

The investment required for building the information infrastructure has been considerable and the connectivity rates differ markedly between countries and continents. For example, political, economic and geographical factors have combined to slow the development of the information infrastructure across the African continent relative to other regions. In many geographically remote areas the rollout of satellite-enabled wireless infrastructure may circumvent the problems associated with land-based telephony systems that cross borders and hazardous terrain. An effective infrastructure needs to be able to support high rates of interactivity and is reliant on robust hardware and software, continuous power supplies, state-of-the-art telecommunications systems and the availability of efficient maintenance and support systems. An important infrastructure initiative that addresses the issue of high demand and the need for quick and efficient access to internet services is the development of broadband.

Broadband

Broadband has been part of communications terminology for a number of years but few consumers of media are aware of what it is or what it does. Since interactive television arrived in the 1990s consumers have been absorbing the products and services that new technology has brought to the home. Similarly, governmental bodies and the communications industries have been on a steep learning curve, as the pace of change has posed difficult questions regarding regulation of industry structure, issues of content, wider access and increasing competition.

Broadband is a term used to describe the bandwidth of a transmitted communications signal. The bandwidth describes a range of frequencies that the signal occupies (Rao and De Backer, 2000). The bandwidth for digital and analogue corresponds to the amount of information received or sent over a particular time unit. Higher bandwidth increases transmission speeds and facilitates the communication of much greater volumes of information (Brennan, 1999). For consumers, broadband has numerous delivery platforms for accessing the internet including personal computers, television and mobile telephones.

With cables, high-capacity optical fibre networks provide greater speed and volume of information. Existing telephone networks also provide a similar platform through the technique of multiplexing. This allows more information to be channelled through old copper wires. ADSL (Assymetric Digital Subscriber Line) is the specific technology for making broadband transmissions on existing telephone networks. Essentially, broadband hugely increases the range of services that can be offered via the internet and digital television.

An important issue relating to broadband rollout is the method of dealing with local-loop unbundling. This is the process that permits smaller firms into the competitive market for ADSL services. Unbundling allows firms to access and install the necessary technology in British Telecom (BT) exchanges to compete in the 'last mile' of the telecommunications link between provider and user. However, demand for access to local exchanges has been lower than predicted because of a combination of poor sites offered and a lack of robust business models. BT has now opened up more of its infrastructure to make investment in broadband more attractive to smaller firms.

The UK government set out its plans for broadband rollout in the document *Broadband Britain* (1997). ADSL technology was the preferred option for introducing broadband services in the UK starting in 2001, with countrywide availability set for 2002. However, for technical and economic reasons ADSL fell short of expectations and the government had to rethink their broadband strategy. Other forms of delivery have been tested for economic and technical efficacy including DSL (Digital Subscriber Line), cable and the existing copper wire in telephone lines. Fibre-optic cable is the most efficient, but also the most expensive option. The business plans of many e-businesses have been built around new business applications facilitated by broadband infrastructure.

Access to broadband has become a vital component for e-businesses. This is especially the case for firms located in geographically remote areas. Most of these firms tend to be small and medium sized enterprises (SMEs) that rely on high-speed internet access to circumvent their geographical isolation. However, in the UK there is evidence that a significant number of businesses are being denied access to the broadband infrastructure on economic grounds. In 2005, BT estimated that there were 565 small-scale exchanges in the UK that were uneconomic for broadband installation. Combined, these exchanges serve around 100 000 customers (the number of people affected rises considerably when employees are added to the list).

Although BT has removed geographical limits for 512 k/bits per second broadband, the majority of businesses need access to 2M/bits per second and this can only be guaranteed within four miles of an exchange. At the Labour Party conference in 2004 Prime Minister Tony Blair underlined the Government's commitment to deliver broadband technology to every home by 2008. This may prove an overly ambitious target unless the economic investment in broadband infrastructure is bolstered by subsidies.

Electronic Data Interchange (EDI)

Electronic Data Interchange (EDI) describes the exchange of documents between organisations in standardised electronic form directly between computer applications. Many routine and procedural processes between organisations are automated and completed electronically using EDI. Purchase orders, invoices and material releases are just some examples of these processes where EDI can result in cost savings and increased efficiency. Another advantage of EDI is the standard format of communication between organisations that it offers. This circumvents the need for each organisation to deal with the internal data formats of other organisations, thereby allowing integration among dispersed organisations.

The origins of EDI stretch back to the early 1960s but the development of the internet gave the use of EDI an added boost. Transmitting EDI via the internet has seen its application extending across many industries such as engineering, electronics, metals, petroleum, chemical and the pharmaceutical sector. The early use of EDI in industry was characterised by closed systems whereby agreements were put in place restricting the number and type of users to a particular industry. Since the development of the internet, systems deployed use international standards that enable organisations to deal with any interested party via that standard. However, there are numerous standards in operation and this constitutes an impediment to the universal online access to all organisations. A detailed analysis of the issue of standardisation is featured later in this chapter.

Minoli and Minoli (1998) summarise the key features of EDI as:

- The use of an electronic transmission medium;
- The use of structured, formatted messages based upon agreed standards;
- The fast delivery of electronic documents from sender to receiver; and
- The direct communication between applications and systems.

The key benefits associated with EDI include:

- Lower costs in administration and processing;
- Lower costs in posting and preparation of transactions;
- Increased efficiency in transaction processing;
- Eliminating paper-handling tasks;

▨ Reducing errors;

▨ Quick exchange of documents which reduces the business cycle;

▨ Lower inventory costs;

▨ Increased customer service.

Use of EDI has been a feature of business strategies of many firms as they seek competitive advantage. However, the cost of implementing EDI and its architectural limitations has resulted in its failure to achieve universal acceptance across industry. For example, there are many EDI standards that are significantly divergent from each other. The United Nations sponsor the EDIFACT (Electronic Data Interchange for Administration, Commerce and Trade) standard, whereas in the United States the ANSI X12 standard is the most commonly used. Each standard requires users to map the data items of the standard with their own system.

EDI systems run on a network infrastructure called 'Value Added Networks' (VANs). These VANs were built for commercial return but have been undermined by the internet, where costs are lower because the development work was paid for through public funds. EDI cannot compete with the internet either on scope of applications, reach or economic criteria. For EDI to be a viable proposition there has to be agreement on standards between participants and even then there has to be sufficiently large volumes of applications taking place to justify the investment costs.

Program languages

Technology development lies at the heart of e-business. In order to communicate with others via a computer it is necessary to access a program language. A program language facilitates the development of a set of instructions from the programmer that constitutes a computer program. The instructions must be translated by a language translator into the computer's own machine language before they can be processed. Types of language translators include 'assemblers' that translate symbolic instruction codes, and 'compilers' that translate high-level language codes. These two types of language translators produce a complete machine language program, unlike an 'interpreter' that translates and executes each statement in a program individually. There are many program languages, and each has their own form of language translator, vocabulary and user characteristics. It is possible to discern four levels of programming languages that have been developed. These are listed below.

Machine languages

The initial and most basic form of program language used binary numbers as codes for instructions. This first generation of program language was slow, cumbersome and prone to error because instructions were required for every switch and indicator used by the program.

Assembler languages

The second generation of program languages was developed to overcome the problems associated with writing machine languages. Assembler languages require translator programs (assemblers) that enable a computer to convert the instructions into machine language. Assembler languages use letters of the alphabet and symbols rather than binary numbers as codes for instruction.

High-level languages

Third generation languages use statements, or arithmetic expressions as codes for instruction. This language is termed 'high-level' because it uses high-level language translator programs that allow each statement to generate numerous instructions when converted into machine language. High-level languages are simpler to learn than assembler languages since they are less formal and rules based, however it requires longer computer time to translate into machine language.

Fourth generation languages

There are many languages available that are less procedural and formal than the ones previously outlined. Fourth generation languages (4GL) place the onus on programmers to specify the results they are looking for. The computer then works out the sequence of instructions that achieve the stated results. 4GL makes the programming process simpler and uses more conventional language as spoken by humans in everyday conversation. Advances in artificial intelligence (AI) technology means that program languages are available in many natural spoken languages.

Object-orientated programming (OOP) languages

Object-orientated programming (OOP) languages include languages, such as Java and C++, that are tools for software development. OOP languages bind together the data elements and the procedures to be performed upon them to create objects. For example, an object could be personal financial data and the actions to be performed may convert the data into a graph. This capability has a number of attributes including ease of use, increased efficiency and increased quality of presentation. Importantly, once objects are programmed, they can be reused.

Java

One of the most important and widely used program languages that enables the building of websites, web pages and web-based applications is Java. Launched in 1995 by Sun Microsystems, Java is an extensive, object-orientated programming language that is widely used to facilitate e-business applications, whether via the World Wide Web or intranets and extranets. Apart from its attributes of simplicity and security, Java offers real-time, interactive, web-based network applications that are the keys to enabling e-business and e-commerce activity.

XML

The program language XML (eXtensible Markup Language) is a subset of the Standard Generalized Markup Language (SGML) and applies identifying tags to the data in web documents to describe the content of web pages. There are very many applications of XML.

For example, online share companies who list companies and movements in share prices can use hidden XML tags headed 'company' and 'share price' to categorise current share prices in real-time for clients. A great many firms use XML for product inventory labelling with tags based on product size, price, availability and brand. XML also helps users to find what they are looking for much more efficiently by categorising a large number of data sets. The automatic electronic exchange of information that XML enables between suppliers, buyers and partners has given a boost to e-business and e-commerce. The case for XML to become the industry standard is analysed later in this chapter.

XML was developed by the SGML Editorial Board formed under the auspices of the World Wide Web Consortium (W3C) in 1996. The designers of XML had to incorporate a number of key characteristics including:

- Ease of use over the internet;
- The capability of supporting a wide range of applications;
- Compatibility with SGML;
- Legibility to the human eye;
- Minimal optional features; and
- Ease of program writing for processing XML documents.

Jini

Sun Microsystems introduced the Jini initiative that allows communication across different devices. These may include PCs, mobile phones, Personal Digital Assistants (PDAs), interactive television or any other device with interactive capability. A feature of Jini is the 'JavaTones' (similar to dial tones on a telephone) it supplies to confirm access to any device connected to the network. The biggest advantage associated with the Jini network is the flexibility it offers for access to its resources using a wide range of devices. The lookup services of Jini, called the 'Directory Service Layer', allow resources to discover and interface with each other. Participants register with the lookup service and this confirms their availability on the network. Other users can download objects placed on the network by any participant via the 'JavaSpace' layer allocated to each registered participant. Once registered the technology facilitates communication using common standards.

Common Gateway Interface (CGI)

The Common Gateway Interface (CGI) facilitates interactivity via the internet. CGI works through extensions to the web server that allow server-side scripts to be run. These scripts process information that is communicated via websites. An advantage of CGI is that any program language can be used to process data. The most commonly used language for CGI is Practical Extraction and Report Language (Perl). However, it is limited by its simplicity. CGI performs a routine process for a single application. Once the application is complete a new process has to start up for the next one. This has proved to be laborious and slow, leading program developers to seek a more scalable solution. Microsoft's Active Server Pages (ASP) is one such solution. ASP comprises of HTML documents that are encoded to run at the server. Originally designed for Microsoft's IIS server, other web servers can now process ASP using third-party products.

Industry standards

The internet allows a wide range of applications and functions through a single interface. The quality of service is enhanced by developing an integrated system that allows the free flow of information between all parties in the supply chain. Despite the real benefits that integration would bring, an all-encompassing and universally acceptable system has yet to be developed. Although there are some technological reasons for the lack of a common standard most arguments revolve around business concerns in general and sustaining competitive advantage in particular.

E-business has made some advances towards standardisation with the XML schema leading the way. However, currently there are over 500 'types' of XML schemas and many overlap others in terms of application. Nevertheless, the issue of standardisation is one that remains high on the agenda of Web-based developers. The formation of the Web Services Interoperability Organisation (WS-I) underlines this, with organisations such as Microsoft, IBM, Oracle, SAP, Intel, Hewlett Packard and other computer heavyweights joining forces to lend impetus to the pursuit of internet standards. The system that incorporates the largest number of business capabilities alongside technology applications criteria will be the model most likely to be adopted as standard. Figure 2.1 lists the main business capabilities that firms require from an integrated system.

1. Reduce the cost of doing business.

2. Reduce the cost of entry into e-business.

3. Provide an easy-to-use set of tools.

4. Improve data integrity and accessibility.

5. Provide appropriate security and control.

6. Provide extendable and controllable technology.

7. Integrate with current systems.

8. Utilise open standards.

9. Provide interoperability.

10. Be globally deployable and maintainable.

Figure 2.1
Key business
capabilities of
integrated
e-marketplace
systems

Assessing the multiple and single interface for e-business

In order to implement an e-business strategy effectively all firms need to interface with those they transact business with. It is possible to determine the total amount of work required to implement a total supply chain by breaking down the amount of work required for implementing one data interface. There are some business models where a single data interface can connect all participants in the e-marketplace; others require a separate interface for each participant. The lower the number of interfaces the less work is required to communicate between firms. A single interface minimises human and financial resources and speeds up the implementation of the supply chain process. In order to expand the interfaces without incurring prohibitive costs requires all firms to operate a standard system of integration. There are many models for integrating e-marketplaces vying with each other for dominance and universal acceptance and it is worth assessing the value of some of the more prominent ones.

Electronic Data Interchange (EDI)

One of the first e-marketplace models proposed for integrating systems was that of the Electronic Data Interchange (EDI) communication system between partners participating in the supply chain. Assuming no standardised system of communication exists then for n partners in the supply chain there are $n(n-1)/2$ possible different communication interfaces (number of partners $\times$ n $-$ 1 communication interfaces/2). The Hubs are the major manufacturers, distributors and retailers. The partners are all those firms engaged in the trade along the supply chain.

The EDI system of implementations required a huge amount of work across the entire supply chain in order to integrate and align communications standards between each partner. If all partners co-operated in using the same standard, the amount of work for the supply chain is n (i.e. one interface per partner). In reality, however, firms are characterised by differences in operating processes and, therefore, communications differences are propagated across the supply chain despite the move to standardisation. Thus, n level of work for a single interface becomes an n and $n(n-1)/2$ level of work to implement an entire supply chain communication system. The complexity and cost of implementing this model undermined confidence in its ability to successfully integrate firms on a global basis.

As EDI faded the next generation of integrated systems had to have a viable method of overcoming the work overload in setting up a system. The portal or nexus method ensured that each partner communicated using the same standard. However, it proved to be unfairly biased towards well-resourced operators. Effectively, the implementation of the system was inversely related to the ability of firms to meet the resource demand it placed on them. The nexus model was essentially a stopgap in the quest for a universally acceptable system.

XML

The Extensible Markup Language (XML) is a class of data objects that are stored on computers. XML goes some way to describe the behaviour of programs that process these objects. XML is a restricted form of the Standard Generalized Markup Language (SGML). The reason for the development of XML was to allow SGML to be applied on the internet in much the same way as Hyper Text Markup Language (HTML) is now. XML is designed for interoperability of both SGML and HTML. The ease of implementation lies at the heart of XML design. It also supports a broad range of applications, has few optional features and is legible, lucid, concise and human-friendly. XML paved the way for a more technological-centred acceptance of standardisation as a concept among a global business community still coming to grips with the implications of the internet.

XML still had a problem integrating small and medium sized enterprises due to the prohibitive costs of participation. It is not just in the realm of technology that an integrated e-marketplace may be judged, but also there are a number of key business level criteria that any system must address before being deemed viable.

The systems outlined have a number of key attributes including:

- Providing an easy set of tools to engage in e-business applications;
- Reducing the cost of entry into e-commerce;
- Technical adaptability to integrate with current systems;
- Use of open standards;
- Provision of at least some measure of interoperability;
- Being deployed on a global basis.

Where differences do occur is in the area of security where the EDI and e-marketplace models do not offer improvements in data integrity. To lend weight to the argument for a common standard, designers had to overcome fears over lack of security, whilst maintaining other attributes such as providing extendable and controllable technology. By 2000 there were moves to develop and implement a system for integrating e-marketplaces that would close in on meeting all the business criteria outlined above. This gave rise to the development of ebXML.

ebXML

ebXML is an attempt to overcome restricted applications by operating a horizontal standard that can be developed for use in any vertical industry, with the main users being small and medium sized enterprises. The ebXML system is one of the most promising attempts at introducing an integration standard to date. This system is a joint development between the United Nations (Trade Facilitation and Electronic Business) and the OASIS (Organization for the Advancement of Structured Information Systems). Eight project teams make up the working groups developing the system and include: ebXML requirements; business process methodology; technical architecture; core components; transport and packaging; registry and repository; technical co-ordination and support; and a marketing division.

The keys to the success of ebXML are:

- That the standards implemented must remove human involvement historically required in the set-up of the exchange of information between two entities;

- ▦ That much greater speed be applied to the standards development process to accommodate need and the pace of change in e-commerce;
- ▦ That implementation of a standard set of communications characteristics overcome integration problems and have benefits industry-wide.

Another key attribute of the ebXML system is its adherence to many of the business capability criteria outlined in Figure 2.1.

The overriding aim of the initiative is to lower entry barriers into e-business for small and medium sized enterprises. The system is characterised by processes as well as transactions such that a standardised set of definitions are stored in global registries. This allows small firms to gain access to application solutions whilst avoiding the cost of complex modelling. One of the key aims of ebXML is to enhance interoperability by allowing firms to create files outlining their e-business and process capabilities to be stored in the central repository. This goes beyond simple exchange of documentation. Thus, all firms involved in an exchange will know the capabilities of each other's systems. Contacts and process descriptions of firms within a relevant sphere of activity will be ready and waiting for those willing to register.

Universal Business Language (UBL)

Universal Business Language (UBL) stands alongside ebXML as the most comprehensive effort to standardise to date. UBL was formally accepted by the OASIS technical committee in October 2001. The main attributes of UBL are experienced and proven leadership qualities, broad industry and vendor support and a solid technical foundation.

UBL uses the horizontal business library developed by Commerce One called 'xCBL'. UBL harmonises xCBL with a host of other business libraries. Also, official liaisons have been appointed to UBL from several vertical standards organisations to ensure that the basic UBL documents will work across multiple industries. However, UBL is not without its critics who assert that the task facing the developers is verging on the impossible. The main concern is that the requirements of companies across different industries will entail more than a single interface to meet the needs of every participant. Companies across different industries, regions and trading conventions use different documentation and procedures. Thus, the criticisms of previous attempts at standardisation still surface. That is, while new formats such as xCBL offer ease of use at lower cost, they still have to be customised through a manual process. Again, this poses a competitive disadvantage for small businesses and undermines fast paced e-commerce.

Rosetta Net

Rosetta Net is an industry specific system geared towards vertical standards in the IT, electronics and hi-tech industries. This e-business initiative is geared towards creating an industry standard that helps to leverage efficiency and cost savings across the supply chain. The pace of change that characterises the participating industries means that firms are under pressure to deliver state-of-the-art products to meet customer expectations and make good their marketing and promotional promises. Rosetta Net is designed to improve the speed and efficiency of the supply chain to meet these challenges.

To explain how Rosetta Net works, May (2000) made the analogy between layered human communication via telephone and a system-to-system communication via Rosetta Net. In human-based commerce, sound enables communication using the alphabet to compile words, words form grammar; and grammar is transformed into dialogue. The dialogue in this analogy is around business processes and the transmission mechanism is the telephone. The same process can be undertaken electronically using Rosetta Net via the internet. The alphabet is the language used (HTML, XML, ebXML etc). Dictionaries define a range of inputs such as products, partners and processes. Effectively, the dictionary provides a framework for undertaking e-business in the domain. The Partner Interface Process (PIP) allows participants to input data on catalogues. Finally,

Telephone	← →	Application
Business process		E-business process
Dialogue		Partner Interface Process (PIP)
Grammar		Framework
Words		Dictionaries
Alphabet		HTML/XML
Sound		Internet

Human-to-human business exchange   System-to-system e-business exchange

Figure 2.2
The Rosetta Net model of e-business exchange. Adapted from *The Business of E-Commerce: From Corporate Strategy to Technology* by Paul May (2000) with permission of Cambridge University Press

any application through which e-business takes place is the systems equivalent of the telephone. Figure 2.2 illustrates the Rosetta Net model of e-business exchange.

UDDI

Universal Description Discovery and Integration (UDDI) is a rival to ebXML. UDDI is the initiative developed by a consortium comprising Microsoft, IBM and Ariba. This system also seeks depth to the interconnections between e-businesses. However, the main difference between ebXML and UDDI is that the latter aims for a standard registry for firms that accelerate the integration of systems for e-marketplaces. The ebXML is aimed at standardising how XML is used in general B2B integration. The UDDI model has middleware connectivity as its main focus and also uses XML to describe the systems that interface with each other. This is achieved by storing information about the integration profiles and capabilities of companies in a shared directory that other companies can access. UDDI was developed specifically to provide large-scale organisations with the means of managing their network integration with small-scale business customers.

Wireless technology

Wireless technology has been the catalyst for structural change in the internet economy since it first emerged as a viable e-business channel in the 1990s. The lack of mobility is a shortcoming of traditional e-business models (Ropers, 2001). Wireless technology is driving the emergence of new business models that exploit opportunities beyond the e-business paradigm.

The emergence of mobile internet networks can be viewed as one of the most significant media opportunities presented to firms across a wide range of industry sectors. Enabling synchronous and asynchronous interconnections via many devices and multiple information Webs, the mobile internet is capable of broad-based applications in business including the tracking of assets, accessing customer information, initiation of transactions and the leveraging of brands off the 'wired' internet to widen connections with their customer base (Kalakota and Robinson, 2001). Essentially, business opportunities derived from the mobile internet, usually termed 'm-commerce', depend on value-adding services that facilitate the communication of information or transactions via public or private mobile telecommunications networks (Rayport and Sviokla, 1995).

Projections of global growth rates in mobile phone use vary between analysts, but the industry expects continuing growth at least until the end of the first decade of the millennium. Nokia, the Finnish providers of mobile devices, predict that the total number of people using mobile phones will break through the two billion mark by the end of 2005 (Wray, 2005). The firm also predicts that mobile phone use worldwide will be at the three billion mark by 2010, almost half of the world's projected population. The prospects for 3G mobile phones has also improved since the industry addressed the drawback of bulky handsets with poor battery life. A new generation of slimline mobile handsets were rolled out at the 3GSM World Congress in Cannes in February 2005. There are several key drivers of the growth and development of the mobile wireless industry. These include:

- The huge investment in infrastructure;
- The technological advances in software;
- The investment capital flowing into the industry;
- The growth in demand for mobile wireless devices;
- The demand from businesses for mobile and real-time communications.

Developments in wireless technology

WAP

Wireless Applications Protocol (WAP) is a standard that transfers data and information to wireless devices. The WAP rollout in 2000 was the first effective standard specifically aimed at mobile devices using a stripped down version of HTML called 'Wireless Markup Language' (WML). WML is designed for making data, information and limited graphics legible on small hand-held devices such as mobile phones.

3G

The rollout of third generation (3G) mobile phone technology in 2003 has provided high-speed data transfer enabling video calling.

Each new technology for accessing mobile internet applications has its own transmission speed. 3G operates at 384 k/bits per second, a tenfold increase since second generation (2G) rollout only a few years previously in 2000.

Bluetooth

Bluetooth is a specification for short-range radio communications among mobile devices (May, 2000). Mobile devices operating Bluetooth can communicate when they come within range of each other and establish a network relationship. Where Jini needs to be hooked up to a network, the Bluetooth initiative allows devices to be connected anywhere within the communications range without cables. Bluetooth also has built-in security features such as encryption and authentication functions, even though research has found that most users do not use these (see Chapter 6).

Wi-fi

Wireless-fidelity, or wi-fi, is a high-speed local-area network enabling wireless access to the internet for mobile, office and home users. Its main attribute is its flexibility since it can be used in built-up urban areas without the need for a fixed connection. Intel, the computer-chip company, has been active in designing a chip that smoothes the way for wi-fi access on laptop computers. Wi-fi can be found in public places such as airports, restaurants, hotels and hospitals. These places provide so-called 'internet hotspots' where mobile devices can hook up to the internet without needing a fixed wire. However, there have been concerns expressed by some security professionals regarding the ease to which wi-fi can be hacked into by anyone within range and using the same wireless frequency. This is discussed in more detail in Chapter 6.

Wimax

Wimax is a broadband service that can support data transmission at speeds of up to 10 Mb a second, twenty times faster than conventional 512 kb/s available on copper wires. The higher data rates will allow firms to transmit large amounts of information faster as well as making it easier to use services that rely on video. The Wimax initiative offers greater reach than wi-fi broadband technology.

Wi-fi can reach up to 100 feet whereas Wimax promises to be available within a range of twenty-five miles.

Wireless standards

The standard protocol for sending data between wireless devices is the Wireless Application Protocol (WAP). WAP uses a version of HTML called Wireless Markup Language (WML) and is designed specifically for small devices such as mobile phones and PDAs. WML allows text to be readable on mobile devices that would be indecipherable using HTML. Users of WAP-enabled devices have to accept some compromises compared to fixed networks. First, the bandwidth is much narrower. Although it is possible to broaden bandwidth on mobile devices, it is at the expense of battery life. Second, HTTP messages do not translate well on mobile devices since they are written in human-readable text that is too bulky for wireless-enabled devices.

When wireless technology was first rolled out in the early 1990s, mobile phones operated on the Global System for Mobile Communication (GSM) standard that offered a minimum transmission speed of 9.6 k/bits per second. By 2000, GSM speed was increased to 64 k/bits per second by aggregating channels in a scheme called High-Speed Circuit Switched Data (HSCSD). This brought mobile devices into line with transmission speeds of fixed networks.

There quickly followed a further initiative called the General Packet Radio Service (GPRS). This standard offered a minimum transmission speed of 43 k/bits per second and potentially 170 k/bits per second. GPRS works by combining packets of data from different calls in order to optimise use of capacity. The evolution of standards has continued at a rapid pace since 2000. The GSM standard has subsequently been enhanced by Enhanced Data Rates for Global Evolution (EDGE) at 384 k/bits per second and third generation (3G) Universal Mobile Telecommunications System (UMTS) with a possible 2000 k/bits per second. Figure 2.3 summarises the evolving standards for mobile devices.

For telecommunications firms such as Nokia, Eriksson, BT and Orange, the importance of acquiring a license to operate on frequencies for mobile phones cannot be underestimated. Across Europe, and including the UK, telecommunications firms had to bid for the rights to own a license in a closed auction. The result was to

2003	**UMTS**	Universal Mobile Telecommunications System 2000 k/bits per second
2002	**EDGE**	Enhanced Data Rates for Global Evolution 384 k/bits per second
2001	**GPRS**	General Packet Radio Service 170 k/bits per second
2000	**HSCD**	High-Speed Circuit Switched Data 56 k/bits per second
1992	**GSM**	Global System for Mobile Communications 14.4 k/bits per second

Figure 2.3
Evolving standards
for mobile devices
(maximum k/bits per
second)

ratchet up the cost of acquiring a license as firms had to bid a price that gave them a realistic chance of gaining the much sought after access to the mobile phone market. Much of the cost has been passed on to customers in the initial rollout phase of 3G mobile phones as firms strive to recover the costs of acquiring a license.

Mobile wireless-enabling capabilities

Mobile wireless technology provides the capability for overcoming some of the problems associated with 'wired' e-commerce. These typically centre on customer service criteria and value-adding activities, both of which combine to determine efficiency and, ultimately, competitive advantage. Mobile wireless technology offers the opportunity to address efficiency gaps so prevalent in the e-commerce space. Firstly, innovators can utilise wireless technology to create new products and services. Efficiencies can be gained in wireless portals by disintermediating retailers and distributing directly to subscribers.

Wireless also enhances monitoring and management of the supply chain process by improving the flow of information for ordering, stock control and payment. The mobile characteristic of wireless increases efficiency in operational productivity. All of these contribute to value-adding services to customers whether in business-to-consumer (B2C) or business-to-business (B2B) sectors. Mobile wireless smoothes transactions between suppliers and customers and provides a mechanism for developing customer relationship management business models, the efficacy of which will play a crucial role in determining the long-term viability of mobile commerce (m-commerce).

Other emerging technologies

Internet protocol

Internet protocol (IP) is a system that facilitates the convergence of voice and video with existing forms of internet communication (e-mail, databases, etc.). IP is linked to a common infrastructure that unifies the computer and IT infrastructure of organisations. This allows workers to communicate with anyone else in any part of the globe using a choice of communications media including video conferencing, mobile phones or laptop computers. IP also extends to mobile communications. Beyond 3G technology comes mobile IP-based network developments that allow users to access any other network using mobile telephones. This will form part of the next generation of mobile phone technology (4G).

Voip

A challenge to mobile telecoms companies is the prospect of the development of internet telephony, and in particular, voiceover internet protocol (voip). Voip is a means of making telephone calls over the internet and is set to have a considerable impact on the telecoms market. Internet telephony works by breaking down the voice call (in similar fashion to the dismantling of data for online contact), sending it over the internet and then reassembling it at the receiver's end. Voip offers free telephone calls by allowing broadband users to download software on to their computers and call other broadband users with exactly the same software anywhere in the world. Free calls are, of course, only available to those users who share the same technology. Nevertheless, voip has attracted the interest of some of the biggest names in telecoms and internet industries including Wanadoo (www.wanadoo.com) and AOL (www.aol.co.uk/ aim). In January 2005 BT (www.bt.com/btcommunicator) announced a £9 billion investment in upgrading its network to facilitate the voip delivery system.

Internet Service Providers (ISPs) can see opportunities by encouraging their customers to switch to internet telephony. Google, one of the world's most high profile ISPs has introduced a strategy to increase its revenues by offering broadband internet users access to cheap phone calls over the internet. By providing a telephony service Google would also gain a greater insight into the customers who use their website. This valuable information could be used to improve the service they provide for their advertisers. The firm also intends to introduce new services such as 'click-to-dial'. This is where an advertiser's web page has a special button that connects an internet phone call straight to a call centre.

Voip may spell the end for telephone charges per minute with the likely replacement being a monthly service charge. This has become possible because of the convergence of telecoms with computers with call traffic moving to the internet. Using the internet for telephony reduces the marginal cost of calls to zero and allows firms to offer phone calls for free. Customers pay a fixed monthly rate and can make as many local or national calls as they wish. This has significant savings potential for businesses who use telephone services extensively throughout a normal working day. Using traditional communications infrastructure, firms require separate network connections at each of their office locations for data, video, fax and standard calls, making the whole process complex and expensive. Voip allows for voice, video or data to be transmitted using the same dedicated network. The technology also includes additional services such as voicemail, call diversion, caller display and three-way calling.

Voice recognition

A great amount of time, energy and resources has been poured into developing voice recognition technology, with IBM leading the way in both research and design. Once voice recognition becomes widely available it will offer a further value-added dimension to communicating via fixed or mobile internet.

Internet television

Internet television (IPTV) enables viewers to choose from a vast archive of film and television programmes. IPTV is to be rolled out in America in 2005 and is likely to reach British shores in 2007. Internet television has been in development for over a decade with Microsoft being one of the leading firms investing in this new technology. BT has agreed a deal with Microsoft to develop the underlying technology for providing a television network delivered over phone lines. The aim is to deliver a range of existing TV channels alongside video-on-demand services through a set-top box. Two technical factors have made this possible. Firstly, increased broadband speeds make the launch of video-based services viable. Secondly, there have been significant advances in developing television picture quality on PC screens. Previously, the fonts and pixels used to deliver text and images on a PC screen were incompatible for television. Developers of IPTV have largely solved this problem such that the picture quality on a PC resembles that of conventional televisions.

Mobile phone television

Major telecommunications businesses are involved in providing mobile television services. For example, Orange provide a mobile phone TV service in France using 3G technology. Vodaphone already provides a mobile phone TV service in Germany and intends to roll out similar services in the UK to try to boost demand for its 3G services. In Finland, Nokia have been active in experimenting with mobile TV services to determine what their customers want from the service, how they use it and how much they are willing to pay. The development of mobile phone television provides another channel for telecommunication companies, content providers, broadcasters, advertisers and other businesses to reach customers.

Interactive television

Television as a medium has been enhanced by computer functions (Stipp, 1999). Instead of competing with each other, television and computers have a vested interest in each other's welfare. The exploitation of synergy between the two media has created new business opportunities for firms across the supply chain of multimedia. Interactive media is a prime example of new technology driving change across many industries including broadcasting, communications, manufacturing and advertising.

Interactive television is a manifestation of the convergence of television and new interactive technologies such as the internet. The main characteristic of interactive television is the engagement of the viewer in the television experience since it offers the possibility of interaction between consumer and content. The development of digital television has opened up a whole new range of interactive applications in the communications and broadcasting industries through extending transmission systems, increasing technical standards and broadening the range of content provision. Developments in television and computer technologies are driving the communications and broadcasting industries towards structural convergence of internet and television. The significance of this on e-marketing and advertising is covered in Chapter 5. As the television and the internet become one, the viewer/consumer will be able to connect directly to the website of the product being offered.

Interactive television technology

Interactive television requires a set-top box to decode digital messages sent via satellite or cable and transform them into pictures on screen. The set-top box is also equipped with a modem that facilitates interactivity. The key difference between traditional analogue television and digital television is that the latter facilitates interactivity. Interactivity requires greater bandwidth and digital technology provides this. New broadband technology has increased bandwidth further thereby allowing an even greater number of channels and wider scope for interactivity. Digital television can be delivered via satellite, cable or terrestrial means. Satellite delivery requires a satellite dish and a set-top box and terrestrial delivery requires the installation of a set-top box. There are three main components to interactive television technology. These are the:

- Platform: the underlying system and standards that makes up the set-top box. The platform enables interactivity and other applications. Platforms can include interactive television related software, middleware and/or hardware.
- Middleware: a general name for any program that serves to bring together the interactive engine and databases. Middleware provides the software for services between server and end-user.
- Software: software adds features to the set-top box.

The UK has been at the forefront in developing and implementing interactive television services. Digital television is experiencing dramatic growth in the UK, with services available through satellite, terrestrial, cable and ADSL platforms. These are driving the development of digital technology and the growth of television-based interactive services. Both government and firms have been active in encouraging UK consumers to switch to digital and use interactive services. In February 2005 the UK Government announced its intention to bring forward the switch off of analogue such that by 2010 all televisions in the UK will be digital. In the UK, increasing numbers of consumers are buying products via interactive television, mostly via BSkyB and their US middleware operator Open TV.

Forrester Research predict continued growth of interactive television services to at least 2010. This will be driven mostly by interactive video, which will become more ubiquitous, as opposed to proprietary 'walled gardens' (where tenant companies pay fees to be present on individual carriers) offering services and content which proliferate at present. UK households are being offered a range of services, including e-mail, games and shopping, by this method. The dominance of 'walled gardens' is diminishing and being replaced by electronic programming guides (EPGs) and interactive video.

In Europe consumers have grown used to clicking on television screens for services such as the UK's Teletext – an early interactive television platform for delivering news, weather, financial services and ticketing services for theatres and airlines. Europe has also been

Electronic programme guides (EPG)

Interactive entertainment guides (IEG)

Answer questions in real-time during interactive game shows

Home shopping, banking, etc.

Customised and localised information, e.g. traffic, weather

View multiple screens simultaneously

Interactive polls and surveys

Interactive sports

Gambling and betting

Video-conferencing

Interactive advertising

Distance learning

Photo display services

Interactive music selection

Instant messaging

E-mail

Direction control, e.g. switch cameras during a sports broadcast

Figure 2.4
Interactive television applications

quick to roll out digital television, which better lends itself to interactive services, making the Continent a testing ground for both content and technologies. There are many ways that interactive television can add value to consumers through the applications it can offer. Figure 2.4 outlines some of the applications of interactive television.

Payment systems

There are many payment service providers such as WorldPlay and Kaji, but it is PayPal that leads the market. Most businesses accept payments via their website and companies such as PayPal facilitate safe methods of transacting. Online traders can open a payment service by accessing the website of the payment service provider and simply click through for details relating to online trading. From there, online traders need only complete an application form to become a client of the payment service provider. Most providers offer some level of protection for their client's customers should there be a problem with a transaction such as fraud or non-delivery of goods.

One of the most important aspects of secure payment systems for e-business and e-commerce is the authenticity of transactions. The most common software used for this purpose is Secure Sockets Layer (SSL) developed by Netscape. SSL makes use of digital certificates to authenticate transactions. Most credit card transactions are protected by SSL. Another authenticity system is Secure Electronic Transaction (SET). This is a payment mechanism for confirming authenticity of both buyer and seller. Each party to a transaction has to obtain a digital certificate from a registered certification authority (the post office and BT are two examples of these). The certificate is contained within a relevant machine, and the credit card details contained within it can only be decrypted by the issuing card company. These secure payment systems are discussed in more detail in Chapter 6.

Just as there is no common standard in e-business, likewise there is a lack of standardisation of payment systems. There have been attempts at introducing standard payment systems but, inevitably, these have been competing rather than collaborating ventures. The two main standards are:

 The Open Buying on the Internet; and
 The Open Trading Protocol.

The Open Buying on the Internet (OBI)

The system managed by CommerceNet called 'The Open Buying on the Internet' (OBI) (www.openbuy.com) is, perhaps, the most advanced e-business standard available and is aimed specifically at business-to-business (B2B) procurement. OBI provides an open architecture that brings buyers and sellers together for the transaction of high-volume, low value products between companies that form the majority of trade between businesses. However, despite offering a detailed and comprehensive service that is easily used, OBI has failed to gain universal acceptance as a standard. The main reason for this lies not in the technology but the differing needs of buyers and sellers. Buyers can use the interoperability of the catalogues to compare and contrast prices, quality and availability of products. This undermines sellers' ability to build and maintain long-lasting relationships with buyers that can lead to brand loyalty and competitive advantage. Of course, this problem is not confined to OBI, but affects all open systems for B2B transactions.

The Open Trading Protocol (OTP)

Leading developers of smart card digital money, Mondex, introduced the Open Trading Protocol (OTP) in 1997. OTP is designed to deliver a virtual analogue of the traditional trading environment across the supply chain from negotiation to delivery of products. Participants can undertake any of the key roles in effecting a transaction including offer, payment, delivery and authentification. OTP can support a range of payment systems including SET and Mondex. This means that consumers have a choice of payment systems and may take advantage of offers, discounts or price differentials between competing systems.

Summary

E-business and e-commerce are technology-driven industries. The development of the internet and its commercialisation through the World Wide Web has opened up an important channel of communication between buyers, sellers and partners in the supply chain of products and services. The huge growth in internet usage has only been possible because of the information infrastructure that supports such a large amount of information traffic. There are concerns that if internet usage continues to grow at levels seen during the last decade, then further infrastructure development will be required to support the demand. However, the introduction of broadband technology has helped alleviate congestion on the internet by accommodating greater numbers of users as well as offering high-speed services.

There have been considerable developments in the technologies that facilitate the transmission of data and information between computers since the use of EDI in the early 1960s. Program languages have become more sophisticated and offer flexibility and efficiency for users. Java, the XML suite of languages and Bluetooth are just some of the numerous program languages available to users in the modern era, each possessing their own set of attributes. Technological developments have also increased the number of channels through which e-business communications can take place. Mobile wireless internet and interactive television are two examples of these increasingly influential channels of communication.

One of the barriers to the growth of e-business and e-commerce has been concerns over security. Much work has been undertaken to increase the security of transactions over the internet. In particular, interested parties such as companies, financial institutions and security experts have developed robust payment systems that both authenticate buyers and sellers, and offer privacy and security. Nevertheless, fraud on the internet remains a problem. A heightened level of vigilance is required from consumers alongside technology-based security measures to build trust and confidence in e-business.

Finally, the issue of standardisation has been the source of much debate among technologists, policy makers and e-business partners since the emergence of the internet as an important channel for communication. There have been numerous attempts at integrating industry standards across a range of technology-based applications such as program languages, mobile wireless devices and interactive services. Although there would be clear advantages of having a single interface between all parties to e-business and e-commerce transactions, the attempts at standardisation have failed because large-scale corporations have been battling each other for supremacy in their particular industry sector. Companies have good commercial reasons for seeking to ensure that their system becomes the industry standard. While this continues, standardisation is likely to remain elusive.

Questions

1. What are the main technologies that have contributed to the growth and commercialisation of the internet?
2. What advantages does broadband access have for e-businesses?
3. Identify the main attributes of XML.
4. How can interactive television add value to customers?
5. What are the main barriers to the adoption of an industry standard for internet systems?

References

Brennan, J. (1999). Open Broadband Access: An Essential Facility Doctrine Analysis. University of Kansas.

Broadband Britain (Report for the Department of Trade and Industry, 1997). HMSO: London.

Kalakota, R. and Robinson, M. (2001). m-Business: The Road to Mobility. *eAI Journal*, pp. 44–6.

May, P. (2000). The Business of E-Commerce: From Corporate Strategy to Technology. Cambridge University Press: Cambridge.

Minoli, D. and Minoli, E. (1998). *Web Commerce Technology Handbook*. McGraw-Hill: Maidenhead.

Rao, B. and De Backer, R. (2000). The Broadband Debate: Legal and Business Implications. *Journal of Media Management*, Vol. 2, No. 3 and 4, pp. 116–24.

Rayport, J. F. and Sviokla, J. J. (1995). Exploiting the virtual value chain. *Harvard Business Review*, November/December, pp. 75–85.

Ropers, S. (2001). New Business Models for the Mobile Revolution. *eAI Journal*, pp. 53–6.

Stipp, H. (1999). Convergence Now? *International Journal of Media Management*, Vol. 1, No. 1, Autumn/Winter, pp. 10–14.

Wray, R. (2005). Nokia upbeat as it predicts mobile users to reach 3bn. *The Guardian*, 15 February, p. 32.

Further reading

Barron, D. (2000). *The World of Scripting Languages*. Wiley: Chichester.

Bocij, P., Chaffey, D., Greasely, A. and Hickie, S. (2003). *Business Information Systems. Technology, Development and Management* (2nd edition). Financial Times Prentice Hall: Harlow.

O'Brien, J. A. (2002). *Management Information Systems: Managing Information Technology in the E-Business Enterprise* (5th edition). McGraw-Hill: New York, NY.

E-business markets and models

Introduction

Chapter 3 identifies and discusses the key markets that exist for e-businesses and the types of business models that can be developed to take advantage of the opportunities that internet trading can provide for achieving competitive advantage and profitability. The chapter starts with an overview of the types of businesses that use the internet as a channel of communication and transaction. The focus is on firms that exist only because of the internet and those traditional firms that use the internet as an added channel of communication between suppliers, partners and customers. This is followed by the identification of the key benefits that the internet offers for e-businesses. The chapter identifies the types of e-marketplaces available to e-businesses, and the advantages they offer to participating firms, before going on to highlight the key characteristics of e-business markets. Although there are many types of e-business markets the discussion in this chapter focuses mainly on business-to-business (B2B), business-to-consumer (B2C) and consumer-to-consumer (C2C).

The discussion on e-business models starts with an overview of what they are and what they are designed to achieve. This is followed by an outline of some of the most prominent e-business models that have been applied across e-business markets. The emergence of new models for mobile wireless applications is included. The chapter concludes with a framework for analysing the development and implementation of e-business models.

E-businesses

Firms using the internet for business and commerce can be split between those who exist because of the internet (firms born on the net, sometimes referred to as 'internet pureplays') such as lastminute.com (www.lastminute.com) and those who use the internet as an addition to their core business (firms who migrate to the net) such as the supermarket Tesco (www.tesco.com). Some firms 'born on the net' have expanded to incorporate a traditional 'bricks-and-mortar' aspect to their business. For example, Amazon.com has expanded to include the storage and distribution of products among their activities. However, the trend is for most traditional businesses to incorporate an e-business aspect to their activities, either as a complementary service, such as the online bookselling facility of Barnes and Noble (www.barnesandnoble.com) or as a dominant means of trading, such as in airline ticketing. These firms are referred to as 'clicks and mortar' or 'bricks and clicks'. Some traditional firms invest or merge with dot.coms to achieve synergy with online and offline activities.

The mid to late 1990s saw a huge rise in the number of firms setting up to take advantage of the opportunities that trading via the internet could bring. These firms were termed 'dot-coms'. The dot-coms adopted numerous types of business models to gain revenue and achieve growth. The dot-coms only exist because of the commercialisation of the internet and some were able to attain high valuations based on the hype and optimism that surrounded the internet economy during that period. Almost inevitably, the fledgling internet economy could not support the large number of dot-coms who were attracted by the prospects of making money quickly. The dot-com crash of 2000 is discussed later in this chapter.

E-business environment

Key elements of the e-business environment

The internet has transformed the competitive environment for firms and requires managers to understand its distinctive attributes in order to build effective models and exploit the opportunities that its use presents. The internet economy works by a different set of rules from the traditional economy and managers of both traditional bricks-and-mortar firms and internet-based firms have had to face the challenge of either transforming their business model or building their business model around the key attributes that the internet exhibits. Lee (2001) outlines the main attributes of the internet that present both a challenge and an opportunity for businesses. These include:

Economics of exchanging information

Firms can take advantage of both richness and reach of information using the internet. The cost of sending additional units of information via the internet is practically zero and the reach is global.

Connectivity and interactivity

The number of people that have access to the internet is rising year on year on a global scale. Connectivity extends the reach of electronic communication and interactivity allows two-way communication in real-time among parties to electronic communication.

Network economies of scale

The network effects are stronger in the internet economy. There are opportunities for achieving a critical mass of customers by accessing a wider customer base electronically at low cost. The marginal costs of sending information are close to zero so firms can achieve economies of scale by providing value-added products or services to customers cheaply, quickly and efficiently using the internet. Network economies of scale are discussed in more detail in Chapter 4.

Speed of change

The internet has speeded up the transactions process and raised expectations of customers. Firms need to readjust their lead times, response times and distribution and delivery times in order to meet the exacting demands of customers, suppliers and partners across the supply chain in the internet economy. Firms who are able to meet or exceed these raised expectations can create a brand loyalty and, hence, a competitive advantage over rivals.

Economics of abundance

Information is a valuable asset in the internet economy. Revenue can be created by the dissemination of information based on its value to consumers (Rayport and Sviokla, 1995). Firms with exclusive rights to the ownership of valuable information can gain a good revenue stream through the production and protection (copyright) of such information. However, much of the information that drives the internet economy is widely available and ubiquitous. As noted previously, information can be reproduced and distributed at near zero marginal cost. This creates an abundance of information where the value can actually decline. These are termed 'diseconomies of scale' and can occur when the consumer becomes so overwhelmed by the sheer volume of information available that the search costs of finding the information they want increase.

Merchandise exchange

The internet provides a mechanism for displaying a huge array of products and services without having to incur the costs of display that traditional stores incur. Search facilities can channel consumers to the exact types of products and services they are interested in and the website can offer additional services such as discount facilities, links to complementary products, product reviews, transactions, payments and delivery. Compared to traditional forms of shopping the internet offers much greater convenience at lower cost and potentially better service delivery.

Prosumption

The internet can be used as a means of communicating with customers and enriching the relationship between buyer and seller. This can lead to customising or personalising products or services to match the requirements of individual customers. The internet facilitates the ability of customers to determine the design, development and production of products and services (Tapscott, 1996).

Industrial context

In the traditional economy value is created within industrial sectors, such as manufacturing or retailing. In the internet economy value generated in e-business communities transcends industrial sectors (Tapscott, 1999).

The economic implications for e-businesses of these key attributes of the internet are discussed in more detail in Chapter 4. E-business models adopted by companies are designed to exploit the advantages that using the internet can bring. There are three types of channels through which e-business activity takes place. These are communications, transactions and distribution channels.

Communications channel

The efficient exchange of information between buyers and sellers is the most important advantage offered by the internet. The internet, and the WWW in particular, has proved to be an effective medium for accessing, organising and communicating information. The key characteristics of the internet that improve the communications channel include:

- The ability to store vast amounts of information;
- The ease of access to information;
- The scope for interactivity;
- The ability to provide information on demand;
- The improved visual presentation of material.

The internet provides almost instant information and is available around the clock in any location. Customers benefit from quicker response times and access to a wider range of services provided by companies via their website. This, in turn, encourages interactivity between customers and sellers through several forms of communication including e-mail, mailing lists, newsgroups and chat rooms. Sellers can also adjust their marketing strategy in response to customer feedback. This feedback also helps sellers in developing new products, developing the application of existing products or offering personalised and customised products to individual customers. The process of relationship building is boosted and sellers can benefit from customer loyalty.

Transactions channel

The internet smoothes the whole transactions process between buyers and sellers, increases efficiency and can lower costs. The potential for reducing transaction costs is covered in more detail in Chapter 4. Transaction costs for customers are reduced because of the ease of access to market information on a wide range of products including, price, quality, availability and discounts. The time and effort expended searching for products and comparing prices is significantly reduced. Companies can also increase internal efficiency by using the internet to: reduce the amount of paperwork and administrative tasks associated with traditional forms of transacting; manage inventory and stock control; and reduce the procurement cycle time of inputs.

Distribution channel

Companies who produce digital products can use the internet as a distribution channel to offer instant supply at significantly reduced delivery cost. Products and services such as financial information, news, music, software, ticketing and reservations, and consultancy services are just some of the multitude of information-centred products that can be delivered quickly and cheaply to online customers. Figure 3.1 highlights the key advantages the internet offers in each of the channels.

Channel functions	Advantages
Communication	Improved product information
	Improved price information
	Constant availability
	Low cost of communication
	Interactive capability
	Information on demand
	Real-time inventory update
	Online technical support
	Quick response times
	Customised orders
	Post-sales service
	Communication across the supply chain
Transaction	Ease of access to all internet users
	Low transaction costs
	Improved transaction processes
	Reduced administrative costs
	Improved procurement cycle times
	Improved inventory and stock control
	Low establishment costs
Distribution	Instant delivery of digital products/services
	Low cost of delivery
	Distribution tracking capability for customers

Figure 3.1
Advantages of the
internet in channel
functions

E-marketplaces

Electronic marketplaces (e-marketplaces) are electronic exchanges where firms can register as buyers or sellers and undertake business activities using the internet. Typically, e-marketplaces attract firms from each element of an industry supply chain to enhance the efficiency of communications and to undertake transactions. There are many different types of e-marketplaces and each one operates a business model that suits the aims and objectives of the proprietor. Some may be set up as a business offering with an intermediary providing an added-value service such as payment systems. Others may operate on a cost-recovery basis by an industry third-party (industry associations are an example of this). There are a large number of services offered by e-marketplaces, including business directories, transaction services and electronic catalogues, for listing inventory of products and services. There are three main types of e-marketplaces:

- Public exchanges: independently-operated B2B trading platforms for facilitating online transactions between trading partners. These are open to any business or group of businesses.
- Consortium exchanges: an exchange owned and operated by a group of competing businesses who combine their buying power to gain group-wide savings on the supply of materials.
- Private exchanges: an exchange owned and operated by a single firm to link its trading system directly to that of its suppliers.

The key advantages offered by e-marketplaces include:

- Much greater scope for firms to form trading partnerships;
- Opportunities for lower costs associated with the negotiation and transactions of products and services through the use of automated systems;
- Benefits from a more open and transparent pricing environment;
- Opportunities presented by access to value-adding services using electronic systems;
- Opportunities for access to global markets, particularly for small and medium sized enterprises (SMEs).

E-marketplaces can be used by firms to acquire inputs, and sell outputs, electronically, thereby saving on search costs and transaction costs. Since most products bought and sold in the B2B marketplace require transportation, the exchange models invariably include automated multi-party transactions facilities. For example, a buyer of chemical products can acquire transport services simultaneously. E-marketplaces have been the catalyst for structural change in industries too. Previously fragmented industries now benefit from the network integration that e-marketplace exchanges have brought about. Examples include steel, chemicals, office supplies, flowers, plastics and electricity. The exchange of information and products has been greatly simplified by the development of industry-specific e-marketplaces. Figure 3.2 illustrates this process.

Alongside online exchanges, most e-marketplaces also feature online catalogues and online auctions. In online catalogues, sellers provide a list of their products along with other relevant data relating

Old economy

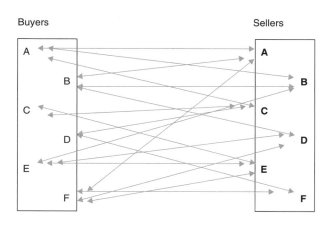

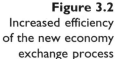

Figure 3.2
Increased efficiency
of the new economy
exchange process

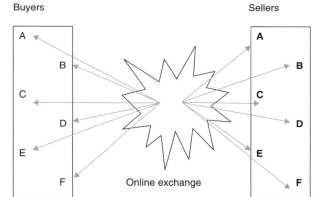

to price, specifications, availability and delivery terms. Buyers can order via the website. The auction model is based on the successful B2C model so effectively developed by firms such as e-Bay. In the B2B market firms can auction off excess inventory to improve revenue and ease storage costs. Figure 3.3 illustrates the dynamic between buy-side and sell-side relationships in an e-marketplace exchange.

E-business markets

Business-to-Business (B2B)

Business value can be enhanced through applications of the internet. This is particularly the case in the B2B sector where clear benefits

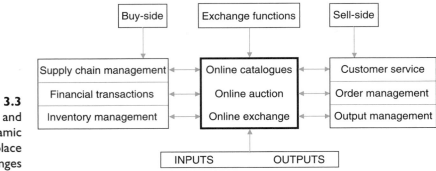

Figure 3.3
Buy-side and
sell-side dynamic
of e-marketplace
exchanges

accrue to suppliers through greater capabilities. It also enhances their asset base and creates potential for sustaining competitive advantage. These assets manifest themselves in a myriad assortment of business and technology advantages. Most notably, it provides a lower cost base such that keener prices ensue or transaction costs reduce. It also reduces the time it takes to bring products to market, thereby increasing response times to emerging opportunities in the global market (Choi et al., 1997). Figure 3.4 illustrates the three distinct stages that can be discerned in the development of B2B business to date.

	Method	Outcome
Stage 1	Buying and selling online	Cut costs and increase speed of supply
Stage 2	Third-party exchanges	Firms bring together buyers and sellers
Stage 3	Consortia	Large firms create a virtual market

Figure 3.4
B2B business
development stages

Stage 1 (c1997) of the development of e-commerce in B2B markets has the characteristics that account for the dramatic rise in entry to the sector. The cost savings from ease of access to market information has reduced procurement times as well as the transaction costs. As the application of the internet to business became more fully understood the next stage produced a rash of firms pitching for the role of middleman. Stage 2 (c1998) saw independent firms specialising in bringing together buyers and sellers within the B2B sector. As specialisation grows, firms will be able to target the best deal in the shortest time as well as ordering to specification. Stage 3 (c2000) has seen large corporations creating consortia to produce virtual markets in their supply chain. The US car industry has been at the forefront of developing these systems (GM/Ford/Chrysler/Daimler) whilst in the UK Alfred McAlpine, Pilkington and BPB have set up a net company for construction-materials procurement.

Much value-adding activity can be conducted in the B2B market-place. Primary activities of a value chain can all provide markets for B2B activity. This ranges from the e-procurement of raw materials (inbound logistics), information-driven content (operations), delivery status and tracking facilities (outbound logistics), e-marketing, transactions and customer relationship management (marketing, sales and after-sales service).

Business-to-Consumer (B2C)

The B2C market has been the most high profile of the e-business markets, principally because of the global brand awareness of firms such as Amazon.com and e-Bay among others. From the mid 1990s there was a surge in the number of firms setting up to take advantage of the developing e-marketspace, the so-called dot-com firms. The staggering rise in the global use of the internet attracted the interest of the business community, as the commercial possibilities that this new means of communication offered became evident.

The first commercial websites emerged in 1994 and soon became the most ubiquitous on the Web. Information-driven industries, and the media industry in particular, were quick to use the Web to market and sell their products. The print media offered online versions of their newspapers and magazines, film and music companies used the internet to promote the latest releases and the first mover in the online bookselling industry, Amazon.com, was founded in 1994. By the mid 1990s, retailers, manufacturers and distributors were being attracted by the ever-increasing commercial possibilities that internet use could provide. Some of the most high profile names in the online industry emerged at this time including e-Bay (auctions), Ask Jeeves (search engine) and Priceline.com (reverse auction).

Two key factors attracted business to the internet. Firstly, it provided a mechanism for instant commercialisation of products and services to potential customers on a global scale. Secondly, the cost of establishing a presence on the internet was low. By the end of the 1990s, the migration of firms to the internet had become a stampede as more and more firms viewed the internet as a quick, cheap and efficient route to making money. Investors were similarly seduced by the potential returns of internet trading and the share values of the so-called 'dot-com' firms rose sharply. The scenario that followed is a familiar one to economic historians.

The *Collins Dictionary of Economics* describes speculation as 'the purchase or sale of assets, real or financial, to achieve a capital gain'. A speculator is described as 'a dealer in markets characterised by rapidly changing prices who buys and/or sells commodities or securities not because he trades in them, but in the hope of making short-term gain from movements in the prices of these commodities or securities'. The activities of speculators can have a stabilising or destabilising effect on a market depending on whether they take a collective view about future price movements. In the 1995 to 1999 period investors in the rapidly growing internet economy did take such a collective view on the future and that view was that the value of dot-com firms was only going to increase.

The internet boom and crash followed a distinct pattern. A new technology emerges that changes the business environment and with it people's expectations about the future. First-movers in the industry, such as Netscape and Amazon.com, initially made money for a few investors. Even though they failed to make profits, the expectations about their future value was enough to attract investors. The dividends gained by early investors attracted other investors and this further ratcheted up the value of the, as yet unproven and fledgling, dot-coms.

There then followed a stampede of investors towards the growth industry as greed replaced pragmatism in the decision-making processes of investors. Fear of losing out on a golden opportunity drove ever-increasing numbers of investors towards the internet industry. By 1999 the prices of dot-com firms bore no resemblance to their actual value. Shares of high profile dot-com firms were offered to the public. In March 1999 Priceline.com was valued at $10 billion despite having little in the way of physical assets (Cassidy, 2002). Investors had staked their savings on a firm with a good brand name and an interesting, but unproven, business model.

In 2000 the dot-com bubble burst; many firms went to the wall and the industry experienced a major rationalisation. The fledgling e-business industry simply could not sustain the large numbers of firms who had flocked to the Web in search of riches. Demand for products and services was still in the early stages of development as consumers were absorbing the benefits of conducting transactions online. However, the level of demand did not match the burgeoning supply created by the large numbers of dot-com firms that characterised the competitive structure of the industry in the late 1990s. Only those firms with robust, differentiated and adaptable business models that captured the imagination of consumers and offered distinct added value were able to survive.

Since the industry 'shake-out' of 2000, the e-business and e-commerce industries have been showing growth at an impressive rate once again. However, this time around firms have come to the market with much more understanding of how the e-business and e-commerce environment works. Both entrepreneurs and investors have focused their attention on the profitability of enterprises. Many firms have reinvented their business models by targeting new markets, expanding into the traditional bricks-and-mortar trading environment, forming alliances, licensing software, and reassessing their value propositions for customers (Chircu and Kauffman, 2000).

Consumers have also undergone a learning process since the commercialisation of the internet in the mid 1990s, and have become more knowledgeable about the buying process online. In the USA the B2C market generated some $120 billion in 2004 with sales of clothing, travel services and pornography leading the way. Some of the internet's most high profile businesses, such as Amazon and e-Bay, have become truly global brand names and have expanded their operations to all continents on Earth. The price transparency associated with e-business and e-commerce means that firms have to work ever harder to gain brand loyalty and offer best value to customers. Much of this is achieved through additional services offered and guaranteed fulfilment. Many e-commerce sites have gained high scores for customer satisfaction. The B2C market is again buoyant and is showing all the signs of remaining that way for the foreseeable future, as online shopping becomes an increasingly important channel for consumers' buying habits.

Consumer-to-Consumer (C2C)

The success of e-Bay as an online auction site and the widespread (and illegal) downloading of MP3 files for music are two catalysts for the expanding consumer-to-consumer (C2C) market. Such direct C2C contact is likely to have profound economic implications for a number of industry sectors. For example, the income generated by classified advertising in newspapers and magazines may be undermined by direct consumer contact; estate agents may find themselves disintermediated, as house buyers and sellers deal with each other directly.

The increasing importance of C2C marketplaces has been recognised by firms in the B2C or B2B markets, with many seeking to participate in the supply chain. Sponsorship of C2C auction sites has been one strategy that firms have adopted to enable participation. Some e-businesses have a hand in facilitating C2C e-commerce such as electronic classified advertising on e-newspaper sites or providers of consumer e-commerce portals.

E-business models

A business model can be defined as the organisation of product, service and information flows, and the sources of revenues and benefits for suppliers and customers. An e-business model is the adaptation of an organisation's business model to the internet economy. A business model is adopted by an organisation as a framework for maximising value in this new economy. Through use of a business model, an organisation can identify where and how in its value chain it can create added value and profit. A business model also enables a firm to analyse its environment more effectively and thereby exploit the potential of its markets; better understand its customers; and raise entry barriers for rivals. E-business models utilise the benefits of electronic communications to achieve these value-adding processes. The internet has increased the number and combination of possible business models that link consumers, public and private organisations, and government bodies. Figure 3.5 is a framework summarising the main e-business markets around which business models are constructed. The channels relevant to the discussion in this chapter are highlighted in bold.

There are many examples of business models designed for the internet. There is a wide range of sophistication associated with business models, some are complex and require collaboration between partners, whereas others are easily set up and operated by few people. E-business models have also had varying levels of commercial success. Some have been spectacular success stories, such as the auction site model operated by e-Bay, and others have been spectacularly unsuccessful, such as online fashion retailer boo.com. E-business models can be linked to e-business markets. Some may be operated across different markets, (e.g. e-auctions can be undertaken in B2C, B2B or C2C markets), whilst others are aimed at one specific

	Government	**Business**	**Consumer**
Government	G2G (Co-ordination)	G2B (Information)	G2C (Information)
Business	B2G (Procurement)	**B2B** **(e-business)**	**B2C** **(e-commerce)**
Consumer	C2G (Tax compliance)	**C2B** **(Compare price)**	**C2C** **(Auctions)**

Figure 3.5
A framework for
e-business markets

e-business sector (e-procurement in the B2B market). The e-business models relating to e-business markets can be summarised as:

- Business-to-Consumer (B2C): e-shops, e-malls, e-auctions, buyer aggregators, infomediaries, classifieds, portaling, manufacturer model, subscription;
- Business-to-Business (B2B): e-auctions, infomediaries, e-procurement, e-distribution, portaling, e-marketing, trading communities, third-party marketplaces, collaboration platforms, value chain integrators, value chain service providers, affiliates;
- Consumer-to-Consumer (C2C): e-auctions, virtual communities.

Types of e-business models

Brokerages

Brokers are intermediaries who bring together buyers and sellers for transactions purposes. There are several forms of brokerage models and they are operated across all e-business markets. In a simple buy/sell fulfilment model, revenue is gained by the brokerage through charging a fee for each transaction completed. In a market exchange model the broker charges the seller a fee based on the value of the sale. Brokerages take on many forms of e-business models. As noted previously, the e-marketplace model is one of the most prominent in the B2B market, but there are many types of e-business models based on brokerage and they involve all types of e-business markets. The ones discussed here include e-shops, e-malls, e-auctions, trading communities, distributors, virtual communities and buyer aggregators and classifieds.

E-shops

Websites are designed to promote the firm and the products or services it sells. However, most e-businesses have gone beyond the basic marketing and promoting of their products and services via their website to incorporate facilities for transactions. E-shops provide firms with a channel of communication to customers and provide valuable information about what products and services are sought by customers. E-shops can also be a first step to competing in global markets since the cost of entry is small and there are economies of scale to be gained from extending the market reach.

For consumers, e-shops provide a quick, efficient and convenient route to accessing information on products and services and undertaking transactions. Repeat business opens up the possibility of customisation and personalisation of products and services as the relationship builds between customer and seller. E-shops are ubiquitous on the internet and cover a huge range of products and services. Some of the many examples of e-shops include: nursery-goods (www.nurserygoods.com) who specialise in baby clothes and accessories; empiredirect (www.empiredirect.co.uk) who specialise in electrical products; onevillage (www.onevillage.com) an online shop for home accessories; and spoilt4choice (www.spoilt4choice.co.uk) an online shop for the buying and delivery of gifts.

E-malls

An electronic mall is a collection of e-shops. Normally, the e-shops that comprise the e-mall have some commonality between them. This may include the types of products or services offered, the type of payment system used or a common market segment targeted. The benefits sought by firms operating in e-malls stem mainly from supporting activities such as advertising, additional services or supporting technologies. Customers benefit from the ease of access to a number of e-shops in the same business category. Increasingly, brokers who organise e-malls are adding services that facilitate transactions, tracking down orders, billing and invoicing of customers. Firms who combine these services with organising e-malls are termed 'metamediaries'.

E-malls have been set up by firms who have traditionally inhabited the bricks-and-mortar trading environment but who seek to expand their online services. Examples include giant department stores such as Bloomingdales, Costco and K-Mart in the USA. Search engines such as AltaVista have also been active in setting up e-malls in partnership with a large number of retailers. The e-mall run by AltaVista is called 'shopping.com' (www.shopping.com). Another firm that has created a successful e-mall is iQVC. The company has built upon its experience of offering products and services via interactive television and linked their business to the internet to create an e-mall where shoppers can browse for a huge array of product and service categories.

E-auctions

The internet is an ideal medium for the exchange of information about products and services. Electronic auctions provide a channel of communication through which the bidding process for products and services can take place between competing buyers. E-businesses gain income from the technology platform that facilitates the bidding process, from a percentage of the transaction fees and from advertising on the website. Consumers benefit from ease of access to a large amount of information on a wide range of products, low transactions costs and efficiency in the transacting process. E-auctions exist in several e-business markets. For example, businesses can auction excess to stock to either consumers (B2C) or other businesses (B2B) and consumers can use auction websites to trade products and services between each other (C2C).

Some auction sites are industry-specific such as eutilia (www.eutilia.com), a European utility marketplace that auctions components in the energy sector. Others focus attention on the consumer market such as onsale.com (www.onsale.com) who specialise in auctions for computer software, hardware, components and digital products. Reverse auctions are another way of generating revenue for firms. Here, buyers make a final bid for a product or service and the broker seeks fulfilment. The revenue generated by the broker comes from the difference between the final bid and the fulfilment price and an administration fee.

Trading communities

Sometimes referred to as a 'vertical web community', trading communities provide a source of information and communication that is necessary for e-business activity to take place in a particular industry. The participants in the industry form a trading community where specific information is accessible to members in buyers' guides, directories of products, lists of suppliers as well as up-to-date industry news, articles and job listings. Members pay a subscription to the developers and operators of trading community sites. VerticalNet.com (www.verticalnet.com) were pioneers of the trading community concept by providing sites for B2B exchanges of information.

Virtual communities

Customers are attracted to websites because of the added value they offer. Specialist websites appeal to customers with a particular interest. The shared interest of customers provides the basis for virtual communities to emerge. This is a community of customers who share a common interest and use the internet to communicate with each other. Amazon.com provides websites for the exchange of information on a wide range of subjects relating to their portfolio of products and services. Virtual communities benefit from network externalities whereby the more people who join and contribute to the community the greater the benefits that accrue, but without any additional cost to participants.

Buyer aggregator model

The buyer aggregator brings together large numbers of individual buyers so that they can gain the types of savings that are usually the privilege of large volume buyers. Mercata (www.mercata.com) was the first American company to receive a patent for group buying over the internet (Business Wire, 2000). As a group, buyers can potentially wield more economic power and gain discounts on large volume sales from sellers. Brokers who organise the collective bargaining of buyers in this way gain revenue by charging the seller a percentage of each sale made to the group of buyers. However, this e-business model has had limited success because most firms have been unable to deliver unique value to customers (Cook, 2001). The group-buying websites have generally been unable to achieve the volume of transactions that is needed to generate the low price proposition that drives the e-business model. Mercata, the first-movers as buyer aggregators, failed to sustain initial customer interest and folded after only two years because of a fatal flaw in their business model – the inability to achieve a critical mass of customers (Kauffman and Wang, 2002).

Classifieds

Online classified advertisements run on the same principles as newspaper classifieds. Content providers list items for sale by sellers and purchases wanted by buyers. Revenue is gained by listing charges and is collected whether or not a transaction takes place.

Infomediaries

Infomediaries specialise in gathering valuable information about customers and selling it on to third parties. These third parties analyse the data and use it to support marketing campaigns. The simplest form of gathering data is through requiring users to register for access to free-to-view content sites. This facilitates the monitoring of user's site viewing patterns and the data generated can then be used for a more targeted marketing campaign. Infomediaries may offer incentives to customers to divulge information about their profile and buying habits. These may take the form of free software or hardware or free internet access for a specified time period.

Infomediaries also serve consumers by offering a range of services including specific information about websites in a market segment and price comparisons. Infomediaries also operate recommendation sites where users exchange information regarding the quality of products or services. Some infomediaries integrate the recommendation site into a web browser. The infomediary can then monitor users' habits and, therefore, increase the relevance of its recommendations to the user's needs whilst adding value to the data it then sells on to third parties.

E-procurement

The internet provides the mechanism for businesses to procure the raw materials they need to create outputs and to help run their businesses efficiently. E-procurement is the management of all procurement activities via electronic means. Business models based on e-procurement seek efficiency in accessing information on suppliers, availability, price, quality and delivery times as well as cost savings by collaborating with partners to pool their buying power and secure best value deals. E-procurement infomediaries specialise in providing up-to-date and real-time information on all aspects of the supply of materials to businesses.

Car manufacturer Ford developed an online B2B exchange that specialises in e-procurement of supplies for a consortium of US car manufacturers that includes Ford, Daimler-Chrysler and GM. This e-procurement infomediary, called 'Covisint', provides information on the many thousands of potential suppliers of component parts for the car industry and uses the huge purchasing power of the consortium to gain best value deals. The supply costs to the members of the consortium are significantly lower compared to the fragmented and competitive arrangements that existed under traditional procurement systems.

Distribution model

The distributor model brings together product manufacturers with high volume (e.g. wholesalers) and retail buyers. Buyers benefit from gaining access to catalogues of manufactured goods and the broker acts as intermediary between distributors and their trading partners. The value to buyers is in the increased efficiency in bringing products to market and the reduction in procurement costs. The buyer can reduce transaction costs by comparing prices between distributors and finding the best deals available.

The e-distribution model helps distributors to achieve efficiency savings by managing large volumes of customers, automating orders, communicating with partners and facilitating value-adding services such as order tracking through each point in the supply chain. An example of a firm specialising in e-distribution is wipro.com (www.wipro.com) who use the internet to provide fully integrated e-business-enabled solutions that help to unify the information flows across all the major distribution processes including sales and marketing automation, customer service, warehouse logistics, purchasing and inventory management, and finance.

Portaling

A portal is the internet equivalent of a broadcaster. Portals are the channels through which websites are offered as content. The control of content can be a source of revenue for firms through charging firms for advertising or charging consumers a subscription for access. There are different types of portal models and they include:

General portal

General portals carry high volume traffic with millions of website visitor hits per month. Examples include search engines such as Google and Lycos or content-driven sites such as AOL. The high volume of traffic makes it attractive to advertisers and generates income streams for the portal owners. There is great competition for website traffic and consumers are invariably offered a number of incentives to choose a particular portal and remain with it for future use. These can include free access to content or services.

Personalised portals

To encourage user loyalty beyond offers of free access to content or free software, some portal owners develop a customised interface that allows users to personalise the website. The content and website design is geared towards the tastes and interests of the users. The information derived from users is a source of value to the portal owner as is the volume of traffic that such personalised portals can generate. Examples of personalised portals include My.Yahoo! and My.Netscape.

Vortals

A vertical portal, or vortal, is a specialised portal that is designed to attract a particular market segment. Vortals may be set up to attract traffic from users with similar interests, experiences or have similar buying habits. The success of a vortal is not determined so much by volume of traffic, but rather the ability to attract a well-defined user base. This is of particular interest to advertisers who seek a more targeted audience for specific offerings. Owners of vortals can charge advertisers a premium for access to a target audience.

Collaboration platforms

Collaboration between organisations is a key feature of the modern business environment and the internet can play a role in the communication between partner organisations. Collaboration platforms provide the technological tools for information to pass quickly and efficiently between organisations. These tools can be designed for specific functions such as sharing customer information for joint marketing ventures, logistics for the tracking of supplies and inventory between partners or creating an information environment for the exchange of ideas among design consultants. Businesses that create collaboration platforms charge users for access and for the tools they use for underpinning their relationship with partners.

Examples of collaboration platforms include Account4.com (www.account4.com) an e-business set up to help automate the business process of firms in the professional services and IT sectors. MatrixOne (www.matrixone.com) sells software tools that facilitate the sharing of product ideas and designs among employees, customers and suppliers for global businesses. CoVia (www.covia.com) offers a collaboration platform for document management, project planning and personalised interactions solutions for partners, clients and colleagues in a range of consultancy businesses.

Third-party marketplaces

Some firms specialise in using the internet to market and promote products and services on behalf of client organisations. These client organisations may have experience of marketing and selling products through traditional channels but lack the specific expertise and experience to transfer this knowledge to the e-business environment. A third-party marketplace is a channel through which firms can extend their sales pitch to customers by making available their product catalogue on the website. The entire transaction process can be undertaken through the third-party marketplace since most include applications for ordering, distribution and payment. Some third-party marketplaces are industry-specific and cater for the needs of clients involved in specific industry activities or processes. For example, spec2000 (www.spec2000.com) is a third-party marketplace that facilitates the electronic exchange of technical and business information related to the purchase and repair of aircraft.

Value chain integrators

Further value can be added to a value chain by integrating the elements that comprise it. Value chain integrators improve the efficiency and quality of information flows between the elements that comprise a value chain. Microsoft (www.microsoft.com) is a value chain integrator through its initiative Microsoft Insurance Value Chain. This value chain integrator service is aimed at the insurance industry and comprises many partners including hardware firms such as EDS and HP as well as independent solutions vendors. These companies use Microsoft products and services to develop and deliver integrated solutions for the insurance industry that can increase efficiency and quality of service. The integration of value chain activities can result in reducing claims settlements and costs, improving underwriting and customer service or streamlining processes. Improving the efficiency of the value chain activities can lead to faster and more accurate policy insurance delivery, expanded policyholder services and, ultimately, greater customer satisfaction and profitability.

Value chain service providers

Value chain service providers focus on one or more functional elements of the value chain and provide specific and customised electronic services such as payment solutions, logistics systems, maintenance or product advice services or after-sales support service. Financial institutions, customer support service providers and distribution firms are well placed to use their skills and expertise to incorporate value chain service provision into their portfolio of business activities.

Manufacturer model

The manufacturing model brings about the process of disintermediation in the supply chain by creating a direct line of communication between manufacturers and consumers. Wholesalers and retailers are eliminated from the distribution process. The resulting savings on transaction costs can then be passed on to consumers in the form of lower prices. Alternatively, the manufacturers can increase revenue by retaining transaction costs savings and offering the consumer added value service in the form of quicker delivery of goods or customisation of products to meet specific consumer preferences. The manufacturing model is particularly effective when dealing with perishable goods that could diminish in quality and value if transported through the entire supply chain. Food items such as fish, fruit and vegetables retain their value over a short timeframe and, therefore, benefit from compressing the supply chain to reach the consumer quicker.

Affiliate model

The affiliate model offers buying opportunities for internet users across many different websites. The firm organising the affiliate model offers financial incentives to affiliate partner sites to participate in the venture. US website befree.com (www.befree.com) is an example of a firm specialising in organising affiliates. The affiliates provide the purchase-point click through to the sellers of products. The economic viability of an affiliate model depends on the level of sales that an affiliate generates. The more products sold the greater the returns to all parties concerned. However, if no sales are generated there is no cost to the seller. The affiliate gets a small percentage of revenue if customers who browse the affiliate's site actually buy something from the seller. In essence, the affiliate model helps many other websites to share revenue with firms who gain sales as a result of other website's traffic.

Subscription model

Revenue is generated through subscription to access particular websites. To generate subscriptions firms have to offer high value content to users. The majority of websites do not run on a subscription basis because of the ubiquity of information available and the low switching costs for consumers. If one firm offered content by subscription only, a rival firm could easily offer free access to the same information and operate a different pricing model. Subscription sites are used where operators own exclusive rights to valuable content or where there is added service such as up-to-the-second financial information. However, research shows that most internet users would not pay to view content on websites.

Models for mobile wireless technology

The development of mobile wireless technology is driving the emergence of new business models. The most important advantage that mobile wireless technology offers is its portability. It provides a channel of communication anywhere at any given time. Two main players dominate in the mobile wireless environment. These are mobile service providers (MSPs) and primary service providers (PSPs). MSPs are the owners of the network that provides a range of services to users. PSPs are firms who already use the internet to provide services, sell products to consumers or match buyers and sellers. MSPs can create business models to fully exploit the added flexibility of mobile devices. Mobile wireless devices have a number of attributes that add value to businesses and customers. These include:

- Portability: mobile wireless technology frees users from the constraints of fixed line computers. This means that e-business can take place anywhere at any time (as long as it is within range of a network operator). New technology, such as Wimax, is extending the reach of mobile wireless devices to move towards the 'anytime, anyplace' goal;
- Multi-channel: the flexibility of mobile wireless devices to communicate with other devices, such as PDAs, interactive television, fax or PC is a further boost to the 'anytime, anyplace' goal. The mobility aspect refers to both people and devices. Users can access different devices in different locations because they all have equal access channels for electronic services;
- Security: the security of mobile wireless communications and transactions is enhanced because subscribers to the network can be located and identified at any given time. Network operators can link a device directly to a subscriber's identity that is already being used for transactions and thereby authenticate that user;

■ Additional services: mobile network operators offer voice services to users along with a host of complementary services including message alerts, account management and browsing facilities for accessing information.

Mobile wireless technology opens up opportunities for primary service providers (PSPs) to rework their business models to exploit the attributes associated with it. These business models may be based on a number of value-adding activities such as consumer transactions, consumer information, access to after-sales services or links to other products and services. Business models can support business activities via the mobile phone such as providing information to employees, ordering equipment, accessing business information, communicating with partners and suppliers via a database stored on the mobile device or supporting the network integration of the business by feeding in information anytime and from any place.

Successful business models built around mobile wireless technology are likely to combine the value-adding attributes of the technology (Ropers, 2001). For example, PSPs can use MSPs' authentification capabilities to offer secure transactions of products and services, or they can use the customer profile database supplied by MSPs to provide personalised services. Combined, MSPs and PSPs can offer customers added value in a wide range of different products and services including payment solutions, banking, brokerage, travel arrangements, calendar management services and contact management. Some business models can be created to integrate the user role (consumer, employee, club member, business associate, etc.) with the type of application (informational, transactional, etc.).

A framework for analysing e-business models

Business models are designed to help firms add value to customers and achieve their stated objectives. To succeed, firms need to understand their external environment, utilise their resources effectively and build distinctive capabilities that leverage competitive advantage over rivals. Figure 3.6 illustrates the process linking a business model with competitive advantage.

Developing and implementing business models help firms to compete in a marketplace. Analysing the business model helps firms identify what activities in the value chain contribute to

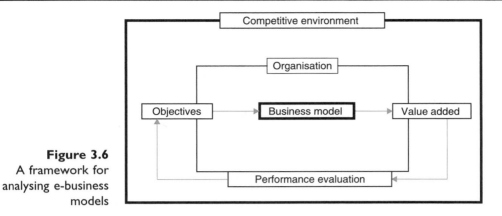

Figure 3.6
A framework for
analysing e-business
models

profit and help create a competitive advantage. The effectiveness of a business model is determined by the ability of firms to exploit market opportunities, match or exceed customer expectations and achieve stated aims and objectives. Lee (2001) sets out the key characteristics of a viable e-commerce model. Firms must:

- Design programs that take advantage of the internet network effects and other disruptive attributes to achieve a critical mass of installed customer base;
- Leverage on a single set of digital assets to provide value across many different and disparate markets;
- Build trust relationships with customers through e-business communities to increase their costs of switching to other vendors;
- Transform value propositions and organisational structures for enhanced value creation; and
- Generate synergy effects on e-commerce product and service offerings.

In developing and implementing an e-business model firms must meet three critical success factors. They must:

- Understand and exploit the e-marketspace characteristics;
- Add value to customers; and
- Achieve economic viability.

E-marketspace characteristics

The e-marketspace comprises supply and demand characteristics. The supply of products and services into the e-marketspace depends on the competitive structure of each industry sector. There are some

B2C markets that are characterised by many hundreds or even thousands of firms all competing for the attention of customers. This competitive structure features a high level of differentiation as firms seek to gain customers through offering discounts, free software, repeat business rewards, free internet access and a host of other incentives to build brand loyalty.

In other B2C markets the competitive structure may be more restricted because of the ability of firms to erect entry barriers through specialist services, such as having access to highly-valued financial information or offering access to specialist advice and consultancy. Entry barriers may also be achieved through first-mover advantages whereby the firms who are first to market have been able to build a critical mass of customers and a global brand name. In other cases barriers to entry may stem from technological superiority or the ability to attract key skills that underpin the value proposition presented to customers. In some cases, exclusive rights to information or products and services may be the determinant of competitive advantage. Entry barriers can be used to build a dominant position in the industry sector by offering lower prices to customers that potential rivals cannot match.

The structure of demand is determined by the number and characteristics of customers for each product or service available on websites. Both new and existing customers make up the demand function for products and services sold over the internet. The e-business model must tap into the key influencing factor or factors that attract customers to, firstly, the website, and secondly, to the products or services being offered. They should be designed to take account of the key characteristics that comprise the structure of demand. Here, market research reveals the nature of demand according to a range of different characteristics that create market segments including income, gender, age, socio-economic groups, geographical location of customers or groups of customers, tastes and fashions, etc.

The B2B market e-business models are built around relationships with partners along the supply chain. Businesses that sell products or services to other businesses must be able to offer added value to their business customers beyond that gained from traditional forms of business transactions. The business models that B2B firms adopt can be built around value-added characteristics such as:

- Increasing efficiency of procuring raw materials;
- Reductions in product costs;

> ▦ Better communications with supply chain partners;
> ▦ Increased efficiency from streamlining the supply chain process;
> ▦ Better quality service provision and delivery;
> ▦ Better information on product availability, quality and price.

Adding value to customers

The drivers of added value determine how firms meet or exceed expectations of customers. The key drivers include the value proposition based on the types of products or services offered, the price of those products and services, and the level of differentiation that supports the unique selling proposition. The added value to customers may be in the design or application of the products or services themselves, or it may derive from the distinct advantages that the internet offers as a means of communication and transacting. The internet has a number of value-adding characteristics for consumers. Gascoyne and Ozcubukcu (1997) highlight the main ones as being:

> ▦ Convenience;
> ▦ Continuous availability;
> ▦ Price transparency;
> ▦ Interactivity;
> ▦ Wider choice;
> ▦ Quicker fulfilment;
> ▦ Personalisation;
> ▦ Customisation;
> ▦ Access to a huge amount of information.

The delivery mechanism also has a role to play in adding value to customers. Here, the collaboration with partners in the value chain may help smooth the supply chain process to quicken fulfilment times; the information gathered on customers can be used to inform more targeted marketing campaigns; and the interactive aspect of the internet allows two-way communication to take place resulting in a better understanding of customers' needs. The delivery mechanism also increases internal efficiency through better communications, automating processes, storing valuable information on customers and suppliers, and providing data for the monitoring of performance.

Achieving economic viability

Firms must set performance targets and evaluate the effectiveness of the e-business model to determine whether changes are necessary or if the model has to be completely reworked or abandoned. The e-business has to be economically viable. A good e-business model can gain a firm the goodwill of financial backers but all investors or venture capitalists will seek a return on their investment sooner or later. Amazon.com took many years to register a profit but retained the confidence of financial backers because of the potential for profit that the e-business model could generate. Not all firms benefit from such goodwill and most have to show returns on investment quickly.

To determine economic viability, a number of indicators from the profit model and the financial model can be used. The profit model comprises the profit and loss results, the cost structure and the revenue generated through the application of the e-business model. The financial model centres on the cash flow of the firm, the value of assets owned by the firm and the financial structure of the business. Close inspection of the data generated by the profit and financial models reveals the performance of the e-business model. Financial analysis is an important performance indicator and is discussed in more detail in Chapter 10.

Decisions on the viability of the venture usually hinge on the performance indicators. There are a number of factors that can determine the economic viability of an e-business model. Three of the most important factors are as below.

Achieving a critical mass of customers

The most important factor that determines the viability of an e-business model is the number of customers that the value proposition attracts and who return for repeat business. Successful e-business models exploit network effects and combine various value-adding characteristics of the internet. Many online customers prefer to have a one-stop-shop for their buying needs. Online customers also perceive value in shopping with a well-known and trusted vendor. The most successful e-business models have been able to gain the trust of customers by offering low prices, quick and

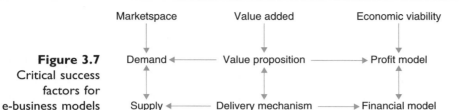

Figure 3.7
Critical success
factors for
e-business models

efficient service, a wide choice of products and services, and security of transactions.

Continuing to innovate and add value

The e-business model must be able to continue to add value to customers by innovation and creativity. This may involve the marketing and promotion of the products or services, the types of discounts and incentives that can be offered, tie-ins with other products and services, access to further sources of information, access to virtual communities of buyers, interactivity, customisation and so on. These benefits create switching costs for customers and can help to build a level of brand loyalty that underpins attaining a critical mass of customers.

Design for flexibility

The e-business model must be able to be adapted to suit related and unrelated business opportunities. The e-business must be able to gain revenue from providing value across many different and disparate markets. For some firms it is important to design an e-business model that can be integrated with other business models so that alignment of all business components can be achieved. Economies of scope can be gained through the synergy of product and service offerings (Rowley, 2002). Where customers seek value from one-stop-shopping online then firms can integrate business models to take advantage of cross-selling opportunities. The viability of the e-business model would depend on where the greater revenue could be derived; that is, if the revenue generated from a single general website was greater or less than the revenue generated from some combinations of two or more specialist single-product providers.

Summary

The e-business environment offers a number of opportunities for firms to present unique value propositions to customers. The e-business industry structure has been through three distinct phases. Firstly, there was a surge of interest from internet start-ups leading to the so-called dot-com era. There followed an industry 'shake-out' as the forces of supply and demand meant that many firms were unable to achieve economic viability. Only those with robust business models were able to survive and prosper. The current industry structure is characterised by an increasing number of entrants seeking a market share in all the e-business markets. However, unlike in the late 1990s, the demand for products and services online has been rising rapidly as consumers become increasingly aware of the benefits that the internet can provide.

The increase in interest in online shopping has led to a burgeoning B2C market. Businesses have also benefited from electronic trading across the supply chain via e-marketplaces and this has boosted the B2B sector. Other markets have emerged in recent years. These include the C2C market where consumers use the internet to deal with each other directly. Technological developments such as mobile wireless devices and interactive television have also opened up opportunities for firms to link their e-business models to the strategies they adopt for exploiting the advantages that these newer communications channels offer.

There are numerous e-business models available to firms. Some involve a form of brokerage, others are information based, while some are revenue models based on access to content or delivery mechanisms. Each e-business model is designed to add value to customers by offering a unique selling proposition. However, the high level of competition in the e-business industry means that achieving uniqueness is often very difficult. Consequently, firms seek to gain a competitive advantage through a mix of factors including differentiating the product or service, offering best prices or discounts, building brand loyalty, offering additional services such as facilitating virtual communities, or by increasing efficiency and lower costs through partnerships and alliances. Whatever e-business model is chosen, and whatever way it is designed, it needs to be economically viable. To achieve this requires the e-business to achieve a critical mass of customers, to continue the process of innovation and adding value to customers, and to add flexibility to the e-business model in order to take advantage of opportunities in different markets.

Questions and tasks

1. Explain how e-marketplaces work and discuss the advantages that they provide for participants.
2. Using examples, identify the main value-adding characteristics of the internet for e-business.
3. Find an example of a firm that operates in the B2C market. Identify the characteristics of the firm's e-business model.
4. What are the key attributes of mobile wireless internet devices that add value to users beyond those offered by fixed internet connections?

References

Business Wire (August, 2000). Mercata Receives the First Internet Group Buying Patent; First Patent in Group Buying Space Issued to Mercata for Business methods and Technology. www.findarticles.com/cf_0/m0EIN/2000_August_9/63962501/p1/article. jhtml.

Cassidy, J. (2002). *dot.con: the greatest story every sold*. Penguin Books: London.

Chircu, A. M. and Kauffman, R. J. (2000). Reintermediation in Business-to-Business E-Commerce. *International Journal of Electronic Commerce*, Summer, 4, 4, pp. 7–42.

Choi, S. Y., Stahl, D. and Whinston, A. (1997). *The Economics of Electronic Commerce*. Macmillan Technical Publishing.

Collins Dictionary of Economics (1993). Harper Collins: Glasgow.

Cook, J. (2001). Venture Capital: Where Mercata Led, Consumers Were Unwilling to Follow, January 12, *Seattle Post Intelligencer*, Seattle, WA.www.seattlep-inwsource.com/business/vc122.shtml.

Gascoyne, R. J. and Ozcubukcu, K. (1997). *Corporate Internet Planning Guide: Aligning Internet Strategy With Business Goals*. International Thompson Publishing: New York, NY.

Kauffman, R. J., Wang, B. and Miller, T. (2001). Strategic morphing and the survivability of e-commerce firms. Proceedings of the 35th Annual Hawaii International Conference on System Sciences (HICSS '02), IEEE Computer Society: Washington.

Kauffman, R. J. and Wang, B. (2002). Bid Together, Buy Together: On the Efficacy of Group-Buying Business Models in Internet-Based Selling. In *The E-Business Handbook* (P. B. Lowry, J. J. Cherrington and R. R. Watson, eds), pp. 99–137, St Lucia Press: Boca Raton, FL.

Lee, C. (2001). An analytical framework for evaluating e-commerce business models and strategies. *Internet Research: Electronic Networking Applications and Policy*, Vol. 11, Issue 4, pp. 349–60.

Rayport, J. and Sviokla, J. (1995). Exploiting the virtual value chain. *Harvard Business Review*, Vol. 73, No. 6, pp. 75–85.

Ropers, S. (2001). New Business Models for the Mobile Revolution. *eAI Journal*, February, pp. 53–7.

Rowley, J. (2002). Synergy and strategy in e-commerce. *Marketing Intelligence and Planning*, 4(20), pp. 215–20.

Tapscott, D. (1996). *The Digital Economy: Promise and Peril in the Age of Networked Intellegence*. McGraw-Hill: New York, NY.

Tapscott, D. (1999). *Creating Value in the Network Economy*. Harvard Business School Press: Boston, MA.

Further reading

Gulati, R. and Garino, J. (2000). Getting the right mix of bricks and clicks for your company. *Harvard Business Review*, May–June, pp. 107–14.

Kalakota, R. and Robinson, M. (2000). *E-Business: Roadmap for Success*. Addison-Wesley: Reading, MA.

Plant, R. (2000). *E-Commerce: Formulation of Strategy*. Prentice-Hall: Upper Saddle River, NJ.

Timmers, P. (1999). *Electronic Commerce Strategies and Models for Business-to-Business Trading*. Wiley: Chichester.

E-business economics

Key issues:

- Towards perfect competition;
- The effect of the internet on the competitive environment;
- Key economic characteristics of the internet;
- Cost of production and distribution;
- Disintermediation and reintermediation;
- Economics of information;
- Connectivity and interactivity;
- Economies of scale;
- Economies of scope;
- Transaction costs;
- Network externalities;
- Switching costs;
- Critical mass of customers;
- Pricing.

Introduction

The economic implications of using the internet for business purposes are the focus of this chapter. The chapter begins by explaining how the internet for e-business and e-commerce pushes markets closer to the perfectly competitive model. The discussion is then broadened to include the effects of the internet on the competitive environment. This is followed by an overview of the key features of internet economics.

Towards perfect competition

Economics is concerned with the efficient allocation of resources. Italian economist Vilfredo Pareto (1848–1929) gave his name to a definition of efficiency where a situation arises in which it is not possible to make someone better off without making someone else worse off. Pareto efficiency can relate to production – where it is impossible to increase output of one good without decreasing the output of any other, and to exchange – where it is impossible to increase consumption of one good without decreasing consumption of another. Maximum efficiency requires the Pareto principle to be evident in production, exchange of goods and services, and in the output mix of goods and services (Hardwick et al., 1999). The conditions necessary for Pareto efficiency to be realised are those relating to perfect competition.

Perfect competition refers to a market where no individual buyer or seller can influence the market. That is, the market forces of supply and demand determine the price and output of goods and services. Perfect competition is a theoretical market structure based on a number of key assumptions. Only when these assumptions are fulfilled can Pareto efficiency be achieved. The assumptions include that:

- There are many buyers and sellers;
- There is freedom of entry into and exit from the market;
- There is perfect mobility of the factors of production;
- There is perfect knowledge of the market;
- There is a homogeneous product.

Perfect competition describes an efficient market because it leaves no excess supply or demand of goods or services. In the real economy this rarely, if ever, happens. Most markets fail to match supply with demand and, therefore, operate at less than optimal efficiency. There are numerous reasons why markets fail. There may be a lack of information and knowledge pertaining to the supply of goods and services into a market; there may be excessive transaction costs (where the costs of making a transaction outweigh the benefits to consumers or suppliers); transactions may be prevented by geographical distance between buyers and sellers; or one seller may have greater economic power than others in the industry and can influence the market price.

The effect of the internet on the competitive environment

The internet has provided a mechanism for edging markets closer to that of perfect competition. In particular, the ease of access and lack of regulation means that there are many buyers and sellers in the market. The abundance of information on websites means that buyers and sellers have access to greater market knowledge. Transacting via the internet ensures a more cost-effective way of matching supply and demand since there are no geographical or time constraints.

One of the key characteristics of the e-business environment is the ease of entry for firms. The cost of entry and exit is low relative to traditional industries, as firms do not require large sales teams, costly investment in infrastructure or high sunk costs in order to compete effectively. Increasing connectivity among potential customers has led to increasing competition among firms engaging in e-business and e-commerce as more and more are attracted to the source of potential revenue.

The nature of competition has been altered by the emergence of the internet. Both cost structures and the types of products and services being offered to customers differ from traditional industries. Reductions in cost can be achieved through smoothing transactions between customers and suppliers and there are opportunities for customising products to specific needs and building communities of buyers. The communications between interested parties is ratcheted up and may bring network externalities where the benefits accrued by increasing information on the website are not reflected in the cost of usage or the price of products.

The internet can change the relationship between buyers and sellers where switching costs play a crucial role in determining the balance of power. The reduction in transaction costs of searching for products or services makes comparisons of prices easier for customers and intensifies price competition among firms.

As noted earlier, the internet is characterised by the abundance of information available. This abundance poses challenges for traditional economic theory where scarcity forms the critical under-pinnings. Easy access to a huge array of information facilitates consumers' comparisons of prices and availability of products and services. The availability of market information contrasts with traditional markets where consumers are reliant on firms to provide them with such information. Conventional wisdom has it that this leads firms to compete more on price because of the absence of significant search costs. The bargaining power lies with the customer. However, some researchers dispute that price transparency leads firms to lower prices.

Muhanna (2005) used an analytical model based on game theory to predict the behaviour of online retailers. The results of the survey showed that making it easier for consumers to compare prices can lead to increased prices. The rationale for this is explained in the behaviour of online retailers. When every competitor is aware of what others are doing, prices remain relatively stable. Each online retailer is reluctant to lower prices in case they set off a price-cutting war that would disadvantage all the sellers. Only buyers would benefit from such a scenario. Any window of opportunity for cutting prices without an immediate response from rivals has been removed because the internet abounds with price comparison sites. The close scrutiny of prices has led online retailers into what can only be described as tacit collusion. According to Muhanna, although each seller acts independently, the combined effect of all sellers' behaviour is to keep prices stable. Although this may be the case in some isolated studies, the overwhelming evidence from price studies reveals that price reductions are a feature of online trading.

Key economic characteristics of the internet

Classical economic theory views information as a resource to reduce uncertainty. However, the development of the internet has led to increasing emphasis on information as a productive element and a product. Economic analysis of information as an asset should view it from both the demand and supply sides. Demand in the form of customers and businesses seeking information on products and services, and supply side in the form of businesses providing information to customers and other businesses.

On the demand side, the internet can be used as a means of accessing information about organisations and the products and services they sell. Customers usually access the website, scan the range of products available, perhaps compare prices on other websites, and then make a decision on whether to buy or not. The internet helps smooth the transaction process. Once an offer to buy has been received by an online business the process of distribution takes place and the physical product is delivered to the customer.

Inspection of the goods can only be done visually via the website. It is possible to search for information regarding the quality of certain products through online reviews. Some examples include consumer review specialists www.reviewcentre.co.uk and school standards website www.ratemyteachers.co.uk. One of the most successful review websites is www.imdb.com, a film review website that registers around twenty million hits per month. However, the products are not tangible until received or experienced.

On the supply side, the internet can be used as a means of marketing, promoting and selling products and services. The potential for reducing production and distribution costs has been outlined above. These are relevant to the process of bringing physical and tangible goods to market. Intangible goods such as those that are information-driven have different economic characteristics from those associated with physical products. Producers can determine how scarce or abundant they wish the information output to be; they can manipulate and alter the content to suit different markets; they can offer consumers access to parts of the product as a 'taster'; they can reproduce and distribute the product at low cost; and they can protect its value through copyright and intellectual property rights.

Cost of production and distribution

The internet can help to reduce production and distribution costs and make firms operate more efficiently. Market information on customers and logistics information gathered from suppliers, distributors and manufacturers form the basis for improving efficiency. The cost of marketing and advertising can be reduced using customer information effectively. Information on customer segments, the types of products demanded, trends in tastes and fashions, etc. form the basis for a more targeted marketing effort. This is discussed in more detail in Chapter 5.

The internet is an effective channel of communication and a source of information storage and retrieval. These attributes can form the basis for potential cost savings in the internal operations of firms. This may include inventory management where the electronic monitoring of stock movements adds to process efficiency in providing products for customers and ordering replacement stock in good time. This also applies to the logistics of distribution where electronic monitoring of all goods movements helps ensure that delivery times are met. Information on the supply of raw materials, the capacity of manufacturing and orders from wholesalers, distributors and retailers all combine to enhance supply chain management. Also, the internet can be used to improve the internal efficiency of organisations by automating administrative tasks that are procedural and repetitive.

Disintermediation and reintermediation

Disintermediation refers to the removal of an intermediary somewhere along the supply chain of products and services from seller to consumer. Disintermediation has become a feature of the e-business and e-commerce environment because the internet facilitates greater communications between suppliers and customers. For example, as more and more information becomes available on the internet (Shapiro and Varian, 1999), customers can override retailers and communicate directly with manufacturers. One of the key driving forces behind the growth of e-business and e-commerce is the cost savings that can be gained by transacting via the internet. Disintermediation is a method of reducing the cost of bringing products and services to customers. Cost reduction is achieved by reducing the number of intermediaries in the supply chain. Firms can use this cost saving to offer lower prices compared to traditional markets. This can help build up a critical mass of customers, increase customer loyalty and create a competitive advantage. Figure 4.1 illustrates the difference between a typical supply chain and one that features disintermediation.

Disintermediation has been evident in many industry sectors. Information-driven industries have been particularly affected by disintermediation. In the media sector there has been disintermediation of publishers, broadcasters and music publishers. Figure 4.2 highlights examples of disintermediation.

The savings from disintermediation can only be realised if the benefits of removing the intermediary outweigh the costs. Intermediaries along the supply chain add value as well as cost. Much will depend upon how dispensable the service they provide is to the customer. Intermediaries provide benefits for suppliers by specialising in marketing and promoting products, searching for

Traditional supply chain

Disintermediation in the supply chain

Figure 4.1
Disintermediation
in the B2C
supply chain

Physical goods flow ⟶

Information flow ⟶

specialist information, feeding back valuable customer information and bringing to bear their experience of dealing in particular products for specific markets. Intermediaries also provide benefits for customers in the form of specialist knowledge of the application, price, quality and availability of products (Turban and King, 2002).

Disintermediation was a feature of the early development of e-commerce markets. The intermediaries, who had the traditional role as a conduit between buyer and seller, were being increasingly marginalised in the new economy. However, the role of intermediaries did not become obsolete. Many intermediary firms have reinvented themselves and re-entered the supply chain by offering specialist knowledge or services for the online market. This process is referred to as 'reintermediation'. Sometimes termed 'infomediaries', these firms specialise in surfing the internet for the most competitive

Media sector	Disintermediating effect
Printing	Electronic books
Publishing	From author direct to reader via internet
Music	Downloading music files from the internet
Video	Online video on demand
Broadcasting	From content direct to viewer

Figure 4.2
Disintermediation in
the media industry

deal on offer for their clients. This revives the specialist nature of their business and creates cost savings.

For example, OneSwoop (www.OneSwoop.com) is a pioneering online car buying firm who acts as middleman between dealers across Europe and UK customers. The business model adopted by OneSwoop relies on arbitrage – finding and capitalising on imbalances in the market in order to secure the best deal for customers. The company never comes into contact with or owns a single car. This is just one of many examples where processing information is more cost-effective than moving physical products. The so-called 'infomediaries' transform raw data into valuable information, provide customer assistance or technology-based buying aids and increase market efficiency.

Mini Case Study: www.oag.com

Prior to the development of the internet the leading authority of airline timetables was Official Airline Guide (OAG) who published the definitive guide to all commercial air travel on a global scale. The OAG publication of timetables ran to three volumes and was updated every month. For many years prior to the commercialisation of the internet OAG was the industry authority on all aspects of airline timetabling and a source of valuable information for travel agents, business travellers, airline executives and even plane spotters. However, by the mid 1990s the company's market dominance came under threat from new entrants into the market who were adopting new technology in the form of the internet to collect, store and disseminate up-to-the-minute information on airline timetabling.

OAG was being disintermediated from the supply chain of information. In particular, airlines had developed their own computerised inventory system that allowed agents to see flights and book them directly. The emergence of budget airlines, such as Ryanair (www.ryanair.com) and easyJet (www.easyjet.com), enabled customers to cut out the middleman and book flights directly using the internet. The decline in sales for OAG meant that the publishers, Reed Elsevier, decided to sell the business to a venture capitalist company for $1.

To survive, OAG had to pursue reintermediation into the supply chain of information. By 2002 the company had invested some £15 million in new technology that was to be the basis of the business transformation. The key added value OAG could offer to business clients and customers was their expertise in the compilation of timetables. With 30 million flights annually, managing the data is a complex and precise process. The company electronically alters around 13 000 units of data in timetables every day. The technology allows OAG to manage and distribute the data more effectively. The company has developed integrated systems so that customers can access information via numerous devices including interactive television and mobile phones. Information is also available in many different languages and packaged to appeal to different types of customers.

Economics of information

Information economics is distinctly different from the economics of physical products. Information is easily produced and can be distributed among a large number of recipients including suppliers, customers and firms. The ease and scale of distribution does not diminish the value or quality of the product (Slater, 1998). Information is easily manipulated and altered to suit different needs of customers in different markets. Information that is in high demand, such as financial data, prices of stocks and shares and news items, constitutes high-value assets.

Where traditional economic theory is concerned with scarcity of resources, the internet is characterised by an abundance of information. Information-driven products and services can be reproduced and distributed for near zero marginal cost (the cost of producing an additional unit). However, there may be diseconomies of scale associated with the abundance of information available to consumers (information overload) as the time and effort involved in searching for the right information may prove a deterrent to use of the internet for transaction purposes. This adds a further reason for previously disintermediated firms re-emerging as information intermediaries, or 'infomediaries'.

The online market for information-driven products and services is characterised by high reach and richness (Evans and Wurster, 1999). Reach is the number of people and products that are accessible quickly and cheaply via online markets. The lack of geographical boundaries in the internet environment greatly extends reach. Richness is the depth and detail of information that can be gathered, offered and exchanged between parties in the market

(Amit and Zott, 2001). Information is easily stored and manipulated at low cost and electronic networks offer advantages in mixing, matching, bundling and unbundling of information contents from many different sources (Bhatt and Emdad, 2001).

The internet has had a profound effect on the economics of selling information, especially in the form of media products such as music, film and books. Most publishers and film producers look to achieve a money-spinning blockbuster to generate huge revenues and offset the costs of less successful ventures. However, the internet provides a mechanism whereby the misses can be just as valuable as the hits. The economics of abundance already forms the basis of the business models of some of the internet's most successful firms, including Amazon, e-Bay and Google. The way the economics of abundance works is best explained by the theory of the long tail as described by Jack Schofield in *The Guardian* on 24 March 2005.

The long tail is named after a type of power law curve created when sales of a product (CDs, computer games, films, etc.) or the popularity of a website are plotted on a graph. The observation made was first determined by Harvard University Professor of Linguistics, George Kingsley Zipf. Zipf noted that there are a small number of words that occur very frequently (such as 'to', 'a', 'of' and 'the') and that, thereafter, there is a steep decline, followed by tens of thousands of words that appear very infrequently (such as 'lapidary', 'contumacy' or 'stertorous'). When plotted on a graph these rare words form a long tail that tapers off to the right of the graph. The Zipf curve is also evident on the internet. Although all websites are equally accessible, visitors to them are not equally distributed. Research by Adamic and Huberman (1999) reveals that the distribution of visitors per site follows a universal power law that is characteristic of a 'winner-takes-all' market. Thus, a small number of sites, such as Google, Amazon and e-Bay, have many millions of visitors per month, whereas, the vast majority of websites attract only a handful of visitors per month. Indeed, the more choice that becomes available, the more pronounced the curve becomes. Figures 4.3 and 4.4 illustrate the short tail of traditional markets compared to the long tail of online markets.

The long tail theory has a real and significant impact on e-businesses. In the physical world traders are constrained by the physical limitations of their shops. Bookstores can only stock so many books, film and music stores can only stock so many CDs, videos and DVDs. They are governed by the economics of scarcity. This drives storeowners to stock only those products they think will sell in large numbers. This limits the choice for customers and

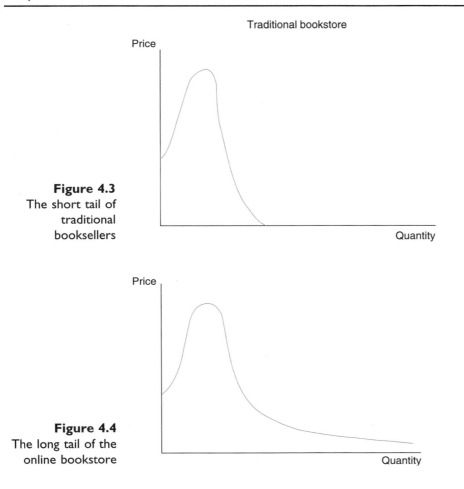

Figure 4.3
The short tail of
traditional
booksellers

Figure 4.4
The long tail of the
online bookstore

stifles innovation in the creative industries. However, if those products can be stored and sold online there is no such constraint on the
number of products available. The economics moves from issues
of scarcity to abundance.

An example of the long tail can be seen in film distribution. Cinema
releases are almost wholly based on maximising capacity in theatres
in order to create profits. This means that a relatively small number
of films are actually shown. The ones that are shown tend to be big
budget productions backed by significant marketing and promotion
efforts. The market for films shown in cinemas has no tail, they either
succeed or they fail. However, if films can be distributed on DVDs or
even downloaded online then the economics changes. Firms can offer
many thousands of films to customers and the vast majority will only
sell a few copies. Nevertheless, the long tail ensures that the numbers
mount up and contribute significantly to overall revenues. In other
words, the less successful films are, economically, as important as

the blockbusters. Firms who distribute media products via the internet incur no shelf space costs, no manufacturing costs and minimal distribution costs. The sale of a product of low popularity achieves the same margin as a widely popular product.

The music industry provides another good example of a long tail market. Retailers can only stock a few thousand CDs, whereas an online music store can easily stock a million. The hits will always sell more than the misses, but the majority of sales will come from the long tail of less popular songs since each one is likely to find at least a few buyers. The long tail is evident in many online markets and provides the basis for successful business models. Online auction site e-Bay is an example of a long tail business. A few transactions take place that involve considerable sums of money, but the vast majority of transactions on e-Bay are for a few pounds or dollars. The success of the site stems from the long tail market made up of large numbers of people transacting small sums.

The long tail markets consist of many millions of niche markets. Although they do not merit mass-market advertising, firms can still make them visible by facilitating virtual communities. Bringing together people who have displayed similar tastes or may be persuaded to buy similar or related products can drive forward niche markets and make them profitable. Websites that collaborate with customers in reviewing and recommending products can also give a boost to niche markets. Successful websites are likely to offer the full range of products, both mainstream and popular and a wide range of products for niche markets. The mainstream products bring in most of the revenue for firms but once 'locked-in' customers may be encouraged to try niche products further down the long tail.

Connectivity and interactivity

In e-business and e-commerce, connectivity exists between information systems, and communication is two-way and in real-time. These characteristics enable real-time pricing, low cost of distribution of information and digital products, and a high level of interactivity. Interactivity makes the relationships between buyers and sellers richer and more intense (Dutta and Segev, 1998). The high growth rates in connectivity and interactivity have had a transforming effect on business. This is evident in relationships with customers, suppliers and partners; the pricing models used; the types of products and services offered; and the marketing and sales functions.

Economies of scale

When production costs decrease with the number of units produced then firms benefit from economies of scale (Chandler, 1990). Where once economies of scale were viewed as the preserve of large industrial units selling large volume products in the traditional economy, the internet has provided a mechanism for firms of all sizes to exploit this economic advantage. This is especially the case with information-driven products because the marginal cost of production is almost zero. There are also demand-side economies of scale that benefit consumers. This occurs where the value of a product increases the more people buy into it. This process is called 'network externalities' and is discussed in more detail later in this chapter.

Firms benefit from economies of scale because the average cost of production declines as the number of units sold increases. In the B2C market, the global reach of the internet presents firms with the possibility of extending the customer base and achieving economies of scale in the number of products sold relative to the cost of producing and distributing them. Also, there are marketing economies of scale available to firms who use the internet for advertising and promoting their range of products and services. In the B2B market economies of scale can be achieved through increasing the number of orders for products or services or, in the case of a portal, an increase in the number of web pages served. Economies of scale can be derived from faster servers, more data storage availability or wider applications functionality.

Economies of scope

Economies of scope are the rate at which relationships are leveraged to add value to customers. In e-business firms can exploit market information gathered from customers to provide added value across other markets (Rayport and Sviokla, 1995). The internet can help achieve economies of scope in relation to customers. These are derived from the knowledge gained about individual customers. The more expertise any single firm has with respect to meeting the needs of a particular individual customer, the greater that firm's economies of scope will be for selling that individual a series of products both in terms of different products and repeat sales over a period of time (Peppers and Rogers, 1993). For example, Amazon.com gain economies of scope by using its customer relationship management system to offer additional services in both B2C and B2B sectors. In the B2C sector they use book reviews received by customers as an additional service to other customers; in the B2B sector they offer information on customers' tastes and preferences to book publishers.

Firms can also gain economies of scope by sharing common inputs over a range of activities or by collaborating with other firms in promoting or distributing products. The knowledge and know-how possessed by collaborating firms represents a shared input that can find a variety of end product applications. For example, Teece (1980) recognised that the transfer of proprietary information to alternative activities can generate economies of scope if organisational modes can be discovered to conduct the transfer at low cost. By the 1990s the emergence of the internet provided the means of achieving this.

Transaction costs

Transaction costs are the costs incurred in using the market system for buying and selling goods and services. Transaction costs include the costs of locating suppliers or customers and negotiating transactions with them. Firms engaged in e-business have been able to reduce the transaction costs at one or more stages of the buying and selling process. The key issue addressed by transaction costs theory focuses on why firms internalise transactions that might otherwise be conducted in markets. Ronald Coase (1937) pioneered the concept of transaction costs and it was further developed by Williamson (1975, 1979, 1983) in an effort to understand the reasons for firms internalising transactions that are normally transacted within the marketplace. There are six types of transaction costs.

Search costs

These are the costs associated with buyers and sellers finding each other in the marketplace. The sheer number and diversity of goods and services available in the modern marketplace can make the cost of searching for them quite considerable. The internet provides a quick, efficient and cost-effective way of searching for products using search engines such as Google, Netscape and Lycos. Suppliers can advertise their goods or services on websites or through banner advertising. For more precise targeting of buyers they can access buyer groups, develop and utilise customer relationship management systems, and pursue permission marketing where the buyers permit the channelling of product information to them via their PC or mobile phone.

Information costs

This is the cost incurred by buyers of gaining market knowledge on the price, quantity, quality, availability and characteristics of goods and services offered by sellers. For sellers, information costs are incurred through the process of learning about the financial condition and need characteristics of buyers. Many e-businesses have reduced this transaction cost by providing up-to-date product information on their website for potential customers to access.

Bargaining costs

This is the cost incurred by buyers and sellers when negotiating a contract for a transaction to take place. This may include the cost of using equipment to contact and communicate with the other party to the transaction, the marketing of information, and the legal costs of drawing up contracts. E-mail has become a cheap and effective way of communication between buyers and sellers. There are now many websites offering goods and services where the whole transaction can be completed online. Auction site e-Bay is a prime example of an e-business model based on the quick and efficient completion of transactions online.

Decision costs

The buyer incurs a cost of comparing prices in the marketplace and ensuring that the goods or services match needs. For suppliers the decision costs are incurred when deciding whom to sell to or whether to refrain from selling. E-businesses can speed up the evaluation process by specialising in providing price information on a wide range of goods and services provided by many competing firms.

Policing costs

These are the costs incurred by buyers and sellers ensuring that the goods or services provided and bought match the terms under which the transaction was negotiated and contracted for.

Enforcement costs

These are the costs incurred by buyers or sellers in the event that the terms of the negotiated contract are not met.

Network externalities

In economics, externalities refer to gains or losses incurred by others as a result of actions initiated by producers or consumers or both and for which no compensation is paid. Externalities can be either positive or negative. For example, the pollution created by chemical plants is a negative externality for the community affected because everyone has to bear the burden of the cost of the pollution without being compensated for it. Alternatively, positive externalities may arise when benefits are derived where no additional cost is incurred.

The business models of many e-businesses are built around the idea of website communities. People with similar interests will naturally migrate to websites that serve their interests well. Community-based websites cover every interest and hobby imaginable. Some examples include stamp collecting (www.stamp.co.uk), ornithology (www.birdguides.com), steam trains (www.steampics.com), plane-spotting (www.aeroflight.co.uk), orchids (www.orchid.org.uk), and wine-making (www.homewinemaking.co.uk).

Network externalities occur when the benefits of using one technology increase as the network of adopters expands (Katz and Shapiro, 1994). This is the economic phenomenon at work in the development of web-based communities. In the first instance, a firm will set up a website that caters for a specific customer segment. This may be based on particular tastes and fashions, interests, hobbies or shared experiences. The members of the initial community contribute to the bank of knowledge and information on the website by relating their experiences and knowledge of the subject matter that the website specialises in. The increasing information directed to the website attracts other users with similar interests. The new users may add further to the bank of knowledge and information on the website, thereby making the website even more attractive. There are positive network externalities for users because they gain increasing benefits in the form of increasing amounts of information they are interested in without incurring any additional costs (Choi et al., 1997).

E-businesses are interested in creating communities of buyers because they constitute an additional service that is valued by customers. Firms may have chat-room facilities for customers to review products and services and to offer advice on prices, quality, availability, substitute products or any other aspect of the consumer process. Firms sometimes use the feedback from customers posted on their websites for marketing purposes. There is a strong correlation between market performance of products sold online and the positive or negative feedback given by customers. The more positive the feedback for a product the greater the market growth and sales of that product is likely to be. Negative feedback invariably leads to the rapid decline of sales. Positive feedback is referred to as the virtuous cycle because the benefits accruing to customers communicated via the website creates a momentum that leads to more and more sales. Conversely, negative feedback is referred to as the vicious cycle because the disappointments expressed by contributors to the website invariably lead to diminishing sales. Figure 4.5 illustrates the positive and negative cycles.

In the case of network externalities it is not the product or service that acts as the catalyst for adding value, but rather the external factors related to the network with which the product or service is associated (Chen, 2001). The use of 'Metcalfe's Law' illustrates the economic phenomenon of network externalities. Metcalfe's Law states that the utility (satisfaction) of a network increases with the square of the number of users. This concurs with the assertion that as more users join the network, so it becomes increasingly attractive for others to join too.

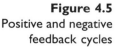

Figure 4.5
Positive and negative
feedback cycles

Metcalfe's Law gives rise to another and related economic phenomenon – that of increasing returns. Economic theory states that as additional units of a variable factor are added to a given quantity of fixed factors, a point will be reached beyond which the resulting addition to output will begin to decline. However, in the internet economy, there are instances where this logic is turned upside down. That is, successive increases in inputs, lead to successive increases in outputs, or increasing returns. In the case of Metcalfe's Law, increasing returns will be evident for as long as the website remains attractive to new users. However, the process will not continue forever since the number of users is finite, and the number of users interested in one particular website may be relatively small. There will come a point when the number of additional users will start to slow down. The rate at which this happens depends on a number of factors including the connectivity and interactivity of those with an interest in the website subject matter, the overall number of people with an interest in the website subject matter, and the rate at which additional users join the website community.

Switching costs

Switching costs include those borne by the consumer to switch suppliers and those borne by the new supplier to serve the new customer (Lee, 2001). The switching costs of customers may include the inconvenience associated with switching suppliers, such as the time and effort involved in evaluating the value of a product or service. The switching costs incurred by suppliers may include the marketing for new customers and research and development costs. E-businesses need to include switching costs into their business model in order to achieve customer loyalty through 'lock-in'. The 'lock-in' of customers refers to a situation where switching costs incurred by customers of changing supplier exceeds the benefits of switching to that alternative supplier. Firms can achieve 'lock-in' in several different ways including:

- Involving consumers in the design and productive processes;
- Creating network externalities through website community building;

- Ensuring ease of navigation of websites;
- Ensuring ease of transactions;
- Building trust in customer relationships;
- Creating a standard for integrating systems.

Critical mass of customers

Lock-in of customers and customer loyalty are two critical factors that determine the economic viability of an online venture. Firms must achieve a critical mass of customers before profits can be gained from e-business or e-commerce. To achieve a critical mass of customers requires successful management of three phases:

Customer attraction

The website must be attractive to gain the attention of customers. Here, the design, navigation and transaction process all play a role. However, to attract customers effectively the website has to tempt customers with an attractive product offering. Firms may adopt marketing and sales techniques to attract customers such as offering discounts, free gifts or reduced prices to initial buyers (loss leaders); added-value services such as personalisation or customisation of products may be attractive to customers. Firms also have to ensure their website is highly visible on search engines. This may involve a cost in buying a prominent position in search lists.

Customer retention

The products and services provided by the e-business must be of sufficient quality to meet or exceed customer expectations. This builds customer loyalty and offers the best chance of repeat business. Firms must also offer security in transactions and ensure privacy for customers in order to build trust in the online relationship. These help to boost confidence in the internet as a means of transacting, which is necessary for achieving customer loyalty and repeat business.

Chapter 4

New customer bases

To reach a critical mass of customers it is necessary to search for new customers whilst retaining existing ones. The e-business should be able to utilise feedback from existing customers to help the marketing effort for finding new customers. This may involve adapting products to target new customer bases, achieving a greater understanding of customer segments or diversifying into related products and services to broaden the customer base.

Mini Case Study: Online gambling

If reaching a critical mass of customers is a prerequisite for success in e-business then the online gambling industry has succeeded in spectacular fashion. In a survey carried out by YouGov, research reveals that there are some four million Britons using the internet for gambling purposes. Between 30–40% of these are female aged between 18–29. Of all the gambling sites available, online poker has experienced the biggest growth. There are an estimated 256 online poker rooms operating on the internet and they generate some £2.3 million commission on a daily basis for their owners. The top online poker site is PartyPoker.com (www.PartyPoker.com) with a market share of about 50%. Its main rival is ParadisePoker.com (www. ParadisePoker.com) an online poker website that was bought by Sportingbet (a subsidiary of the Hilton Group) for $297 million in 2004. In 2004, online gamblers lost a total of £4.1 billion (*The Sunday Times*, 2005).

Poker websites receive revenue from collecting a 'rake' from each pot of cash that gamblers feed into. This usually amounts to between 1–3% of the total cash gambled. Online gambling sites are successful because they meet all the economic and psychological factors necessary to attract and retain customers: customers are in control of their spending (some people may develop an addiction to gambling but most control their spending habits); the activity offers the potential for making money (greed and avarice are powerful motivators in the human condition); there is no face-to-face contact with other gamblers (customers value their anonymity); and the online gambling experience provides a thrill to participants, albeit usually fleeting.

There is also an element of network externalities at play in the online gambling environment. The amount of money available for winning gamblers is dependent on the number of participants. The more people who play the greater the potential rewards for winning. This acts as a powerful attraction to gamblers who seek the highest returns on their 'investment'. The more players who participate the better the service, and better service is likely to attract more players. This dynamic accounts for the huge growth in gambling sites across the world in the last few years. By 2005, the phenomenal growth of online gambling recorded since 2000, started to level off. This led the big operators to look at ways in which the online gambling concept can be extended. To this end, the future is likely to involve gambling on interactive television. UK bookmakers William Hill have already experimented with their own digital television station, showing greyhound racing and offering interactive games such as roulette.

Pricing

It is important to recognise that products offered online differ from standard industrial products. Very often there is no physical productive process involved except for the human and intellectual capital that is employed. Online products are also characterised by interdependence, with standards and compatibilities required as a precursor to successful sales. This is why network externalities play an important role in determining the scale of online product demand. Nevertheless, when determining pricing, the types of considerations applied by traditional 'bricks-and-mortar' firms are relevant to online businesses too. These invariably include:

- Cost price: the cost incurred when producing the products or services;
- Sales price: the price charged to customers;
- Profit: the sales price minus the total costs of production;
- Mark-up: the percentage of the profit based on the cost price (sales price minus cost price, divided by cost price);
- Margin: the percentage profit based on the sales price (sales price minus cost price, divided by cost price).

Other factors are taken into account when determining prices. These include:

- The level of forecasted demand;
- The level of competition;

- The prices of rivals' products;
- The cost of marketing, advertising and promotion;
- The position of the product on the product life-cycle;
- Price elasticity of demand (how sensitive customers are to changes in price);
- The availability and price of substitute products;
- Distribution costs;
- After-sales service costs.

Pricing strategies

Having taken into consideration the key factors in determining price, firms must then determine their pricing strategy. The options available to firms will be dependent on the type of product they produce and the nature and characteristics of the customers targeted. It is possible to divide pricing strategies into four broad categories. These include:

- Premium prices: prices above the industry average are charged. This occurs where the product offers added value to customers in terms of quality, uniqueness, status or availability.
- Average prices: the price charged reflects the market demand and supply dynamic.
- Discount prices: prices are discounted below that of the market price. Sometimes referred to as a loss leader, this may be a short-term strategy to gain market share.
- Free: firms may give away products or services in an attempt to attract customers.

There are a number of other pricing strategies available to e-businesses that can help to improve revenue and maintain the economic viability of the online venture. These include price discrimination, bundling, the pricing of information-driven products, and congestion pricing.

Price discrimination

The internet empowers consumers by allowing them to compare prices, products and services offered by e-businesses. There are a

multitude of price comparison sites such as www.kelkoo.co.uk,
www.pricerunner.co.uk and www.dealtime.co.uk. As noted previously, this can lead to a reduction in transaction costs as searching for products becomes easier. Lower search costs for prices
and products offered leads to more intense price competition
among sellers (Bakos, 1998). This has an effect on profit margins
for e-businesses and affects the level of competition in online
industries.

E-businesses have to employ appropriate pricing policies to
overcome the threats posed by the empowerment of consumers.
Price discrimination makes it more difficult for buyers to compare
prices of competing products. There are numerous forms of price
discrimination that firms can employ. In some instances firms only
allow access to pricing information on receipt of specified information from customers such as post or zip codes or personal profile
information. Others include charging different prices according
to subscriber usage rates (price lining) or smart pricing where the
charge relates to market conditions or differences in how customers
value the product.

Effective price discrimination relies on gaining and using information on customers. This gives rise to differential pricing where a firm
can segment the market and charge different segments different
prices. Differential pricing is a method of gaining additional revenue
from a market that would not be gained using a standard price.
Differential pricing is illustrated in Figure 4.6.

In Figure 4.6, the firm is willing to move from the revenue
associated with Area B, with price/quantity combinations (P_o-P_i)
and (Q_o-Q_{ii}), to a revenue associated with Area A $((P_{ii}-P_o)\ Q_{ii})$ and
Area C $(P_i\ (Q_i-Q_o))$. The producer sells Q_{ii} for P_{ii} and Q_i-Q_{ii} for P_i.

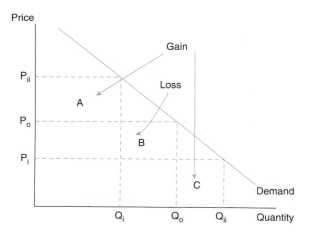

Figure 4.6
Differential pricing

Sinha (2000) suggests two other forms of price discrimination – price lining and smart pricing. Price lining is where the firm offers the same product or service at different prices according to different customers' needs. This is particularly evident among Internet Service Providers (ISPs) who also provide web content such as Compuserve, AOL and Wanadoo. These companies charge different rates according to the level of their subscribers' usage of the service. Smart pricing refers to different prices being charged in different markets. Here, the price charged depends on a combination of market conditions and the perceived value placed on the product or service by the customer. Some customers want to access information at particular times and will place a high value on the access at those times. The price charged will reflect this.

There are some markets where price discrimination is not viable. Products in commodity markets are largely identical and customers can easily compare prices of competitors. Where price discrimination is not feasible firms will have to reduce cost to remain competitive. Where the marginal cost of production determines the lowest price, firms need to reduce production costs to remain competitive. In such markets being the least cost producer (cost leadership) may determine competitive advantage.

Bundling

Another way firms can prevent customers from comparing prices is to bundle products and promote the benefits of a whole package (Shin, 2001). For example, media giants AOL/Time Warner use the convergence of technology to strengthen their bundling strategy by offering interactive services on television, music on computer, and e-mail on mobile phones alongside their existing services. The rationale behind the strategy is that it is less expensive to sell an additional service to an existing customer than it is to attract a new customer (Schiesel, 2001). Product bundling is a form of price discrimination because it disallows the choice of buying single items. Customers are faced with the choice of buying a group of products to access the one they really want or not buying at all.

Pricing information products

Traditional pricing models are not suitable for determining the economic value of information-driven products. Usually, the price of products is determined by production costs, transaction costs and the level of profit aimed for. Information products delivered online incur initial production costs associated with the research and compilation of the information. However, thereafter, additional units have near zero costs. There are also low transactions costs because of the effect of the internet in easing search costs and opening up an effective line of communication for bargaining and negotiating. These factors, combined with the erosion of profits as a result of the empowerment of consumers, means that e-business involved in delivering information products online have had to develop new pricing models.

There are some important economic characteristics relating to online information products that determine the pricing models used. First, there is no clear link between inputs and output of such products. This discounts production costs as a means of determining price. Mass consumption does not require mass production (Loebbecke, 2001). Secondly, economies of scale derive from distribution effects rather than production. The costs of distributing information products online are low, but there are high sunk costs (initial investment) involved in setting up the infrastructure for production as well as the variable costs of researching and compiling the information product. Third, information products delivered online entail unbundling. That is, the content can be priced separately from the medium of communication. Printed material such as books, magazines and newspapers is priced according to production costs, distribution and the aimed for profit margin regardless of the quality of the product. Information products delivered online can be priced according to the value placed on the content. In other words, price discrimination plays a role in online information products.

The characteristics of online information products directly affect the demand function. For example, some information products are time dependent. The value of such information (financial data, stock prices) can diminish rapidly as they can become outdated. The demand function itself may not be a suitable measure for determining price because of the level of copying and sharing of information that exists between consumers. Also, network externalities distort the value of demand since consumers receive benefits that are not reflected in the price of accessing the product.

Congestion pricing

Since the development of the World Wide Web in the late 1990s the use of the internet has grown into a global phenomenon. While this has proved to be a catalyst for the commercialisation of the internet it has also led to congestion. The growth in demand for access to the internet has outgrown the capacity of bandwidth to cope. The development and rollout of broadband alleviates this problem to an extent, but the huge demand for internet access means that the issue of congestion persists. In economics, when a situation arises where there is excessive usage of a resource, the destruction of that resource may result thereby leaving everyone worse off. This is termed the 'Tragedy of the Commons'.

Two approaches have been suggested as a solution to the congestion problem. One is to manage supply at source via Internet Service Providers, telecommunications lines, modems or regional networks. Limiting access would involve complex issues of public policy, freedom, democracy and discrimination. An economic solution is via pricing. The price mechanism acts as a limiting factor for the demand for products and services. The price charged for accessing the internet can be matched with the level of demand at different times during the day. At times of high demand prices rise and at times of low demand prices fall. The electricity industry has operated a similar pricing model for many years. Electricity firms know the patterns of demand for their product during an average day. They operate a peak-load pricing model during times of high demand and lower pricing at other times. Internet firms can do likewise to alleviate congestion. There are, however, issues of public policy associated with congestion pricing. Some may argue that it discriminates against the poor since they are the group of consumers most likely to be excluded on economic grounds.

Pricing policy

The European Commission has also been active in investigating allegations of overcharging of products and services delivered via the internet. In particular, there have been allegations that UK customers are charged higher prices than their mainland European counterparts for online products and services. In 2005 online music service iTunes (owned by Apple) was referred to the competition authorities in

Brussels for charging UK customers 15% more than those in France or Germany for downloading tracks.

Summary

One of the important economic effects of using the internet for e-business has been to push the competitive environment closer to that of perfect competition. The ease and low cost of entry to the internet economy combined with greater amounts of market knowledge for customers and suppliers means that there is a high degree of competition in the market. These factors, alongside the increasing levels of internet connectivity, have resulted in significant year-on-year growth of the internet economy since the dot-com crash of 2000.

There are a number of key economic factors that drive firms towards using the internet for business purposes. Two of the most important factors include the access the internet gives to a broader customer base at low cost, and the reduction in transaction costs. Firms can deal directly with customers and cut out intermediaries thereby saving on costs, then use the saving to lower prices for customers to encourage brand loyalty. One of the keys to the economic success of websites is to build in switching costs that further underpin brand loyalty through 'lock-in' of customers.

The potential for benefiting from network externalities also makes the internet distinct from traditional forms of business. Customers can gain extra benefit at no extra cost if a firm's website includes access to additional services such as facilities for virtual communities. However, customers have to be attracted to the website in the first instance. This is where the economic viability of the e-business model is crucial. Firms have to deliver added value to customers to attract them to the value proposition of the products or services they offer for sale. Building a critical mass of customers is crucial to ensuring a successful e-business venture. One way of attracting customers is to offer lower prices. There are a number of pricing models available to e-businesses and the one chosen needs to reflect the supply and demand dynamic. For example, the high demand for internet services allows some firms to charge premium prices, especially at peak demand times.

The internet has also changed the internal efficiency of firms. Firms can use the internet to improve communications with parties across the supply chain, improve information flows, automate routine transactions and processes and create an intelligent organisation through the collection and analysis of information on customers and suppliers. These cost savings can be used as the basis for creating a competitive advantage.

Questions and tasks

1. Explain how the internet pushes the competitive environment further towards the perfectly competitive model.
2. What are transaction costs and how does the use of the internet lower transaction costs for e-businesses?
3. Using an example, describe network externalities and explain the phenomenon of Metcalfe's Law.
4. What methods can firms use to create switching costs and 'lock-in' customers to their website?
5. Why do firms price discriminate? Give examples of price discrimination.

References

Adamic, L. A. and Huberman, B. A. (1999). Growth Dynamics of the World Wide Web, *Nature*, 401, September, p. 131.

Amit, R. and Zott, C. (2001). Value Creation in E-Business. *Strategic Management Journal*, **22**, pp. 493–520.

Bakos, Y. (1998). The Emerging Role of Electronic Marketplaces on the Internet, *Communications of the ACM*, **41**(8), August, pp. 35–42.

Bhatt, G. D. and Emdad, A. F. (2001). An analysis of the virtual value chain in electronic commerce. *Logistics Information Management*, Vol. 14, Issue 1/2, pp. 78–84.

Chandler, A. D. (1990). *Scale and Scope: The Dynamics of Industrial capitalism*. Belknap Press.

Chen, S. (2001). *Strategic Management of e-Business*. Wiley and Sons: Chichester.

Choi, S. Y., Stahl, D. O. and Whinston, A. B. (1997). *The Economics of Electronic Commerce*. Macmillan Technical Publishing: Indianapolis, USA.

Coase, R. (1937). The nature of the firm, *Economica*, **4**, pp. 386–405.

Dutta, S. and Segev, A. (1998). The global Internet 100 survey 1998, *Information Strategy Online*, June. http://www.info-strategy.com/GI100.

Evans, P. and Wurster, T. (1999). Getting Real About Virtual Commerce. *Harvard Business Review*, November/December, pp. 84–94.

Goodman, M. (2005). Winning Hand. *The Sunday Times: Business Focus*, 27 February, p. 5.

Hardwick, P., Langmead, J. and Khan, B. (1999). *An Introduction to Modern Economics* (5th edition). Longman: Harlow.

Katz, M. L. and Shapiro, C. (1994). Systems Competition and Network Effects. *Journal of Economic Perspectives*, **8**(2), (Spring), pp. 93–115.

Lee, C. (2001). An analytical framework for evaluating e-commerce business models and strategies. *Internet Research: Electronic Networking Applications and Policy*, Vol. 11, Issue 4, pp. 349–59.

Loebbecke, C. (2001). Online delivered content: concept and business potential. In *E-Commerce and V-Business: Business Models for Global Success* (S. Barnes and J. Hunt, eds), pp. 23–45, Butterworth-Heinemann: Oxford.

Muhanna, A. W. (2005). Search and Collusion in Electronic Markets, *Management Science*, Vol. 51, No. 3, March, pp. 497–507.

Peppers, D. and Rogers, M. (1993). *The One-to-One Future: Building Relationships One Customer at a Time*. Currency-Doubleday: New York, NY.

Rayport, J. F. and Sviokla, J. J. (1995). Exploiting the virtual value chain. *Harvard Business Review*, **73**(6), pp. 75–85.

Schiesel, S. (2001). Planning the Digital Smorgasbord: For this Media Conglomerate, the Future is All-You-Can-Eat. *The New York Times*, June 11, Section C, p. 4.

Shapiro, C. and Varian, H. R. (1999). *Information Rules: A Strategic Guide to the Network Economy*. Harvard Business School Press: Boston, MA.

Shin, N. (2001). Strategies for Competitive Advantage in Electronic Commerce. *Journal of Electronic Commerce Research*, Vol. 2, No. 4, pp. 164–71.

Sinha, I. (2000). Cost transparency: the Net's real threat to prices and brands. *Harvard Business Review*, Vol. 73, No. 2, pp. 43–50.

Slater, D. (1998). The power of positive thinking. *The CIO*, August 15, pp. 31–6.

Teece, D. J. (1980). Economies of scope and the scope of the enterprise. *Journal of Economic Behavior and Organizations*, Vol. 1, No. 3, September, p. 223.

Turban, E. and King, D. (2002). *Introduction to E-Commerce*. Prentice-Hall: Harlow.

Williamson, O. E. (1975). *Markets and Hierarchies, Analysis and Antitrust Implications: A Study in the Economics of Internal Organization*. Free Press: New York, NY.

Williamson, O. E. (1979). Transaction cost economics: the governance of contractual relations. *Journal of Law and Economics*, **22**, pp. 233–61.

Williamson, O. E. (1983). Organizational innovation: the transaction cost approach. In *Entrepreneurship* (J. Ronan, ed.), pp. 101–33, Lexington Books: Lexington, MA.

Further reading

Chircu, A. M. and Kauffman, R. J. (2000). Reintermediation in Business-to-Business E-Commerce. *International Journal of Electronic Commerce*, **4**(4), (Summer), pp. 7–42.

Economides, N. (1996). The Economics of networks. *International Journal of Industrial Organization*, **14**(2), (October), pp. 673–99.

Katz, M. L. and Shapiro, C. (1996). Technology Adoption in the presence of Network Externalities. *Journal of Political Economy*, **94**(4), (August), pp. 822–41.

CHAPTER 5

E-marketing

Key issues:

- Internet marketing;
- E-marketing plan;
- The marketing mix;
- Branding;
- Online advertising;
- Targeting online customers;
- Interactive television and e-marketing;
- Customer relationship management.

Introduction

This chapter focuses on key elements of using the internet as a marketing tool (e-marketing). The chapter begins with an overview of internet marketing before going on to discuss the components of an e-marketing strategy including the e-marketing plan, the distinct characteristics of the e-marketing environment, demand and competitor analysis, objective setting and the e-marketing audit. This is followed by an outline of the marketing mix using the product, price, place and promotion model. The discussion then moves on to the issue of branding and the methods used to target customers or customer segments. The chapter also focuses discussion on some of the key issues relating to interactive television as a relatively new medium for marketing products and services and facilitating e-commerce. The chapter concludes by highlighting the advantages and problems associated with the application of customer relationship management systems for marketing purposes.

Internet marketing

The development and use of the internet on a global scale has created opportunities for consumers, suppliers and sellers of goods and services to communicate with each other in the online marketplace. The internet has been the catalyst for organisations to extend their activities beyond traditional boundaries that were characterised by physical constraints. One of these activities is the marketing function within organisations. As a medium of communication, the internet offers a range of benefits that can be exploited by organisations to enhance their marketing strategy. The internet is characterised by ubiquity, information richness and density, global reach, interactivity, customisation and personalisation (Timmers, 1999). Importantly, the internet brings buyers and sellers together in a more cost-effective way than traditional advertising and marketing methods (Chi and Kiang, 2001). The growth in use of the internet for e-business has changed the way suppliers, distributors, buyers and sellers interact.

The purpose of marketing is to identify, anticipate and satisfy customer requirements profitably. The key market variables to be considered when implementing a marketing strategy are price, promotion, place and products. A critical success factor for companies implementing a marketing strategy is to understand the characteristics of the customers they target. They may target a general customer base, but more usually, the marketing effort is aimed at one or more customer segments. Customer segments may be determined by a range of criteria including age; gender; socio-economic groups; geography; employment; tastes and interests; cultural factors and lifestyles (Galvin and O'Connor, 2001).

The internet is an additional mechanism available to companies that facilitates the receiving and sending of information to customers, suppliers and partners. In particular, the connectivity of customers to internet sites provides companies with a huge and on-going store of valuable customer-related information that can be used to inform their e-marketing strategy. E-marketing is the use of electronic communications technology, such as the internet, to achieve marketing objectives. Of course, information on websites also empowers customers and helps them achieve their objectives. For example, they can compare prices of products by rival firms. The internet changes the relationship between buyers and sellers because market information is available to all parties in the transaction.

E-marketing plan

The e-marketing plan is part of a wider ranging plan put in place by firms to achieve stated objectives. The e-marketing contribution forms part of the e-business strategy for achieving objectives and includes market research and communications with customers or customer groups using the internet. The e-marketing plan will be dependent on the level of resources available to the organisation. The plan will be built within the budget allocated and will range in scope according to the perceived benefits it can accrue for the business. The e-marketing plan is designed to identify and set out ways of achieving e-marketing objectives. The plan consists of analysis of the demand function and competitors. These form the basis for developing and implementing strategies for target markets. The marketing mix is the tactic used to target markets. Finally, there is an element of performance measuring and evaluation of the e-marketing plan. This process is illustrated in Figure 5.1.

Figure 5.1
E-marketing plan
model

The e-marketing environment

An important first step in implementing an e-marketing plan is to understand the key differences between traditional marketing and e-marketing. An effective e-marketing plan is built on new perspectives on customers, different interactions with customers and different solutions to marketing products and services. Indeed, customers have come to expect different approaches to marketing because of the internet. Before undertaking an e-marketing plan it is necessary to address some key questions. These include:

How is the marketing function in the new environment different?

   (i) There are no geographical constraints in the online environment;

  (ii) E-marketing models are subject to change depending on the level of technological advance. Traditional marketing is relatively stable and more clearly defined;

(iii) Niche markets are more easily identified and larger in online markets;

 (iv) E-marketing is subject to a customer-pull relationship where the customer decides the time and place of interaction.

What are the critical success factors for e-marketing?

   (i) First-mover advantages are vital;

  (ii) Collaboration with partners to provide added value to customers;

(iii) Customers must perceive added value;

 (iv) Innovation in products and services, e.g. personalisation;

  (v) Maximise customer interactivity.

What is the new organisational position for the marketing function?

   (i) Product development is driven by marketing and information systems;

  (ii) The marketing function is integrated with other functions such as IT and business development;

(iii) How are customers perceived within the new trading environment?

 (iv) Customers have greater awareness of the organisation and its products and services;

  (v) Customer behaviour changes online, e.g. greater impulse buying. This can be monitored and used for marketing purposes;

 (vi) Customers are perceived more as individuals rather than customer groups.

Demand analysis

Once e-businesses understand the key differences between traditional marketing and e-marketing it is then possible to go on to build the e-marketing plan. An effective marketing plan requires an understanding of the demand dynamic of the market. This can involve analysing the current demand and projecting future demand of the whole market or narrowing the scope of analysis to gain knowledge of demand for specific market segments. Demand analysis focuses on a number of key issues including:

- The level of connectivity to the internet by customers;
- The level of interactivity by those with internet access;
- The number of customers who purchase products or services via the internet;
- The number of customers who access websites but who do not purchase via the internet;
- Identifying the barriers to using the internet for purchasing purposes.

Customer segmentation helps to further understanding of different types of customer bases. Some products are aimed at the whole market, such as discount airfares. However, many products and services are aimed at markets with specific characteristics. Some products or services may be designed or adaptations applied to suit particular target markets. Market segments include:

- Socio-economic groups: these divide the population and consumers into six broad groupings as outlined in Figure 5.2.
- Geographic positioning: although one of the advantages of the internet is that geographical distance between buyers and sellers becomes less relevant (especially for

A	Upper middle class, higher professionals
B	Middle class, intermediate professionals
C1	Lower middle class
C2	Skilled working class
D	Working class, semi-skilled, unskilled
E	Under class, unemployed

Figure 5.2
Socio-economic
groupings

information-driven products and services), the location of customers is of interest to e-businesses. This helps to target products and services according to types of location where consumers reside. Important information includes whether consumers reside in areas that are urban or rural, have high or low population density, or have access to infrastructure and distribution outlets.

- Gender: products and services can be targeted to particular customers based on gender. This information links in to other key data on customer behaviour, such as product usage, loyalty, purchasing patterns and the types of benefits sought, and psychographic variables such as lifestyle, attitudes, personality traits, interests and activities.

- Age: the age profile of customers or customer groups is important for e-marketing. This gives rise to market segments such as children, young adults, middle aged, retired people, etc. Travel company Saga (www.saga.com) specialises in holidays for the over 50s age group. The company has been expanding its online service to market its wide range of holidays and travel services to provide an additional channel of communication for its customers. The information received by the company leads to a better understanding of its customers' needs and requirements and provides the basis for a more targeted marketing effort.

- Tastes and fashions: the interests and tastes and fashions expressed by particular customers, or customer groups, provide valuable information for e-businesses when devising an e-marketing plan. This allows a much more specific marketing effort to be implemented knowing that the target market already has an interest in the products or services being offered. Online bookseller Amazon.com has a repository of information on the genre of books that individual customers or groups of customers habitually read. The information customers send Amazon, either by way of clicking on specific parts of the website, or directly through e-mail communication or actual purchases, provides the basis for sending information on books that are likely to be of interest to customers.

- Business sectors: in the B2B sector customers are divided by sectors such as financial services, retail, transport, healthcare, public sector, leisure, etc. B2B involves setting up a web portal for communicating with buyers and suppliers, underpinning alliances in the buying process and auctioning inventory. E-businesses scan the market for selling products or services to other businesses. Companies may specialise in providing products or information to other companies to bolster their supply chain. The internet has given rise to a large number of 'infomediaries' who specialise in providing real-time information on the process of bringing products or services to customers. The level of demand for B2B products and services depends on the added value that businesses as customers receive from e-businesses compared to traditional methods of transacting.

■ Demographics: customers can be divided into a mix of geographical, age and gender criteria. The demographics of the UK suggest that a greater proportion of the population will be over 55 in the next ten years. There is a misconception that the internet is the preserve of young people but more and more e-businesses are undertaking initiatives to encourage the over 50s age group to participate in online activities. There are sound economic reasons for this when one considers that the high proportion of the population represented by this age group in the next decade will constitute a distinct and relatively wealthy customer group.

There are already signs that the numbers of older internet users is increasing. A Forrester Research (2004) survey revealed that there are some 20.7 million internet users in Europe aged over 55. Around a quarter of all people in Europe over 55 have access to the internet. In the UK, McClellan (2004) noted that over 35% of over 50s are internet users. The research points to the growth being mostly in the 50–65 age group. Age Concern (www.ageconcern.org.uk/silversurfer) has formed partnerships with companies such as Microsoft and Cable and Wireless to organise events aimed at giving the over 65s 'taster' sessions on the internet to encourage participation. A roving IT bus visits day-care centres, sheltered housing units and nursing homes for the same purpose.

Competitor analysis

Building knowledge of competitors is an integral part of developing a strategy for both traditional and e-businesses. Sometimes referred to as 'competitor intelligence', the analysis involves gathering information on a wide range of criteria including who the competitors are, what products and services they produce, their market performance, the communications channels used, and their marketing strategies. Competitor analysis helps to determine the impact that the actions of a rival will have on the performance of a business.

Much of the information required for competitor analysis can be gleaned from suppliers and customers as well as from the industry intelligence gathered by employees. Other sources of information include competitors' promotional material, advertisements, industry reports, government reports, press releases and academic case studies. Companies will often buy products from rivals to test and analyse them for effectiveness, or to seek ways of improving or adapting them as a means of creating a competitive advantage through differentiation and innovation. Rival companies' websites are also a valuable source of information. These very often provide information on new products, prices, availability, quality, discounts, promotions, and target customers.

Objective setting

The e-marketing plan is based on clearly defined objectives. These objectives may include increasing sales, establishing new products in the marketplace (Higgins, 2001), broadening the customer base, enhancing customer service, diversifying the product range, reducing costs, or any of the other benefits associated with undertaking the marketing function using the internet. Whatever objective or objectives are chosen it is important to ensure that they are achievable. Many firms have failed in their e-business strategy because they do not understand the capabilities and limitations of the technology when setting objectives. The technology cannot achieve objectives in isolation from other functions within an organisation. Objectives must also be measurable in order to form part of the e-marketing audit. Some objectives, such as improving the company reputation may take some time to be achieved and even then may be difficult to measure. How much of the improvement can be put down to the e-marketing effort?

E-marketing objectives will vary between organisations. Firms who exist only because of the internet derive all their revenue from their online activities, whereas traditional bricks-and-mortar companies use the internet as an added service to customers. Firms 'born on the net' are likely to have more exacting objectives for their e-marketing strategy since it forms a vital role in determining the viability of the organisation. Traditional firms invariably view their investment in online services as a source of additional revenue and a means of enhancing the customer relationship. The viability of the organisation does not depend entirely on the e-business element of their operations.

E-marketing audit

The e-marketing audit is designed to review the performance of the e-marketing plan. In particular, the e-marketing audit assesses the performance of the integrated factors in the objective setting model.

The effectiveness of the company website forms a key part of the e-marketing audit. The analysis of website performance centres on three areas. These include:

- Contribution to business performance: the website has to make a contribution to the economic performance of the company in the form of additional revenue and profitability.
- Marketing effectiveness: the website has to contribute to greater sales and will be subject to monitoring for measures of effectiveness in attracting, retaining and repeating custom. Feedback from customers on quality of service and satisfaction rates also feature in the measures of marketing effectiveness.
- User effectiveness: the website needs to be prominent, attractive and easy to use. User effectiveness can be measured in the number of hits the website receives over a set period of time, the particular pages of the website that are accessed, the length of time users stay on the website and the result of the hit (i.e. a purchase, request for more information, no further contact, etc). Market research in the form of questionnaires, surveys and focus groups can provide valuable information on users' percep-tions of the website experience in terms of accessibility,

navigation, design, quality of information and ease of transaction.

The marketing mix

After identifying the target market, firms develop their marketing strategies by focusing on the marketing mix. The marketing mix is a combination of product, price, place and promotion that helps increase sales to the target market (McCarthy, 1960). The unique mix of the elements that comprise the marketing mix can help firms compete more effectively, ensure profitability and gain a competitive advantage. The internet influences the construction of the marketing mix and therefore e-businesses need to take that influence into account when developing and implementing their e-marketing strategies.

Product

The success of a product or service in the marketplace depends on a number of factors including quality, availability, application, construction, packaging, image, customer service and ease of use. The product has to match or exceed customers' expectations. These expectations have been raised because of the influence of the internet. Consumers have ease of access to information on a wide range of products and services. Information from market research on the type of products consumers demand informs firms as to what products or services to provide.

Usually, to meet the demands of consumers it is necessary for firms to vary the product offerings and/or provide additional features that add value to the customer. This is the difference between a core product that meets basic consumer expectations, and an extended product that has additional features that take the product beyond basic consumer expectations. For example, the *Encyclopaedia Britannica* is now only available online or on CD format. This greatly reduces the cost of delivering a huge amount of information to readers but also enhances the consumers' experience by offering interactive facilities, easy search facilities, moving images for illustration, and access to a greater amount of information. This adds value to the consumer and reduces the cost burden to the seller of what was once a paper-based product. There are some consumers, of course, who prefer the traditional paper-based product for aesthetic reasons. The internet can be used to vary the extended product in numerous ways. Chaffey and Smith (2001) suggest the following examples:

- Endorsements;
- Awards;
- Testimonies;
- Customer lists;
- Customer comments;
- Warranties;
- Guarantees;
- Money-back offers;
- Customer service;
- Incorporating tools for using the product.

Another feature of the internet is the possibilities it provides for mass customisation of products. Mass customisation is a means of personalising a product or service, but on a large scale. Mass customisation relies on technology to create economies of scale where the low average cost of production makes it cost-effective to provide tailored products to individual customers or groups of customers. The increasing demand for e-learning products since the commercialisation of the internet in the mid 1990s has given rise to many educational establishments offering mass customised learning products to individuals and groups of learners around the globe.

Bundling is another way of varying the product. Product bundling emphasises the benefits of the whole product package. As noted previously, one advantage for sellers of product bundling is that consumers cannot compare prices for individual items that, combined, comprise the whole product package. For example, some television broadcasters bundle packages of channels for subscription. Consumers may only want a sports channel but have to pay for a bundle of channels that may include a news channel, a children's channel and a history channel along with sport. Microsoft bundles its software with its operating system thereby maximising the brand exposure across most internet activities. Firms can charge a premium price for the product bundle. These examples have attracted the attention of the courts since many argue that bundling can be anti-competitive and against the consumers' interests.

Price

The only element of the marketing mix that generates revenue is price. All the other elements represent costs (Armstrong and Kotler, 1991). The price at which any product or service is sold depends on production costs, distribution costs, and the level of return on investment and profit margin aimed for by the producer. The reaction of customers to the initial price may influence price changes. The internet has had an effect on the pricing of products and services. There is a great deal of pricing information available online and customers can use this to make comparisons and make better judgements about purchases (Sinha, 2000). As customers become more aware of prices of competing products or services this has the effect of limiting the firms' ability to discriminate on price between different consumer groups. Price intermediaries, such as Pricescan.com, are search engines that undertake price comparisons of products or services and customers can access these to ensure they get the right product for the least price.

The internet allows for a much more dynamic approach to pricing products and services. Dynamic pricing refers to a market where prices can be updated instantly in response to changes in market conditions. The real-time aspect of the internet allows sellers to constantly inform their customers of current prices for the products or services they offer. Potential new customers can be targeted with discounts, free gifts, or other incentives to buy online from a particular website. The more information firms have on customers the more able they are to customise prices towards individual customers or groups of customers.

The interactive characteristic of the internet allows for much greater price negotiation to take place between buyers and sellers. Business-to-consumer (B2C) firms such as QXL offer customers the opportunity to bid for a wide range of consumer products. Negotiation is a key feature of customer-to-customer (C2C) auction sites such as e-Bay, and business-to-business (B2B) exchanges for reverse auctions.

Place

The place element of the marketing mix refers to the channel through which firms bring products or services to the customer.

These channels include a communications channel (e.g. e-mail), a distribution channel to intermediaries (e.g. to customers via wholesalers) or direct selling to customers (disintermediate middle-men in the supply chain). Most firms who use the internet do so mostly for marketing purposes. Firms will have a website that is an electronic version of a storefront. The website has a communications facility that allows information to flow between seller and buyer and vice-versa.

Firms can use the internet to take orders from customers and then use intermediaries such as wholesalers and distributors to deliver the products or services to customers. However, the global reach of the internet means that there are cost savings to be made for information-based products or services that can be sent electronically direct from sellers to consumer. Even so, firms need to exercise caution when engaging in direct selling to customers. Established relationships with wholesalers, distributors and retailers may break down leaving the onus for efficient delivery of products and services in the hands of the seller. This may not present a physical problem for down-loadable products or services but there may be a negative effect of disintermediation on a firm selling products that require physical transportation. There may also be negative consequences for the brand, image and reputation of the business by selling direct to customers unless that firm possesses specific expertise and experience in managing these attributes.

The choice of place depends on a number of factors, including the nature and characteristics of the products or services for sale, the power of intermediaries in the supply chain, the effectiveness of traditional supply chain mechanisms, the scope of channel conflict, and the closeness and depth of relationship firms seek with customers.

Promotion

Promotion is the element of the marketing mix that involves the communication with customers regarding products and services for sale. The internet represents another channel for communication with customers. The promotion of products and services can be undertaken using a number of different methods including branding, advertising, public relations, sales promotions, in-store displays, web promotion, sales promotions and personal selling. These techniques combine to inform customers of products and services for sale, the form of communications required for each stage of the transaction, and the availability of discounts or special offers.

The internet is mostly a 'pull' medium whereby consumers make the decision to visit websites. Techniques such as permission marketing represent the 'pull' element of the marketing effort where firms seek the permission of potential customers to forward marketing material to them. This is discussed in more detail later in this chapter. For the most part, however, the 'pull' element is the medium that informs the promotion strategy. There are a number of ways firms can encourage customers to make return visits to their websites. These include:

- Use of traditional media such as newspapers, magazines, radio and television to promote the website;
- Direct e-mail to promote the website and as a means of attracting customers with details of special offers;
- Providing information on the website to enhance the customer experience or make the transaction smoother for the customer.

The success of promotion is highly dependent on the effectiveness of the website design. Customer loyalty is one of the keys to creating a competitive advantage in the online environment. The website, as the first point of contact between potential customer and supplier, must posses specific characteristics to attract and maintain the interest of consumers. It must be:

- Easily accessible and easy to use: the website needs to be highly visible on search engine lists and easily navigated by consumers when accessed;
- Fast and efficient: the website must provide consumers with up-to-date and relevant information quickly;
- Confidence boosting: consumers must gain confidence that the company and its products and services being offered are genuine. This can involve the use of company logos, brand names, contact details and visual images of premises and people;
- Constantly available: the website should be available at all times;
- Secure: consumers need to be confident that no other third party will be able to access any of their communications and

that the information they provide will not be sent on to any third party without their permission.

Branding

A brand is the name, term or symbol given to a product by a supplier to distinguish the offering from that of similar products supplied by rivals. Branding refers to the process of creating and developing brands that add value to consumers or where consumers perceive there to be added value. Companies need to develop products or services that are differentiated from those of rivals. Choosing a name for the company is an important step in the overall branding effort. The brand name chosen should:

- Identify the unique aspects of the company and its products;
- Communicate the company aims and objectives to a wide audience;
- Help to protect the intellectual property of the company.

The e-business sector is populated with a large number of organisations because of the small start-up costs and ease of entry. There are many examples of branding that reflect what the companies produce, what their aims are and how they perceive their *raison d'être*. Figure 5.3 illustrates the spectrum of brand names.

There are three main types of brand names along the spectrum:

- Free-standing: the name is designed to be unique and memorable;
- Associative: the name is chosen to reflect links with quality or is an abbreviation of the full company name;

Free-standing	Associative	Descriptive
Benetton	Yahoo!	British Petroleum
DeBeers	General Electric	Kentucky Fried Chicken
MacDonald's	Federal Express	General Motors
Tesco	Playboy	Deutsche Telekom
Amazon.com	Toys 'R' Us	Domino's pizza

Figure 5.3
Spectrum of brand names

■ Descriptive: the name of the product or service or the productive process.

To exploit the value of brands it is necessary to match consumer values with brand values. Hart et al. (1998) highlighted three main values that underpin the matching of consumer values and brand values. This is illustrated in Figure 5.4.

	Consumer values	Brand values
Core values	Lifestyle, aspirations, attitudes and beliefs	Shared values of the consumer and brand
Expressive values	Type of personality	How the brand symbolises personality traits of the consumer
Functional values	Demand for types of products	How the brand fulfils consumer expectations

Figure 5.4
Consumer values
and brand values

Effective brand management using the internet requires very different marketing and promotional strategies from traditional marketing. One way of promoting brands is to engage in a dialogue with consumers about products or services. This is called one-to-one marketing. This allows firms to build relationships with customers and gain information about their wants and needs. The firms can then develop or adapt products to suit those needs. Customisation and personalisation are distinct value-adding services for customers. The benefits of personalised promotions are at their greatest when customers are interested in detailed product information (Allan and Fjermestad, 2000). This can be the basis for building customer loyalty. There is evidence to suggest that as consumers become increasingly familiar with using the internet they will only buy products or services that precisely match their needs (Sealy, 1999). To meet these expectations firms need to adopt brand management strategies that go beyond product characteristics but also include criteria such as values, beliefs, emotions, memories and attitudes.

Online advertising

The internet provides an effective means of communication and forms a powerful mechanism for organisations to promote and market products and services to broad-based or targeted audiences. A number of online advertising methods have been developed that enable organisations to use the internet to communicate their value proposition to customers. Three of the most prominent methods include:

- Banner advertising;
- Affiliate marketing;
- Viral marketing.

Banner advertising

Banner advertising appears on web pages and is the most common form of online advertising. The effectiveness of banner advertisements can be measured using the click-through method. This quantifies the number of customers clicking on the advertisement to access the sponsor. This type of advertising was popular during the early years of the commercialisation of the internet, but its potency has subsequently waned as web users tired of the disruptive effects of banner advertising on the web-surfing experience. Consequently, advertising revenues from banner advertisements have not reached levels predicted as many organisations returned to more traditional forms of media, such as radio, newspapers and television, for their advertising needs.

Related forms of banner advertising include

- Interstitials: a method of online advertising using a separate window of advertising that pops up spontaneously and blocks the site behind it.
- Supertials: a method of online advertising where a window that appears during dead time (in the gap between a command and the actual download) grabs the web user's attention for a few seconds;
- Rich-media expanding banners: banners that have some functionality and product identity built into them. This provides immediate benefits for the consumer rather than simply forcing them to link to another site. Some allow customers to perform tasks on the banner such as ordering products or giving permission for receiving more information.

Affiliate marketing

As noted in Chapter 3 (*E-business markets and models*) affiliate marketing is a referral system where two websites agree to have a revenue sharing relationship based on one website owner paying another for referring customers. There are two main types of affiliates, single and multiple tier:

- Single tier affiliates: this is an arrangement where the advertiser pays the host for sales or traffic directly referred to their site. Under single tier arrangements the host site sets a price based on the number of times the advertisement was viewed or downloaded. This is called 'Pay-Per-Click' (PPC). Another may be 'Cost-Per-Click' (CPC) where the advertiser pays the host for the number of clicks the banner advertisement receives. A third method is where the host is paid a commission for the number of sales generated through a direct referral called 'Pay-Per-Sale' (PPS) which is either fixed or varies according to the value of the sale.
- Multiple tier affiliates: the host receives commissions for the direct referrals and also for the referrals generated by these direct referrals.

Viral marketing

Viral marketing is based on word-of-mouth principles where online users of a service are encouraged to refer the site to friends, family or work colleagues. Mail services such as Hotmail use viral marketing to promote their services. The method is relatively simple and has the following steps:

- Give away free e-mail addresses and services; then
- Attach a simple tag at the bottom of every free message sent out stating 'get your free e-mail at http://www.whatever.com'; then
- Wait while people e-mail to their own network of friends, family and work colleagues who seek the message; and
- Sign up for their own free e-mail service and then forward the message still further to their own network of friends, family and work colleagues ... and so on it goes.

The attraction of these types of advertising methods is the relatively low cost compared to advertising in traditional media. It is also a low risk method of communicating messages to a potentially global audience because the advertiser is only paid when the desired results are generated. There are also benefits associated with building a network of websites and e-mail lists of people who refer others to advertisers' websites. Databases of potential or prospective customers are valuable to advertising organisations. Nevertheless, the performance of such advertising methods has not met expectations, largely because of the low number of referrals generated, but also because significant numbers of internet users started using software to block advertisements. There is also a difficulty in tracking each affiliate sale for making the required payments because of the complexity of the system.

Targeting online customers

E-marketing involves targeting customers or customer segments with information about the company, its activities, and its products and services. Traditional forms of marketing have been characterised by the way they interrupt the activities of consumers. For example, banner advertisements on websites or search engines are a disruptive element in the online experience. Increasingly, the e-marketing effort of companies has moved towards less disruptive techniques such as permission marketing, request marketing and opt-in marketing.

Permission marketing

Consumers are increasingly playing an active role in determining the type and content of advertising they receive (Greenberg, 2000). An example is the development of permission marketing as an approach to selling goods and services in which a prospect explicitly agrees in advance to receive marketing information. Opt-in e-mail, where internet users sign up in advance for information about certain product categories, is an example of permission marketing. Permission marketing can be effective because the prospect is more receptive to a message that has been requested in advance. It can also be more cost-efficient because the prospect is already identified and targeted.

Permission marketing is a response to the age-old problem of interruptions as a characteristic of mass-marketing advertising.

Television commercials interrupt favourite programmes, telemarketing interrupts 'family time', a print advertisement interrupts a feature article and so on. Permission marketing is designed to persuade consumers to volunteer attention. Companies sell consumers a little of themselves and consumers respond in kind. The relationship builds over time based on mutual benefits. Permission marketing is based on the rational calculations made by all parties. There is an initial outlay cost in gaining consumers' attention but this is the beginning of the process where attention turns into permission, permission into learning, and learning into trust (Godin, 1999).

Permission marketing can be viewed from both the consumers' and company's perspectives. First, consumers have money they want to spend on products. However, they want to minimise transaction costs by reducing the time spent evaluating both products and the level of trust in the companies that produce them. Since permission marketing is based on self-interest, consumers will grant a company permission to communicate only if they know what is in it for them. A company has to reward consumers, explicitly or implicitly, for paying attention to its messages. From a company's perspective, once a consumer has given permission for channelling marketing information to them the cost of sending additional information via electronic means is zero. In particular, e-mail frequency is free thereby allowing companies to continue communicating with people, continue teaching them and continue turning them into customers.

It is possible to argue the point that permission marketing does not go far enough since it is based on the notion that marketing is the transmission of messages from the business to the consumer. This unidirectional metaphor is also implied by the B2C (business-to-consumer) acronym. Ethical companies will only send people information if they have indicated a willingness to receive it. However, this is unidirectional. The Web and permission marketing work in opposite directions. Whereas permission marketing is business to user, the nature of the Web is from user to the website. It is a customer-driven medium where the company only sends messages users request. In other words it is request marketing.

Request marketing and opt-in marketing

Request marketing and opt-in marketing are ideally suited to the Web or to the mobile wireless internet where intrusive messages are especially deemed to be aggravating and unwanted. Request marketing is where customers proactively seek information on products or services from companies even where no previous communication has existed between the two parties. Request marketing is closely related to opt-in marketing. Opt-in is where customers agree to receive further information from a company after they have already received some information via online promotion techniques such as direct e-mail.

Interactive television and e-marketing

Interactive television is still a relatively new phenomenon. Television and internet-based firms are merging activities to capture viewer attention by offering integrated products. Where there has been competition between computers and television for consumer loyalty, there are advantages to merging the two media (Coffey and Stipp, 1997). Interactive television brings together some of the characteristics that define the computer and television as means of information, entertainment and communication.

Interactive television advertising provides six capabilities that improve customer service above that of traditional methods of advertising. These include:

- Interactive and personalised customer communications;
- Greater speed and accuracy;
- Enhanced ability to track and measure capability;
- Instantaneous and real-time communications;
- A customer-focused business model; and
- Continuous availability.

Combined, these attributes of enhanced service can translate into cost reduction and be used as a platform for gaining competitive advantage.

Interactive television introduces new opportunities in integrating advertising content within traditional programme content and in integrating this with the World Wide Web (Chan, 2001). There is much more direct response to advertising through this medium. The success of interactive television depends on consumer behaviour and the capacity for immediate response and minimal effort on the part of consumers. An example of this is where a viewer is watching a sports programme and decides they like the training shoes being worn by an athlete. By simply clicking on the athlete the screen stops and a window-style drop-down menu appears asking if you want to buy. After clicking 'yes' the next menu offers customisation of the product. The final menu is for address and credit card information. After this process a simple click returns the viewer to the action. There is a multitude of similar applications including downloading ingredients of a cookery programme or having fast food sent to the home (Lee and Lee, 1995). Interactive television favours impulse buying.

Television and the internet: user experience

There are key differences between the PC and the television in terms of the way users engage with the medium (Holmes, 2004). In the case of the PC users are much closer to the screen than those using television. The difference is termed the 'lean forward' (internet) or 'lean back' (TV) experience. Also, the PC is a decentralised medium and usage is normally a solitary activity whereas the television has traditionally been a communal experience in the home (multiple televisions in the home have diluted this tradition in recent years). Television is not an ideal medium for interactivity (Doyle, 2002). Potential consumers do not want to be several feet from the screen when surfing the internet for products they want. Larson (2000) identifies the problem as being one of design. He notes that most internet pages are designed for the PC rather than the television. Although pages for television can be designed using the same HTML language as the Web, it is difficult to turn a web page into one that looks good on television. Consequently, proximity to the PC offers a much more intensive experience.

Interactive television and advertising

Advertisers and marketers have had to respond to the challenges and opportunities presented by the development of digital media. One of the advantages of interactive television for advertisers is the ability of both advertiser and advertising agent to monitor user interaction with the products or services being offered. The relatively simple software that allows monitoring gives advertisers valuable information regarding the type of consumers engaged in interactivity, the length of time the interactivity took place, and the outcome of the consumers' interactivity. The feedback from each press of a button from each viewer/consumer adds to the bank of knowledge that advertisers have and can influence everything from the design of the products offered to the nature of the advertising content. The information forms the basis of customer relationship management capabilities. This is discussed in more detail later in this chapter.

The primary impact of television advertising is to help an entity present themselves and their message to the mass audience. The intention is that buyers notice their television 'presence' and that this is translated into increased sales. This is the 'pull' side of the push/pull marketing effort and involves non-interactive commercials. Here, content is supplied to the user/viewer when they want to be exposed to it and/or will accept being exposed to it. The 'push' side is when businesses actively go out and 'push' customers to actively access additional information about their products. Advertising using interactive television is mostly orientated towards 'push' activities. Importantly, interactive television advertising offers customers the ability to access product information and transact immediately. However, a characteristic of 'push' style advertising is that content is supplied to the user/viewer whether they ask for it or not.

Interactive television advertising mostly takes the form of television commercials offering isolated link areas that are viewed along with, and literally over, the television programme. Viewers can 'click' on these links using a control device such as a remote control, mouse or keyboard, and experience more of the commercial than those who see the commercial without these enhancements. An example being when a commercial is aired and a link to the advertiser's website is presented as part of the commercial, the viewer could then immediately click on the link to the advertisement. Interactive advertising specialists need to anticipate a number of factors before developing and offering interactivity during a particular programme. These include the anticipated:

- Actualised audience;
- Audience flow;
- Ad click-through rates;
- Ad cost per click;
- Conversion rate;
- Return on investment.

The programme's anticipated actualised audience is the estimated number of actual viewers of an interactive television programme. The audience has to have all the necessary equipment, programming and training to participate in the interactive experience.

Another factor is the anticipated audience flow. This is an attempt to determine whether viewers will stay with a channel when the programme they have been watching ends, or when a commercial is presented during a programme, as they naturally tend to interrupt the viewing experience. This can include viewers leaving the programme or channel due to interactivity.

One of the key elements in the development of interactive media, and interactive television in particular, is the ability of firms to target consumers in advance. Chiagouris and Wansley (2000) noted the analogy with nineteenth-century general store owners who knew their customers so intimately that they could sell products to meet their specific needs. New technology in the twenty-first century allows marketing managers to offer the same level of personalised service, albeit via the electronic medium. Identifying and reaching the right audience has become a complex process and has gained in importance with two countervailing trends: while markets expand, market segments are compacting. Thus, running concurrently with the trend towards globalisation in the last decade has been a distinct shift from mass marketing of products to ones targeting smaller segments (Sividas et al., 1998).

Interactive television is one of a host of new technologies that facilitate the advanced targeting of consumers. Consumers communicate their preferences with a range of interested parties in the transacting process including manufacturers, sales people, and retailers. Furthermore, they communicate with other consumers and consumer groups. The information provided forms the 'raw material' for marketing people to engage in compacting market segments, generating new ideas and products or services, and in customising advertising.

Short Message Service (SMS)

Additional interactive services have been created through convergence of television and mobile wireless phones. Applications can now provide a Short Message Service (SMS) and text chat capability. The SMS capabilities enable users to send short text messages to SMS enabled wireless phones. Interactive television middleware vendor Open TV has been prominent in developing SMS services where users are charged by the message. Additionally, Open TV offers the option for cable operators to add banner advertisements to the messages. Broadcasters can also use SMS to send messages that are related to programming. The chat application enables viewers to discuss programmes. Cable operators can have the option of connecting the TV-based chat to internet-based chat rooms. SMS advertising can be used to gain data profiling of the consumer, enhance brand awareness and, ultimately, help achieve higher sales.

In 2002, UK satellite broadcaster BSkyB extended its portfolio of television-based messaging services with the introduction of a two-way SMS. Previously, BSkyB subscribers could only send text messages via their set-top box. The new service enables them to receive SMS messages on-screen and reply to them. The company has a strategy of building a growing portfolio of interactive services around its core broadcast content services to add value to its programme packages and access broader revenue streams. Broadcasters perceive SMS voting/polling in connection with television programmes as an ideal vehicle for engaging with viewers. BSkyB has developed a two-way SMS for this purpose with emphasis on viewers watching live football matches screened on their sports channel. These developments have the potential for fundamentally altering the viewing experience and the relationships between those involved across the supply chain of broadcasting and communications.

Advertiser and consumer relationships

Interactive television technology has enabled firms to transform previously passive promotions of products into a more effective marketing vehicle by creating on-demand advertising. This, in turn, enhances the relationship between advertiser and consumer. Chigouris and Wansley (2000) noted that the nurturing process between advertiser and potential customer relies on a keen understanding of the stage at which the potential customer has reached in the relationship. These stages include:

(i)   Awareness and willingness to initiate a relationship with a company;
(ii) Acquiring an appreciation for that company by knowing what the brand has to offer;
(iii) Moving towards a motivated exchange thereby enhancing positive feelings and trust; and
(iv) Making the transaction which solidifies the relationship.

As firms gain more knowledge in marketing-related content and advertising, interactive television significantly adds value to customers by efficiently satisfying consumers' demand. There are a number of value drivers for consumers. The adoption of new technologies by consumers often follows a well-defined pattern (Johnson, 2001), beginning with a basic need to be in control. Fundamental drivers such as security, reliability, usability and time-efficiency are the foundations for the creation of any new technology-based consumer service. Key to tapping into a mass market is to present technology that empowers consumers. Interactive television ensures that consumers feel more in control of the technology. Consequently, other behavioural and usage drivers gain in importance when determining added value for consumers. These may include convenience, simplicity, participation, impulse buying, access to more information, learning experiences and entertainment.

The market for interactive television in the UK

The growth of interactive television services has accompanied the development of the UK digital television market. Data from the communications industry regulator Ofcom shows that digital television penetration of UK households stood at 53% in March 2004. Of the UK's 13 million homes with digital television, over half already use interactive services every week with over 100 companies already providing interactive services across all digital platforms in the UK. Research by Ofcom points to there being a positive response by consumers to interactive services, with six out of ten consumers agreeing that interactive services enhance television viewing for the viewer. 43% of respondents tend to agree that interactive television offers valuable services to viewers, with a further 12% definitely agreeing.

Customer relationship management

The development of the internet as a means of transacting has spawned a number of business models for creating competitive advantage. The key characteristics of these business models were outlined and discussed in Chapter 3 (*E-business markets and models*). Most of the models are geared towards market, price or cost criteria as the main focus for generating profits. However, more and more managers have become aware of the importance of customer loyalty and the building of long-term relationships with customers as a means of creating a competitive advantage. As Lykins (2002) notes, it costs as much as twenty times to acquire a new customer as to retain one. Consequently, the issue of customer relationship management (CRM) has attracted the attention of managers of e-businesses as they increasingly adopt customer-driven business models for achieving competitive advantage.

There are three component parts to a CRM model. These are:

- Customer acquisition – this is where techniques are used to form relationships with new customers in the online trading environment. These techniques include advertising and promotion; the offering of discounts, loss leaders or other incentives to attract new customers; the offering of value-adding services to new customers; and the targeting of groups of customers through direct e-mail;
- Customer retention – this is where techniques are used to retain existing customers. This may involve using information on customers to offer a personalised service; access to a community of buyers; discounts for loyalty; or access to specialist promotional material;
- Customer extension – this is where techniques are used to encourage customers to become more involved in the activities of the organisation. This may involve sending additional information via direct e-mail relating to the portfolio of products the company has or about the company itself.

There are a number of marketing applications of CRM. Chaffey (2004) highlights the main ones:

- Sales Force Automation (SFA) – sales representatives are supported in their accounts management through tools to arrange and record customer visits;
- Customer service management – representatives in contact centres respond to customer requests for information by using an intranet to access databases containing information on the customer, products and previous enquiries;
- Managing the sales process – this can be achieved through e-commerce sites or through the application of SFA in B2B relationships;

■   Campaign management – managing advertising and promotional material, direct e-mail or other marketing techniques;

■   Customer analysis – technologies for data warehousing and data mining provide the storage and retrieval mechanisms that form the basis for analysis of buyers' characteristics, habits and behavioural responses.

CRM places the needs of customers at the forefront of the business model. Information regarding the buying behaviour and shopping habits of customers forms the basis for developing long-lasting relationships between customer and seller. The bank of information gleaned from direct contact, online, fax or any other medium all passes into a common repository for later use (Dutta and Segev, 1999). The analytics for these multiple channels informs decisions for marketing new or existing products and services. Although building knowledge of the behaviour of customers has a long history in marketing, few firms have a consolidated view of their customers.

To compete effectively, many firms have invested in a central repository for customer information storage. An electronic archive of this nature can help to foster stronger and longer-lasting relationships with customers by providing added value in service based on all previous interactions between the customer and seller. Thus, when customers enquire about issues of post-sales support or delivery times, that interaction is logged and stored in the central repository. Future contact with that customer benefits from the knowledge gained from the previous contact (O'Brien, 2002).

All departments within an organisation should have access to each customer's history of interaction and engage in communication armed with that knowledge. To the customer this may be perceived as customised service and added value, thereby increasing the likelihood of return visits and increasing loyalty. It can also help to create a hierarchy of customers such that everyone is aware of those with preferential status. The corollary of this being where unreliable or non-paying customers are known throughout the organisation and appropriate action can be taken when contact is re-established.

To benefit from important customer information requires the integration of the CRM repository throughout the organisation. Having customer data spread across multiple platforms diminishes an organisations' ability to gather important data on customers, products and services that can improve profitability and create a competitive advantage. For example, top tier customers may be lost in the time it takes to trace important information from disparate sites. Managers need to use CRM data effectively to meet customers' expectations and, simultaneously, minimise the cost of managing relationships. Here, managers must provide clarity on how best to utilise data to support their business goals. This can become complex if there are different groups within the organisation that have different CRM needs and objectives. Much depends on the capability of the CRM system in leveraging a competitive advantage. To this end, there are five key criteria against which firms should review their CRM strategy. These include:

- Breadth – the return on investment of a CRM system is closely correlated to the number of people or groups involved in using the system;
- Repeatability – the potential returns of the CRM system depend upon the frequency of the activity or transaction that the application supports;
- Cost – the cost of the solution must be lower than the cost of the system it replaces;
- Collaboration – CRM applications that support collaboration across organisations can increase efficiency, lower costs and help to leverage a competitive advantage;
- Knowledge – CRM applications that support knowledge sharing can create a competitive advantage.

Problems with CRM

It is important that managers understand the objectives that CRM systems are designed to help achieve. Conflicting objectives lead to confusion, duplication of effort, inefficiency and, ultimately, a waste of resources as the lack of focus and coherence in the rollout of the CRM strategy fails to bring returns on investment. The success rate of CRM is low. There may be a number of reasons for this. There may be hidden problems in usability where staff members require additional training to glean maximum potential from CRM or there may be conflicting ideas about how best to use the data that leads to inefficiency.

Disappointment relating to the performance of CRM systems stem from five main areas:

- Knowledge management capability;
- Measuring CRM performance;

■ Customer expectations;
■ Managing cost reductions; and,
■ Industry saturation.

Knowledge management capability

Most CRM systems are ideal for collecting and managing customer data. However, they lack features for problem solving or handling complex questions. CRM systems lack knowledge management capability and, therefore, additional software (Primus being one example) is required to plug the gap. This allows employees to access the knowledge database, ask questions and get quick replies. They can also add information to the knowledge bank for others to use.

Measuring CRM performance

The poor success rates associated with implementing CRM systems may stem from the economic limitations of their use. The ubiquity of CRM across significant numbers of industry sectors has eroded the potential for competitive advantage by its utilisation. Also, there is no clear causal link between CRM and returns on investment. Measuring the performance of CRM systems is fraught with difficulty. Even firms who report increases in revenues post-CRM implementation cannot be sure how much, if any, of the increase has been garnered through CRM utilisation. Similarly, decreases in revenues of firms utilising CRM may not be wholly, or even in part, the responsibility of CRM systems. Other inflexibilities and inefficiencies in those firms or changes in the external environment may account for the downturn in performance.

Customer expectations

Customer satisfaction has been another measure used to determine the success, or otherwise, of CRM. However, this poses problems too. The advent of the internet has radically altered consumers' expectations. Expectations of reduced delivery times are now fully embedded in the psychology of consumers and firms have had to meet those expectations. There has been some evidence to suggest the internet has increased satisfaction rates among consumers, especially in the USA where internet firms frequently top the American Customer Satisfaction Index (ACSI) compiled by the University of Michigan.

Measuring cost reductions

The extent of cost reductions has been used as a performance measure of CRM systems. The most commonly cited example is the efficiencies gained from increasing the availability of information to customers. Again, there are difficulties associated with this measure because efficiencies can be eroded by the empowerment of consumers by allowing free access to information. Consumers can match prices, determine availability, reduce search costs and build communities to increase their market power based on information garnered from websites. Efficiency gains from CRM utilisation need to be weighed against the potential for diminishing competitive advantage in the face of increasing consumer power.

Industry saturation

A source of potential savings using CRM is in the acquisition of customers. It costs less to increase sales to existing customers than it does to acquire new ones (Birkin and Harris, 2003). However, there is still the process of industry saturation to contend with. Continued acquisition of new customers alongside increasing revenues from existing customers means that the total market is being reduced. Firms may decide to focus on acquiring new customers or on existing customers, but to do both quickly erodes the market. Without tacit collusion (illegal) industry revenues would start to decline. This economic reality determines that firms need to pursue a strategy that brings industry leadership in order to gain and sustain competitive advantage. Consequently, it is unlikely that industries with CRM at the heart of their operations will have a high success rate and this accounts for the disappointments associated with CRM.

Summary

The internet is a valuable tool for marketing purposes. It is a mechanism through which companies can communicate with customers and effect transactions. The characteristics of the internet for business purposes makes it ideal for extending the reach of advertising and promotional material to a greater number of potential customers at relatively low cost. The e-marketing plan has become a vital element in the e-business strategy of many firms who seek competitive advantage. Firms need to understand the differences between traditional forms of marketing and e-marketing, focus on the critical success factors in the e-marketing environment and alter their perceptions of, and relationships with, customers in the new trading environment.

The success of an e-marketing plan is dependent on the ability of firms to use information relating to customers and competitors in ways that contribute to the overall e-business strategy. Firms need to determine clearly defined and measurable objectives for the e-marketing plan such that performance of the marketing effort can be evaluated. The marketing mix is another key element of the e-marketing plan and comprises product, place, price and promotion criteria. The characteristics of the internet play a role in determining the marketing mix adopted by firms when positioning their products or services in the market space.

Two other important aspects of e-marketing are branding and targeting of customers. The internet provides valuable information about customers and this can be used to inform the strategies for branding the products or services and determining the method and form of targeting of customers. Firms are able to collect and use a huge amount of information on customers and their online behaviour to inform future e-marketing efforts. Customer relationship marketing is a way of using such information for enhancing the relationship between buyer and seller online through more targeted marketing.

Finally, technological advances have opened up other channels of communication between buyers and sellers. Mobile wireless internet technology and interactive television are just two media through which e-marketing activity has increased markedly in recent years. Both require firms to think differently about how they engage with customers and adapt their marketing activities accordingly.

Questions and tasks

1. What are the main benefits of using the internet for marketing purposes?
2. Highlight the differences between traditional marketing and e-marketing.
3. Choose an internet-based firm and:
   (i) Undertake a profile of their customer base using demand analysis;

(ii) Undertake a profile of their marketing mix;

(iii) Identify the values that underpin the brand.

4. How can interactive television improve customer service as a medium for e-commerce?

5. Explain how the marketing function of an organisation can benefit from using a customer relationship management (CRM) system.

References

Allan, E. and Fjermestad, J. (2000). E-Commerce Strategies: The Manufacturer Retailer Consumer Relationship. In *Proceedings of the 5th Americas Conference on Information Systems*, Milwaukee, WI, 13–15 August.

Armstrong, G. and Kotler, P. (1991). *Principles of Marketing*. Prentice-Hall: Engelwood Cliffs, NJ.

Birkin, S. J. and Harris, M. L. (2003). E-Business and CRM: Directions for the Future. In *Proceedings of the International Association for the Development of Information Systems (IADIS) Conference*, Carvoeiro, Portugal, 5–8 November, pp. 121–8.

Chaffey, D. (2004). *E-Business and E-Commerce Management* (2nd edition). Prentice Hall: Harlow.

Chaffey, D. and Smith, P. R. (2001). *E-marketing excellence: at the heart of e-business*. Butterworth-Heinemann: Oxford.

Chan, S. (2001). *Strategic Management of e-Business*. Wiley: Chichester.

Chiagouris, L. and Wansley, B. (2000). Branding on the Internet. *Marketing Management*, July, pp. 34–8.

Chi, R. T. and Kiang, M. Y. (2001). A Framework for Analyzing the Potential Benefits of Internet Marketing. *Journal of Electronic Commerce Research*, Vol. 2, No. 4, pp. 157–63.

Coffey, S. and Stipp, H. (1997). The Interactions Between Computer and Television Usage. *Journal of Advertising Research*, Vol. 37, No. 2, pp. 61–7.

Doyle, G. (2002). *Understanding Media Economics*. Sage Publishers: London.

Dutta, S. and Segev, A. (1999). Business transformation on the Internet. *European Management Journal*, **17**, No. 3, pp. 23–34.

Forrester Research (2004). *Consumer Technographics, Q2, 2004*. European Study, Forrester Research, July.

Godin, S. (1999). *Permission Marketing*. Simon & Schuster: New York, NY.

Greenberg, K. (2000). Golden Age of Wireless (Marketing via wireless devices). *Mediaweek*, May, p. 102.

Hart, S., Murphy, J. and Murphy, J. M. (1998). *Brands: The New Wealth Creators*. New York University Press: New York, NY.

Higgins, A. (2001). Designing with the new Internet, *Machine Design*, Vol. 73, Issue 14, pp. 90–4.

Holmes, S. (2004). "But this time you choose!": approaching the 'Interactive' Audience in Reality TV. *International Journal of Cultural Studies*, June, Vol. 7, No. 2, pp. 213–31.

Johnson, K. (2001). Interactive Television Services: marketing strategies to drive next generation technology. Rookwood Consulting: London.

Larson, P. (2000). Interactive TV: several important issues still need to be resolved. *IT Supplement, Financial Times*, 7 June, p. 2.

Lee, B. and Lee, R. S. (1995). How and why people watch TV: implications for the future of interactive television. *Journal of Advertising Research*, Vol. 35, November/December, Issue 6, pp. 11–20.

Lykins, D. (2002). Focus on Your Customers, E-Business Advisor. *Advisor Media*, San Diego, (August), pp. 10–13.

McCarthy, E. J. (1960). *Basic marketing: A Global-Managerial Approach* (13th edition). Irwin: Homewood, IL.

McClellan, J. (2004). On the Crest of a Wave. *The Guardian*, 18 November, p. 24.

O'Brien, J. A. (2002). Management Information Systems: Managing Information Technology in E-Business Enterprise (5th edition). McGraw-Hill: New York, pp. 128–32.

Sealy, P. (1999). How E-Commerce Will Trump Brand Management. *Harvard Business Review*, July/August, pp. 171–6.

Sinha, I. (2000). Cost Transparency: The Net's Real Threat to Prices and Brands. *Harvard Business Review*, March/April, pp. 43–50.

Sividas, E., Grewal, R. and Kellaris, J. (1998). The Internet as a micro marketing tool: targeting consumers through preferences revealed in music newsgroup usage. *Journal of Business Research*, **41**, Issue 3, pp. 179–86.

Timmers, P. (1999). Electronic Commerce: Strategies and Models for Business-to-Business Trading. Wiley: Chichester.

Further reading

Allan, E. and Fjermestad, J. (2001). E-commerce marketing strategies: a framework and case analyses. *Logistics Information Management*, **14**, (1/2), pp. 14–23.

Chaston, I. (2000). E-Commerce Marketing. McGraw-Hill: Maidenhead.

Dutta, S., Kwan, S. and Segev, A. (1997). Strategic marketing and customer relationship in electronic commerce. *Proceedings from the Fourth Conference on the International Society for Decision Support Systems*, Lausanne, Switzerland, 21–22 July.

McDonald, M. (1999). Strategic marketing planning: theory and practice. In *The CIM Marketing Handbook* (4th edition) (M. Baker, ed.), pp. 116–282, Butterworth-Heinemann: Oxford.

Schubert, P. and Selz, D. (2001). Measuring the effectiveness of e-commerce Web sites. In *E-Commerce and V-Business: Business Models for Global Success* (S. Barnes and B. Hunt, eds), pp. 83–103, Butterworth-Heinemann: Oxford.

The internet: law, privacy, trust and security

Key issues:

- The internet and the law;
- Privacy;
- Trust;
- Security.

Introduction

This chapter outlines and discusses issues of law, privacy, trust and security relating to e-business. Key issues include the formation of contracts under English law and European law and intellectual property rights, data protection and privacy. The issue of privacy links in to the section on building trust in the e-business environment. Here, the treatment of trust is from the perspectives of consumer/ business and business/business relationships. The chapter also addresses security issues relating to e-business and highlights types of internet security breaches and the techniques used to combat them.

The internet and the law

Contracts

The development of the internet and the World Wide Web has provided the mechanism for a new type of commercial transaction. The availability of online transactions has raised a number of legal issues, some of which have yet to be fully resolved. In traditional marketplaces, a business contract comes into force when the sale of a good or service is agreed by the buyer and seller. Once the price has been negotiated and agreed upon, then the transaction takes place. The contract provides legal security for the buyer and seller should either party fail to fulfil their obligations associated with the agreed transaction. However, in e-business transactions the legal position is often ambiguous. Sales via the internet may be based on out-of-date information since there is no legal requirement for firms to update the information they provide on any universally agreed timescale. Should a buyer purchase an item based on out-of-date information posted on a website it is likely that courts would employ the *caveat emptor* principle – let the buyer beware. However, courts in different countries may interpret the law differently.

Online transactions under English contract law

E-mail contracts and web-click contracts are the two methods of electronic contracting. E-mail constitutes the electronic equivalent of a written letter since the process is similar – the sender types the message, inserts an address and sends it to the receiver. The receiver's inbox is the equivalent of a traditional letterbox. The web-click contract is an electronic equivalent of shopping in traditional retailers. The supplier advertises a product on a website and specifies the price; the customer ticks a box to select the product and then clicks the 'buy' button. Once the exchange of financial details has taken place and monies exchanged the transaction is complete.

However, there is a problem when a signature is required to complete the transaction. Although it is possible to create an electronic signature based on a scanned digital image of a person's written signature, there is no blanket recognition of electronic signatures under the Electronic Communications Act (2000).

However, Section 8(2) of the Act provides that secondary legislation may be made that facilitates the use of electronic communication for the purposes concerning a person's signature. The Act also made provision for contracts expressed in the form of e-mail to be valid.

To form a contract under English law requires a clear 'offer' and a corresponding 'acceptance'. There also has to be a 'consideration', that is, some benefit passing between the two parties. As noted in McKendrick (2000), 'an offer is defined as a statement of willingness to contract on specific terms, made with the intention that if accepted, these terms should be binding upon the parties'.

However, a distinction has to be made between an offer and an 'invitation to treat'. The display and advertising of goods for sale are generally considered invitations to treat. Two principles underpin this. First, it upholds the rights of sellers not to contract with a customer if they so wish. Second, invitations to treat ensure that sellers do not find themselves contractually obliged to sell more goods than they actually own. The relevance of the distinction between an offer and an invitation to treat in e-business lies in the status afforded an advertisement on a website. It is possible to argue the case for both, however, they are deemed by law to be closer to an invitation to treat (Murray, 2000). The principles that protect the seller, outlined above, apply to advertisements on websites.

The distinction between an offer and an invitation to treat becomes crucial when genuine mistakes are made by e-businesses. This typically happens when online retailers (e-tailers) wrongly label a price for a product. If the price is significantly lower than the intended price it is likely to attract numerous opportunistic buyers. The buyers who place orders have accepted the offer, and this is usually confirmed automatically by the e-tailer. Normally, this is where the contract is formed since there has been an offer and an acceptance. E-tailers and other types of online sellers can protect themselves by entering a clause in their terms and conditions that ensures they reserve the right to withdraw the offer if a mistake has been made and/or the consumer has acted in bad faith. It can be problematic proving that there has been bad faith on the part of the consumer unless there is a clear and significant error made that is recognisable by any reasonable observer.

The moment of formation of a contract is another issue that requires clarification in English law. Acceptance becomes effective when communicated to the offeror (Dickie, 1998). Much depends on the means of communication. If the communication is by post the acceptance becomes effective when sent rather than when it is received. However, acceptance via e-mail becomes effective when the communication reaches the offeror's place of business in office hours.

Virtual trade

One internet-related phenomenon that has exercised the minds of legal experts is the rise of virtual trade. Virtual trade refers to the buying and selling of assets that do not exist in the real world but have value in cyberspace. The assets typically involve weaponry for computer games, non-existent currency or virtual land or property. For example, in 2004, an Australian man paid £14 000 for a virtual island for a game called Project Entropia. Computer games instil levels of passion in some players that induce them to place real value on the assets required to compete and win. Massive multi-player online games (MMOG's) can attract tens of thousands of players each with a determination to win. This creates a value for any asset that helps achieve success as well as the trade in those assets. Players can pay real money for virtual currency that allows them to buy horses, swords, clothes, property, weapons, hunting permits or any other asset that aids their quest to win.

The rise of virtual trade has inevitably brought disputes under contract laws. However, there is no need to change existing laws to deal with disputes over virtual trade. Lawyers view virtual property that is bought and sold in cyberspace as being similar to the trade in domain names or trademarks. Buying and selling items as part of computer games involves entering into contracts in the same way as exchanges in the real world. Since it is possible, or even likely, that the parties to a contract involving virtual trade reside in different countries, it would be necessary to agree the jurisdiction governing the exchange should a dispute arise. Invariably, such contracts include a provision for an agreed form of online dispute resolution that circumvents the need to go to court.

Online transactions and European Union legislation

Directives laid down by the European Commission require member states to pass legislation that then becomes part of their national law. Once adopted, these laws have precedence over national laws.

The European Union (EU) has been active in addressing the legal issues raised by the development and use of the internet for business and transaction purposes. The Electronic Commerce Directive (2000) gives consumers a basic level of protection in e-commerce. This requires e-businesses to provide the consumer with information on the seller, the products being offered for sale and the prices of the products being offered for sale. However, to date, there has been no universal acceptance of this directive by all member states of the EU since some (including the UK) argue that complications can arise in some circumstances.

The ease of access and the global scale of website offerings mean that very often transactions span national boundaries. Cross-border contractual disputes require clarification as to where the contract was made. The Brussels Convention on Jurisdiction (1968) states that the country of domicile of the defendant is the key factor in determining the origin of business transactions. Unless an online contract specifically contains a contrary jurisdiction, companies can only be sued in the courts of their state (art.2). Art.13 and 14 provide that consumers can only be sued in their domicile but can choose to sue either there or in the seller's domicile (Dickie, 1998).

The EU adheres to the Rome Convention of 1980 when addressing the choice of law applicable to contractual obligations for business and consumer transactions. This instrument makes a distinction between contracts that contain an expressed choice of law and those that do not. Under article 1, parties to a business transaction are free to choose the law applicable. The choice can be made explicitly where online sellers include the choice of law in their terms and conditions, or implied from the circumstances of the transaction (article 3 (1)). For consumer contracts, article 5 (2) states that if the contract was preceded by an advertisement (website) the consumer can rely upon their own national consumer protection laws. Unless e-tailers and other online sellers know the country of origin of the buyer then they could, in the event of a dispute, be bound by a foreign law.

The issue of which law applies is complicated by the fact that the seller may be located in a different part of the world from the buyer. In 2002 the European Union (EU) attempted to provide clarity on this issue by adopting the 'country of origin principle'. This meant that in business transactions the contract would be subject to the law pertaining to the EU country where the seller is located. In consumer contracts the applicable law is that of the country of domicile of the consumer.

Intellectual property

E-business and e-commerce are information driven. Consequently, the main legal framework affecting the online business community is that of intellectual property rights. Most countries are signatories to the World Intellectual Property Organization that sets internationally recognized standards for protecting intellectual property (IP).

IP is legislation that protects the investment in time, money and creative input that developers expend on the production of a good or service. IP covers innovation in forms of media, branding, design, products and services, or processes. The main instruments used for protecting IP include patents and trademarks for industrial products, and copyright for literary, musical and artistic works.

Patents

Patents offer protection to unique technical innovations, usually in the manufacturing or productive process. In the UK, patents for software were excluded from the UK Patent Act (1977). Consequently, the huge rise in the development of software and hardware for the computer industry in the intervening years has meant that more and more firms are patenting their products with the European Patent Office (www.european-patent-office.org). Software patenting is important for protecting the investment of firms in developing software that is designed to perform specific functions. Patents provide stronger protection than copyright because they prevent others from utilising specific algorithms underlying a 'display' of information, whereas copyright only protects against the total duplication of a computer program.

There are a number of business processes generic to e-commerce where patents have been sought. Underpinning this position is the belief among some e-commerce entrepreneurs that a new method of undertaking commercial practice using the internet constitutes a unique innovation. However, as May (2000) notes, the generic nature of many of these methods enables competitors to imitate or develop close alternatives without infringing the patents. Legislating for patents is fraught with difficulty because it requires a judgement regarding what is innovative and unique and what can be regarded as ordinary. It can be argued that some processes are so simple that nobody should be allowed to patent them.

Anti-patent campaigners argue that most software innovation stems from refining existing products and that legislation would undermine the development of new products. Those in the pro-patent camp argue that the ability to register software patents is necessary to protect the investment of developers. There are divergent approaches to software patents between European and US legislators. In June 2005, the US Supreme Court came down on the side of copyright holders against technological innovators by ruling that copyright holders could proceed in a lawsuit against two distributors of peer-to-peer (P2P) file sharing software. Almost simultaneously, the European Parliament voted overwhelmingly against a proposed software patents directive, formally known as the Directive on Patentability of Computer Implemented Inventions.

Trademarks

Trademarks offer protection to signs, brand names, and commercial logos and labels. An organisation must be able to protect its brand since this may be a source of value and competitive advantage. An infringement of branding may damage the customers' perception of the quality of a product, the reputation of an organisation or the efficiency with which the organisation carries out its business. For these reasons organisations will usually register a trademark with a designated government body. Trademarks are important to e-businesses because they protect the name and image of the organisation. High profile firms with web content such as Amazon.com, Disney and Fedex need to ensure that customers are accessing their authentic website and not one generated from outside the organisation.

Mueller (1999) identified four categories of domain name conflict:

- Infringement;
- Speculation;
- Character string conflicts;
- Parody and pre-emption.

Infringement

Infringement refers to conflicts over domain names. An organisation will trade from a registered domain name that closely resembles another organisation's trademark. The value of a trademark may also be diminished through association with a domain name adopted by another organisation specifically to benefit from that association. The Internet Corporation for Assigned Names and Numbers (ICANN) oversees the internet's addressing system and officially sanctions domain names. ICANN has approved domain names attached to companies (.com), organisations (.org), industries (.travel), education (.ac) and recruitment (.jobs). There are moves to bring in domains for mobiles only sites (.mob) and pornographic sites (.xxx). These are designed to allocate internet-based activities to appropriate domains to make searching easier and to avoid confusion regarding the content of websites.

Speculation

Name speculation occurs when a domain name is chosen to resemble the trademark of another organisation in the hope that the trademark owner will buy out the registered domain name from its owner. Name speculators are sometimes referred to as 'cybersquatters'.

Character string conflicts

Conflict can arise in cases where there is more than one legitimate, non-speculative user of a given character string as a domain name. This type of dispute usually occurs because of non-registered company names or products. Much will depend on who was first to register a particular domain name. Large companies may buy the registration of a domain name from an individual or organisation who were first to register it if an agreement can be reached.

Parody and pre-emption

Domain names can be used for reasons of parody, pre-emption or expression. In this instance a domain name is chosen to purposefully resemble a company name or trademark as an attempt at satire. In some cases domain names are chosen as a means of expressing a political view or as a weapon for attacking and undermining organisations. Domain names can very closely resemble famous brand names by changing just one character such as Askjeeves.com instead of AskJeeves.com.

Copyright

Copyright laws differ between countries but all are designed to offer protection to literary, artistic and musical works, media and software, cable services and recordings. In the UK, copyright is conferred automatically on a wide range of materials without the need to legally register them with a statutory body. However, copyright does not cover 'ideas' until such time as they are conveyed on paper or computer or have been copied.

Copyright in the UK lasts for the lifetime of the producer of the work plus seventy years. Since copyright is automatic, producers of the types of works outlined above need only insert a copyright symbol (normally a small 'c' within a circle) to protect their asset from being copied. In the case of the internet, website owners can include fictitious information or insert software bugs to enable proof of infringement of copyright. To copy legally requires the copier to gain permission from the Copyright Licensing Agency (for music and films) or the Performing Rights Society.

Under UK law copyright programs and material sent via the internet are protected in the same way as in other forms of media. To use such material commercially requires the user to obtain either an 'assignment', which legally transfers all intellectual property rights to the new owner, or, a 'licence', which provides the licensee with the specified rights to use the material.

The music industry has been particularly active in pursuing cases of copyright infringement. The development and use of MP3 files that allow music to be stored and downloaded on the internet has been the source of conflict between the music industry and those engaged in the process of delivering music via the internet. The industry has had to fight its corner on a number of different fronts. First, against those who develop and distribute the MP3 software that facilitates the downloading of music on to a PC; second, against website owners on whose websites MP3 files have been posted; and third, against internet intermediaries that assist users in locating free MP3 files for downloading.

The most high profile conflict involving the music industry has been their battle against peer-to-peer (P2P) sites such as Napster.com. Napster is a protocol designed to enable online communities of MP3 users to share information derived from content on the hard drives of their computers. Napster can be used to gain an MP3 copy of a song by locating it on the hard drive of a fellow member of the

Napster community and then downloading it to a personal hard drive. To avoid litigation, Napster neither stored nor cached any digital music on its servers and it published a disclaimer repudiating responsibility for the activities of its subscribers.

In December 1999 the Recording Industry Association of America (RIAA) initiated legal proceedings that, ultimately, led to the demise of Napster. Subsequently, Shawn Fanning, the founder of Napster has reinvented his online file sharing business as a legitimate distributor of music on the internet. His new venture, called 'Snocap', includes technology that identifies digital music tracks shared online and creates a system of collection of royalties for copyright owners to the satisfaction of the music industry. Fanning's aim is to build online communities where users can legally swap songs. Much will depend upon the willingness of P2P networks to adopt the technology developed by Snocap. In the meantime other P2P sites for music downloads, such as Kazaa and Grokster, remain prevalent on the internet and continue to pose a problem for the music industry despite tougher laws being introduced to undermine the practice.

Data protection

In the UK, information relating to living people held in electronic form comes under the Data Protection Act 1998. Those holding such information need to register it with the Data Protection Registrar (www.dpr.gov.uk). The Act is designed to regulate the use of automatically processed information relating to individuals as well as the provision of services using such information. The Act provides for individuals to have access to such information and where appropriate to amend or delete incorrect information. Certain information is excluded from the Act and includes information pertaining to national security, company pay-roll information on staff, and mailing lists used only for the distribution of information.

The European Union has also issued Directives relating to data protection. The 1995 Data Protection Directive 95/46/EC (http://europa.eu.int/comm/internal_market/en/dataprot/) is the main EU legislation relating to data protection. The directive is periodically updated to reflect changes in data protection issues. Although individual countries adopt their own data protection legislation they are governed by the guiding principles laid down by the European

Directive (Dickie, 1999). There are eight enforceable principles that ensure that personal data must:

1. Be fairly and lawfully processed;
2. Be processed for limited purposes;
3. Be adequate, relevant and not excessive;
4. Be accurate;
5. Not be kept longer than necessary;
6. Be processed in accordance with the data subject's rights;
7. Be secure;
8. Not be transferred to countries without adequate protection.

Individuals and subjects, on whom information and data is stored, have a number of rights that offer protection. These include the right to:

1. Receive notification whenever data is collected;
2. Approach collectors or receivers of personal data for a copy of the data collected;
3. Have the data corrected;
4. Object to certain types of data.

Data protection legislation is designed to protect the interests of the individual and to ensure deterrence of the misuse of information. Data protection lies at the heart of the issue of privacy of personal information. Privacy and security are influencing factors among consumers when deciding whether or not to buy online. E-businesses have a vested interest in ensuring that the privacy of information on consumers is protected.

Privacy

Privacy refers to the rights of individuals to control the information held about them by third parties. The growth of the information economy has led to increasing interest in the issue of privacy. Research indicates that two-thirds of internet users have concerns regarding confidentiality (NTIA, 2002; Cranor et al., 1999; Hoffman et al., 1999; Pew Research, 2000) and a similar number perceive the internet as being a threat to their privacy (Cole, 2001). To improve privacy standards requires the co-operation of firms and an underpinning legal framework to protect individuals.

Individuals in European Union member states are offered protection via the 1995 Directive 95/46/EC that specifically provides protection for individuals with regard to the processing of personal data and on the free movement of such data.

Elsewhere, regulation has been less robust in dealing with the privacy issue. LaRose and Rifon (2003) note that following the 9/11 terrorist attacks in New York the American government introduced the Patriot Act (2001). They argue that this Act significantly 'lowers the bar' for privacy protection by undermining the established mechanism for privacy protection, the Electronic Communications Privacy Act (EFF, 2001). A further undermining of the principles of individual privacy protection comes from the increasing demands of many commercial firms to be allowed to invade the computer hard drives of individuals to search for copyright violations.

The eighth principle of the European Union Data Protection Directive 95/46/EC, states that: *'personal data must not be transferred to countries without adequate protection'*. In an attempt to provide clarity on what is deemed 'adequate' the EU Information Commissioner issued guidance. For those intent on transferring data abroad, the following guidance is given:

- If the data is meant for transfer (and not transit), it can be accessed from a website in the destination country;
- If the destination country is within the European Economic area (EEA) then the transfer will not be affected by the eighth principle of the directive;
- Names and addresses of customers for delivery purposes are exempt from the eighth principle in the directive.
- The EU publishes a list of non-EEA countries that provide an 'adequate' level of protection.
- Those wishing to export data to countries not on the EU-approved list of countries must perform their own adequacy tests.

There have been a number of efforts made to bolster consumer confidence in matters of privacy. Companies can participate in initiatives designed to set standards and formalise codes of conduct. Membership of organisations that oversee standards and codes of conduct receive a seal of assurance that informs customers of the reliability of the organisation in meeting its obligations in relation to privacy.

Two of the most prominent seal authority organisations in the USA are TRUSTe and BBBOnLine. These are programmes that enable companies to develop privacy statements that outline their policies on information gathering and dissemination. Both are reliant on voluntary compliance with privacy policy standards set out in the guidelines of the Federal Trade Commission (2000) that cover disclosure, choice and data security. The FTC standards require companies to:

- Notify users when data is being collected;
- Give users a chance to 'opt-out' of giving information about themselves;
- Give users access to their information so that they can correct it;
- Provide adequate security for customer databases; and
- Provide access to a live customer contact.

The assurances offered by TRUSTe include:

- Accuracy of information;
- Ongoing monitoring;
- Periodic privacy policy reviews;
- Consumer complaint resolution.

BBBOnLine prohibits the release of personal information to third parties for marketing purposes even if consent is obtained. There are 'opt-in' privacy arrangements relating to health, financial, political or religious information. Opt-in is an arrangement where a customer proactively agrees to receive further information. BBBOnLine undertakes ongoing monitoring, but unlike TRUSTe, posts consumer complaints online as well as the follow-up to those complaints. They may also report violators to the FTC with a view to removing the seal in the absence of a satisfactory resolution to a complaint.

The development of privacy seal programmes in the USA has not been without problems. TRUSTe violated its own standards by using a third party to track identifiable information on its own site (Perfectly Private, 2001). There have been instances where the organisation's seal holders have been found forwarding personal information to marketing companies. TRUSTe has attracted criticism for lacking transparency since the results of the organisation's investigations are never published. The authority of both TRUSTe and BBBOnLine has been compromised at various times after they had approved seals to companies who were already under FTC investigation.

In the UK the British Standard Institution set the standard BS7799 that covers information security. Voluntary schemes include TrustUK, a not-for-profit organisation formed through a partnership between the Consumers' Association (Which?) and the Alliance for Electronic Business that sets codes of conduct for processing online transactions. Another is UK Smart, an internet company that has formed a partnership with the Post Office to enhance trust between e-businesses and consumers, principally through the development and dissemination of digital signature software to consumers.

In Australia, the Australian Privacy Act 1998 (Cwlth) is the legislation through which privacy safeguards are protected. Federal government departments in Australia must adhere to the guidelines set out in the Act when collating, storing, and using personal information. Privacy protection was extended to cover private sector use of personal information through the Privacy Amendment (Private Sector) Act 2000. Of the ten National Privacy Principles (NNPs) that are outlined in the Act the most important is an individual's right to access information to check for correctness. Private companies in Australia are given scope to adopt their own principles, however, they must be compliant with the principle of allowing individuals access to information held. The Australian government has signalled their determination to set guidelines on internet privacy and security issues by putting in place the Australian Federal Privacy Commissioner who sets privacy boundaries for companies.

Privacy statements

Websites often contain pages that explain to customers how personal data will be collected, stored, disseminated and updated. These are called 'privacy statements'. Privacy seals are only given to companies who explicitly state their policy on personal information use. There are good economic and marketing reasons for explicitly stating compliance with data protection legislation and guidelines, as customers are more likely to use websites that respect privacy and some may choose to opt-in to websites channelling information to them.

Consumers are particularly sensitive to matters of privacy and confidentiality on two fronts: the protection of personal financial information; and the passing of information on to third parties. One of the problems relating to sending on information to third parties is the use of electronic tags on the end-user's computer – so-called 'cookies'. Cookies are small programs downloaded to the hard disks of computers used by internet users and are specific to a particular browser or computer. These can be used to trace the internet user's path through websites and the information is then passed back to the website owner. Few website owners inform customers of the type of information they gather or what they intend to use it for.

The information gathered on customers is valuable since it reveals the type of websites that individual customers habitually access, as well as details of personal information of the user. The preferences expressed by internet users can then be used for personalised marketing techniques. The lack of disclosure by website owners means that the user's privacy has been compromised. Disclosure by companies of their intended use of information derived from cookies was not included in the 2002 Data Protection European Directive 95/46EC as it was deemed restrictive to the growth of e-commerce.

Privacy: risks and rewards

As noted, there have been a number of attempts to put in place privacy standards to offer online consumers clear explanations of information practices. This is seen as vital to the continued growth of e-commerce as it provides the first step towards creating trust in the relationship between buyers and sellers. Website proprietors need to meet their duty to inform consumers of their information practices to maintain their confidence and trust. However, some privacy problems stem from consumers themselves. The desire for convenience or pleasure may be the dominant driving force behind consumers' willingness to divulge personal information. This desire may supersede concerns over privacy. Websites are characteristically laden with temptations designed to 'capture' the consumer and can lead to impulsive behaviour on the part of users (LaRose, 2001).

Privacy statements themselves can prove a barrier to ensuring privacy. The complexity of written statements in quasi-legal language can confuse consumers, as can their unfamiliarity with self-protection techniques (Anton and Earp, 2001). Although concerned with matters of privacy, consumers may simply not understand the implications of privacy disclosures or, indeed, may not be motivated to do so. Research points to the fact that most internet users divulge personal information as a routine part of accessing and using websites

(Pastore, 1999). When divulging personal information, consumers make either a conscious or sub-conscious decision to trade off privacy for the benefits they perceive of gaining from websites (O'Neil, 2001). Consumers have to weigh up the risk and rewards associated with the desire to avoid disclosure of personal information and the desire to transact online. For the majority of online transactions there is a mutual benefit between the buyer and seller that smoothes the way for exchange to take place. Transactions that create mutual benefits and mutual satisfaction between the parties encourage interactivity and build trust.

Trust

Very often the issue of trust is equated with security. In fact, these two concepts are different but complementary constructs. Trust can be described as the willingness to accept a level of insecurity for the realisation of future benefits. Trust emerges as a result of sustained interaction in which the parties continually assess the coherence between their own held level of trust or mistrust and the actual behaviour of the partner in the interaction (Introna, 2001).

Trust is a social capital that requires a reciprocal social investment from a partner. If this is the case then e-businesses lack some of the fundamental building blocks for trust to emerge. The virtual element of e-business is not conducive to fostering human relations where judgements on trust are invariably made. Consequently, it has taken much longer for trust to be built up in the e-business environment. This accounts for the reliance of e-business on legal protection and the development of technology for secure systems as methods of controlling the risks associated with collaboration or undertaking e-business.

There are four important trust factors that e-businesses and consumers have to consider when forming relationships online. These include trust involving:

- Product quality;
- Authenticity of information;
- Authenticity of the business or consumer;
- Integrity of the business or consumer.

Since most goods bought online cannot be physically handled, consumers require assurances that the goods bought match the quality advertised on websites. Only through experience can consumers build confidence in buying physical products via the internet. This can pose problems for businesses too. Levi Strauss had to scale back their online ambitions as it became clear that the cost of offering consumers a free returns service proved uneconomic and impractical.

There are some products where tangible inspection is key to effecting a sale. There also has to be authenticity of the business and consumer engaged in transactions online. This ensures that sensitive information on consumers, such as financial information, is kept secure. Likewise, businesses need to be sure that the consumers they deal with are who they say they are. Businesses and consumers need to believe in the integrity of the partner in the transaction. Recourse to the law can help to remedy a complaint. Nevertheless, the impact that both legal and technical protection affords e-businesses is limited (Sultan, 2002). In a survey carried out by CommerceNet (2000) of more than 1000 internet users, the issue of security was cited as the biggest impediment to acceptance of e-business as a means of transacting. Building trust requires a high and on-going level of satisfaction by consumers and businesses if relationships are to be sustained and renewed.

Trust in B2B relationships

Collaboration is an increasing feature across the e-business landscape as firms seek cost savings through synergy in activities and the economies of scale associated with combining expertise and experience in trading online. The economic benefits of collaboration provide an incentive for firms to seek partners. However, this also leaves firms vulnerable should the collaboration break up or turn out to be something other than what was originally planned. Electronic transactions are the measure of effective e-business and include all the activities carried out via electronic networks in the course of an exchange of services, such as the trade in goods, the exchange of information, or providing consultation services.

When two parties are mutually interdependent through collaboration they each start with a view of the trustworthiness of the other partner. Whether this is positive or negative depends on a range of factors including the propensity for risk-taking, the cost of failure, and past experience. The partners monitor each other's behaviour and review their position accordingly. Research by Kuhn (1977) suggests that firms will maintain a particular view long after anomalies appear to contradict the reasons for believing in the prevailing view. However, if the anomalies persist and accumulate then the view shifts from trust to mistrust and the prevailing view is aborted in favour of another. Thus, if the prevailing view is one of mistrust then it will require a large number of anomalies to generate a switch to trust.

However, entrepreneurship thrives on risk-taking and, therefore, there has been an imbalance in the risk/benefit dichotomy in e-business in favour of increased security at the expense of seeking competitive advantage. As the e-business industry matures there is a growing recognition that to achieve competitive advantage requires building trust with partners. The dominance of legal and technical mechanisms for underpinning security in e-business transactions is being challenged by new approaches where trust forms the central issue. Current thinking has it that trust is the ultimate and decisive factor in determining the willingness to transact via e-business networks. This paradigm shift is characterised by the pursuit of greater understanding as to what actually determines the users' trust in e-business transactions and how this develops.

Efforts have also been made to increase trust in security building components (SBCs), and in the corresponding transaction partner, by trust building components (TBCs). Finally, where traditional discussion on security has focused on the development of secure systems, now there is a distinct shift towards considering trust as an essential source of sustainable competitive advantage. The development of TBCs is likely to form an important part of the future structure of e-business and may become as relevant as SBCs in boosting the confidence of users. However, it is the quest for competitive advantage that is driving many firms to develop the concept of trust as a key strategic aim.

Products and services that are information driven have distinct characteristics that require an element of trust between parties involved in online collaboration or transaction. Choi et al. (1997) highlight three specific characteristics of digital information that, ultimately, require trust-forming relationships to sustain their value. These are:

- Indestructibility;
- Transmutability;
- Reproducibility.

Indestructibility

The intangible characteristic of digital information ensures that the quality of the product does not diminish or deteriorate. Although most digital information products do not require to be replaced because of deterioration, many are time dependent, such as up-to-date financial information. This means that the information as a product can quickly become obsolete. However, information products that do not require constant updating are deemed to be indestructible. These can be in the form of digital designs or reference works.

Transmutability

Digital information products are easily altered, modified or even customised. Technology is available to detect where this process has taken place. However, this incurs a cost to the supplier of digital information.

Reproducibility

Digital information products can be reproduced at low cost and without any loss of quality. The same information can be used in different business contexts. However, it is possible to customise digital information products to minimise the risk of reproduction. Most online consultancies and supply chain specialists deal with specific business problems that require a particular solution. Nevertheless, there is great scope for the reproduction of material produced by businesses via their website or online catalogues.

To overcome the risks associated with the characteristics of digital information products, firms need to build trust. The indestructibility of digital information makes it extensive and ubiquitous but cannot guarantee its value if time dependent. The transmutability of digital information products can compromise the reliability and integrity of the information. The reproducibility of digital information products can undermine business models based on open access to large amounts of information on products or services.

Security

Security is one of the most important issues affecting e-business. Secure transactions are of high value to customers. Security also underpins confidence in e-business and e-commerce and helps e-businesses to achieve growth. However, online transactions are inherently insecure (Karmakar, 2003). There is a paradox in the new economy created by the internet. Firms engaging in e-business need to be both open and closed. That is, they need to be open to sharing information with customers, suppliers, distributors, etc., but closed to hackers and other unwanted intruders. There is a balance to be struck between securing information and allowing access to those who need it to undertake transactions.

There are a number of ways internet security can be breached. The most common is the spreading of computer viruses. One of the most damaging examples of this was the so-called 'Sasser' computer worm that was unleashed in 2004 and which brought many computer systems crashing to a halt around the world. The virus crippled hospitals, brought airports to a standstill and interfered with global banking systems. In the UK, the Maritime and Coastguard Agency had to temporarily close, placing at risk seafarers in UK waters. A German teenager was later convicted of spreading the virus from his computer at home.

Other security breaches include unauthorised network entry, denial of service, data loss, information loss, manipulation of software applications or systems programs, fraud, trafficking in illegal materials, theft and piracy. Malicious code is a particularly prevalent and damaging form of security breach. This is software designed to damage, destroy, or deny service to the target system. Examples of malicious code include:

- Virus: a virus attaches itself to another program and is activated to cause damage when the host program is opened;
- Trojan horse: hides the true identity of user. The damaging behaviour is revealed when the program is activated;
- Logic bomb: triggers actions when conditions occur;
- Time bomb: triggers action when a specific time has elapsed;
- Trapdoor: an electronic hole in software that is left open by accident or intention;
- Worm: a virus that replicates on to other machines through a network;
- Rabbit: replicates itself without limit in order to exhaust a resource;
- Pharming: duping online bank customers into revealing account details.

Security in e-business and e-commerce typically entails setting in place systems that ensure:

- Authenticity;
- Data integrity;
- Confidentiality;
- Availability.

Authenticity ensures that the parties to a transaction are who they say they are. Digital certificates, or keys, consist of encrypted numbers that are used to identify users. Data integrity ensures that data has not been modified or altered or interfered with during transmission over the internet. Encryption technology facilitates secure communication in open systems and ensures that only the intended recipient can view the material. Secure systems also ensure continuity and accessibility to internet services. Other forms of security are designed to support the integrity of the application architecture and include:

- Authorisation that ensures only proper users are permitted entry;
- Non-repudiation that ensures proof of receipt of a communication;
- Digital time stamp that ensures the integrity of the message transmission;
- Digital signature that ensures the integrity of senders.

Encryption

Encryption is the most commonly used method of securing transmissions via the internet. There are two main types of encryption – secret key and public key. Secret-key encryption is where parties to a transaction share a common encrypted key number that is known only to them. The same key is used to encrypt and decrypt a message. Public-key encryption is where the encrypted key number used is different for sender and receiver. This method, sometimes known as asymmetric cryptography, uses two keys – one to encrypt the message and the other to decrypt the message. The keys are related by numerical code and the material only becomes readable when the keys are used in combination. Each user has a public key and a private key. No key pair can be transformed into the other. This means that any user remains free to publish their own public key and allow others to communicate with them using that public key to encrypt the message. This security is maintained so long as the user ensures that the private key is not disclosed to anyone else.

Public-key encryption is based on Pretty Good Privacy (PGP) software that encrypts e-mail messages and is available in both free and commercial formats. Most private users of the internet are likely to have a security system called Secure Sockets Layer (SSL) that was developed by Netscape and widely distributed as a means of securing messages across HTTP. SSL-enabled servers use digital certificates as a means of authenticating transactions. Most B2C transactions are secured via SSL.

Secure Electronic Transactions (SET)

One of the biggest impediments to growth in e-business and e-commerce is the customer's fear that their credit card information may be intercepted by a third party. This issue has been recognised as a threat to e-business for some time. In 1996 Visa and Mastercard jointly developed the Secure Electronic Transaction (SET) protocol. The SET protocol uses cryptography to provide confidentiality of information, ensure payment integrity, and confirm the authenticity of cardholder and seller. Both buyer and seller in a transaction receive a digital certificate (or key) from a trusted certification authority (CA). In the UK there are a number of certificate authorities including the Post Office (ViaCode) and BT (Trust Wise).

Of the commercial certificate authorities, Verisign (www.verisign. com) is the most commonly used. These certificate authorities are essentially trusted third parties. Each certificate is stored in a 'wallet' at the relevant machine and the credit card details held within can only be decrypted by the issuing credit card company. The digital certificate confirms the legitimacy of the seller and the provision of digital signatures confirms the legitimacy of the buyer. Combined, these provide a level of trust and security that forms the basis for secure transactions.

There have been a number of problems associated with SET that have hampered its use. SET constitutes an additional operational process to an e-commerce transaction. Users are faced with the cost of installing additional software to operate the SET protocol. Users also need to acquire digital certificates and install them on their client machine. This restricts online transactions to one machine per certificate. The development of Smartcards is designed to overcome this barrier to e-commerce. Smartcards are physical rather than virtual cards that can be inserted into a Smartcard reader in any location with an internet connection. Nevertheless, the lack of portability has been a limiting factor in the use of SET.

As noted previously, most transactions are conducted under the SSL encryption technique. There is competition between SET and SSL for dominance in the market for secure systems. Sellers have to install SET software on their server. The cost of this may be absorbed by the firm or be passed on to customers in the form of higher prices. Either way it may be deemed a barrier to competitive advantage. Also, it is known that SET is slower than SSL in verifying transactions. SET also requires the issuing of a huge number of certificates and this can prove burdensome. However, one key advantage of SET is that credit card details are not stored on the seller's server, thereby reducing the risk of fraud. One of the key differences between SET and SSL is the allocation of risk in the transaction process. SET places the onus on the buyer to verify credentials whereas, with SSL, the onus is on the seller to authenticate the buyers' identity and their ability to pay. This makes SET attractive to sellers because otherwise they run the risk of users simply denying that they have undertaken transactions.

Public key infrastructure

Rather than having competition in the provision of secure systems, there is a compelling argument for having a single standard protocol. The Public Key Infrastructure (PKI) is one initiative that is designed to provide a generic solution to the issue of security. PKI is an e-commerce architecture that combines specialist authorities, digital certificate management systems, and directory facilities to create secure networks on top of unsecured networks such as the internet (May, 2000). PKI is managed by certificate authorities, such as the Post Office or BT in the United Kingdom. The certificate authority records all users of public keys in the form of a digital certificate and oversees all operational aspects of data encryption. Qualifying users of public keys must gain approval from Registration Authorities.

The effective management of public keys and certificates has ensured that PKI is a popular choice of architecture for e-businesses. PKI offers security in three important areas: confidentiality, authenticity and non-repudiation. The public-key encryption provides confidentiality; digital certificates ensure authenticity of identity; and the PKI management systems ensure non-repudiation such that transactions cannot be denied by either buyer or seller.

Other forms of security breach

There are numerous ways in which the security of open systems can be breached, ranging from the irritating to serious criminal activity. Companies are forced to invest in security measures to protect their commercial assets and the trust they have built with consumers. Computer hacking, spam, fraud and misrepresentation of identity are some of the most common security breaches.

Hacking

Computer hacking is where someone deliberately and illegally gains access to a system. Much hacking activity is for criminal gain. That is, hackers seek to gain valuable information, such as credit card details, in order to commit fraud. Others use the information they have gained illegally to deliberately undermine organisations or to disrupt the free flow of goods and services in the market.

However, not all hacking is undertaken with criminal intent (although the act of computer hacking is a criminal offence). Hackers exhibit a range of motivations for their activities. These motivations include the challenge presented by overcoming internet security; the development of computer skills; a direct attack on the capitalist society or as a political gesture or an attack on particular corporate interests whose products or practices are disliked by the hackers. In many cases hackers break into computers simply because they can. Because the motivations for hacking are numerous, so too are the types of hacking activity that can be identified. These include:

- Monitoring of information: hackers introduce a programme to tap into e-mail and other sources of confidential information;

- Accessing databases: hackers have been active in raiding databases of financial institutions for sensitive financial data and credit card numbers;

- Identity fraud: hackers can assume another identity once they have gained access to confidential information on individuals. Fraud from stealing identities of individuals or organisations is on the increase and represents a real threat to the growth of e-commerce. This type of hacking is sometimes referred to as 'spoofing'.

- Denial of service: hackers can inundate an organisation with information traffic such that its internal systems shut down under the strain. These so-called 'DoS' attacks severely disrupt the ability of firms to offer a continuous service to customers but, more importantly, they undermine consumers' confidence in the ability of firms to ensure security. Some of the most high-profile names in e-business have been victims of DoS attacks including Yahoo! and e-Bay.

Hacking has become an increasing problem as technology has advanced. In particular, wireless computers, known as 'wi-fi', are vulnerable to security breaches. Wi-fi technology allows communication between computers by transmitting data across radio waves rather than through cables. Laptops with wi-fi capability are becoming increasingly popular in the business community because of the portability it offers. Wi-fi-enabled laptops are also widely available in hotels, hospitals, airports and other public places. The problem with using wi-fi technology is its reliance on radio waves for transmission. Wi-fi-enabled laptops send out signals to connect to communication beacons emitted from the nearest wireless network. Unencrypted information transmitted via radio waves can be detected and hacked into by tuning into the same frequency. The risk of security breaches is considerable because a high percentage of wi-fi-enabled laptops do not possess encryption as a means of protecting information, or if they do they are invariably not activated (Iredale and Gadher, 2004).

Spam

Spam is unsolicited e-mails that are sent to random and untargeted addresses. Sometimes referred to as 'junk e-mail', spam has become a significant problem for organisations and individuals to deal with.

Firewalls can provide some security against unsolicited e-mails and illegal access and can provide protection of information. The motivation for sending spam e-mails is multifarious and may include initiating a form of direct advertising; a method of spreading viruses; a method of inserting 'cookies' as a means of gathering valuable information that can then be sold on to third parties; a malicious attack on particular organisations or individuals; or as a means of making a political gesture.

The legal framework for tackling the problem of spam has had limited success, partly because of the sheer prevalence of the problem. Companies have had to invest in educating their workers in how to deal with spam messages as well as introducing software that filters e-mail messages based on keywords. However, determined spammers can detect what the keywords are and simply avoid them to continue their practice. In some instances valid e-mails may be filtered out because they have unwittingly used a keyword recognised by the software.

In 2004, search engine company Lycos attempted to put junk mail websites out of business by giving the spammers a taste of their own medicine. The *Make Love, Not Spam* website run by Lycos tried to increase the bandwidth bills of spammers by flooding them with junk mail. Over 100 000 people downloaded the Lycos screensaver from the *Make Love, Not Spam* website. The screensaver deluged spammers with requests for data forcing many offline. The aim of the initiative was to slow down the growth of spammers' websites. However, the company had to abandon the anti-spam idea after a wave of protests and criticism that the initiative was unethical.

Fraud

Fraud represents one of the biggest barriers to the growth of the internet for business and commerce. The true scale of fraudulent activity on the internet may never be known since many victims prefer not to report the crime and firms opt to avoid negative publicity. Nevertheless, the problem is a growing one and this is reflected in the figures released by the Federal Trade Commission (FTC) in the USA for 2004 that revealed losses of $200 million due to fraud (*The Economist*, 2004). According to the FTC the most prevalent form of internet fraud involved online auctions.

The practice of so-called 'phishing' is another growing problem for e-businesses and consumers. This involves fraudsters creating an identical website to target companies with the aim of duping

Auctions:	the buyer pays for goods that are wrong, faulty or do not appear at all.
Internet access:	offers of 'free' internet access may have hidden charges and high cancellation fees.
Credit card fraud:	credit card details are requested by some sites as proof of age; this may result in unauthorised charges.
Personal website:	offers of free website access for one month, but charges via the telephone bill.
Modem scam:	download a 'free' dialer to access adult sites but high charges follow.
Home business:	pay a fee but earn nothing.
Travel bargains:	cheap travel has hidden charges or trip is non-existent.
Investments:	site promises increases in returns on investments that do not materialise.

Figure 6.1
Fraudulent activity
on the internet

consumers into revealing personal financial information. Banks and financial institutions have been particularly targeted and the publicity surrounding the fraud has restricted the growth of online banking. Figure 6.1 highlights the most common forms of fraud on the internet.

A little-known, but increasingly prevalent, fraud is that of the dial-up scam. The chain of events runs from telecom providers leasing premium-rate lines to service providers. However, some of the service providers will be fraudsters. The fraudsters scatter 'free' downloads to attract their victims (usually music, celebrity pictures or software). A piece of software is lodged in the victim's computer once they have downloaded the material. This software reconfigures the computer to dial a premium-rate number and this connects the user to the premium-rate site (usually pornography). Eventually, the premium-rate site bills the telecom provider, which then passes it on to BT who then passes it on to the unsuspecting customer. In 2004 there were some 80 000 victims of dial-up fraud in the UK. Victims who receive bills from BT or any other telephone company may seek redress by citing Section 15 of the Theft Act 1968 that covers the obtaining property by deception. Also, victims may seek redress through the Proceeds of Crime Act 2002 that states it is illegal to handle, transfer or arrange assets derived from criminal conduct.

Misrepresentation of identity

Firms can install sophisticated software to check the authenticity of identity of those they deal with. Nevertheless, it is necessary for firms to maintain vigilance to ensure that security breaches do not occur that undermine their credibility. The internet provides easy access to a wealth of information on a huge array of subjects. However, not all the information posted on the internet is genuine. It is necessary for firms to ensure that the information they use is accurate and genuine. Failure to do this can lead to embarrassment, diminished reputation, legal proceeding or financial loss.

Mini Case Study: BBC

The BBC is one organisation that has been a victim of misrepresentation of identity. In November 2004 the BBC's international news channel, BBC World, broadcast an interview with a man claiming to be a representative of Dow Chemical. This company took over the running of a chemical factory in Bhopal, India from Union Carbide. In 1984 around 20 000 people lost their lives in a chemical leakage from the plant. Dow Chemical have been fighting legal moves to make them accept responsibility for the disaster as well as for the compensation claimed by survivors and the clean up of the plant. The interviewee was a hoaxer who had previously targeted Dow Chemical. Masquerading as a Dow Chemical representative, the hoaxer announced during the broadcast that the company now accepted full responsibility for the Bhopal catastrophe. The interview was broadcast twice on BBC World and on BBC television and radio before the hoax was detected.

The hoaxer was able to pull off an elaborate stunt because a BBC producer had accessed the Dow Chemical website to find a company representative from their media relations department. However, the Dow Chemical website had been hacked into and contact details of the bogus company representative inserted. This was the information that the BBC acted upon and resulted in the booking of an interview with the hoaxer. The BBC issued an apology to viewers, listeners and the company and set up a review of their procedures for dealing with information posted on websites. This case illustrates the need for organisations to be constantly vigilant for breaches of security and to be circumspect in their use of information derived from websites.

Summary

The development of the internet and the World Wide Web has led to a huge growth in online transactions for products and services. The existing legal framework of individual countries and trading pacts, such as the EU, have had to be updated to take account of this particular method of transacting. The EU has been active in setting directives on internet-related issues such as transactions and security.

An important cornerstone of the legal framework protecting firms engaged in e-business or e-commerce is intellectual property rights. The legislation protects the investment in time, money and creative input that developers expend on the production of a product or service. Patents can be registered to protect unique innovations and trademarks protect brand names. Copyright law offers protection for literary, musical and artistic works.

Consumers are offered a measure of protection through data protection legislation that ensures access to information held by organisations. The European Union has issued a directive relating to data protection that all member states must adhere to. The directive also covers issues of privacy. The e-commerce industry has also been active in trying to boost consumers' confidence by setting up privacy seals that formalise codes of conduct for organisations in matters of privacy. This is one method of trying to bolster trust in online relationships. A great deal of e-business and e-commerce activity is based on trust between the parties to a transaction. Technology such as encryption, public keys and secure electronic transactions (SET) offers a measure of security but there needs to be an on-going level of trust to maintain the growth in e-business and e-commerce.

Questions and tasks

1. How can firms protect their investment in developing new information-driven products to be sold online?
2. How do privacy seals work? How effective are they in bolstering the trust of online consumers?
3. How can technology help to build trust and confidence in e-business and e-commerce?
4. Outline three types of breaches of internet security and discuss the problems they can pose for e-businesses.

References

Anton, A. I. and Earp, J. B. (2001). A Taxonomy for Website Privacy Requirements. http://www.csc.ncsu.edu/faculty/anton/pubs/anton TSE.pdf.

Australian Privacy Act (1998). *(Cwlth).*www.privacy.gov.au

Brussels Convention on Jurisdiction (1968). Brussels. http://www.jus.uio.no/lm/ec.jurisdiction.enforcement.judgements.civil.commercial.matters

Choi, S. Y., Stahl, D. O. and Whinston, A. B. (1997). *The Economics of Electronic Commerce*. Macmillan: Indianapolis, IN.

Cole, J. I. (2001). *Surveying the Digital Future: Year Two*. UCLA Center for Communications Policy: Los Angeles, CA.

CommerceNet (2000). Barriers to Electronic Commerce. http://www.commerce.net/research/barriersinhibitors/2000/Barriersstudy.pdf.

Council Directive 95/46/EC. On the protection of individuals with regard to the processing of personal data and on the free movement of such data. European Commission, Brussels, October 24, 1995. http://europa.eu.int/comm/internal_market/en/dataprot/.

Cranor, L. F., Reagle, J. and Ackerman, M. S. (1999). *Beyond Concern: Understanding New Users' Attitudes About Online Privacy*. http://www.research.att.com/resources/trs/Trs/99/99.4.3/report.htm

Data Protection Act (1998). HMSO: London. http://www.hmso.gov.uk/acts/acts/19980029.htm

Dickie, J. (1998). When and where are contracts concluded? *Northern Ireland Legal Quarterly*, **49**, 3, pp. 332–4.

Dickie, J. (1999). Internet and Electronic Commerce Law in the European Union. Hart Publishing: Portland, OR.

Electronic Communications Act (2000). HMSO: London. http://ww.hmso.-gov.uk/acts/acts2000/20000000.htm

Electronic Frontier Foundation (EFF) (2001). EFF Analysis of the Provisions of the USA Patriot Act. http://www.eff.org/Privacy/Surveillance/Terrorism_militias/20011031_eff_usa_patriot_analysis.htlm

Federal Trade Commission (FTC) (2000). Privacy Online: Fair Information Practices in the Electronic Marketplace: A report to Congress. http://www.ftc.gov

Hoffman, D. L., Novak, T. P. and Peralta, M. (1999). Building Consumer Trust Online. *Association of Computing Machinery, Communications of the ACM*, Vol. 42, pp. 80–5.

Introna, L. D. (2001). Recognizing the limitations of virtual organizations. In *E-Commerce and V-Business: Business Models for Global Success* (S. Barnes and B. Hunt, eds), pp. 268–79, Butterworth-Heinemann: Oxford.

Karmakar, N. (2003). Digital Security, Privacy and Law in Cyberspace: A Global Overview. In *Proceedings of the International Association for the Development of Information Systems (IADIS)*, Lisbon, Portugal, 3–6 June, pp. 528–36.

Kuhn, T. S. (1977). *The Essential Tension: selected studies in scientific tradition and change*. University of Chicago Press: Chicago.

LaRose, R. (2001). On the Negative Effects of e-Commerce. *Journal of Computer Mediated Communication*, Vol. 6, No. 3, pp. 20–34.

LaRose, R. and Rifon, N. (2003). Your privacy is assured – of being invaded: websites with and without privacy seals. In *Proceedings from International Association for the Development of Information Systems (IADIS) Conference*, Carvoiero, Portugal, 5–8 November, pp. 63–72.

May, P. (2000). The Business of E-Commerce: from Corporate Strategy to Technology. Cambridge University Press: Cambridge.

McKendrick, E. (2000). *Contract Law* (4th edition). Macmillan Press: London.

Mueller, M. (1999). Trademarks and domain names: property rights and institutional evolution in cyberspace. In *Competition, Regulation and Convergence, Part 1*: Proceedings of the 26th Annual Telecommunications Policy Research Conference, Mahwah, NJ, 29 November, S. E. Gillett and I. Vogelsang (eds). LEA Publishers, NJ.

Murray, A. (2000). Entering into Contracts Electronically: The Real WWW. In *Law and the Internet: Regulating Electronic Commerce* (L. Edwards and C. Waelde, eds), Chapter 2. Hart Publishing: Oxford.

National Telecommunications and Information Administration (NTIA) (2002). *A Nation Online: How Americans are expanding their use of the Internet.* http://www.ntia.doc.gov/ntiahome/dn/html/anationonline2.htm

O'Neil, D. (2001). Analysis of Internet Users' Level of Online Privacy Concerns. *Social Science Computer Review*, Vol. 19, pp. 17–31.

Pastore, M. (1999). Consumers Fear for Their Online Privacy. http://cyberatlas.internet.com/markets/retailing/article/0,,6061_228341,00.html

Perfectly Private (2001). *Privacy Seals Revealed.* http://www.perfectlyprivate.com/newsresources_seals.asp

Pew Research Center (2000). *Trust and Privacy Online: Why Americans Want to Rewrite the Rules.* http://www.pewinternet.org/reports/toc.asp?Report=19.

Sultan, F. (2002). Determinants and Role of Trust in E-Business: A Large Scale Empirical Study. *MIT Sloan School of Management Working Paper* 4282–02.

Iredale, W. and Gadher, D. (2004). Wireless hackers spark computer alert. *The Sunday Times*, 19 December, p. 5.

UK Patent Act (1977). HMSO: London.

US Patriot Act (2001). www.epic.org/privacy/terrorism/hr3162.html

Further reading

Australian Privacy Amendment (Private sector) Act (2000). www.privacy.gov.au

Bainbridge, D. (2000). *An Introduction to Computer Law* (4th edition). Longman: Harlow.

Chadwick, S. A. (2001). Communicating Trust in E-Commerce Interactions. *Management Communication Quarterly*, Vol. 14, pp. 653–8.

Cornish, W. R. (1996). Intellectual Property, Patents, Copyright, Trademarks and Allied Rights (3rd edition). Sweet & Maxwell, London.

Kesh, S., Ramanujan, S. and Nerur, S. (2002). A framework for analyzing e-commerce security. *Information Management and Computer Security*, **10**(4), pp. 149–58.

Laudon, K. C. and Traver, C. G. (2002). *E-Commerce: business, technology, society*. Addison Wesley: London.

Pavlou, P. A. (2002). Trustworthiness as a Source of Competitive Advantage in Online Auction Markets. In *Best Paper Proceedings of the Academy of Management Conference*, Denver, Colorado, August 9–14, pp. 9–14. http://www-scf.usc.edu/~pavlou/14735.pdf

Pfleeger, C. P. and Pfleeger, S. L. (2003). *Security in Computing* (3rd edition). Prentice Hall: London.

Reed, C. (2000). *Internet Law*. Butterworths: London.

The Economist (2004). A Survey of E-Commerce. *The Economist*, 14 May, pp. 3–18.

Treleaven, P. (2000). E-Business Start-Up: The Complete Guide to launching Your Internet and Digital Enterprise. Kogan Page: London.

The management of e-business

Key issues:

- Managing knowledge;
- Managing applications systems for e-business;
- Customer Relationship Management (CRM);
- Supply Chain Management (SCM);
- Management skills for e-business;
- Managing risk.

Introduction

Chapter 7 focuses on the management of e-business from the perspective of knowledge sharing, applications systems, the skills set required of managers in e-business and the management of risk. The chapter begins by emphasising the important role that knowledge has to play in many modern businesses. It features discussion around the key elements of knowledge management that include communication, co-ordination and collaboration. There are many applications systems available to enable knowledge sharing and support activities in organisations. The chapter identifies and discusses the main advantages offered by some of the more prominent applications systems used for e-business and how they can be managed effectively to achieve specific organisational aims.

The key to successful utilisation of technology in e-business is determined by the quality of management. The chapter includes analysis of the key management skills required to link human resources with effective use of technology. This is followed by discussion on the issue of leadership in the e-business environment. The chapter concludes with a systematic overview of managing risk in e-business. This includes identifying key elements of a risk assessment framework, identifying the requirements for achieving stated aims within the context of each element, and identifying the risks associated with each element. The overview also includes possible solutions to overcoming or minimising risks associated with undertaking e-business.

Managing knowledge

For many modern organisations the route to competitive advantage lies in their ability to share knowledge and become a learning organisation. Firms need to have creativity and innovation at the heart of their organisational culture that helps create a constant stream of new knowledge, disseminates that knowledge throughout the organisation and uses it to create new and differentiated products that add value for customers. This is especially cogent in the new economy where technological obsolescence, rapid change and market volatility are some of the key industry characteristics.

There are different types of knowledge, including:

- Explicit knowledge: information stored as data or documents;
- Tacit knowledge: information stored in the human mind, 'know-how', intangible assets such as intellectual and creative abilities;
- Theoretical knowledge: knowledge that furthers understanding, 'know-why';
- Strategic knowledge: knowledge that furthers decision-making, 'know-what'.

Managing knowledge is an important aspect of any organisation's activities and managers need to put in place techniques, technologies and reward systems that facilitate and encourage employees to share both explicit and tacit knowledge. Since knowledge sharing permeates all levels of the organisation and is increasingly central to creating a competitive advantage, so knowledge management has become a key strategic issue in many organisations.

An organisation that bases its strategy on knowledge can create a competitive advantage by producing the skills, competencies, products and processes that competitors do not possess and find difficult to emulate. Knowledge can be embedded in technology and products or in customer service or in a brand. The value of knowledge is that it grows exponentially when shared and adds greater value than physical factors. Also, there are a number of trends evident in the business environment that make knowledge management critical to success. These include:

- The increase in the knowledge content of products and services;
- The fast obsolescence of knowledge in the information age;
- The growth of the internet and the resulting speed of business;
- The increasing focus by companies on knowledge assets; and
- The focus on growth, as more and more organisations realise they cannot achieve competitive advantage through 'downsizing'.

Technology plays a key role in the process of managing knowledge. Knowledge management systems (KMS) assist in the process of building a learning organisation by facilitating the gathering and dissemination of business information throughout an organisation.

Knowledge management relies on three key attributes within an organisation. O'Brien (2002) identifies these as:

- Communication: the ability to share information;
- Co-ordination: the ability to control and co-ordinate work efforts and use of resources;
- Collaboration: the ability to work co-operatively on joint projects and tasks.

These three attributes form the basis of successful workgroups and teams within the organisation. Workgroups are where two or more people work together on the same project or task. A team is a collaborative workgroup. The members of a team rely on each other to contribute to the completion of tasks in a co-operative way. Collaboration is the co-operative work of a team that produces an end product greater than the sum of its parts. The members of a team form relationships and understandings that contribute much greater knowledge compared to that contributed by any one individual working alone. The development of systems such as the internet, intranets and extranets has facilitated the emergence of virtual teams.

That is, members of the team do not have to be in the same location to work effectively and collaboratively on the same project. All the relevant information for communication, co-ordination and collaboration can be provided online.

Technologies for knowledge management

Three important technologies that support knowledge management are data warehousing, data mining and knowledge management portals. Data warehousing is the use of a large database that combines all the data generated and required by an organisation. It allows users to access the data directly. Data warehousing is an improvement on traditional methods of storing data where information was stored in separate systems and there was no facility for sharing the information. Organisations can store literally billions of bytes of data in data warehouses. Searching for the correct information is aided by data mining. Data mining is software that uses decision-making processes to search raw data for patterns and relationships that may be significant. Managers can analyse data and identify trends in online buying behaviour by a particular market segment. A knowledge management portal is a single point of access for employees to multiple sources of information that provides personalised access on the organisation's intranet.

The key to success for many modern businesses is having teams of workers collaborating on projects. Technology can assist in this process. Enterprise Collaboration Systems (ECS) use hardware, software and network resources to support the three key attributes of communication, co-ordination and collaboration within organisations. Examples of ECS include e-mail, web publishing, video-conferencing, chat rooms and document sharing. An important software for supporting ECS is called 'groupware'. Groupware is a collaboration software that enables users to share information with each other and work together on numerous projects. Groupware can be customised to the needs of individual firms and supported through their intranet or extranet. Figure 7.1 highlights the key ECS capabilities supported by groupware packages.

As the importance of knowledge management gains currency so managers seek ever more sophisticated systems for improving the knowledge-based environment of their organisations (Plant, 2001). One example is enterprise document management (EDM) systems.

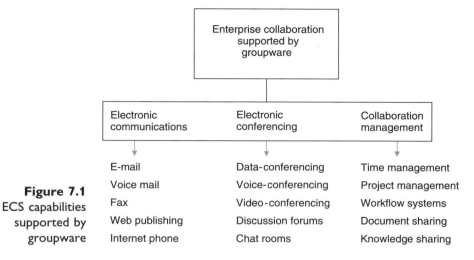

Figure 7.1
ECS capabilities
supported by
groupware

The first generation of this system automates filing systems across the organisation. The system builds vertical silos of files and there is an indexing mechanism to meet the organisation's needs. The EDM system is geared towards enhancing four key knowledge-sharing relationships.

These are:

- document to document;
- document to processes;
- people to communities;
- people to documents.

The second generation of EDM systems, commonly referred to as Enterprise Information Portals (EIP), has been developed to converge with second generation, browser-based Enterprise Resource Planning (ERP) systems. ERP focuses on processing back office transactions and is discussed in more detail later in this chapter. These second generation systems facilitate greater flexibility for users by developing tools and applications designed to co-ordinate activities in functional areas such as logistics or stock control. They also provide data and information via the portal so that managers can analyse performance and make better-informed decisions. A third type is collaboration portals. These bring together both structured and unstructured information from multiple sources. This portal facilitates group interactivity, reporting and problem solving through knowledge sharing.

Managing applications systems for e-business

Technology provides the mechanism for e-business to take place and there are numerous ways in which it can be applied both for business purposes and transactions and the internal activities of organisations. However, technology has to be managed effectively if firms are to realise the huge potential that it can yield. Poor management of technology has led to many firms operating a mix of disparate systems throughout their offices, installing different PCs and running different applications on different communications networks. Some firms have numerous applications that cannot communicate with each other, while others have separate networks for data and telephony. Not only is this inefficient but it is also costly to support. Such firms are unable to use technology in a way that helps them to solve problems, work flexibly and quickly, and save on costs.

One of the keys to success for e-businesses is to integrate their technology by unifying their computer and IT infrastructure. This makes for a more simplistic technology portfolio and creates an efficient communications system throughout the entire organisation. The internet can provide a common system for communications. The main attributes of the internet are its high level of connectivity, its interactive capability, including voice, data and video services, and its real-time capability. Developments in internet protocol have greatly enhanced the quality and range of services that the internet can deliver for businesses. Modern internet protocol solutions can converge just about any type of data. This makes communication with suppliers, customers and partners quick, efficient and cost-effective for businesses. It also helps to increase productivity, offers a greater degree of flexibility to the firm and provides a platform for extending business relationships. There are many systems available to firms that support e-business applications. Some of the most prominent ones include intranets, extranets, Enterprise Resource Planning (ERP), Enterprise Application Integration (EAI), Customer Relationship Management (CRM), and Supply Chain Management (SCM).

Intranet

An intranet is a firm's network that is based on the model of the internet. It uses internet technologies for the purposes of electronic internal communications. Access is restricted to the internal organisation. An intranet can be used to disseminate useful information such as:

- Directory of staff and contact numbers;
- List of company rules and regulations;
- Information on company procedures and processes;
- Up-dated information on products, prices, availability and quality;
- Staff development information;
- Company news;
- Job vacancies.

An intranet is also useful for sharing information on customers, suppliers and partners within an organisation. Information that becomes available to one department may be useful to others and the intranet is a quick and efficient way of sharing such information. For example, if market research reveals that customers want a broader range of applications in a specific product, this information can be spread to research and development and manufacturing divisions using the intranet. This may result in better customer service and, ultimately, a competitive advantage.

Intranets can also be used as a platform for business applications. The total cost of ownership (TCO) is the overall cost of managing information systems. Using an intranet can reduce the TCO compared to using multiple software programs that are more complex to manage, install and maintain. Some of the other benefits of using an intranet include:

- The global reach of the medium;
- Low cost of access;
- Low cost of software;
- Low cost of hardware;
- Capability for being run on all platforms;
- Standardised file transfer, document creation and network protocol;
- Reduction in paper costs.

Mini Case Study: Ryanair

Ryanair was formed in 1985 as a low-cost, low-budget airline. Today it carries some 27 million passengers annually to ninety-one airports across seventeen countries. The company headquarters is based in

Dublin and it operates from a series of 'hubs' such as Frankfurt, Rome, Milan and London Stansted. The generic strategy of Ryanair is cost leadership. To create a competitive advantage in their highly competitive environment requires being the least cost producer in the industry. There are numerous ways in which Ryanair seek to reduce costs to the bare minimum. These include flying to secondary airports, no-frills service, minimal advertising costs, minimal training of staff, and quick turnaround of aircraft to minimise time spent on the ground, when airlines incur most costs. Another method of reducing costs is to encourage customers to book their seats online. This saves on administration costs and quickens the process of filling seats. In 2005 around 98% of the firm's income was derived from online booking generating some £400 million in profit.

Another method of controlling costs within the firm was the development of an intranet system that all staff could use. The company's intranet links all fourteen corporate offices located at the hub airports as well as the flight simulator facility in the UK midlands and the headquarters in Dublin. The value of the system lies in its speed and capacity, allowing the IT function to be based in Dublin. No head office functions are performed at any of the other locations, leaving employees to do it themselves. This saves on administration costs. A wide range of operational activities can be undertaken by staff using the company intranet. These may include pilots obtaining latest weather reports, check-in staff monitoring demand conditions or cancellations, or engineers prioritising maintenance jobs. The intranet not only increases efficiency but, with no administration staff, the operating costs are greatly reduced.

Extranet

An extranet is a network that links selected resources of a company with its customers, suppliers and partners, using the internet or private networks to communicate with other organisations' intranets. One of the key characteristics of the modern e-business environment is the high level of collaboration that exists between different firms who can gain mutual benefits from sharing knowledge. An extranet is a way of facilitating partner inclusion in information flows from an organisation. The information made available may vary in depth and richness according to the nature of the relationship between partner organisations. It may simply involve giving access to information on prices, availability of products, specifications, delivery times, etc.

However, some partnerships are much closer and require the sharing of information that is both process-orientated and strategic.

One of the most common uses of extranets is to enhance efficiency in supply chain management. An extranet can be used to communicate with all parties along the supply chain to ensure that inputs are transformed into outputs and delivered to customers in the most cost-effective and efficient way. Very often a firm will have to link their intranet with another firm's intranet via an extranet to integrate business applications. This is achieved using middleware as a systems integrator. Middleware is software that is designed to facilitate communications between business applications. The application of this technology is referred to as Enterprise Application Integration (EAI) and is discussed in more detail later in this chapter.

Enterprise Resource Planning (ERP)

Enterprise Resource Planning (ERP) is an integrated cross-functional software that re-engineers manufacturing, distribution, finance, human resources and other business processes of a firm to increase its efficiency, flexibility and, ultimately, profitability. For example, a firm can use ERP software to electronically manage their procurement needs including gathering information on availability of supplies, costings, delivery times, quality assessments and price comparisons between different suppliers. ERP software has become a vital component of firms' e-business architecture and is an important tool in meeting customer expectations. ERP helps firms meet expectations by integrating back-office processes that result in better customer service, maximising production capacity and increasing distribution efficiency. ERP also supports management decision-making by providing the necessary data on cross-functional activities that forms the basis of determining business performance.

Enterprise Application Integration (EAI)

EAI is a cross-functional e-business application that integrates front-office applications, such as CRM, with back-office applications, such as enterprise resource management. Figure 7.2 illustrates the interconnections between front- and back-office applications supported by EAI software.

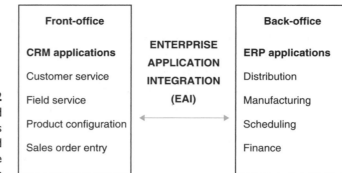

Figure 7.2
EAI-enabled
interconnections
between front- and
back-office
applications

EAI software (often described as 'middleware') enables users to control business processes involved in interactions between different business applications. There is also a middleware component to EAI that facilitates data conversion and co-ordination, application communication and messaging services. EAI offers the flexibility that allows firms to integrate numerous enterprise applications by facilitating the exchange of data according to the derived business process models put in place by the software designers. For example, the rules can regulate the entire supply chain process. That is, when an order is received a series of process applications kick in including inventory control, billing, delivery and fulfilment. Relevant departments within an organisation are alerted automatically, such as accounting, distribution, warehousing, etc., thereby integrating both front- and back-office applications.

There are real benefits to be derived from such a seamless and integrated way of linking applications in an organisation. First, it allows firms to respond quickly and efficiently to changing business conditions and variations in customer demand. EAI integrates access to all relevant product and customer information. Second, the sales process is quicker and more effective using EAI and it helps match the needs of customers to the products available, thereby adding value to customers and helping to build brand loyalty. Third, EAI benefits all parties along the supply chain, as well as customers, because of the quicker response times and better co-ordination that it facilitates.

Customer Relationship Management (CRM)

Customer Relationship Management (CRM) is a cross-functional e-business application that integrates and automates many customer-related processes such as sales, direct marketing, account handling, order management and customer support. The development of e-business as a method of transacting has spawned a number of business models for creating competitive advantage. Most are geared towards market, price or cost criteria as the key focus for generating profits. However, in recent years more and more managers are becoming aware of the importance of customer loyalty in providing the basis for long-term viability of their organisation's e-business ventures.

A significant number of business managers report a reluctance to adopt a CRM business model because of the perceived high cost of introducing new technology. However, the cost of not doing so can be severe. Large numbers of businesses operate multiple interaction channels that undermine consistency in service to both customers and in-house information needs.

There are a number of identifiable critical success factors for the successful implementation of a CRM strategy. The first of these is invariably the most difficult to achieve. Senior managers must have the commitment to drive cultural change geared towards a clearly defined customer-orientated business strategy. High rates of customer attrition have characterised the e-business environment adding to the costs incurred by firms. A CRM strategy begins the process of reversing this trend by focusing on retention and increasing customer lock-in and loyalty.

A key cultural change factor is the need for everyone in the organisation to have a customer-orientated view of the business. The bank of knowledge regarding customer profiles, relationships and buying habits forms the basis of building an enhanced understanding of customers and their needs. This necessarily involves understanding how each customer prefers to communicate those needs to the firm. Thus, method, type, content and outcome of each customer communication should be entered into the central repository for future reference by any department within the organisation.

A successful CRM strategy also needs a robust and flexible architecture. In the initial phase of adopting a CRM strategy managers need to develop the central repository for all customer information. However, to gain a competitive advantage this may not be sufficient. The key to success is likely to lie in the flexibility of the architecture in incorporating other systems such as ERP or EAI. Combined, these systems present a powerful mechanism for creating good order information, increasing efficiency and enhancing customer value. Again, the added value to customers is conducive to retention and loyalty. To alleviate the fears of spiralling costs, managers can invest in ready-made CRM solutions from the myriad of vendors in the marketplace. This very often proves a cheaper and more efficient method compared to building one in-house. Although developing a CRM infrastructure internally can help create a competitive advantage it requires superior analytical and technical skills that few firms possess.

Acquiring the technology and building an appropriate and flexible CRM architecture goes only part way to determining a successful CRM strategy. The technology can be seen as both the enabler of CRM and its downfall. Technology can help reduce costs by standardising the information seen through the buying and selling process. Crucially, though, it is how the technology is implemented that will determine the extent to which firms can achieve the benefits associated with CRM. Too often, too many firms have failed to capitalise on the potential that the technology offers because of failures in managing one or more of the critical success factors. For example, firms may install the right technology but fail to adapt their corporate culture to one that is customer focused. Chief Executives may enthuse over CRM but fail to lead staff in its implementation.

Mostly, firms do not spend enough on the technology and fail to acquire or train staff to utilise it effectively. Thus, another critical success factor is human resources. Technology offers the capacity to succeed but not the ability. A successful CRM strategy relies on highly motivated staff to maximise the potential that the technology brings to the business.

Finally, to bring these criteria together requires strong leadership skills. The issue of leadership in e-business is discussed in more detail later in this chapter. However, it is worth noting that a critical success factor for implementing a CRM strategy is the effective and inspirational leadership that should stem from the apex of the firm. The leader fulfils a number of crucial roles in driving forward the strategy, including that of information visionary, trouble-shooter, change agent and motivator. One of the most difficult tasks facing managers has been to effect a change in corporate attitudes towards one where a technology enabled customer focus is the dominant culture within the organisation.

Since the mid 1990s, firms have been active in investing significant amounts of time and money ensuring that the critical success factors for implementing their CRM solutions are in place. And yet much of the expenditure has been wasted. The worldwide success rate for CRM is low. The vast majority of firms have yet to realise any return on investment in CRM. Business models built around CRM need to go further than meeting the basic success factors. For most, this entails overcoming barriers that prevent positive returns on investment. These barriers invariably cluster around issues of cost, deployment time, maintenance and the value of information.

Supply Chain Management (SCM)

Supply Chain Management (SCM) refers to the management of interrelationships with other businesses along the supply chain that combine to produce and sell products to customers. Normally, SCM involves co-ordinating and communicating across a network of business relationships from suppliers of raw materials, to manufacturers, distributors and retailers. Figure 4.1 in Chapter 4 included an illustration of a traditional supply chain. Distinction can be made between the downstream supply chain, which involves transactions between a firm and its customers and intermediaries (sell-side e-commerce), and the upstream supply chain, which involves transactions between a firm and its suppliers and intermediaries (buy-side e-commerce). Figure 7.3 illustrates the upstream and downstream dynamics of a supply chain.

Before discussing the merits of electronic SCM systems it is worth noting the characteristics of traditional SCM systems in order to emphasise the difference that new technology has made to this process.

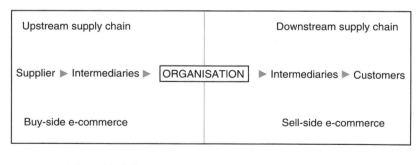

Figure 7.3

Upstream and downstream dynamics of a supply chain. Adapted from *E-business and E-Commerce Management* (2nd edition) by E. Chaffey (2004) with permission from Pearson Educational Publishers

The traditional supply chain consists of a network of partners through which materials flow from suppliers to consumers (Warkentin et al., 2000). An important aspect of managing the supply chain is the management of information flows between partners in the supply chain (Lummus and Vokurka, 1999). Traditional supply chain management linked partner firms in a linear and inefficient way. Suppliers of raw materials would sell to manufacturers, who would then distribute the finished product to wholesalers, distributors, dealers and then on to consumers via retailers. In the traditional supply chain, the communication of information had to traverse several layers of intermediaries before reaching the manufacturer. This invariably led to the diminution of quality of information as it passed through each layer and made the management of the supply chain inefficient. The distortion in information flows very often resulted in firms carrying excess capacity, having poor allocation of resources, and failing to maximise production scheduling.

The linear relationship between firms and their suppliers was restrictive. Information flowed from one firm to its suppliers (upstream) or immediate distributors (downstream). Typically, firms had a fixed number of suppliers with whom they had built up a relationship. There was no direct link to consumers. Information did not extend beyond one link in the supply chain. Furthermore, there was no standard data representation scheme to facilitate this anyway. The lack of knowledge sharing across the supply chain led to inefficiencies in managing the needs of customers.

Many firms use third-party logistics firms to manage their supply chain, but this requires an effective communications system if it is to bring real benefits. The use of the internet can provide this. Modern SCM systems integrate information systems between firms and their downstream partners, their suppliers and even their suppliers' suppliers. SCM systems provide the tools to manage huge amounts of information and data that exist across the supply chain. There are clear benefits to be gained in managing the supply chain including:

- Greater visibility across the supply chain, improving inventory management;
- Better understanding of demand conditions through electronic point-of-sale (EPOS) technology. This increases efficiency in planning and maintains stability in the supply chain;
- Streamlined order processing that promotes supply chain lead-time reduction.

The development of e-business applications has facilitated the integration of the myriad forms of media that connect the supply chain, whether from a fixed PC, mobile phone or interactive television. Using the internet adds value by removing the constraints of geography, time, and space. This creates so-called 'value-webs' where customers drive the formation of flexible dynamic networks by their demands and firms can build real-time links with partners located anywhere in the world. The value-webs provide the mechanism for delivering products to customers cheaply and efficiently.

Intranets and extranets can also be used to build relationships between suppliers, partners and customers, and EAI can integrate the business applications that underpin supply chain management. The aim of SCM is to reduce costs, increase efficiency and improve supply chain cycle times. A supply chain life-cycle includes a process of committing to a contract to deliver a product; undertaking a schedule for delivering the product; manufacturing the product and then, finally, delivering the finished product. Again, software designed for SCM helps firms become more flexible and responsive to the needs of their customers and business partners. Figure 7.4 illustrates an integrated solution for SCM.

It is possible to identify a number of important steps that organisations must take to implement a successful supply chain strategy based on collaboration with partners. These steps include:

- Ensuring that the internal logistics processes are fully integrated and co-ordinated with procurement and manufacturing functions;
- Identifying key partners and focusing collaboration efforts on those; and build relationships and integrate activities with key suppliers, partners and customers through trading networks;

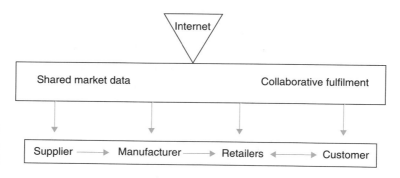

Figure 7.4
Integrated solutions for SCM

- Building co-operation and trust to enable knowledge sharing and access to information;
- Synchronising key activities with partners in existing trading networks; and explore further efficiency gains by building collaborative relationships through other trading networks;
- Identifying the activities that are critical to the success of the supply chain and focus collaborative activities on those to improve performance and gain a competitive advantage.

Management skills for e-business

The type and range of skills in the labour force have undergone significant change as a result of changing information technologies and the development of internet and intranet use in the workplace. The impact of rapidly changing Information and Communications Technologies (ICTs) has radically altered the scope and process of business operations and reconfigured the skills base firms need to maintain competitiveness. The development of ICTs has presented challenges in the workplace where learning and applying new skills are key. This has been particularly evident in knowledge-intensive industries (Silvestri, 1997) where demand for technical skills is high. Computer scientists and systems analysts are two such examples where employment growth has been high to meet demand for ICT skilled personnel (Colecchia and Papaconstantinou, 1996). However, increasing demand for technical skills and changes to the type of occupations in the workplace are only two manifestations of the development of ICT.

Another important issue relates to the changing role of management. Managers are increasingly faced with the challenge of creating added value via investment in human resources and use of knowledge as an asset. Managers are increasingly called upon to perform as organisational designers, coaches and teachers (Davies et al., 1998). Increasingly, there is a need for management to display attributes of social and cultural awareness allied to ICT skills in a business context. These have largely superseded demand for managers with technical expertise (Hansen, 1998).

However, in the case of e-business, where the exploitation of new technology is the key to competitive advantage, there is a need for synergy of technical and social skills. Different industries have experienced different imbalances in their management skills port-folio. Knowledge-based industries, where high technical skills are traditionally evident, have had to acquire management with added social and cultural skills. Conversely, industries where social skills predominate have had to acquire managers with good technical skills (Hansen, 1998).

Firms have not only been engaged in correcting the imbalance of management skills but they have also been actively involved in determining the characteristics of new management within a knowledge-based industry sector. Lundvall and Johnson (1994) provide a checklist of combinations of skill sets incorporating contextual, tacit, social and technical skills. These must be added to general management skills such as communications, creativity and flexibility. The transition to effective management within an e-business environment requires a combination of most, if not all, of these skills.

The level of involvement in e-business activities largely determines the type of management skills demanded across different industry sectors. According to Davies et al. (1998) two main types of management skill sets can be identified for e-commerce. These are technically-orientated skills sets and relationship skills sets. The former is more prevalent in industries with a history of implementing ICT systems, such as distribution and logistics. The latter is more likely to be the realm of senior strategists within organisations where a combination of technical understanding and social skills drive the e-commerce strategy both internally and externally.

At the simplistic incremental level there is an isolated application that facilitates local exploitation of a particular technology – unskilled labour is replaced by automated processes. The integration of IT applications forms the next, and more complex, level. This adds to the co-ordination and co-operation within the organisation. Enterprise Resource Planning (ERP) software applications facilitate integration across business functions. An ERP system is a simple concept but one that takes management skill to implement. The basis of an ERP system is where all organisational activities that involve information processing are stored and maintained in a database through one image; that is, the data is stored once and uniquely as a set of tables (Plant, 2001). This system allows all the information content of an organisation to be represented and manipulated efficiently. The decision to move to an ERP system is a critical one for management. The skill of management is to identify the driving force behind the potential added value of adopting an ERP system and understanding the key sources of the firm's competitive advantage.

ICT applications also facilitate the third level, which is the re-engineering of business processes. This involves the re-evaluation of the organisation's value chain and production processes. The fourth is business network reconfiguration. At this level, co-ordination and co-operation extend beyond the boundaries of the organisation (Clarke, 1994). ICT at this level enables changes to the scope and tasks of the business network involved in the creation and delivery of products and services. The fifth level involves a redefinition of the scope of the business and is characterised by the migration of functions across the organisation's boundaries to such an extent that it alters the core business activity of the firm.

All but the simplest applications of ICT have increasingly greater increments of organisational and technological change. Firms experience difficulty cultivating and gaining added value from relatively small increments of ICT-induced change. Under-taking e-business means incurring increasing risks, as it requires concurrent reconfiguration of internal business processes and external business relations within a rapidly changing technological environment. Understanding the functionality of technology and the value-adding application of it in a business context are the key criteria needed of modern management engaged in e-commerce.

Leadership

As e-business develops it alters the nature of organisations and the speed at which transactions and other business operations take place. Consequently, the nature of leadership within e-commerce and e-business-orientated organisations has changed. Each firm must adapt to the evolving rules of the new economy. To be successful and create competitive advantage it is necessary for firms to develop or refine each aspect of the business that affects, or is affected by, ICT. It is incumbent on leaders within organisations to maximise the 'e-space' available to them by developing strategies capable of operating in the new environment. Crucially, these strategies must enable firms to:

- Protect their brand;
- Optimise shareholder value; and
- Maximise opportunities for enhancing revenues and reducing costs.

To maintain shareholder and customer confidence in a rapidly changing environment requires distinct leadership skills in organisations where ICT plays a crucial role in creating competitive advantage. To understand leadership in an e-business context it is necessary to make the distinction between the new economy and traditional bricks-and-mortar firms. Where the former requires leadership, the latter is characterised by management. Old economy firms have managers who can design and implement strategies over a period of time (Cope and Waddell, 2001). The new economy relies on intellectual or knowledge resources and the main role of management is to link competencies and resources to create and sustain competitive advantage.

Leadership in e-business means initiating and implementing a new set of company aims based around e-business initiatives. Where, traditionally, the focus has been on profitability, the new economy requires leadership that focuses on competitiveness and customer satisfaction. Successful e-business requires leaders who can develop cultures and teams that can realise the potential of the internet for their business.

Clearly, investing in technology is important, but the critical success factor is getting people to use it effectively. This is where leadership makes the difference. Leaders need to communicate their vision of the role that the internet will play in achieving the company aims. The extent to which the workforce understands and embraces the vision determines the effectiveness of the leader. That is, it is the followers that attribute leadership. If there are no followers, then there is no leadership (Grint, 2005).

In many modern businesses the requirements of leaders are multifarious and complex. This is particularly the case in e-business where the engagement with technology permeates the entire organisation. To maximise efficiency requires all staff to use the same tools so that an integrated and collaborative approach to problem solving becomes the dominant culture within the organisation.

Managing risk

As firms spend ever-increasing amounts of money on e-business, so the risks associated with such activity increase. The first risk to be considered by managers is to determine the extent to which they want their organisation to participate in e-business, if at all. The risk assessment is likely to focus on the likely impact of non-participation on performance, the extent to which their competitors are likely to participate in e-business and the impact on relationships with suppliers and customers of non-participation.

A second risk factor is deciding on the level of investment in e-business applications technology appropriate for the organisation's aims. The cost implications of training staff or hiring new staff to operate the systems have to be taken into account, as does the speed of change in technology and the likely impact this has on achieving a competitive advantage.

Thirdly, the widespread use of the internet for business purposes has led to increasing collaboration between firms who share information and knowledge to effect mutual benefits. Firms are no longer isolated in the business environment but are part of a wider, more integrated, business community. However, the benefits of participating in this business community have to be weighed against the risks.

Finally, there are technical risks associated with e-business including systems failures and breaches of security. Typically, the types of risks managers need to consider cluster around operational, technical, managerial, legal and customer-orientated functions. Figure 7.5 highlights the main risks associated with each of these functions.

Operational	Technical	Management	Legal	Customer
Staff training	Security costs	Identifying core business activity	Copyright	Understanding the market
Recruiting qualified staff	Access to information and data	Integration of business and marketing plans	Advertising standards	Branding
Ensuring high visibility of the website	Client/server relationship	Identifying cost-saving activities, increasing efficiency	Intellectual property rights	Customer service
Handling product defects	Electronic documentation of all business transactions	Increasing customer service	Different buyer/seller jurisdictions	Integration of business processes
	Automating processes	Benchmarking	Tax issues	Transactions
	Continuous system testing	Investing in new technology	Privacy	Payment system
	Data loss prevention	Improving distribution	Regulatory compliance	Complaints procedures
		Building relationships with partners	Domain name registration	Market research
		Evaluating e-business performance	Contractual issues	Changes in demand conditions

Figure 7.5
E-business
risks

Risk assessment framework

Corporate leaders have to undertake risk management assessments before committing fully to e-business. As noted in Chapter 6 (*The internet: law, privacy, trust and security*), firms need to ensure security, privacy, high availability and accessibility to gain the confidence of customers, suppliers and partners. Managers need to be fully satisfied that their business processes are reliable and that the technology they have in place can execute transactions at any given time. These issues form the basis of a risk assessment framework for firms.

The risk assessment framework can be used as a basis for determining the quality of business processes that the firm undertakes. However, it also acts as an enabler of e-business strategy by focusing attention on a number of key issues. These include:

- Determining the appropriate level of risk that the firm needs to absorb to achieve its aims;
- Focusing attention on the appropriate organisational culture to achieve its aims;
- Forming appropriate relationships with customers, suppliers and partners;
- Understanding the external competitive environment;
- Recruiting staff with the correct skills to drive forward the e-business strategy;
- Creating an appropriate organisational structure for sharing knowledge and making decisions;
- Putting in place contingency arrangements for dealing with systems failures;
- Putting in place appropriate security measures to prevent malicious attacks.

A risk assessment framework needs to be operated from the outset of a firm's e-business strategy so that it can compete effectively in the business environment in which it exists. Risk management in e-business needs to address both technological and strategic factors. Although there are many different areas that firms could focus on when defining business risks, it is possible to narrow the focus to six key elements of a risk management framework. These are:

- E-business strategy;
- Implementation of e-business risk management;
- Policies and procedures;

■ Applications infrastructure;
■ Technology infrastructure.

The risk management framework is built around understanding what the requirements are for achieving the stated aims of the organisation in the context of each element, and then determining what the key risks are that could potentially lead to failure. From there, it is possible to devise ways of managing the reduction in risk.

E-business strategy

E-business strategy, IT and risk management need to be clearly defined, aligned and supported by all levels of management and knowledge shared throughout the organisation. The strategy should be underpinned by maintaining relationships with partners and suppliers to maximise efficiency in bringing products and services to customers.

Risks: failure to see initiatives through to completion; channel conflict.

Managing risk:

Management need to undertake a thorough internal and external analysis and follow a systematic process of evaluating their strengths and weaknesses before committing to an e-business strategy. Once committed, firms need to follow through with effective resource allocation to key operational activities in order to successfully implement the strategy. The strategy needs to be understood and supported by management at all levels throughout the organisation. To achieve this requires leadership from the apex of the organisation. The CEO must be able to communicate the strategic vision to other managers throughout the organisation and ensure that operational processes are in alignment with their decisions at the strategic level. Managers also need to evaluate the performance of the strategy at regular intervals, implement change where necessary or abandon completely if it proves to be failure. However, once committed to a strategy managers need to back their convictions with a determination to see it through to completion.

It is not only internally that managers have to communicate their strategy and build relationships. Many organisations have built up relationships with suppliers or partners over a number of years. The internet may offer the opportunity for disintermediating erstwhile partners by facilitating direct contact with consumers. Managers have to think of the long-term consequences of this action and the likely response from disintermediated firms. It may be in the interests of the firm to avoid channel conflicts and continue to maintain relationships with partners. Channel conflict arises when a medium like the internet presents a disruptive element to existing arrangements between partner firms. The internet has three main channels of communication, namely, as a communications channel only; a distribution channel for intermediaries or as a direct sales channel to customers. Managers need to choose the appropriate channel for achieving their long-term aims.

Implementation of e-business risk management

The structure, resources and skills needed to execute the risk management strategy are defined and in place.

Risks: inability to plan for and react to events; inability to develop and support e-business initiatives.

Managing risk:

Organisations need to assign a designated office to oversee the implementation and monitoring of the risk management strategy. Perhaps the most important element of the risk management team's remit is being able to recruit the right people to undertake the tasks that help achieve the firm's stated aims. Technology provides a useful mechanism for helping to achieve aims but requires highly trained, skilled and motivated staff to realise its potential. The recruitment of high quality staff is a top priority for managers who then need to put in place policies that help to develop and direct the capabilities of staff towards achieving the aims of the organisation. Importantly, managers must be able to communicate the strategic vision of the organisation and influence an organisational culture that is orientated towards knowledge sharing, collaboration and teamwork. To this end managers must be innovative in the reward system within the organisation. This may go beyond financial rewards for high performance to include promotion, peer recognition, greater autonomy in decision-making, and a role in the strategic decision-making process.

Other key elements of the risk management team's remit are likely to include setting aims and putting in place methods of measuring and evaluating performance in achieving stated aims; putting in place an organisational structure that defines roles and responsibilities; establishing financial and budgetary procedures and clear processes for dealing with legal, contractual and competitive risks. These key elements of risk management help organisations deal with rapid changes in the competitive environment. In combination, they establish a mechanism for supporting the initiatives that are developed to create a competitive advantage.

Policies and procedures

Policies, procedures and guidelines are developed, implemented and communicated to all staff.

Risks: some staff members operate in a manner that is not aligned to the e-business strategy.

Managing risk:

Organisations need to clearly define the policies and procedures they put in place to minimise the risks associated with any aspect of their e-business strategy. These policies and procedures will likely cover a wide range of activities centred round business processes, technology and security. Staff members need to be aware of the policies and procedures through training programmes and a review of staff awareness, undertaken periodically. An internal audit of policies and procedures will determine if the existing framework is appropriate for achieving the firm's aims.

There should also be policies and procedures in place for monitoring performance in the various activities carried out by the organisation. These may typically involve monitoring and evaluating customer satisfaction, incidents of security breaches, returns on investment, personnel development, partner agreements and financial support for initiatives. For many of the organisation's activities the use of quantitative metrics to monitor and evaluate performance can be used.

Applications infrastructure

Applications need to be reliable, secure and accurate to support transactions and data integrity, confidentiality and availability.

Risks: inefficient business processes; susceptibility to security breaches; unreliable availability for technical reasons.

Managing risk:

As organisations expand their e-business applications so the risks associated with inconsistent approaches or security breaches increase. To overcome these, firms need to put in place a secure and robust applications infrastructure that supports their e-business strategy. Crucially, the applications infrastructure must be integrated with those of partners, suppliers and customers. The sharing and receiving of information, knowledge or functionality with third parties requires a high level of vigilance among partners. There have to be clear rules and procedures in place for managing access to information across integrated systems.

Technology infrastructure

Technical infrastructure should be able to support strategic aims and include hardware, software, middleware, communications and other technologies that ensure availability, security, reliability, scalability and flexibility.

Risks: systems failures.

Managing risk:

To minimise the risk of systems failure requires effective Information Systems (IS) operations management. IS operations management focuses attention on the use of hardware, software, network issues and the links with human resources within an organisation. The types of operations that are supported by IS include computer systems, network management and production control and support. Many organisations now utilise software to automate and monitor the performance of their computer systems. The software monitors how effectively the computers process a large number of tasks and feedback data to managers for analysing performance. The data not only allows managers to monitor performance, but also helps them to anticipate problems, reduce cost and, ultimately, enhance performance by ensuring quality thresholds are maintained.

An e-business risk management framework forms the basis for organisations to achieve added value in the e-business environment. This is evident across organisations' activities including product development, operations, marketing, customer relationships and communicating both internally and externally. A risk assessment should be carried out with the aims of achieving a high level of security, accuracy of information, completeness and integrity of information and guaranteed 24/7 availability of processes and transactions.

Summary

For many modern organisations, the creation and sharing of knowledge is the key to gaining a competitive advantage.

The development of the internet has provided a means of enhancing the process of sharing knowledge both within organisations and with business partners. Specifically, the internet facilitates greater communication, co-ordination and collaboration in e-business. It is the responsibility of managers to incorporate the appropriate applications systems into their business as well as ensuring the recruitment of properly trained and qualified staff to maximise the potential of the technology and achieve the organisational aims. There are many applications systems available. One of the keys to successful e-business is the integration of applications systems to fully support the organisation's activities. This is likely to include front- and back-office activities, and communication with customers, suppliers and partners.

Acquiring and implementing technology is vital to the success of an e-business. However, technology is only useful if managed properly. Fundamentally, it is the quality of management within organisations that will determine how successful they are. This applies to the management of technology and the people that use the technology. E-business has presented challenges to managers by increasing the requirements of their skills and knowledge base. Managers have to display a synergy between human skills and technical skills in order to gain maximum returns from their e-business venture. This means that they have to understand where value can be gained from the functionality of technology as well as motivating, leading and communicating the vision of the organisation to staff.

Engaging in e-business incurs risks for organisations and this too has to be managed effectively. To this end firms need to build their strategy around a risk assessment framework. This typically includes some combinations of assessing risk in the context of strategy, the implementation of e-business risk management, the policies and procedures of managing risk and the risks associated with the applications and technology infrastructure.

Questions and tasks

What is knowledge management? How can technology enhance the ability of firms to share knowledge?

1. Identify and discuss the critical success factors for implementing a CRM system.

2. How has the development of ICT changed the skills required by managers of e-businesses?

3. Choose an organisation that is engaged in e-business and undertake a risk assessment analysis using the key elements of a risk assessment framework.

References

Chaffey, E. (2004). *E-business and E-Commerce Management* (2nd edition). Pearson Educational Publishers.

Clarke, R. (1994). The Path of Development of Strategic Information Systems Theory. http://dossantos.cbpa.louisville.edu/courses/imba/strategy/

Collechia, A. and Papaconstantinou, G. (1996). *The Evolution of Skills in OECD Countries and the Role of Technology*. STI Working Paper 1996/8, OECD, Paris. http://www.oecd.org/dsti/sti/prod/wp_8.htm

Cope, O. and Waddell, D. (2001). An audit of leadership styles in e-commerce. *Managerial Auditing Journal*, Vol. 16, Issue 9, pp. 523–9.

Davis, C. H., Hajnal, C., DeMattereis, D. and Henderson, M. (1998). *Management Skill Requirements for Electronic Commerce*. Report prepared for Industry Canada.

Gint, K. (2005). Leading from the front. *The Sunday Times: Smarter Business*, 6 February, p. 7.

Hansen, W. (1998). *The Transition of the Skill Base of the Workforce in Three Service Sectors. A Decade of Change, 1986–96*. MERIT: Maastricht.

Lummus, R. and Vokurka, R. J. (1999). Managing the demand chain through managing the information flow: capturing the 'Moments of Information'. *Production and Inventory Management Journal*, **40**(1), First Quarter, pp. 16–20.

Lundvall, B. and Johnson, B. (1994). *The Social Dimension of the Learning Economy*. Alborg University: Denmark.

O'Brien, J. A. (2002). *Management Information Systems: Managing Information Technology in the E-Business Enterprise* (5th edition). McGraw-Hill: New York, NY.

Plant, R. (2001). *E-commerce: formulation of strategy*. Prentice-Hall: Upper Saddle River, NJ.

Silvestri, G. (1997). *The 10 Occupations With The Fastest Employment Growth, 1996–2006*. US Bureau of Labor Statistics. http://stats.bls.gov/news.release/ecopro.table6.htm

Warkentin, M., Bapna, R. and Sugumaran, V. (2000). The role of mass customization in enhancing supply chain relationships in B2C e-commerce markets. *Journal of Electronic Commerce Research*, Vol. 1, No. 2, pp. 45–52.

Further reading

Birkin, S. J. and Harris, M. L. (2003). E-Business and CRM: Directions for the Future. From *Proceedings of the International Association for the Development of Information Systems (IADIS) Conference*, Lisbon, Portugal, 3–6 June, pp. 121–8.

Boddy, D., Boonstra, A. and Kennedy, G. (2001). *Managing the Information Revolution*. Financial Times/Prentice-Hall: Harlow.

Dutta, S. and Segev, A. (1999). Business Transformation on the Internet. *European Management Journal*, Vol. 17, No. 3, pp. 23–34.

Huang, K., Lee, Y. W. and Wang, R. Y. (1999). *Quality Information and Knowledge*. Prentice-Hall: Upper Saddle River, NJ.

Rayport, J. E. and Sviokla, J. J. (1994). Managing in the Marketspace. *Harvard Business Review*, November/December, pp. 141–50.

Tapscott, D. (1996). *Creating Value in the Network Economy*. Harvard Business School Press: Boston, MA.

Tiwana, A. (2001). *The Essential Guide to Knowledge Management*. Prentice-Hall: Upper Saddle River, NJ.

Venkatraman, N. (1994) IT-enabled Business Transformation: From Automation to Business Scope Redefinition. *Sloan Management Review*, (Winter), pp. 73–86.

E-business strategy: formulation

- Strategic management and objective setting;
- The strategic process;
- Internal analysis;
- External analysis;
- Competitive strategies for e-business.

Introduction

Chapter 8 is the first of three chapters that focus on the strategic elements of undertaking e-business. The chapter begins by defining what strategic management is and highlights the key elements of objective setting for organisations in an e-business environment. This is followed by an explanation of the strategic process that firms can follow as a framework for choosing and implementing strategies to achieve stated aims. The chapter then offers an overview of the internal analysis as part of the strategic process. There are many factors that form a typical internal analysis and the most important ones are highlighted and discussed. However, emphasis is placed on value chain analysis to determine what activities undertaken by an e-business can lead to added value and, ultimately, competitive advantage.

There then follows discussion of the external environment as part of the strategic process. This section uses Porter's (1985) five forces model to identify the key factors that determine the e-business competitive environment. The chapter concludes with analysis of competitive strategies in the context of e-business. This chapter is the precursor to analysing the implementation of strategy in Chapter 9 and the strategy evaluation in Chapter 10.

Strategic management and objective setting

Strategic management is about determining the purpose and aims of an organisation, choosing the most appropriate courses of action towards achieving those aims, and fulfilling the aims over a set period of time. Chandler (1962) describes strategy as 'the determination of the basic long-term goals and objectives of an enterprise, and the adoption of courses of action and the allocation of resources necessary to carry out those goals'. The first part of Chandler's definition relates to objectives setting. This includes:

The mission statement: communicates the overriding purpose of the organisation.

The vision: managers have to be able to communicate a vision of what the organisation is all about and where it wants to be in the future; it describes the aspirations of the organisation.

Objectives: communicates the specific outcomes that need to be achieved such as sales, turnover, market share, rates of growth, etc.

In an e-business context the vision of organisations will be determined by how managers view the future of the industry. A wide range of issues will be analysed in order to form judgements on how the e-business environment will evolve into the future. Some examples may include:

   ▪ The market domination of a few globally recognised brands in providing products and services online;
   ▪ The rate of growth in demand for online products and services;
   ▪ The emergence of a dominant marketplace for e-business and e-commerce;
   ▪ The impact of increasing regulation in the online industry;

- The changes in the technological environment;
- New opportunities and threats in the e-business environment.

The vision of an e-business organisation must reflect the ability of managers to position the organisation to exploit opportunities in the marketplace, in technology utilisation and through building relationships with partners and customers. The vision should also stem from the organisation's ability to influence the structure of the industry, either through building market share, embracing change and being innovative, or by seeking industry leadership in technology, management skills, marketing or any other key element-driving industry structure.

Objective setting can be built around both closed and open statements. Closed statements are objectives that are capable of being measured and achieved. Open statements are objectives that are not easily quantified or measured. For example, for an e-business to state that one of its objectives is to become the technological leader in its industry sector is not an unreasonable aspiration. However, actually quantifying and measuring technological leadership is problematic. There is no obvious criterion for measuring technological leadership. It may be possible to make inferences based on such things as investment in new technology and the corresponding financial performance of the organisation, or the number of new customers attracted to a website after introducing new software for improving design and navigation, but there is no direct measure of technological leadership. Nevertheless, technological leadership is a valid objective for organisations engaged in e-business.

Objectives based on closed statements are the most commonly used by organisations. Having measurable targets for revenue, market share, number of new products developed, or increase in customers, makes them prescribed and the results are transparent. There is a clear link between the objective set and the performance indicator. Examples of objectives and performance indicators for an e-business are outlined in Figure 8.1.

The strategic process

Strategy can be viewed as a series of decisions and actions that are taken to achieve stated aims and objectives. These decisions and

Objectives	Performance indicator
Increase revenue from new marketing campaign	Conversion rate increase by 1% by end of 12-month period
Retain existing customers	Retain 95% of existing customer accounts
Reduce cost of procurement	Reduce procurement costs by 12% over next 12-month period using existing ICTcapability
Improve delivery times	Meet 99% of delivery time targets over next 12-month period
Improve customer satisfaction	Improve customer satisfaction ratings by 12% through market research and customer feedback
Improve efficiency in supply chain	Form partnerships and alliances with two key supply chain firms
Increase market share	Expand into growing markets and create new innovative services that add value to customers. Make an acquisition of a rival firm

Figure 8.1
Objectives and performance indicators in e-business

actions are based on analysis of key elements of the strategic process. The strategic process is illustrated in Figure 8.2.

The analytical part of the strategic process comprises internal (strengths and weaknesses) and external analysis (opportunities and threats). These are discussed in more detail later in this chapter. Combined, the internal and external analysis forms the basis for a SWOT analysis (strengths, weaknesses, opportunities and threats). It is from the SWOT analysis that the key strategic issues should be identified. The key strategic issues are the ones deemed most important that require attention and are given a high priority rating.

Once the strategic issues have been identified the next stage involves the evaluation of the options available and the selection of strategy. The understanding gained from the strategic analysis helps managers to narrow down the range of options available to the organisation. Each option will be examined in relation to the identified key strategic issues. Evaluation of each option is undertaken using the criteria of:

■ Suitability: the option is only suitable if it enables the organisation to achieve its objectives;
■ Feasibility: the option has to be possible within the skills, competences and resources available to the organisation;
■ Acceptability: the option must be acceptable to shareholders. The level of power and influence held by different stakeholder groups (directors, shareholders, managers,

customers, etc.) and their willingness to exercise that influence and power will determine the acceptability of options. Mostly, it is executives in private organisations who have the most influence and power and who determine the choice of options;

▪ Scope for gaining a competitive advantage: the option must result in superior performance leading to a competitive advantage over rivals.

The implementation of strategy involves the practical measures taken to action the selected strategic option or options. The implementation of a chosen strategy invariably means communicating the strategic option to other levels of management within the organisation. Strategy is decided at corporate level and communicated to business level managers. The practical implementation of strategy is usually carried out at the business or functional level of

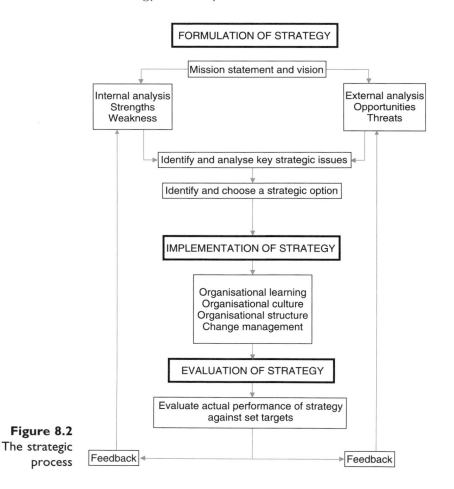

Figure 8.2
The strategic process

management in organisations. There are four critical success factors relating to the implementation of strategy. These are that:

- The strategy is translated into implemented action and guidelines that form the daily activities of staff within the organisation;
- The strategy must be reflected in the way the firm is organised and structured;
- The strategy must be reflected in the culture and values of the organisation;
- The managers must direct and control all actions and outcomes relating to the implementation of strategy.

Finally, evaluation of the performance of the chosen strategy is a monitoring process that stretches from the implementation of strategy back to the analysis. Every organisation exists in a dynamic environment characterised by rapid change. Sometimes change is predictable, mostly it is not. Change affects the internal and external environment and can have consequences for strategy that may require action. It is necessary for firms to review their strategic analysis periodically to ensure that their current strategy still fits the options criteria and can achieve their stated aims and objectives.

Internal analysis

Internal analysis is undertaken to provide managers with a detailed account of the effectiveness of the current strategies. It also reveals how efficient the organisation has been in deploying its resources (physical, financial, and intellectual) in supporting its strategies. Crucially, the internal analysis should provide information that helps managers understand where the strengths and weaknesses are in the organisation. The analysis also sheds light on the organisation's ability to gain a competitive advantage. Other reasons for undertaking an internal analysis include:

- To identify resources, competencies and core competencies to be exploited;
- To evaluate the effectiveness of the organisation of value-adding activities;
- To evaluate the performance of products;
- To evaluate the performance of the functional areas of the business.

Value chain analysis

Value chain analysis focuses on how much value an organisation's activities add to its products or services compared to the costs incurred in utilising resources in the productive process. Every product produced is the result of organising and using resources in a particular way. There may be many different ways of organising activities to produce a product. Value chain analysis helps managers to focus attention on configuring and co-ordinating resources on those activities that produce the product in the most efficient and effective way. Specifically, the value chain analysis determines how much value is added in the process of turning inputs into outputs. The analysis of the value chain also includes activities associated with links to suppliers, partners and customers. A typical value chain analysis is likely to include:

- A breakdown of all the activities that are undertaken by the organisation;
- Identification of the core activities of the organisation and their relationship with the current organisational strategy;
- Evaluation of the effectiveness and efficiency of individual activities;
- Identification of linkages between activities for additional added value;
- Identification of blockages that prevent the organisation achieving competitive advantage.

The main questions managers have to address from conducting a value chain analysis are:

- What activities should the firm perform, and how?
- What is the configuration of the firm's activities that best enables adding value to the product and allows the firm to compete in its industry?

The concept of the value chain described by Porter (1985) was constructed with a manufacturing business in mind. The value of activities were concerned with the physical flow of materials including acquiring the raw materials, manufacturing the products, packaging and distributing the products, marketing the products and, finally, selling the products to customers. Ultimately, value is determined by the amount buyers are willing to pay for what a firm provides them.

That is, value is measured by how much total revenue exceeds the costs involved in producing the product.

The two principal methods of adding value are through:

- Differentiating the product or service so that customers perceive added value in the product compared to similar ones produced by competitors, and are willing to pay a higher price to acquire it;
- Reducing the cost of producing the product or service below that of competitors who produce a similar product.

The drivers of product differentiation are the policy choices made (what activities to undertake and how), linkages (within the value chain or with suppliers, partners or customers), and the timing of activities (in what sequence should the activities be undertaken). Other factors that can drive a strategy of product differentiation include the location of activities, the sharing of activities across different business units, the scale of activities undertaken, and learning within the organisation. Porter and Miller (1985) assert that information technology creates value by supporting the differentiation strategies of organisations.

The virtual value chain

Virtual markets refer to settings in which business transactions are conducted via open networks based on fixed and wireless internet infrastructure (Amit and Zott, 2001). The virtual value chain has a strategic role in gathering, organising, selecting, synthesising, and distributing information (Rayport and Sviokla, 1995). The characteristics of virtual markets are wide ranging and include high connectivity (Dutta and Segev, 1999), a focus on transactions, and emphasis on information goods and networks. Crucially, both electronic and mobile wireless business models that use open standards to support networks can exploit the breakdown of traditional boundaries between firms along the value chain. New forms of connecting buyers and sellers in existing markets creates value and offers increased efficiencies as transaction costs diminish (Dyer, 1997).

Virtual markets are also characterised by high reach and richness of information (Evan and Wurster, 1999). Reach refers to the number of people and products that are reachable quickly and cheaply in virtual markets. This links into the richness of information where the management of that information leads to better-targeted efforts in satisfying demand.

E-business value chain

In e-business, firms conduct their business through electronic means. Information is the raw material that organisations use to add value whether it be as a medium of communication, an asset for sale, or as a support activity in the form of marketing and transactions. The added value that can be gained from engaging in e-business and e-commerce is determined by the extent to which different value chain activities of a firm are interconnected with suppliers, partners and customers, facilitating a simultaneous flow of business information along the supply chain (Bhatt and Emdad, 2001).

In traditional businesses the value chain refers to the physical value chain of the organisation (Porter, 1985). Porter describes how the value chain uncovers the strategically relevant activities through which a firm conducts its business. The model proposed by Porter divides the activities of a value chain into primary and support activities. The primary activities directly add value to the final product and include inbound and outbound logistics, operations, marketing and sales, and service. Support activities indirectly add value to the end product by providing support for the successful execution of the primary activities. Support activities include the firm's infrastructure, human resource management (HRM), technological development and procurement. The value chain model is illustrated in Figure 8.3. The internet has had a transforming effect on each of the activities comprising the value chain.

Primary activities:

Inbound logistics

Inbound logistics are the activities associated with acquiring, storing and disseminating inputs. Value-adding activities typically involve warehousing, material handling, inventory control and returns to suppliers. The internet can add value by providing a control and monitoring facility to maximise the efficiency and speed of the process. For example, internet-based inventory control

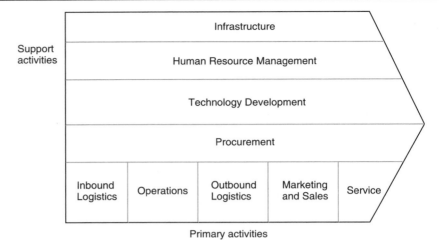

Figure 8.3
The value chain. Adapted with the permission of The Free Press, a division of Simon & Schuster Adult Publishing Group, from *Competitive Advantage: Creating and Sustaining Superior Performance* by Michael E. Porter. Copyright 1985, 1998 by Michael E. Porter. All rights reserved

systems help managers monitor the flow of inputs, maintain stock levels to ensure continuous production and maximise capacity in warehousing.

Operations

Operations are activities associated with transforming inputs into the final product. There are many aspects to the operations element of the value chain, including manufacturing, packaging, assembly, testing for quality, and printing. Many of the manufacturing processes in modern organisations are automated with applications software used for quality control.

Outbound logistics

Outbound logistics are activities associated with collecting, storing and distributing the product to wholesalers, retailers or direct to customers. An extranet facilitates communications between the manufacturer and wholesalers, distributors or retailers. This can improve efficiency by matching demand with supply of products. Retailers, for example, can give manufacturers an up-date on their delivery needs in real-time well in advance of running out of stocks. This adds value to both the manufacturer and the retailer. This emphasises the principle that competitive advantage can be gained not only from internal value-adding activities, but also by overlapping the value chains of other organisations along the supply chain.

Marketing and sales

Marketing and sales are activities associated with promoting and selling the product or service. The internet can play an important role in the marketing process. First, it provides another channel through which organisations can communicate with customers. As firms build their knowledge of customers, so they can target marketing campaigns much more closely to the needs of customers. This improves the efficiency of marketing and lowers the cost. Second, it adds value to customers who receive information on the range of products and services that they have traditionally been interested in buying.

The internet allows firms to use customer relationship management (CRM) systems to store, analyse and disseminate information relevant to the marketing and promotion of their products or services. This has been discussed in Chapter 5 (*E-marketing*) and in Chapter 7 (*The management of e-business*). Third, the internet has also provided the means of introducing more innovative forms of marketing. Permission marketing allows customers to determine what information they are sent regarding products and services. This can be done via fixed or mobile internet.

Service

Service relates to activities associated with providing pre or after-sales service to increase or maintain the value of the product. The internet provides an effective means of communication between organisations and customers. Customers can feed back their views on a wide range of issues including the quality of the product or service, the efficiency of delivery or the availability of other products. Some e-businesses set up chat rooms for customers to compare, review and judge the quality of products and services.

Support activities:

Procurement

Procurement relates to the purchasing of resources required to turn inputs into outputs. Key to the success of organising procurement are the relationships formed with suppliers. Organisations are likely to have relationships with a wide range of suppliers covering everything from components for assembly to advertising space in the media. E-procurement systems can lead to savings by linking into other sites that identify and compare prices, availability and quality of service provided by different suppliers. It also helps to increase efficiency, control and planning of the purchasing of inputs. The control function is important because it prevents unauthorised spending that can prove wasteful to firms.

E-procurement also reduces administration costs by automating orders and transactions. Efficiency savings can also be gained by limiting the number of suppliers used. Research shows that most firms prefer to transact with just a few well-chosen suppliers. As well as helping to build trust, many organisations believe that chosen suppliers are encouraged to invest in technology infrastructure that enables and supports the buyer–supplier relationship (Bakos and Brynjolfson, 1993). This investment can lead to reduced costs through improving the co-ordination of information exchanges between buyers and suppliers.

Internet-based e-procurement systems can be linked to B2B electronic marketplaces (e-marketplaces). They are open systems that allow firms to reach and transact with suppliers and customers in virtual markets (Dai and Kauffman, 2000). Some e-businesses specialise in e-procurement services for particular industry sectors, others provide procurement information on a wide range of industry sectors. E-marketplaces support a range of mechanisms for e-procurement including e-catalogues and e-auctions allowing firms to achieve their procurement needs by comparing thousands of suppliers and choosing the best one for their purposes (Bakos, 1998). E-marketplaces have been developed in many industries including steel (www.e-Steel.com), chemicals (www.ChemConnect.com) and cars (www.Covisint.com).

However, although there have been some notable successes, the e-marketplace concept has not met expectations. The main reason for the disappointing participation rates of firms using e-marketplaces is the preferred strategy of many firms to build long-term relationships with a few trusted suppliers rather than sift through tenders from many unknown ones. Firms also found it unnecessary to deal with the reintermediated middlemen in the procurement process – the infomediaries that organise and co-ordinate the information on the many thousands of suppliers. Instead firms contacted suppliers directly using the internet. Nevertheless, e-marketplaces retain a powerful presence in e-business and some are flourishing as a vehicle for e-procurement. For example, the e-marketplace for retailers, the World Wide Retail Exchange has some sixty members including Tesco and Marks and Spencer, and claims to have made £1 billion worth of savings for its participants since its formation in 2000.

Technology development

Technology development is the technological support mechanism for developing new products, improving processes and monitoring performance. This involves investing in research and development programmes that improve processes or lead to new products or extending applications of new products. Much will depend on the knowledge-sharing culture within the organisation and the ability of managers to effect positive collaborative relationships that lead to value-adding technology development.

Technological development has been at the forefront of determining the evolving structure of e-business itself. Chapter 2 (*E-business technology*) highlighted just some of the vast array of applications that technology offers in supporting e-business. One of the most prominent technological developments affecting e-business is the emergence of the mobile wireless internet as an additional channel for communicating and transacting business. It is worth discussing how the value chain of this newer medium differs from fixed internet networks.

The mobile wireless internet value chain is more complex than its fixed network predecessor, with more players and more interactivity involved. Figure 8.4 illustrates the mobile wireless internet value chain. As applications increase and content providers flock to take advantage of the higher capabilities of the networks, so the complexity of the mobile wireless value chain increases. The evolution from second to third generation mobile devices adds to this process. When one includes the added standards (WAP and WML) and technologies (PDAs and cell phones) involved, alongside issues of bandwidth, provisioning, billing, voice and data applications, then an appreciation emerges of the complexity of the mobile wireless value chain.

The value chain of a network differs from that of a manufacturing organisation principally through the sequential characteristic of the primary activities. For the network to function efficiently each of the constituent parts of the primary activities has to operate simultaneously.

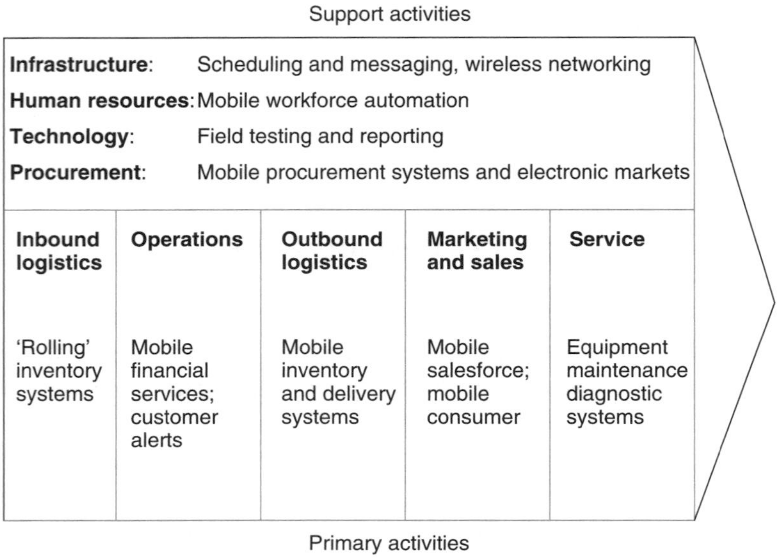

Support activities

Infrastructure:	Scheduling and messaging, wireless networking
Human resources:	Mobile workforce automation
Technology:	Field testing and reporting
Procurement:	Mobile procurement systems and electronic markets

Inbound logistics	Operations	Outbound logistics	Marketing and sales	Service
'Rolling' inventory systems	Mobile financial services; customer alerts	Mobile inventory and delivery systems	Mobile salesforce; mobile consumer	Equipment maintenance diagnostic systems

Primary activities

Figure 8.4
Mobile wireless
internet value chain

Network promotion and contract management involves marketing the network to potential users and providers, administering contracts, customers' accounts and subscriptions, and screening potential members for suitability. Mobile wireless enablement for customers adds value by the efficient use of network promotion centred round content and customer relationship management (CRM). In terms of content, value-adding activities are evident in a host of activities including advertising and branding, product and service information, personal information management, location-based services, and remote monitoring. These can lead to increased revenues, reduced costs, increased customer satisfaction and brand loyalty. Each element benefits from the increased flow of information that the mobile wireless internet provides and creates efficiencies in transactions.

In the B2C arena the mobile wireless internet is providing value-adding services. This is particularly evident in the financial, travel, entertainment, news and media sectors. Content providers offer a range of services including news headlines, travel deals, hotel reservations and financial and market data. These fit neatly into the mobile wireless applications platform and provide customers with information-driven services when and where they want them. For example, banks have been collaborating with mobile phone networks to offer customers a WAP (wireless application protocol) mobile banking service. Customers can access their accounts via branches, the telephone, the internet, interactive television – and now via WAP-enabled phones. Using WAP phones, customers can track their finances, pay bills and access location-based services, such as the nearest automatic telling machine or branch.

Infrastructure

The infrastructure of an organisation refers to the planning, finance, technology and information systems, and general management. While other support activities focus on individual parts of the value chain, infrastructure is distinctive in that it supports all the value chain activities. All primary activities require management, planning and resourcing. As has been noted, each of the activities benefits from the use of information systems to increase efficiency and lower costs. For example, the firm's intranet provides a quick and efficient means of communicating information relevant to the various functions carried out internally. In terms of management, very often it is the leadership qualities of the Chief Executive that set the tone for the organisational culture, values and beliefs. The core values, vision and ambition of Jeff Bezos for his company, Amazon.com, permeates throughout to the organisation's management philosophy.

In e-business there is a need to build an infrastructure that is conducive to blending the skills of people with technology and information systems. Managers need to either recruit key personnel who can develop the information and technology infrastructure in-house, or outsource the task to specialist technologists. The information infrastructure includes building all the databases and information systems required to facilitate communications and processes within the organisation.

Chapter 2 (*E-business technology*) and Chapter 7 (*The management of e-business*) identified and discussed a range of technology and information systems applications that commonly feature in the infrastructure of e-businesses. The technology infrastructure has to be able to support the chosen software applications. The efficiency of the software applications is determined by the way they are integrated and work together to form a communications infrastructure that encompasses both internal and other organisation's systems.

Human resource management

The function of human resource management (HRM) is concerned with attracting and recruiting people with the correct combination of skills, capabilities, values and attitudes that will add value to the organisation and help achieve stated aims and objectives. HRM also involves the continuous development of staff in the form of training, education and appraisal. This helps employees fulfil their potential and maintains motivation levels, especially if development is linked to rewards such as promotion, status or financial rewards. The reward system and the working conditions within the organisation largely determine the ability of firms to retain staff.

The function of HRM has become increasingly important since the development and use of the internet as a means of doing business. More and more it can be seen that competitive advantage is gained through the creation and sharing of knowledge. The recruitment of large numbers of knowledge workers has been the key to increasing performance for many organisations in the last decade. This has presented some stiff challenges for HRM departments as they seek to attract and retain the best staff. Of relevance here is the observation made by Champey and Hammer (1993) that 'an important technology first creates a problem, and then solves it'. To this end the internet can help in the process of recruitment of workers who add value to organisations.

The cost of recruiting staff can be high for many organisations, especially ones who traditionally have large numbers of employees such as the National Health Service (NHS) in the UK or the civil service. One method of ensuring that the best people are recruited is through psychometric testing of candidates. The cost of under-taking such testing for large numbers of candidates can be prohibitive. However, the internet can help by facilitating online psychometric testing. This has been rolled out in the NHS with some 4500 potential recruits undertaking the test in a two-month period between November and December 2004. The results of the tests increase efficiency and lower costs of recruitment for organisations. It helps firms to quickly identify suitable candidates, focus resources on a smaller number of potential recruits and speeds up the process of recruitment.

Lloyds TSB receive around 3800 applications for 102 graduate positions annually. Before online testing was introduced the firm had to use 500 staff members to conduct some 1300 interviews. There was also a significant cost of bringing potential recruits to the interview location. Now candidates can complete a twenty-minute online test on numerical reasoning from the comfort of their own home. The online testing is also fairer for candidates since they are all subjected to the same questions and the results are turned around much quicker.

External analysis

An external analysis is undertaken to provide a clearer understanding of the competitive environment that firms face within their industry sector. The competitive environment comprises many factors that will influence a firm's choice of strategy. The main factors concern existing or potential competitors, suppliers and customers. One way of analysing the competitive environment is by using Porter's (1985) five forces model of industry competition. The model comprises five key elements that form the basis for describing the competitive environment. These are:

- The threat of new entrants into the industry;
- The bargaining power of buyers;
- The bargaining power of suppliers;
- The threat of substitute products or services;
- The intensity of rivalry among competing firms in the industry.

The five forces model is illustrated in Figure 8.5. Each of the forces that comprise the model has an effect on a firm's ability to compete in the market. Combined, the five forces determine the potential for achieving profit within an industry sector. Consequently, it helps managers decide whether or not to stay in a particular industry. It is also the basis around which decisions on resource allocation can be made. The five forces model is also important in helping

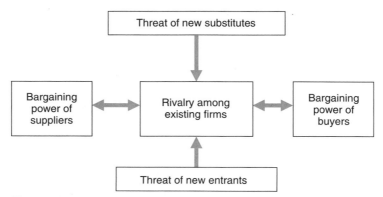

Figure 8.5
Five forces model. Adapted with permission of The Free Press, a division of Simon & Schuster Adult Publishing Group, from *Competitive Strategy: Techniques for Analyzing Industries and Competitors* by Michael E. Porter. Copyright 1980, 1998 by The Free Press. All rights reserved

firms achieve a competitive advantage by focusing analysis on areas where the firm can improve its competitive position.

The development and use of the internet for business purposes has presented a number of strategic challenges to managers as they contend with a rapidly changing competitive environment. This can be seen in the speed of change in technology, the shifting patterns of demand, alterations to the relationship arrangements with suppliers, partners and customers, and the global effects of increasing connectivity. To gain a competitive advantage in such a dynamic environment requires managers to develop strategies to exploit the opportunities that new information technology can facilitate. Firstly, however, managers need to understand the competitive environment. Using the five forces model in the context of e-business can shed light on the competitive environment in the new economy.

Threat of new entrants into the industry

The threat of new entrants into an industry refers to the possible reduction in profitability for existing firms as a result of increased competition by new rivals. The existence and effectiveness of entry barriers as a deterrent and the competitive response of incumbent firms will determine how successful potential new rivals are in entering the industry. There are five main entry barriers: capital requirements; economies of scale; product differentiation; switching costs; and access to distribution channels. These can be used to analyse entry conditions in the e-business competitive environment.

Capital requirements

One of the characteristics of e-business is the low cost of entry to the industry. It costs relatively little for firms to set up a web page and introduce applications systems that facilitate communications and transactions with suppliers, partners and customers. The sunk costs of investing in a web presence are significantly lower than those associated with setting up traditional bricks-and-mortar firms because there is no need for high expenditure on buildings, large numbers of staff, printing and administrative costs or shop fittings.

The low cost of entry has resulted in many thousands of businesses setting up in cyberspace and using the internet to gain a market share by promoting and selling their products online. Although the crash of 2000 saw many so-called dot.coms fail and exit the market, the growth in the number of firms using the internet for business purposes has been growing year on year ever since. Incumbent firms need to create barriers to entry through means other than start-up costs.

Economies of scale

Firms in e-business can create a barrier to entry through economies of scale. This is where the costs of production are spread over the number of units produced. The greater the volume of units produced the lower the average costs of production. New entrants would have to match the scale of production of incumbents in order to compete effectively. This can be difficult if incumbent firms have been able to build customer loyalty and create switching costs. These ensure their products are likely to remain in high demand by a critical mass of loyal customers who provide repeat business.

In e-business sectors where economies of scale is the criterion for gaining competitive advantage then the threat of entry will be low. This can be seen in the online provision of financial information and information on stocks and shares movements. Firms who gain exclusivity of access to such information can package and sell it at high volume and low cost to many different markets around the globe. The cost of disseminating the information is low and the negligible marginal cost of production gives scope for considerable economies of scale that potential entrants would find almost impossible to match.

Product differentiation

Established firms can create a barrier to entry by differentiating their products or services. This may entail building a strong brand name and image, creating added-value designs and applications of products, or providing the customer with superior service such as access to customised or personalised products. A new entrant would have to overcome the customer loyalty that incumbent firms will have built through exploiting product differentiation. The first or early movers in e-business will have had an opportunity to exploit their market share by building a strong brand name and creating ubiquitous web presence that acts as a marketing and promotional tool for their products or services. Established firms are more likely to have been at the forefront of developing applications and software that underpins their e-business venture. This can also be a differentiating feature as it facilitates a wider range of services available to customers, thereby further increasing brand loyalty.

Switching costs

Customers incur a cost when switching from one product to another. This cost can be financial if there is a contract broken, but more likely the cost will be reflected in the time, energy and administration of switching allegiance. E-businesses can exploit switching costs to bolster brand loyalty. For example, customers may have to undertake a process of entering details and passwords to gain initial access to a website. Customers will be reluctant to undertake the whole process again to switch to a rival unless there are significant benefits to be gained from doing so. Switching costs act to 'lock-in' customers to a website. New entrants would have to offer the established firms' customers sufficient incentives to persuade them to switch. This is likely to prove costly, at least in the short term, while they try to establish a critical mass of customers. Where switching costs are high the threat of entry will be low.

Access to distribution channels

Fulfilment is the ultimate obligation of organisations that offer products or services for sale. Delivering the product or service to customers requires effective logistics management and access to distribution channels. Unless organisations are selling information-based products or services, such as financial information, music downloads or providing gambling opportunities, then firms will have to ensure that the physical product is physically delivered to the customer. This is where the new economy meets the old economy. Customers can easily access a huge array of products and services online and undertake the transaction process in quick-time. However, access to the internet has ratcheted up expectations on delivery times. Customers' expectations place onerous demands on firms engaged in e-business and e-commerce. Consequently, organisations have been competing vigorously for access to distribution channels that can help them match or exceed customer expectations.

Access to distribution channels can provide a formidable barrier to entry. Successful firms in e-business have been able to establish relationships and form partnerships with distributors to ensure that their products reach customers within the timescale promised. This is vital to maintain customer loyalty, ensure repeat business and achieve performance targets. The world's most prominent delivery service organisations, such as Fedex, UPS and DHL, are heavily involved in the supply chain of e-business and e-commerce and have formed formal partnerships with a large number of firms selling products online.

The issue of access to distribution channels is less relevant to firms who sell information-based products or services. These firms can directly send their products or services to the customers via the internet. This has huge cost advantages because there are no distribution costs, the costs of sending the material are low, and customers gain almost instant delivery. All firms can easily distribute information-based products to customers. With no entry barriers in distribution, firms seeking competitive advantage may have to rely on exclusive rights to information, or on differentiating the information in such a way that consumers perceive added value, or on selling the product or service at least cost.

The bargaining power of buyers

The profitability of an industry can be eroded when buyers exert power over suppliers. This usually takes the form of forcing firms to lower prices or adding costs by insisting on better quality. The bargaining power of buyers depends on certain conditions. Key issues to consider are:

- How concentrated the buyers are or if they buy in large volume;
- If the products bought are undifferentiated buyers will seek to ensure suppliers compete on price;
- The existence of switching costs 'locks-in' the buyer and reduces their bargaining position;
- If buying firms have low profits they will seek to lower the cost of buying;
- If firms who are buyers become integrated backwards along the supply chain then they can improve their bargaining position;
- If the products sought make no difference to the buying firm's products or services.

Large-volume buyers can wield significant power in the market. The internet provides a communications channel for buyers to coalesce and exert their combined economic influence on suppliers in order to secure better deals. As noted in Chapter 3 (*E-business markets and models*), some firms have become specialists in organising and co-ordinating buyer groups to gain economic benefits from aggregating their market power. However, buyer aggregator business models have not proved to be successful among consumers. Even so, individual consumers have greater market knowledge because of the internet and they can use this to their advantage. Price comparison sites and the huge array of product information available means they can enter into negotiations with suppliers in a better position than previously existed in traditional markets.

The bargaining power of suppliers

The power of suppliers depends on the nature of competition in any industry. The internet has both positive and negative effects on supplier power. On the positive side, the internet provides suppliers with access to a larger number of customers, both B2C and B2B. However, two main factors limit supplier power. First, the ease of entry into the e-business industry increases competition and, second, the empowerment of customers who have access to market information, such as price comparisons, makes customer retention more difficult.

Suppliers can try to increase their bargaining power by differentiating their service through specialist procurement systems or by using technology to improve their products or services. For example, Amazon.com has developed its applications software, such as the One-Click purchasing technology, to deal with the logistics of bringing products and services to customers quickly and efficiently. The company is in the logistics business and it has built its competitive advantage by being a first-mover in developing a logistics infrastructure capable of gathering, organising, co-ordinating and disseminating information to and from customers, other suppliers and partners. However, it is difficult for most suppliers to achieve competitive advantage through differentiating the service because of the inevitable imitation of the business model, or widespread diffusion of the technology used to create the advantage across the industry. These tend to erode any advantage gained by any one firm.

Some suppliers may be able to improve their bargaining power at the expense of other suppliers. If customers use the internet to deal directly with manufacturers this has the effect of disintermediating some suppliers from the supply chain. The manufacturer as a supplier of products direct to customers can achieve cost savings by dispensing with intermediaries and negotiating more favourable deals with customers based on their increased power in the supply chain. However, customers too will seek benefits from dealing directly with manufacturers and so a balance needs to be struck between the two parties to ensure mutual benefits persist. The increase in bargaining power of suppliers in this instance would only continue so long as customers perceive an added value of dealing directly with manufacturers.

The threat of substitute products or services

The threat of substitute products or services is high because of the ease of entry into the e-business industry. The internet provides an additional channel of communication and transaction between suppliers and customers and the ease of entry ensures that there are many competitors selling similar types of products. This is advantageous for consumers because they can easily compare the price, quality and availability of competing products or services. They have a wider choice and their buying decisions will be based on what products meet or exceed their expectations. Brand loyalty will persist until a substitute product or service becomes available that outperforms the existing one to which customers are loyal. Suppliers can create switching costs to deter customers from switching allegiance to substitute products or services.

The intensity of rivalry among competing firms in the industry

One of the key characteristics of the internet has been the intense level of competition brought about by ease of entry, access to large numbers of potential customers, cost savings in functional activities, and the scope for adding value to customers and gaining a competitive advantage. Key to gaining a competitive advantage is the ability of firms to offer customers a distinctive or unique product or service that clearly adds value. Few firms have been able to achieve this because imitation of the business model, technology or process, quickly erodes any advantage gained.

Even if firms focus on customer service as a means of differentiation, their performance is likely to be monitored through one of the many websites that rank firms in terms of service provided. There has also been a proliferation of websites dedicated to customers' reviews and recommendations of products and services. Interestingly, these comparison and recommendation websites are most likely operated by suppliers who were originally disintermediated from the process because of the internet. These suppliers have been reintermediated into the supply chain in the form of infomediaries. Infomediaries specialise in searching the internet for key information on firms' products or services that are of interest and value to customers.

Since differentiating products or services is difficult, firms may decide to compete on price. However, the availability of price comparison sites has made the market more transparent for customers and they can simply search for the best offer available. Another characteristic of the internet is its accessibility on a global scale. The broad-based geographical market and the high connectivity rates, has led to a large number of firms undertaking e-business and e-commerce activities. All these factors contribute to the high intensity of rivalry among competing firms in the industry.

Competitive strategies for e-business

Competitive strategies are the courses of action that firms choose to implement in order to achieve stated objectives and gain a competitive advantage. Porter (1980) developed a generic strategies model designed to help firms overcome the constraints evident in the five forces and to achieve better performance than rivals in their industry sector. The generic strategies are cost leadership, differentiation and a focus strategy. Porter recommends that firms choose either differentiation or cost leadership and stay consistent with that choice or be 'stuck in the middle'. However, there are some firms who operate both generic strategies simultaneously. For example, some car manufacturers, such as Honda, reduce costs through effective use of technology for manufacturing, communications, logistics and marketing, but they also differentiate their products to narrowly defined market segments.

This section explains the key elements that comprise the generic strategy model as illustrated in Figure 8.6. The way organisations use generic strategies to gain competitive advantage in the e-business environment is discussed in Chapter 11 (*Gaining and sustaining a competitive advantage*).

Figure 8.6
Generic strategy model. Adapted with permission of The Free Press, a division of Simon & Schuster Adult Publishing Group, from *Competitive Advantage: Creating and Sustaining Superior Performance* by Michael E. Porter. Copyright 1985, 1998 by Michael E. Porter. All rights reserved

Cost leadership

Firms who achieve competitive advantage through overall cost leadership are able to create a lower-cost position compared to their rivals in the industry. To achieve this normally requires firms to reduce costs throughout all activities in their value chain. Firms who adopt this generic strategy use their experience and learning in order to seek cost reductions. This may take a number of different forms including seeking economies of scale in production, minimising marketing and promotional activities, controlling overheads, and imitating rather than developing new products.

Differentiation

A generic strategy based on differentiation requires firms to create differences in their products or services that set them apart from those of their rivals. These product differences need to be perceived by customers as offering added value. Advertising, marketing and promoting brands play a key role in differentiating products and services. This helps to improve the brand image and prestige of the firm. Other methods used for differentiating products and services include creating products based on superior technology; innovation and creativity for unique product features; superior customer service; and superior supply chain management.

Focus

A focus strategy is where firms choose a segment of a market to target sales of their product or service rather than aiming at numerous markets or the whole market. Firms may focus on a particular group of customers based on distinct profiles and target their products or services at that market. Once the market segment has been identified firms will then operate either a cost leadership or differentiation strategy within that segment.

There are some key benefits that can accrue to firms adopting a focus strategy. First, it is less costly than targeting many markets or a whole market. Second, firms can build specific knowledge and market expertise based on the particular characteristics of a market segment. The firm can use this knowledge to specialise in meeting the needs of customers in the market segment. It also makes entry to a new market less costly and less complex.

Summary

Formulating a coherent strategy is an important first step for any business seeking to achieve stated aims and objectives. Undertaking a formal strategic process helps to put in place a systematic set of policies that provide the basis for implementing a chosen strategy. Once firms have determined their aims and objectives they have to understand their internal and external environment.

One of the key models for understanding the internal environment is the value chain. The e-business value chain differs from traditional value chains found in the physical world. The e-business value chain highlights activities stemming from information flows between firms and their suppliers, customers and partners. E-businesses use the virtual rather than the physical value chain. There are opportunities for e-business to use the information flows in each stage of the virtual value chain to help create a competitive advantage. This involves gathering, organising, selecting, synthesising and distributing information from the primary and support activities that comprise the value chain.

Firms have little control over the factors that determine the external environment, such as the macroeconomy, political decision-making and the evolving demographic changes in society. However, firms can have an influence on the structure of the industry in which they reside. First-movers in an industry can influence the technology used to create products and services, the distribution channels, and the relationships with customers and suppliers. Firms need to understand their competitive environment in order to formulate and implement strategies to achieve their aims and objectives within that environment. Porter's five forces model provides a useful framework for analysing the key factors that determine the competitive environment.

Once firms have undertaken the internal and external environmental analysis they need to choose a suitable strategy that will help to achieve their aims and objectives. Porter's generic strategy model points firms in the direction of differentiation, cost leadership or focus as a basis for achieving competitive advantage. Porter recommends that firms choose either differentiation or cost leadership as their strategy and stick with it. However, some firms operate a hybrid strategy that incorporates both of these elements of generic strategy. Firms also have to decide to focus their differentiation or cost leadership strategy on a narrow market segment or opt for selling to a wider market.

Questions and tasks

1. Choose an e-business and identify the key elements of its mission statement.
2. Highlight the key components of a formal strategic process.
3. Explain the key differences between the virtual value chain and a physical value chain. How can firms exploit the virtual value chain to gain a competitive advantage?
4. Undertake a five forces analysis of the online food retailing industry.
5. Find examples of e-businesses who have adopted a generic strategy based on:
   a) Differentiation;
   b) Cost leadership;
   c) A narrow-based differentiation focus;
   d) A broad-based cost leadership focus.

References

Amit, R. and Zott, C. (2001). Value creation in E-Business. *Strategic Management Journal*, **22**, pp. 493–520.

Bakos, J. Y. (1998). The Emerging Role of Electronic Marketplaces on the Internet. *Communications of the ACM*, **41**(8), August, pp. 35–42.

Bakos, J. Y. and Brynjolfsson, E. (1993). From Vendors to Partners: Information Technology and Incomplete Contracts in Buyer-Supplier Relationships. *Journal of Organizational Computing*, **3**(3), December, pp. 301–28.

Bhatt, G. D. and Emdad, A. F. (2001). An analysis of the virtual value chain in electronic commerce. *Logistics Information Management*, Vol. 14, Issue 1/2, pp. 78–84.

Champey, J. and Hammer, M. (1993). Re-engineering the Corporation: A Manifesto for Business Revolution. Harper Business: New York.

Chandler, A. D. (1962). *Strategy and Structure*. MIT Press: Cambridge.

Dai, Q. and Kauffman, R. J. (2000). Business models for Internet-based e-procurement systems and B2B electronic markets: an exploratory assessment. In *Proceedings of the 34th Hawaii International Conference on Systems Science*, Maui, HI, 3–6 January, Vol. 7, p. 7004.

Dutta, S. and Segev, A. (1999). Business transformation on the Internet. *European Management Journal*, **17**, No. 3, pp. 23–34.

Dyer, J. H. (1997). Effective Interfirm Collaboration: How Firms Minimize Transaction Costs and Maximize Transaction Value. *Strategic Management Journal*, **18**(7), August, pp. 535–56.

Evans, P. and Wurster, T. S. (1999). Getting Real About Virtual Commerce. *Harvard Business Review*, November/December, pp. 84–94.

Porter, M. E. (1980). *Competitive Strategy*. The Free Press: New York, NY.

Porter, M. E. (1985). *Competitive Advantage: Creating and Sustaining Superior Performance*. The Free Press: New York, NY.

Porter, M. E. and Miller, V. E. (1985). How Information Gives You Competitive Advantage. *Harvard Business Review*, **63**(4), July/August, pp. 149–60.

Rayport, J. F. and Sviokla, J. (1995). Exploiting the virtual value chain. *Harvard Business Review*, November/December, pp. 75–85.

Further reading

Cartwright, S. D. and Oliver, R. W. (2000). Untangling the value web. *Journal of Business Strategy*, **21**, Vol. 1, January/February, pp. 22–7.

Deise, M., Nowikow, C., King, P. and Wright, A. (2000). *Executive's Guide to E-Business: from Tactics to Strategy*. John Wiley and Sons: New York, NY.

Dess, G. G. and Lumpkin, G. T. (2003). *Strategic Management: creating competitive advantages*. McGraw-Hill: New York, NY.

Hackbarth, G. and Kettinger, W. (2000). Building an e-business strategy. *Information Systems Management*, Vol. 17, No. 3, Summer, pp. 78–93.

Porter, M. E. (2001). Strategy and the Internet. *Harvard Business Review*, March, pp. 63–78.

Plant, R. (2000). *E-Commerce: Formulation of Strategy*. Prentice-Hall: Upper Saddle River, NJ.

Willcocks, L. and Sauer, C. (2000). *Introduction to Moving to E-Business*. Random House: London.

E-business strategy: implementation

- Strategic controls;
- Organisational learning;
- Organisational culture and e-business;
- Organisational structure and e-business;
- Change management.

Introduction

Chapter 9 focuses on the implementation of an e-business strategy. The first section outlines the type of strategic controls that are required to link the chosen strategy with performance. Two main types of strategic controls discussed are information control and behavioural control. This is followed by discussion of organisational culture. The key issues raised include the determinants of organisational culture, the main influences that organisational culture has on firms, and the attributes that an organisational culture must have if it is to help firms gain and sustain a competitive advantage. The discussion extends to explaining how firms can implement policies to build a knowledge sharing and collaborative organisational culture. The section on organisational culture links into discussion of developing a learning organisation.

This chapter also includes a section on the types of organisational structures that are evident in the e-business environment. The section starts with an overview of traditional structures before highlighting those that have evolved as a result of the development of information technology and the internet, such as network organisations and virtual organisations. The chapter concludes by identifying and discussing the key elements of change management in the e-business environment.

Strategic controls

Once a strategy has been formulated, the next stage is implementation. Strategic implementation is the practical measures taken to execute a strategic choice. However, in order to implement a strategy successfully, firms need to put in place effective strategic controls that link strategy with performance. Traditionally, firms undertook the strategic control function after the strategy had been formulated and implemented. The strategic control constituted the evaluation of performance against pre-determined targets. Contemporary thinking in management emphasises the integrated approach to strategic controls. Figure 9.1 illustrates this approach.

Two key elements form the strategic control process: informational control and behavioural control. Informational control focuses on monitoring the effectiveness of linking what actions have been decided upon with those that are actually carried out. Information control helps managers determine the strategic fit between the firm's objectives and the chosen strategies. Consequently, it is an on-going process of information gathering and analysis to improve organisational learning. Simons (1995) highlights four key characteristics that determine effective information control as part of a strategic control system. These include:

- A focus on constantly changing information that has potential strategic importance;
- The information is important enough to warrant frequent and regular attention of managers at all levels of the organisation;

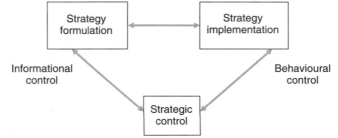

Figure 9.1
An integrated
approach to
strategic controls

- The information generated is best interpreted and discussed by face-to-face meetings of superiors, subordinates and peers;
- The control system is a catalyst for on-going debate about underlying data, assumptions and action plans.

Behavioural control focuses on the extent to which the actions undertaken are correct and meet set performance standards. Traditionally, firms placed an emphasis on rules, regulations and procedures to control behaviour and achieve aims and objectives. However, contemporary management thinking has a focus on culture and reward systems as a basis of achieving these. The catalysts for this have been the rapidly changing business environment and the development of technology that speeds up business processes. There is a need for firms to be more agile, flexible and responsive to change (or proactive in influencing change).

Organisational learning

Implementation of strategy requires firms to effectively leverage organisational learning. Organisational learning occurs through experience, building and sharing knowledge, expertise, ideas and insights. Different types of organisational learning can be identified. Argyris (1992) developed the concept of 'double loop learning' where learning does not simply involve finding solutions to immediate problems but also develops principles that inform and determine future behaviour. Senge (1990) identified 'adaptive learning' and 'generative learning' in leading organisations. 'Adaptive learning' means changing as a result of changes in the business environment. 'Generative learning' means building new competencies or having the ability to create new competencies for leveraging existing competencies in new competitive environments.

Organisational learning is linked to leadership, organisational structure and culture. Effective leadership should entail creating a vision for the firm that incorporates the learning process. Leaders should also set the tone for developing an organisational culture around learning. The key features of a learning culture are curiosity, experimentation, freedom to explore new ideas, creativity, innovation and sharing of knowledge. Organisational learning should also create a cultural environment that embraces change and seeks continual improvement.

Figure 9.2
Three key elements
of organisational
learning

One way of influencing culture is to build an organisational structure that facilitates the key features of a learning culture. This may include organising work schedules and projects around small groups or teams of workers, empowering those workers to take charge of their project and creating an integrated and free-flowing communications system that incorporates internal employees and external suppliers, partners and customers. Figure 9.2 illustrates the three key elements of a learning organisation.

There is value to be derived in a learning organisation by developing an organisational structure that comprises a series of self-directed teams of workers. The individuals that make up the teams are likely to have different backgrounds, skills and experiences that, when combined, add value to the process of achieving objectives. Tasks that were previously the responsibility of managers higher up a traditional hierarchical structure are now incorporated into the work schedules of teams of workers. This empowerment of workers entails giving them the freedom, resources and decision-making authority to organise, co-ordinate and manage their own projects. These tasks may include organising training, work schedules, rewards, safety, and the co-ordination and communication with other teams. Team members are given the scope to carry out these duties and responsibilities, thereby reducing or eliminating the need for middle management.

The co-ordination and collaboration that is a necessary part of a learning organisation is facilitated through an integrated system of electronic communications. Workers benefit from access to a wide range of information on their own project as well as other projects. They have access to information at organisational level and with external suppliers, partners and customers. This helps to identify problems and opportunities quicker, contributes to better and faster decision-making, and generates a greater learning capacity. Integrated information systems enable the gathering and dissemination of a large volume and range of information that can be built into databases covering items such as industry, organisational, financial, customer, demographic and supplier information. The integrated approach is vital in knowledge-based firms where the sharing of ideas, solutions and knowledge forms the basis of creating a competitive advantage.

First- and second-movers

Many of the first-movers in the e-business environment started with a leader who communicated a vision based on learning. When the internet was commercialised for business purposes in the mid 1990s it provided a new channel of communication and transaction. This presented opportunities and challenges for firms. One of the challenges was to learn quickly from the experience of using the internet for e-business and e-commerce and channel this learning into adding value to activities such as technology applications, branding, customer relationships, internal processes and supply chain management. Some firms such as Priceline.com and Amazon.com were successful in leveraging their organisational learning to build a sustained competitive advantage. Others, such as boo.com, failed to transfer their learning into a strategy that sustained a competitive advantage. Some firms adopt a strategy of 'wait and see' and benefit from second-mover advantages. That is, they deliberately delay entry to the industry until incumbent firms have put in place strategies that they can learn from.

Cost advantages of a learning organisation

There are also cost advantages associated with a learning organisation. The learning curve points to the cost advantages that are derived from accumulating knowledge, experience and expertise. Learning occurs at both the individual and organisational levels. Workers' performance is improved through building and using their experience to improve the efficiency and quality of their activities. At the organisational level, learning can improve value chain activities. For example, Tesco.com use their customer relationship management systems to learn about the types of customers that use their online facilities, what they buy, when and in what quantities. The information is the basis of gaining knowledge, knowledge forms the basis

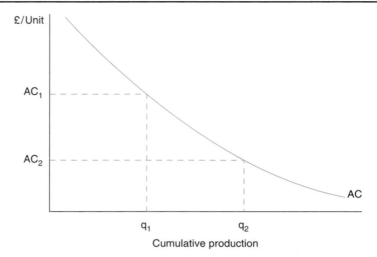

Figure 9.3
Learning curve

of learning and the learning is transformed into improving their marketing campaigns, supply chain management, inventory and delivery services.

Organisational learning can result in lower costs, increased efficiency and better quality service. Figure 9.3 illustrates a learning curve.

The extent of the benefits derived from learning is expressed in the slope of the learning curve. In this example the slope for a given production process is determined by the extent to which average costs decline as cumulative production increases. Using cumulative output better reflects the learning effects rather than successive increases in output. In Figure 9.3 the firm has a cumulative output of q_1 with an average cost of production AC_1. If the firms' cumulative output increases to q_2 with an average cost of AC_2 then the slope of the learning curve is AC_2/AC_1.

Organisational culture and e-business

Organisational culture is the set of beliefs, values, norms of behaviour, and attitudes shared by members of a firm that influences individual employee preferences and behaviour. These bases of culture are very often difficult to observe and measure. Nevertheless, culture plays an important role in determining performance by providing a guide to employee behaviour that is not governed by contractual duties but that, nonetheless, constrains and informs the managers and employees. There are many factors that determine organisational culture. Some of the more prominent ones include:

- The vision of the person or people who established the organisations;
- The historical precedence set by previous generations of managers and workers;
- The type and range of activities a particular firm undertakes;
- The nature of interpersonal relationships within the organisation;
- The management style: autocratic, consensual, participative;
- The control mechanisms: freedom of association and movement, monitoring;
- The reward structure: financial, promotion, status, freedom, peer acceptance;
- The level of technological dependence;
- The geographical location: national and regional characteristics.

Very often it is difficult to pinpoint exactly what determines the organisational culture because of the complexities involved in the combined effects of all the key elements that influence the culture. Nevertheless, it is important for managers to understand and influence culture because it plays an important role in achieving organisational aims and objectives. Organisational culture influences:

- The ability to recruit staff with key skills and experience;
- The motivation and morale of workers;
- The level of output;
- The quality of work and output;
- Industrial relations;
- Attitudes, beliefs and values of managers and workers;
- Innovation, creativity and the sharing of knowledge.

Managers in e-business are concerned as to whether the organisation's culture affects its performance. Linking the two can be problematic since, although culture may be associated with high performance, it may not necessarily cause high performance. A firm may be seen as having a strong culture, combining customer service, employee development and professional standards that contribute to its success. However, if it has strong competitive practices that result in high earnings, then this may have created an environment where a strong culture could develop and persist. In this instance it remains ambiguous as to whether the culture caused the firm's high performance or vice versa.

Barney (1986) describes conditions under which culture can be a source of sustained competitive advantage. He concludes that the culture must:

- Be valuable to the firm;
- Be particular to the firm. If the culture is common to most firms in the market it is unlikely to lead to relative competitive advantage since most rivals will share the same cultural attributes;
- Be inimitable. If a culture is easy to imitate, other firms will begin to emulate it, thereby undermining any competitive advantage gained by the firm that first developed it. The more complex the set of factors that determine culture the more difficult it is for rivals to imitate it. However, complexity also makes it difficult for managers to modify the culture of the firm to significantly improve performance.

One of the key determinants of creating a competitive advantage based on organisational culture in e-businesses is the way in which knowledge is shared among workers. Traditionally, businesses have operated on the basis of rewarding individual performance rather than around principles of collaboration and sharing. A feature of traditional businesses has been a culture where employees recognise knowledge as providing them with a strategic advantage (Katzenbach and Smith, 1994). These knowledge-based advantages are protected rather than shared.

The task facing managers in modern knowledge-based industries is to create an environment where the organisational culture is built around employee recognition that shared knowledge rewards the group as well as the individual. This enhances teamwork, creates a mutually supportive working environment and boosts efficiency.

To create a collaborative and knowledge sharing culture requires a specific organisational design built around core values that underpin sharing, alongside an implementation strategy based on incentives for participation in achieving organisational goals. Managers can rate performance based on each employee's co-operation and participation in the knowledge sharing working environment. Rewards, whether financial, status orientated or peer acceptance, can be linked to the level of participation observed. Meanwhile, managers need to be constantly emphasising the benefits of knowledge sharing.

There are practical measures that managers can take to shift the culture of a firm towards that which has knowledge sharing at its core. Two key measures are:

- Setting aside specific time slots for learning; practicing knowledge management and knowledge sharing such that employees witness the real benefits that can be gained;
- Commiting to developing and implementing the culture throughout the organisation and not just in some well-chosen, isolated departments. The ultimate goal is for collaboration and the sharing of knowledge to become the dominant culture within the organisation, so that it becomes a naturally occurring process.

Organisational structure and e-business

Successful implementation of strategies requires an appropriate organisational structure to determine how activities and tasks are divided, supervised and co-ordinated (Boddy, 2002). An organisational structure acts as a controlling mechanism by formally detailing lines of authority, span of control, responsibilities and duties, the allocation of tasks and the different levels of management within the organisation. Traditionally, large complex organisations were characterised by tall, hierarchical structures with an emphasis on rules, regulations, procedures and clearly defined levels of authority. Figure 9.4 outlines traditional types of structure.

Teamwork

Traditional structures have largely been superseded by a trend towards adopting flatter structures where more people are involved in the decision-making process and communications are more fluid. Modern organisations are typically characterised by multi-skilled staff, teamwork, geographical dispersion of functions, and fewer layers of management. The organisational structure has to reflect these changes and facilitate the co-ordination of activities within the new working environment.

One of the key trends in recent years has been for organisations to increase employee involvement through the creation of teams.

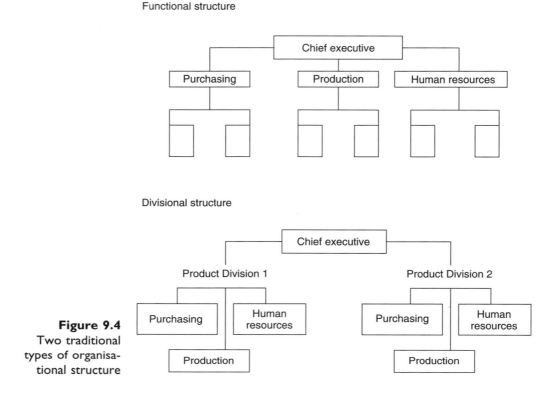

Figure 9.4
Two traditional types of organisational structure

Since the development of the internet in the mid 1990s employees have gained greater autonomy in managing their own work. Some have evolved into problem-solving teams where employees from the same department meet regularly to discuss and solve problems and seek to improve the quality and efficiency of their activities. Problem-solving teams can further evolve into self-directed teams. This consists of a group of employees (usually between 5–20) who are multi-skilled and who rotate jobs to produce an entire product or service. The team itself directs, controls and co-ordinates all the activities required to produce the intended output. They also monitor performance, manage behavioural aspects and determine the reward system.

Virtual teams

Information technology has opened up opportunities to expand the concept of teamwork to that of virtual teams. A virtual team uses information technology and telecommunications to facilitate collaboration between geographically dispersed members who work on the same project. Virtual teams are usually made up of employees from the same organisation but can consist of other workers from partner organisations such as consultancies or suppliers. Virtual team members access a wide range of communications technologies including e-mail, video-conferencing, internet, intranets, extranets, mobile wireless technologies and collaboration software for generating cross-functional information.

Virtual teams can be brought together either permanently or for a specific project then disbanded. One of the key characteristics of virtual teams is the flexibility it offers. For example, the leadership of the virtual team can change according to the mix of managerial and technical skills required at different stages of the productive process. Team members may join for a period of time to undertake specific tasks and then leave the virtual team when their contribution to achieving aims is completed. A virtual team is a dynamic arrangement designed to maximise efficiency in the use of resources. The critical success factors in virtual teams include the:

- Ability to quickly assemble the correct mix of skills for each stage of the project;
- Building of trust between all members;
- Creation of a knowledge sharing culture;
- Ability to apply technology to optimise communications.

Global teams

Virtual teams can be comprised of workers from around the globe. A global team brings together people from many different countries and cultures and their activities span many different countries. Virtual global teams comprise members from many different countries who remain geographically dispersed and who communicate electronically. The biggest challenge for managers who organise virtual global teams is to co-ordinate activities around significant time, language and cultural differences. Different countries may use different technological standards and there are likely to be considerable differences in work-based culture regarding authority, decision-making, timeliness and etiquette. The critical success factors for virtual global teams include the:

- Recruitment of skilled and culturally sensitive staff;
- Communication of organisational objectives;

- Communication of roles and responsibilities to each team member;
- Provision of training and education;
- Implementation of a robust and reliable integrated communications system.

The boundaryless organisation

The development of information technology (IT) in general, and the internet in particular, has played an important role in determining the shape and character of modern organisational structures. IT has a strategic role to play in helping firms increase efficiency and gain a competitive advantage. The organisational structure can be designed around the IT infrastructure. For example, the concept of the network organisation is based on the ability of staff to use technology to communicate with each other, collaborate as part of a team and co-ordinate activities from different locations (Laudon and Laudon, 1998). The internet provides a mechanism for facilitating a global network of communications. This has had the effect of broadening the span of control of managers, allowing them to co-ordinate and control more workers spread over a wider geographical area.

The development of a global network of communications has redefined the boundaries facing organisations when conducting business. Traditional organisations have boundaries that create barriers against their ability to compete. These can be external or internal barriers. An external boundary is the geographical constraint of being physically distant from markets and customers. Internally, firms face barriers created by the hierarchy that characterises their organisational structure. These can be horizontal boundaries created by work specialisation or the formation of departments, or they can be vertical where there is separation between different levels of workers and management.

The boundaryless organisation is one where the structure is not defined by, or limited to, the boundaries imposed by traditional structures. The main advantages that organisations gain from a boundaryless structure are that it:

- Improves the scope for co-operation, co-ordination and collaboration among the functional areas that comprise the organisation;
- Allows greater knowledge sharing across the organisation;

    ■ Allows organisations to respond more quickly to changes in the environment;

    ■ Helps co-ordination and collaboration with partners, suppliers and customers;

    ■ Empowers staff members and encourages a culture of innovation and creativity.

A typical example is that of a network organisation where vertical, horizontal and inter-organisational barriers are broken down to create an organisation that is more flexible and adaptable to rapid changes in the environment. Firms engaged in e-business can benefit from an organisational structure based on the concept of the network organisation.

The network organisation

A network organisation is one that outsources or subcontracts some of its functions to other organisations and co-ordinates their activities from its own central headquarters. Figure 9.5 illustrates the network organisation structure.

The hub firm in the network organisation is where the strategic decisions are made and where the strategic controls are co-ordinated and monitored. The network organisation consists of the hub firm around which numerous subcontracted firms perform functions, such as design, accountancy, distribution, transportation, etc. The specialist organisations are connected to the central headquarters electronically. The IT infrastructure and the internet facilitate the exchange of a vast array of information between the hub firm at central headquarters and the specialists firms.

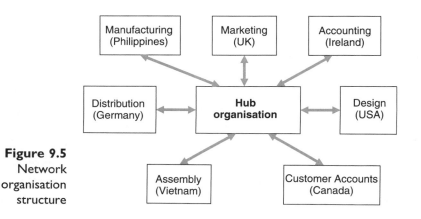

Figure 9.5
Network organisation structure

A robust and efficient IT infrastructure allows the network of participating organisations to operate as if they constitute one seamless organisation. The rationale behind adopting a network structure is that it allows an organisation to commit resources to its core activities and contract out other activities to specialists. There are a number of important advantages that network organisations have. These include:

- No geographical constraints on outsourcing functions;
- Increased competitiveness on a global scale;
- Flexibility in workflows; no permanent staff undertaking non-core activities;
- Flexibility in dealing with changes in market conditions; can outsource work according to need;
- Cost savings in minimal supervisory or administration staff.

Hub firms necessarily relinquish some of their control when they outsource functions to geographically dispersed organisations and this can be a drawback. Where control is deemed important to the hub firm, then this type of arrangement would not be appropriate. The loyalty of employees is likely to be weakened because of the distance from central headquarters and the perception that the hub organisation is a client not an employer.

There may also be economic drawbacks to becoming a network organisation. If one of the subcontractors under-performs or becomes bankrupt, this will have an economic impact on the hub organisation because of lost work and the time and cost of making alternative arrangements. Nevertheless, network organisations have flourished since the development of the internet for business purposes. The network effect has also been extended to create other forms of business arrangements based on collaboration – most notably the virtual organisation.

The virtual organisation

The network organisational structure can be extended to create a virtual organisation. Virtual organisations consist of groupings of units of different organisations that have formed a temporary partnership to achieve the same strategic objectives. A virtual organisation brings people together temporarily to exploit specific opportunities, and then disbands them when the objectives are met (Daft, 2003). Consequently, this type of organisational arrangement is a continually evolving network of independent companies. The members of a virtual organisation achieve more by pooling resources, skills and knowledge than any one individual organisation could achieve operating alone. Collaboration can bring long-term gains for each of the participants.

The development of the internet as a means of conducting business has proved a catalyst for the growth of virtual organisations because it is an ideal medium for communicating and co-ordinating collaborative business activities at a significantly lower cost than traditional bricks-and-mortar firms could achieve. The main characteristics of a virtual organisation include:

- No physical structure;
- Emphasis on knowledge creation and sharing;
- Reliance on electronic communications;
- Geographically dispersed and mobile workforce;
- No organisational boundaries;
- Temporary working relationships.

A virtual organisation typically employs few people since its approach is to hire in the skills it needs from specialist organisations. This saves on overheads and administration costs relating to employing a permanent workforce. Savings can also be made on the costs of providing in-house training for staff. However, the main reason firms join virtual organisations is to be able to compete effectively on a global scale by exploiting opportunities for collaborating with other organisations in complementary activities that achieve mutual benefits (Doz and Hamel, 1998).

The success of virtual organisations depends largely on what each participant can offer to the collective group. Each participant contributes what it does best – its core competencies. Each firm can then mix and match the range of core competencies available to add value and achieve strategic objectives. The advantages of a virtual organisation can be summarised as:

- Offering the scope for firms to access a wide range of skills, experience and knowledge;
- Increasing the flexibility and responsiveness of firms to meet changes in the environment;
- Helping firms grow by allowing them to compete on a global scale;
- Increasing competitiveness by reducing overheads and the cost of employing a large workforce.

There are some disadvantages associated with virtual organisations and the main one centres on the loss of direct control. Collaboration with partners necessarily means relinquishing some control in favour of interdependency. Consequently, there is a need for strong management to maintain a focus on objectives and a high standard of contributions from participants. Managers of virtual teams must also be flexible and adaptable to deal with constant change as groups form and disband quickly. Virtual organisations can easily fail if managers are unable to communicate the objectives to each successive group of participants or fail to motivate them effectively. Since the medium for carrying out these management tasks is electronic, the scope for misunderstanding, confusion or conflict is increased.

Mini Case Study: Sure Start

Business analysts at telecommunications giants BT calculate that it costs the company an average of £435 to run a meeting. This includes travel and accommodation costs and an estimate of the time spent by workers attending meetings at the expense of core activities. Considering the amount of meetings scheduled in an average year the total cost to BT runs into millions of pounds. This is true of the public sector too where many meetings have to be arranged that bring together multiple agencies.

Sure Start is a national initiative that brings together health, social services and education to create neighbourhood nurseries, post-natal care and adult training. The success of the initiative depends on the ability of council staff across multiple departments to collaborate effectively. The logistics of organising meetings consisting of many busy local managers is a formidable challenge. The solution has been to abandon face-to-face meetings and replace them with video-conferencing and instant-messaging technology. The local managers use technology to become a virtual team charged with managing the provision of services to mothers of young children. The format encourages local managers to prepare more thoroughly for the virtual meetings, deal more directly with issues, and action decisions more speedily.

Change management

Change management refers to major alterations to an organisation's processes, structure, technology, staff or culture.

Change management is necessary when firms seek to improve their current performance through changing their infrastructure and internal processes and activities. Usually, change management is necessary when a performance gap emerges. That is, when there is a disparity between existing and desired performance levels. To effect change management it is necessary for managers to understand what forces drive change and what forces restrain change. These form the basis of a force-field analysis.

Force-field analysis

Force-field analysis is a method of looking at change proposed by Kurt Lewin. The analysis is based on the competitive forces that drive change and restrain change. Lewin (1952) suggests a three-step approach to understanding these forces. These are:

- Unfreezing: finding ways of making the need for change so clear that most people will understand it and support it.
- Changing behaviour patterns: bring to bear new attitudes, values and behaviour that become the dominant culture within the organisation.
- Refreezing: introduce supporting mechanisms that consolidate and maintain the new behaviour patterns.

These steps are used to form the basis of the force-field analysis. Figure 9.6 illustrates a force-field analysis.

Each arrow is labelled and the arrow size reflects the strength of the force, either a driving force or a restraining force. The number of arrows reflects the breadth of the force. The length of the arrow

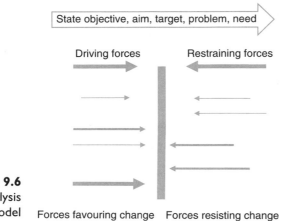

Figure 9.6
Force-field analysis
model

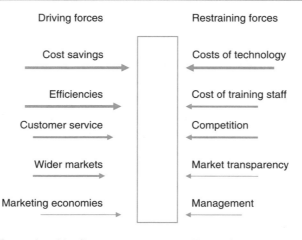

Figure 9.7
Force-field analysis
for an e-business

Forces that drive firms
towards e-business

Forces that restrain firms
from adopting e-business

represents the length of time taken to put into operation a driving force or overcome a restraining force. Managers can use a force-field analysis to complement market information that illustrates the competitive position to employees in an effort to reinforce the need for change. This can be the catalyst for changing behaviours that form the basis for improved performance.

Refreezing can be achieved by creating a culture of continuous change whereby innovation and creativity can flourish. This can be achieved in a number of ways including developing teamwork, emphasising peer group acceptance as part of the reward structure, empowering workers to take responsibility, and authorising workers to make decisions. Eventually the new culture means that workers become proactive in the change management process. Many firms seek to understand the force-field that drives or restrains their efforts to achieve their aims. In e-business there are many such forces evident. Figure 9.7 outlines some typical driving forces and restraining forces that affect firms seeking to engage in e-business.

Key aspects of change

The key factors to be taken into consideration when undertaking change management in e-business include the:

- Scope of change required;
- Timeframe for undertaking each successive stage of change;
- Financing of change;

- Identification of resources required for implementing change;
- The resources to be retained and the procurement of new resources;
- Design of the most appropriate organisational structure;
- Human resource management implications of introducing large-scale change;
- Level of technology required for effective e-business change;
- Level of risk and the likely benefits involved in implementing change management.

There are a number of important aspects of change that firms have to address when undertaking change management. In e-business, technology infrastructure plays a prominent role in determining efficiency and performance. An audit of the performance of technology informs the need for the change. Just as strategy is a process, so the implementation of technology must follow a systematic pathway. For example, there is a series of implementation activities that are undertaken to transform a newly acquired or developed information system into an operational system for end-users. Figure 9.8 illustrates implementation activities for the rollout of an information system.

The implementation process can only begin once a thorough evaluation of appropriate activities has taken place. This ensures that the correct hardware and software has been selected, that the systems have been rigorously tested, that an efficient user documentation system has been developed and that all staff have received suitable training. The implementation process also involves the conversion from a previous system to the new system. Conversion methods smooth the transition from old to new systems and include:

- Parallel conversion: old and new systems run in tandem until the development team and management agree to switch permanently to the new system.
- Phased conversion: only parts of a new system or only a few departments, offices, or business units are converted at a time.
- Pilot conversion: one department or business unit acts as a test site for conversion.
- Plunge conversion: the whole organisation converts to the new system at the same time.

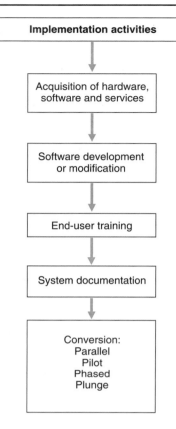

Figure 9.8
Implementation
activities for a new
information system

Other key aspects of change that need to be addressed include the business model adopted for achieving competitive advantage, and the organisational structure and culture that exists within the organisation. Change management is used to alter the culture and behaviour of workers and this can be facilitated by structural change. As noted previously, structural change can influence culture by altering control functions, decision-making processes, lines of authority and span of control.

Scale of change

Managers have to determine the appropriate scale of change that is necessary for firms to undertake in order to achieve their aims. Change can differ in scale and intensity ranging from a paradigm shift to radical change through Business Process Re-engineering (BPR), then to the lower scales of incremental change through Business Process Improvement (BPI) and automation. Each level of change brings with it its own level of risk and reward.

Paradigm shift

A paradigm shift refers to a radical rethinking of the nature of the business and the nature of the organisation. This scale of change usually occurs when the organisation finds it difficult to compete effectively in the industry sector. Its inability to compete will be reflected in poor performance, loss-making and low market share. Firms need to reassess their entire *raison d'être* under circumstances where their current capabilities are inadequate to make returns on investment.

The e-business environment is highly competitive and many firms have failed to achieve their objectives. In the wake of the dot-com crash of 2000 many firms ceased to exist. Others, however, were able to undertake a paradigm shift by reinventing the organisation based on an entirely new business model. In some instances, firms who adopted an e-business aspect to augment existing bricks-and-mortar activities simply reverted to being a traditional business.

Mini Case Study: Levi Strauss

Levi Strauss, one of the world's leading brand name clothing manufacturers, launched its first website in 1994. The company was one of the early movers in supporting their marketing and sales via the internet. However, by late 1999 the company had a paradigm shift in its approach to its e-commerce venture. By 2000 Levi's had largely opted-out of the online method of selling jeans. The main reason for the change was the need to preserve relationships with their retail partners. The internet posed a competitive challenge to retailers by offering customers an additional channel through which to transact.

The website service had cost implications for the company too. Customers did not want to incur shipping costs and they wanted to be able to make returns to traditional bricks-and-mortar stores. Levi's were unable to meet these customer demands because of the extra costs that the company would incur, both in terms of distribution and operations. The website was not advertised effectively due to a company-wide cost-cutting exercise during a downturn in performance in the late 1990s. This resulted in the website failing to attract a critical mass of customers to make the venture viable.

Levi's had to radically rethink their whole online strategy in light of the operational difficulties experienced and the increasing costs incurred of providing an online service. A paradigm shift in thinking resulted in the firm exiting the e-commerce industry and deciding to refocus on their traditional business methods for designing, manufacturing and selling jeans. This, they decided was their true *raison d'être*. However, by 2002 Levi's had again reassessed their strategy. Not wanting to be seen as laggards in the e-commerce environment, the company took the decision to re-enter the online market. This time they received the support of retailers who now sell Levi jeans online via their own websites that are attached to the Levi website.

Business Process Re-engineering

Business Process Re-engineering (BPR) is a relatively new concept developed by Michael Hammer in 1990. Hammer argued that computerising existing processes wasted the opportunity to use modern IT systems as a means of remodelling business processes from scratch. He believed that waste and duplication of effort between departments could be avoided by entirely rethinking processes. Hammer advocated a plunge approach to conversion whereby the changeover to a new system should occur in one radical swoop.

BPR has become an important method of implementing strategies in e-business. BPR involves radical alterations to the design of business processes to improve the firm's costs, product quality, efficiency of production and service to customers. It has an emphasis on linking innovation to improvements in business processes to improve the performance of the firm and helps achieve a competitive advantage. In e-business, BPR has most commonly focused on technology as a means of implementing change management. For example, the types of applications software described in Chapter 7 (*The management of e-business*), including ERP and EAI, are used to re-engineer, automate and integrate functions in the organisation such as production, inventory, distribution and human resources management. This has enabled firms to create new ways of working. However, installing new technology may not, in itself, bring improved performance.

The redesign of organisational structure is an enabler of BPR. This has become an integral part of change management in e-businesses alongside that of introducing new technology. As noted previously, the trend in the e-business industry is for firms to organise projects around teams of workers who are empowered to make decisions affecting their project management. These teams are invariably cross-functional or multidisciplinary groups who can communicate electronically within the organisation (using the intranet) or with external partner organisations (using the extranet). The technology and the structure combine to make the organisation more flexible, responsive to change, innovative and efficient.

Business Process Improvement

Business Process Improvement (BPI) is a less radical approach to change than BPR. It is incremental in scale and involves introducing change to optimise existing processes using information technology. BPI offers an alternative to the more radical scale of change represented by BPR. Small incremental changes are easier to manage and control since they focus attention on identified activities within an organisation. For example, new applications software may be introduced to increase efficiency and service in distribution. This improves a current business process by investing in a particular information technology that is designed for that chosen process.

Over a period of time other business processes can be improved by introducing appropriate information technology. The risks and rewards associated with BPI are less than those associated with BPR. BPI may be an option for firms who lack the resources, either financial or human, to undertake radical change. Alternatively, incremental change may be the most appropriate approach for the organisation – it may be risk averse but need to take measures to improve performance over time.

Automation

As noted previously, automating business processes can bring cost savings and increase efficiency for organisations. Most modern organisations have some element of automation of processes even if this only entails simple answerphone software. The attraction of e-business to many firms is the scope it offers for using technology to improve their operations and to undertake a large number of tasks that previously required human resources.

Although automation can bring distinct benefits to organisations, its implementation requires careful planning and analysis. Automation can improve business processes, but those business processes have to be the right ones. A poor choice of business model or business process means automation serves only to improve the process of doing the wrong thing. This will undermine the organisation's ability to achieve its strategic aims. Organisations need to address the issue of what business processes need to be improved before investing in the information technology that can facilitate the improvement.

Practicalities and tactics for implementing change

There are a number of practical measures that managers of an e-business can take to implement change. There are also a number of tactics that can be used to manage resistance to change. The key to successful change management is to choose the correct practical measures and tactics that ensure the smoothest transition from the status quo to where the organisation wants to be. Practical measures for change include:

Changing personnel

Firms operating in the e-business environment seek to reduce costs of labour by automating many process functions traditionally carried out by humans. Personnel employed in an e-business need to add value otherwise they are a liability. Change management may involve promoting some highly valued staff and/or removing those who do not add value.

Forming partnerships and alliances

One of the key characteristics of the e-business environment is the importance attached to forming partnerships and alliances with other organisations along the supply chain. Change management can be implemented more effectively when influential people in partner organisations lend support. The relationships formed with partner organisations can prove invaluable when seeking to resource change through the skills, expertise and experience they bring to the partnership or alliance.

Changing the technology infrastructure

The way in which an organisation's technology infrastructure is set up plays a significant role in determining work schedules, activities and communications within an organisation. Alterations to the technology infrastructure can force personnel to change their behaviour such that it is in alignment with proposed change at the organisational level. For example, an aim of change management may be to leverage competitive advantage through superior use of analytics in customer relationship management (CRM). Investment in a CRM system, alongside training of existing staff and recruitment of new staff with specific analytical skills, could form the basis for change management towards a more knowledge-based organisation.

Training and education programmes

Training programmes are an important aspect of educating and communicating to staff the rationale, need and benefits of change. Training is also a useful practical measure of ensuring that staff update their skills so that they continue to add value to the organisation. Training is also necessary for staff to cope with the challenges that change presents. Developing the skills of staff through training is also a cost-effective way of maximising returns from investment in human resources. It may be too difficult to attract new skills or too costly to hire new staff so it makes economic sense for firms to concentrate on developing the skills base that already exists within the organisation.

Alongside training programmes designed to enhance skills and knowledge, change management should include a broader-based educational programme for workers. Champey and Hammer (1993) note that a broad-based approach to education is necessary for staff to deal with a wider variety of tasks and challenges. This is particularly relevant to knowledge-based organisations where greater emphasis is placed on self-directed teams. Here, it is not just increasing the technical skills of workers that is important; understanding the role of leadership and the decision-making process have become key elements of change in many modern organisations in the e-business environment.

Alongside practical measures, managers need to adopt specific tactics to implement change. The tactics chosen will depend on the attitude of workers to the proposed change and the level of resistance to the proposed change. There are five main tactics available to managers for dealing with resistance to change. These are:

Education and communication

This tactic is appropriate when the proposed change and its consequences require clarification and explanation. A clearer understanding of the rationale for implementing change is likely to encourage acceptance.

Participation

This tactic involves workers in the design of change. Participation helps workers understand the need for change better and their involvement in the process of change acts as a motivator and encourages acceptance of change.

Negotiation

This tactic is a formal approach to achieving the co-operation of workers. Negotiation uses formal bargaining to gain acceptance for a proposed change. In effect, this tactic 'buys' the acceptance of change by workers because the organisation has offered concessions in exchange for the goodwill of workers. The danger of negotiating acceptance is the potential for setting a precedent whereby workers seek concessions for every proposed change. This is likely to be costly, time-consuming and will erode industrial relations.

Manipulation

This tactic involves covert attempts to influence people regarding change. Managers may seek to target particular individuals or groups of workers to emphasise the benefits that change will have for them. This creates divisions within the workers and undermines collective resistance. This tactic is likely to have long-term negative effects on industrial relations.

Coercion

This tactic involves the use of formal powers to force change. Coercion may include the removal of rewards, sanctions or even job losses if workers refuse to accept change. This tactic points to a failure of management to develop a culture where change is introduced by means other than the threat of sanctions.

Responses to change

Change brings about different emotions in different people but it is important for firms to recognise the general response to change exhibited by workers. Worker responses vary within organisations and between different organisations. However, it is possible to establish a series of responses that help managers choose the appropriate tactic for implementing the change. These include:

- Acceptance;
- Grudging acceptance;
- Passive resistance;
- Active resistance.

Acceptance

Acceptance is the best-case scenario for managers, since workers recognise the need for change and embrace the proposals for seeing it through. In modern businesses where competitive advantage is sought through innovation, creativity and knowledge sharing, the concept of change should be an integral part of the working environment and should inform the dominant culture. Acceptance of change is a pre-requisite for success in e-business and a necessary characteristic of workers in the e-business environment.

Grudging acceptance

Grudging acceptance is an unsatisfactory response from workers in an e-business environment and requires managers to choose an appropriate tactic to remedy the situation. In e-business only a full acceptance of change will achieve success. First of all managers have to understand why full acceptance is not forthcoming. This can be for a number of reasons including:

- Fear of losing something valuable;
- Fear of the unknown;
- Fear of losing status or privilege;
- Belief that change is not good for the organisation;

■ Belief that change requires skills and experience not currently possessed;

■ Fear of being made redundant.

In this situation managers have to clarify what change means for the workers and outline the benefits that change will bring to both themselves and the organisation. A programme of education to explain the rationale for change is an appropriate tactic. Where workers already possess the skills to bring about the proposed changes then a tactic of participation in the process of change is appropriate. The increased involvement of workers encourages acceptance.

Passive resistance

Passive resistance is similar to grudging acceptance from an operational perspective. However, passive resistance suggests a deeper mistrust among workers to the proposed change. Here, managers may have to go beyond education, communication and participation to bring the workforce around to embrace change. It may be necessary to engage in negotiation in order to 'buy' commitment to change. However, the benefits of this are likely to be short-lived since it does not address the real underlying problems. In an e-business context, if workers adopt an attitude of passive resistance to change then it is likely to stem from management failure in recruiting the right people for the challenges presented by the e-business environment.

Active resistance

Active resistance is where workers refuse to accept change and actively seek to undermine it by refusing to carry out tasks, not accepting responsibility and, in extreme cases, by destroying the means of carrying out new tasks. This is clearly an extreme situation and requires managers to completely revamp their human resource strategy in order to create an entirely new organisational culture that is geared towards accepting change.

Summary

The success of an e-business depends crucially on having a viable business model, a coherent strategy and the ability to implement the strategy to achieve stated objectives. Implementation refers to the practical measures that managers can take to translate a chosen strategy into action. Implementation of strategy has to be carried out within a controlled environment. Two types of control mechanisms include informational and behavioural control. The former links the chosen strategy with those actions that are actually carried out. The latter focuses on determining the extent to which actions carried out meet set standards.

Organisational learning forms an important element in the implementation of strategy and is linked to leadership, structure and organisational culture. Leaders should set the tone for organisational learning by communicating the vision of the organisation and emphasising the need for learning as part of the working environment. This should inform the organisational culture such that workers embrace change, continually seek improvement and share knowledge.

The structure of the organisation should enable learning and be conducive to supporting the desired organisational culture. Many modern organisations have flat structures that comprise of self-directed teams of workers who are empowered to make decisions affecting their own project. Integrated information systems facilitate the cross-functional communication within teams, with other teams and with external partners and customers. Information systems have contributed to eliminating geographical and organisational boundaries that previously constrained organisations.

In some instances organisations have to undertake radical change in order to realign their strategy for achieving competitive advantage. Change management is a process of undertaking changes designed to make the organisation more competitive. Before undertaking change, firms need to identify the factors that both drive and restrict change. A force-field analysis is one method of doing this. Organisations then have to decide on the scale of change necessary to achieve strategic aims and then undertake a series of practical measures to ensure that change management is translated into actions. The appropriate management actions to be undertaken will depend on the workers response to the proposed change.

Questions and tasks

1. What measures can managers take to enhance organisational learning?
2. Choose an example of an e-business and, using the factors that determine organisational culture as a guide, determine the dominant culture within the organisation.

3. What are the advantages and disadvantages associated with a network organisation?
4. What practical measures can managers take to implement change management?

References

Argyris, C. (1992). *On Organisational Learning*. Blackwell: London.

Barney, J. B. (1986). Organizational Culture: Can It Be a Source of Competitive Advantage? *Academy of Management Review*, **11**, pp. 656–65.

Boddy, D. (2002). *Management: An Introduction*. Prentice-Hall: Harlow.

Champey, J. and Hammer, M. (1993). *Re-engineering the Corporation: A Manifesto for Business Revolution*. Harper Collins: New York, NY.

Daft, R. L. (2003). *Management* (6th edition). Thomson: Mason, OH.

Doz, Y. and Hamel, G. (1998). *Alliance advantage: The art of creating value through partnering*. Harvard Business School Press: Boston, MA.

Hammer, M. (1990) Re-engineering work – Don't automate, obliterate! *Harvard Business Review*, July/August, pp. 104–12.

Katzenbach, J. R. and Smith, D. (1994). *The wisdom of teams: creating the high performance organization*. Harper Business: New York, NY.

Laudon, K. C. and Laudon, J. P. (1998). *Management Information Systems: New Approaches to Organization and Technology*. Prentice-Hall: Upper Saddle River, NJ.

Lewin, K. (1952). *Field Theory in Social Science*. Tavistock/Routledge and Paul: London.

Senge, P. (1990). Building learning organisations. *Sloan Management Review*, Fall, pp. 7–23.

Simons, R. (1995). Control in an age of empowerment. *Harvard Business Review*, **73**, pp. 80–8.

Further reading

Deal, T. and Kennedy, A. (1982). *Corporate Cultures: The Rites and Rituals of Corporate Life*. Addison-Wesley, Boston, MA.

Peters, T. and Waterman, R. (1982). *In Search of Excellence*. Harper & Row: New York, NY.

Peters, T. (1992). Rethinking scale. *California Management Review*, Vol. 35(1), Fall, pp. 7–29.

Romanelli, E. and Tushman, M. L. (1988). Executive leadership and organisational outcomes: an evolutionary perspective. In *The Executive Effect. Concepts and Methods for Studying Top Managers* (D. C. Hambrick, ed.), pp. 75–106, JAI Press: Greenwich, CT.

Roos, G. and Roos, J. (1997). Measuring your company's intellectual performance. *Long Range Planning*, **30**(3), pp. 413–26.

Schein, E. H. (1983). The role of the founder in creating organisational cultures. *Organisational dynamics*, **12**, Summer, pp. 13–28.

Schein, E. H. (1992). *Organizational Culture and Leadership* (2nd edition). Jossey-Bass: San Francisco, CA.

E-business strategy: evaluation

- The evaluation process;
- Organisational control and evaluation;
- Financial evaluation;
- Technology evaluation;
- Human resources evaluation;
- Website evaluation;
- Business model evaluation;
- E-business strategy evaluation.

Introduction

Chapter 10 focuses on evaluation as part of the strategy process. Although it appears after formulation and implementation, the evaluation of strategy should be continuous throughout the strategy process. Managers must evaluate the performance of all activities that take place within the organisation so that they can identify areas for improvement, make the necessary adjustments and achieve the objectives.

The first part of this chapter gives an overview of the evaluation process. This is followed by an outline of the role that evaluation plays in organisational control. Thereafter the chapter focuses discussion on the key evaluation criteria relevant to firms engaged in e-business. These include evaluating performance relating to finance, technology, human resources, the website and the business model adopted for achieving competitive advantage.

The evaluation process

After implementation, the strategic process includes the evaluation of the performance of the chosen strategy. The actions that are implemented need to be monitored, assessed and evaluated to determine the effectiveness and efficiency of the strategy (Coulter, 2002). The evaluation should reveal whether or not the organisation's strategy is achieving the stated objectives. The most common feature of evaluation is comparing set targets with performance achieved. This is likely to include quantitative measures on sales, profit, turnover and market share. Firms in e-business and e-commerce evaluate the performance of the website in attracting customers and transforming 'hits' into sales (conversion rate). Evaluation is part of a control process within organisations. Figure 10.1 illustrates the key elements of the evaluation and control process.

Once the performance of a strategy has been measured, the evaluation needs to address the reasons for the performance outcome in relation to the set target. This will reveal competitive strengths or weaknesses and help to inform future strategy. Evaluation combines both internal and external factors. The use of the organisation's resources and capabilities will be scrutinised alongside any changes to market and competitive conditions.

The strategy evaluation should reveal whether or not change is necessary. If change is necessary then the evaluation should also point to the extent to which change should be implemented. Change can range from minor alterations to the business model or the way the internal functions are carried out, to radical change management or even a paradigm shift in thinking about what the business is all about. Redesigning strategy is likely to prove risky, expensive and time-consuming since it requires the redeployment of resources

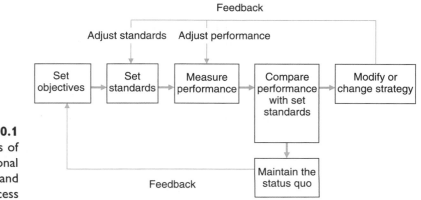

Figure 10.1
Key elements of
the organisational
evaluation and
control process

and capabilities. More often than not, organisations will modify their strategic actions. This forms part of the process of increasing competitiveness for a large number of businesses. Modifications can achieve desired outcomes but with limited risk and disruption to the organisation.

Organisational control and evaluation

Organisational control is a systematic process that allows managers to regulate internal activities and match their performance with set targets. The control function within an organisation is dependent on the information generated on performance standards and performance achieved. Consequently, it is necessary for managers to determine what information is required, how it is to be generated and the appropriate response to the outcomes based on analysis of the information.

There are three main ways of looking at the control process in organisations. Feedforward control refers to controlling human, material and financial resources flowing into the organisation. The focus is on anticipating problems. An example is in e-recruitment where firms use the internet to set tests for a large number of prospective employees. This filters the applicants' skills, qualifications and experience and reduces the number of final interviews to manageable proportions. E-recruitment testing prevents problems associated with the costs of administering and interviewing non-suitable applicants.

Concurrent control is another type of control process. This type attempts to solve problems as they happen. For example, concurrent control may focus on monitoring the activities of employees to ensure that they consistently match set standards. The monitoring of activities of operators in call centres is an example of concurrent control. These two types of control may feature as part of developing and operating a strategy. However, in terms of evaluating strategy, the most commonly used type is feedback control. Figure 10.2 illustrates the three types of organisational control.

Feedback control

Feedback control focuses on an organisation's outputs with an emphasis on the quantity and quality of products and services

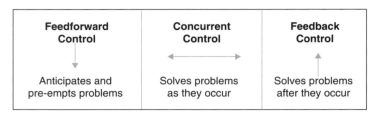

Figure 10.2
Key elements of
organisational
control

produced (Daft, 2003). Also, feedback control is used as a basis for matching actual performance against set targets. In e-business, targets may include financial, customer satisfaction, sales, quality, number of 'hits' on the website, advertising revenue, or number of new customers. The feedback information helps managers make decisions and undertake the appropriate course of action to ensure the organisation achieves its objectives.

Set standards of performance

Organisations have to develop a strategic plan and establish objectives for each of the functional areas. In each of the functional areas a standard of performance will be set, against which actual performance can be measured. The set standards should contribute to the organisation's strategy for achieving its objectives. It is important that the set standards are clearly defined and are achievable. The standard performance may be linked to the reward system in the organisation and should be set high enough to present a challenge to workers but not so onerous as to make it unachievable. In some instances it may be necessary to adjust the set standards to better reflect the resources and capabilities within the organisation.

Measure actual performance

There are activities that take place within organisations that can be measured quantitatively. Managers can monitor the performance of the functional activities by preparing formal reports on the actual outputs achieved over a set timescale. The types of activities measured should relate to those that have an established set standard of performance. However, not all performance criteria can be quantified.

Managers need to gain an understanding of the value of resources and assets that are not easily measured. For example, gaining competitive advantage may stem from the intellectual capital within an organisation. When this is translated into innovation and creativity, which help produce new products and services, the value to the firm is significant. However, it is not easy to determine an actual measure to reflect this input. Managers need to use their skills and experience to recognise and value a host of qualitative information that contributes to achieving established set standards of performance. Both the quantitative and qualitative information are noted and will form the basis for the compilation of formal reports on performance.

Compare performance to set standards

Over time, the formal reports will reveal trends that help managers to identify areas where change or modification is required to realign performance with set standards. The actual performance may meet, or exceed, set standards in which case no change may be necessary. When comparing actual performance with set standards it is important that managers use a combination of quantitative information and their own experience to determine the meaning of any variance. The type of change or modification undertaken will depend on managers' ability to correctly interpret what the information is telling them about how the organisation is performing across different functions.

Assess the need for action

The final step in the feedback control process is to determine whether or not actions to change or modify the strategy are necessary. Where performance dips below set standards it will require change or modification to the strategy. The analysis undertaken of the reasons for, and level of, the under-performance and the identification of the activities that are under-performing will determine the scale of change that is required to remedy the situation.

Sometimes it is the case that the set standard of performance has to be changed rather than the strategy. It may become evident that the standards expected are unrealistic or that the environment has changed thereby making previously set standards redundant. Where standards are met or are exceeded then managers will likely stick to the status quo. Where performance meets or exceeds set standards managers may reward workers for their efforts as a means of recognising their contribution and reinforcing the positive culture within the organisation.

Financial evaluation

One of the first measures that managers look at to evaluate the performance of their e-business are figures contained in the financial reports. This gives an immediate overview of the health of the organisation and tells the managers if their current strategy is paying dividends in the form of increasing returns on investment and profitability. Most e-businesses struggle to make money in the start-up phase and therefore cash flow is an important measure for determining if the business can stay afloat. The finances of any business are part of the control function and it is vital that managers keep monitoring and assessing the financial health of their organisation. The main elements of financial control include:

- Cash flow: the level of short-term working capital or liquidity that the firm has to ensure it can operate on a day-to-day basis.
- Assets: refers to short- and long-term assets.
- Customers accounts: refers to credit control, terms of credit and payment control.
- Suppliers: controlling the risks associated with the supply chain.
- Stock: methods of controlling and monitoring stock levels.

There are two main financial statements that provide the basic financial information for control and evaluation of performance. These are the balance sheet and the income statement.

Balance sheet

The balance sheet is a financial statement that outlines the organisation's financial position by focusing on assets and liabilities at a given point in time. Three types of information comprise the balance sheet. These are:

- Assets: both current assets (those that can be converted into cash quickly) and fixed assets (building, machines, etc.);
- Liabilities: the short- and long-term debt owed by the firm;
- Equity: the difference between assets and liabilities. Gives the company's net worth in terms of stocks and retained income.

Income statement

The income statement is a summary of an organisation's financial performance over a given period of time. This is sometimes referred to as the profit and loss account. The income statement outlines all sources of income coming into the firm over a period of time and subtracts all the expenses and costs to derive the net income (profit or loss) for the period.

Evaluating the financial position of an organisation can be achieved by calculating some simple financial ratios. Some of the most commonly used ratios include:

Liquidity and gearing

The financial resources that firms use to produce outputs are called capital. The main measures of the performance of working capital are liquidity (cash flow) and gearing. The measure for liquidity is called the current ratio.

$$\text{Current ratio} = \frac{\text{Current assets}}{\text{Current liabilities}}$$

Gearing is the level of borrowing (debt) owed by a company measured against its equity.

$$\text{Gearing (debt to equity)} = \frac{\text{Long-term liabilities}}{\text{Total capital}}$$

There are a number of measures of profitability. These are:

$$\text{Gross margin} = \frac{\text{Gross income}}{\text{Sales}}$$

$$\text{Gross profit} = \frac{\text{Cost of sales}}{\text{Sales revenue}}$$

$$\text{Profit margin on sales} = \frac{\text{Net income}}{\text{Sales}}$$

$$\text{Net profit} = \text{Gross profit} - \text{explicit costs}$$

$$\text{Net profit after tax} = \text{Gross profit} - \text{explicit costs and tax}$$

Every time a business invests capital in a business venture the aim should be to achieve a return on that investment that is greater than the initial investment. Return on investment is important because it gives investors confidence to continue to invest in the company in future and it provides finance for the firm to further invest in the business venture. It also increases the goodwill of potential investors and lenders who may provide additional investment funds for the company. The two main ratios that measure return on investment are:

$$\text{Return on capital employed} = \frac{\text{Net profit}}{\text{Capital employed}} \times 100$$

$$\text{Return on shareholder capital} = \frac{\text{Net profit}}{\text{Shareholder capital} + \text{retained profits}}$$

Managers use financial reports to evaluate the performance of the firm and to help them make decisions regarding future strategy. Current financial statements can be compared and contrasted with previous financial statements to determine whether performance has improved, declined or remained static. This will offer an insight into how competitive the organisation is and how effectively it can compete against rivals in the industry.

Technology evaluation

Technology is one of the key drivers of e-business so it is important for organisations to understand their current position regarding the stage of technology adoption and what can be achieved from it. There are various different levels of e-business applications and organisations will adopt those that help achieve their objectives within the constraints of finance and skills (Daniel et al., 2002). Most organisations start with general information on a website then

STAGE 1:   Electronic information search and content creation
Find new suppliers
Find products and services
Advertise the company and/or its products and services
Find new customers
Provide information on products or services

STAGE 2:   Electronic transactions
Purchase products and services online
Sell products and services online
Order products and services from suppliers
Access suppliers database of products and services
Process customer orders
Provide after-sales service to customers

STAGE 3:   Complex electronic transactions
Buy products and services via electronic auctions
Sell products and services via electronic auctions
Buy products and services via electronic call for tenders
Sell products and services via electronic call for tenders
Negotiate contracts with suppliers
Negotiate contracts with customers
Make electronic payments to suppliers
Receive electronic payments from customers
Allow access to company inventories
Gain access to customers' inventories

**STAGE 4:   Electronic collaboration in product design, distribution
and logistics**
Transfer documents to customers
Transfer documents to suppliers
Undertake collaborative online customisation with suppliers
Undertake collaborative online customisation with customers
Electronically manage distribution and logistics

Figure 10.3
Stage model of
e-business adoption

progress to having an internet presence. The next stage is the development of distinct value-adding services for customers followed by the integration of systems for supporting communications and transactions with customers, suppliers and partners. The final, most technologically demanding, stage is the development and use of technology for collaboration with suppliers and partners. Figure 10.3 outlines the activities that each stage of e-business adoption facilitates.

The information technology infrastructure that underpins the activities of an e-business comprises of hardware and software. To achieve stated objectives it is vital that the investment in technology enables organisations to improve internal processes, communicate and transact with customers, collaborate with partner organisations and store data for analytical purposes. The key to a successful IT strategy is for managers to understand exactly what technology is required for helping the organisation achieve its objectives.

Other technological factors will also feature in the evaluation process including connectivity rates among customers, suppliers and partners, access to broadband and compatibility of systems used by organisations and customers in different parts of the globe. The evaluation of technology includes the assessment of the quality and capabilities of technology prior to investment, and an evaluation of the performance of the technology once it has been implemented. The main factors comprising an evaluation process for computer hardware include:

Capability

The capability of computer hardware will determine the scope of use that it is put to. Capability includes speed, capacity and throughput. An e-business has to evaluate what speed and capacity is required for the volume of business and the types of business it expects to handle over a given period of time.

Cost

The cost of acquiring and installing the technology influences the decision about what type of technology is appropriate within the set IT budget. The cost of installation also includes the likely disruption during the changeover from the old to the new system. The cost of putting into operation and maintaining the hardware forms part of the evaluation of its performance. A set standard of performance relative to cost projections will determine the cost-effectiveness of the chosen hardware. This informs future decisions on choice of hardware.

Reliability

The performance of the hardware is constantly monitored and any malfunctions noted. The information relayed to managers will include the number of malfunctions, the type of malfunctions and the time factor relating to resolving the problem. Managers will set a minimum threshold for reliability and take action to replace the hardware should it fall below the threshold. Managers need to be satisfied that the problem lies with the hardware and not with the people who operate it.

Obsolescence

The rate of technological advance in computing hardware could represent a cost to organisations if the suite of current computers becomes obsolete or outdated relative to those used by competitors. When evaluating the performance of the technological infrastructure managers have to account for the longevity of current stock and the rate of obsolescence over given periods of time. This will be closely linked to the types of activities carried out within the organisation and the reliance on technology to carry out those activities. It may well be the case that an organisation develops a strategy for growth that requires additional capability and reliability of hardware. In other instances, current stock may be of sufficient operational capability and capacity to meet the needs of the organisation.

Scalability

As firms experience growth so the demands on technology increase. Vendors of IT systems will normally guarantee scalability to set levels as part of the sales agreement. However, managers still need to evaluate the performance of the technology infrastructure in handling increasing demands from an increasing number of end-users. Scalability and reliability are linked and form important measures of technological performance in organisations that seek to achieve growth and competitive advantage.

Risk

Technology is the cornerstone of e-business and plays a pivotal role in determining how successful organisations will be. The greater the benefits of installing a new technology infrastructure the greater will be the associated risks. For example, the technology may be capable of facilitating an improvement in customer service but the organisation may lack the necessary skills to realise its potential. An e-business may seek competitive advantage by investing and installing the very latest technology infrastructure. However, this increases risks because it may not have been 'live' tested elsewhere. Managers need to weigh the benefits of being first to roll out a more efficient system against the risks of malfunction, installation or usability.

Organisations can reduce risk by installing new technology incrementally. However, this may give rivals time to catch up. The greatest benefits and risks derive from a radical approach to changing technology. Increasingly, organisations are taking advantage of the convergence of technology and the integration of systems to cut costs and improve efficiency. The convergence of technology links voice, data, mobile and video, and Internet Protocol (IP) sets an industry standard for facilitating communications across different media. The investment in new systems to take advantage of convergence and integration would constitute a high risk for many organisations but the risk of losing out may be even higher. Ultimately, organisations have to determine whether the costs of a new system are covered by the extra revenue it generates.

Evaluating software uses similar criteria to evaluating hardware. Capability, cost, reliability and compatibility are as relevant to software evaluation as they are to evaluating hardware. However, there are some specific factors that have to form part of the evaluation process both before and after investment in software. These include:

- Quality: The software has to be free of viruses, have security mechanisms built in to prevent improper use and be free of errors in the program code;
- Efficiency: The software should be a well-developed system of program codes and it should not take up excessive memory, capacity or disc space;
- Flexibility: The software should be able to process all e-business demands placed on it without requiring major modification;
- Connectivity: The software should be Web-enabled for access to internets, intranets and extranets;
- Language: The software must be written in a language that is familiar to IT developers in-house;
- Documentation: The software must be well documented and include items such as help screens, reports, forms and data entry screens. Documents should be easily created and changed since they form an important method of communication among staff responsible for developing, implementing and maintaining the IT infrastructure.

The evaluation of technology, both before and after the investment decision, is an important element in determining an e-business strategy. Since many of the activities that take place in an e-business are reliant on technology, the choice and implementation of specific systems play key roles in determining the success of the organisation. Consequently, evaluation of the performance of technology is a continuous process, as is the testing of new technologies before committing to investment. Before deciding on such an important investment, organisations have to ensure that costs and risks are controlled and that training of staff, or the recruitment of new staff, is in place to ensure immediate usability of the new technology.

Human resources evaluation

One of the most commonly cited reasons managers put forward for adopting e-business are the cost savings that can be derived from reducing the number of people employed. E-business applications can process many jobs that were previously undertaken by humans. Many firms who have engaged in e-business seek to employ fewer, but more specialised, workers. The development of network organisations and virtual organisations means that firms can cast their net much wider to attract and recruit suitably skilled staff. The evaluation of human resources in e-business is undertaken at four different levels. These are:

- The evaluation of human resources policy;
- The evaluation of the recruitment process in attracting and retaining key skills;
- The evaluation of human resource performance against set targets;
- The evaluation of feedback from human resources.

Evaluating human resources policy and planning

Every organisation has to develop and implement a human resources policy. The policy will incorporate the overriding criteria that determine the type of skills and experience the organisation needs to attract, the reward system, the training and staff development process and the system for monitoring, assessing and appraising staff performance. There are wide differences in approach to determining the types of skills and experience required. Much depends on the objectives of the organisation, the products or services produced and the strategy that is put in place to achieve organisational objectives. The type of skills and experience sought by firms in e-business may cover a multitude of specialist activities including:

- Web design: design web structure, graphics and navigation;
- Web developer: initiates web-based projects, programming;
- Webmaster: managing and developing the website using web technology;
- Computer technician: solves computer problems and ensures hardware and software reliability;
- Online marketer: manage online marketing and promotional campaigns;
- Network manager: controls and co-ordinates staff across the network organisation;
- Project manager: develops, controls and manages the delegation of projects to teams of workers;
- Logistics manager: manages the electronic control of inbound and outbound logistics.

In modern e-business working environments the reward system is likely to go well beyond simple financial reward for time spent in the office. Rewards will reflect innovation, creativity and contributions to developing new products and services and ways of improving internal efficiency. This may include promotion, peer acceptance, greater autonomy in work scheduling or greater decision-making powers.

The evaluation of human resources also entails reflecting on how closely matched the actual human resources performance is to the forecasts for human resource needs. Human resource needs form part of human resource planning. In e-business, firms need to address some strategically important issues. These include forecasting the impact that new and emerging technologies will have on the working environment over a given period, the likely volume of business over the period and the likely rate of attrition in the workforce over the period. Forecasts for these are used to determine an organisation's human resources strategy for a given period of time. Key issues to be addressed include:

- How many senior managers will be required;
- How many new workers will be required to operate in key functional areas;

- What type of skills and experience will be required over the period;
- What organisational structure will support the new working environment.

Evaluating the recruitment process

An e-business has to be able to attract and retain skilled staff who possess the correct qualifications and experience to add value to the organisation and help achieve the stated objectives. Organisations have to put into place a recruiting policy that is designed to bring in the right people for least cost. Recruitment refers to all the activities that help to define the characteristics of applicants for specific jobs.

The aim of the recruitment process is to find the right people for the right job. First, the process begins with a job analysis where all relevant information on the tasks, duties and responsibilities is gathered and interpreted. This is followed by the compilation of a job description that summarises the specific tasks, duties and responsibilities. Lastly, the job description details the knowledge, skills, qualifications and experience required to perform the tasks, duties and responsibilities to a satisfactory standard.

Evaluating human resource performance

When organisations recruit staff they expect a return on their investment. All staff should add value to the organisation and be prepared to use their skills, experience and expertise to contribute to the organisation achieving stated objectives. Managers need to set performance targets and evaluate staff performance in the form of appraisals. Performance appraisal is a process of observation, evaluation, recording outcomes and providing feedback to workers. The rigour to which performance appraisal is undertaken varies between different types of organisations, but it is important to put in place a formal appraisal system so that set standards are widely known, employees understand the benchmark performance expected and managers can observe when performance falls below standard and take action.

Information systems have opened up the possibility of constant monitoring of performance in many work tasks. For example, in call centres managers can constantly monitor and assess the response times and quality of information given to clients by operators. E-business is orientated towards information technology to communicate with customers, suppliers and partners.

However, it can also be used to monitor the performance of workers. Time spent online and the content of communications is information that may form the basis for assessment and appraisal by managers. This type of monitoring raises some ethical and industrial relations questions. Some workers resent being constantly monitored. It may be contrary to the successful development of an organisational culture based on innovation, creativity and knowledge sharing. Constant monitoring may also be detrimental to implementing an organisational structure based on the empowerment of workers in self-directed teams.

Evaluating feedback from human resources

As noted previously, one of the key characteristics of modern organisational structures is the development of self-directed teams with authority and power to make decisions relating to their own projects. Part of the responsibility offered to teams is to feedback all relevant information to senior managers to help in the process of making strategic decisions. This requires an effective communications system where workers can easily and efficiently feedback relevant information on a regular basis.

Some organisations will put in place formal systems that determine the time and type of feedback to be delivered to senior managers. This may include feedback on how strategic decisions affect the workers' ability to achieve their objectives. From this, managers can make necessary adjustments or implement change as required. One way of gaining human resources feedback is through the intranet. The intranet is an ideal mechanism for allowing staff from geographically dispersed parts of the organisation to communicate with each other and senior managers. Most organisations have a forum for discussion and feedback as part of their intranet.

There is also specific applications software available that is designed to facilitate feedback. For example, Amazon.com uses the eePulse software to electronically poll workers on a biweekly basis on their opinions and attitudes to specified developments in the company (Welbourne, 2000). The poll allows workers to rate the effect that company developments have on their work duties. Responses range from 'no impact' to 'overwhelmed and need help'. Workers can also feedback general comments on their working environment. All the information is collected in real-time and sent to managers for analysis. The information is vital for managers to keep abreast of workers' attitudes and responses to change so that appropriate action can be taken where necessary. Managers at Amazon can use the eePulse to feedback their response to observations and views expressed by workers. To maintain the relevance of the poll to workers requires managers to respond quickly and consistently to the feedback.

Finally, there has to be some evaluation of those whose responsibility it is to choose and implement strategy. The executive level of management is responsible for creating the vision of the organisation, developing and implementing strategies and achieving stated objectives. The evaluation of the performance of the organisation has to include an audit of top management. An audit of top management should focus on both economic and non-economic factors.

The economic performance of the organisation refers to profitability, return on investment, market share, etc., whereas the non-economic factors refer to the ability of top managers to develop a strategy, create a positive organisational culture, build effective teams of workers, and provide leadership and vision. The evaluation of top management should be linked to the stated strategic objectives. The evaluation of top management is usually a task undertaken by the board of directors and is most often seen in large organisations with an e-business element to their activities. However, most 'pure play' e-businesses have no discernable hierarchy of authority and are characterised by empowerment of workers. Here, an independent audit may be necessary from consultants brought in to evaluate the performance of the senior managers and executive officers.

Website evaluation

In e-business it is the website that generates interest from customers and drives the business model. The design and application of the website is of vital importance to organisations engaged in e-business and e-commerce. The first step in developing an effective website is to ensure the design is attractive to browsers. Positive first impressions are crucial since browsers are only a click away from moving on. The design has to capture the attention of users. Secondly, the website has to be easily navigated. Internet users will quickly move on if they are unable to work their way around the website quickly and efficiently. Thirdly, the website has to offer fast access to information required by internet users. Finally, the website needs to offer 24-hour access and security.

Determining what and how much information to put on the website are important decisions that designers have to make. A balance has to be struck between highlighting the range of products and services offered and overcrowding the website. Overloading the website with technical applications, service requirements and many different brand promotions can slow down the website processes and make the website more complicated for customers to use. This may have the effect of failing to establish a customer base, failing to attract new customers or losing the loyalty of existing customers. Fletcher et al. (2004) offer some simple website design principles that can help an e-business avoid these pitfalls. These include:

- Keeping graphs to a minimum;
- Offering visual pictures of products;
- Keeping the layout design simple;
- Simplifying navigation;
- Limiting or dispensing with banner advertisement.

The internet may offer organisations access to a global market, but their websites need to reflect local conditions. Website design needs to take into account differences in language, culture, technical experience and the types of products and services demanded in different regions of the globe (Dowling, 1999). The traditional model of selling to a global audience was based on selling fairly homogeneous products using similar marketing techniques and distributing and selling products globally. This model has now broken down and has been replaced by one that emphasises local needs in a global market.

Website design needs to recognise the key characteristics that define demand conditions in the areas in which a particular company wishes to do business. This may involve offering translations into different local languages (for example, there are dozens of different regional languages in India); using relevant local symbols; linking products with established local brands; and having local contact details.

There are a number of advantages of using the internet as a means of gaining information on customers and their behaviour online. Automating data on online customers saves time and can reduce costs of gathering information. Some research points to customers being more amenable to participating in online surveys compared to traditional hardcopy ones (Shu and Wong, 2001). Although care has to be taken in ensuring that a representative sample of customers is achieved, the use of online surveys has become commonplace in the marketing function of e-business.

Hosting

One of the stages of implementing a website strategy is deciding on the hosting of the site. Hosting is the physical location where an organisation's website is stored, maintained and monitored. There are several options available to e-businesses regarding hosting. These include:

- Self-hosting: the organisation operates and manages the website;
- Co-location: the organisation operates and manages the website but physically locates its systems in a hosting company's facilities;
- Dedicated hosting: the organisation outsources the management of its systems and support activities to a third party, but the website and systems are physically located on a server dedicated solely to the organisation;
- Shared hosting: similar to dedicated hosting, except that the website resides on a shared server.

Organisations need to consider a number of factors when making a hosting decision, including those relevant to website performance. Plant (2000) highlights the main factors as being:

- Performance: the long-term returns on investment in systems;
- Scalability: capability of a system to grow in size to service increasing demand;
- Availability: the capability for meeting continuous demand;
- Reliability: the technological robustness of systems;
- Simplicity: ease of navigation and usability;
- Integration: extent to which the systems are linked with other systems;
- Security: protection against criminal or malevolent attacks.

Website performance indicators

In e-business, the evaluation of the performance of the website has to be a continuous process. In a rapidly changing marketplace, characterised by high levels of competition, organisations have to assess the performance of their website on a daily, weekly, monthly and yearly basis. This includes gathering information on:

- The number of 'hits' on the website by potential customers;
- The length of time the potential customer stayed with the website;
- Which types of products or services were viewed by potential customers;
- The navigation of the website, whether one-stop or multiple browsing;
- The number of 'hits' transformed into actual sales;
- The value of sales made;
- The types of products and services sold;
- The number of repeat customers;
- The characteristics of customers – age, gender, employment, location, etc.;
- Comparisons between website performance indicators in one time period set against another similar time period.

The last of these information gathering elements is an important one for evaluating the performance growth of the website. This information tells managers if the website is working to attract increasing numbers of browsers and customers over a given period, if it is largely static or if the website is failing. Managers should set realistic and achievable targets for attracting customers to the website and compare the actual results with those targets. If the numbers fall short of target then the managers have to decide on their response. This may include changing the targets, changing the website design, changing the business model or rethinking their strategy. A failing website may be symptomatic of a deeper malaise within the organisation relating to an inability to recruit and retain quality staff, technical inefficiency, management failure or a negative organisational culture.

The website evaluation cannot rely solely on information on users' online behaviour. There is a host of other information that is required in order to fully evaluate the performance of the website. This will include customers' perceptions of the website design and usability, the accessibility and speed of access to the website, the quality of service, the quality of products, the efficiency of delivery and after-sales service. Although most firms have online facilities for feedback from customers this is not used in a systematic and controlled fashion. The responses may vary in number over different periods of time making analysis more difficult.

Effective evaluation requires firms to complement information gained online with traditional market research methods such as questionnaires, surveys and focus groups. Focus groups, in particular, are a useful method of gaining a deeper insight into customers' perceptions, attitudes, buying behaviour and use of the internet. Although focus group discussions can take place online, the electronic version lacks the spontaneity, synergy and non-verbal communication that face-to-face discussions generate.

Business model evaluation

The business model adopted defines the types of activities that an e-business undertakes to achieve a competitive advantage. Chapter 3 (*E-business markets and models*) outlined a number of examples of commonly used business models for e-business. The performance of the business model will be continuously monitored and evaluated. One of the purposes of creating a business model is to generate revenue so that the e-business can survive and grow. Thus, the income-generating capability of the business model is the most prominent of the performance measures carried out by e-businesses. An e-business will set targets for income generation over a set period of time and compare it with actual income received.

Even though the business model may not generate much income in the short term, managers in e-business must remain true to their convictions and not abandon the business model too early. Unless an e-business has first-mover or other market advantages it can take some time for e-business models to generate income. However, the period of grace may differ significantly between different organisations. Some investors or lenders may wish to see some evidence of income generation from an e-business model over a shorter period of time than others. This will influence the decision-making process and evaluation of the business model by managers. In this case it is not only managers of the e-business that undertake an evaluation, but their financial backers too. Much will depend on the views held by backers regarding the medium to long-term prospects for profitability and whether they think the business model can generate sufficient funds to allow the e-business to remain viable in the short term.

Mini Case Study: Amazon.com

Amazon.com is a prime example of a globally recognised dot-com who, in 1994, was first to market in the online bookselling business. Subsequently, the firm has expanded rapidly to e-tail a vast number of products and services. However, for the majority of the time Amazon.com has been trading, the company has been registering year on year losses. Only in 2004 did the company finally announce a trading profit. The reason for their continued existence throughout the loss-making years is down to investor and lender goodwill. Investors and lenders take a dispassionate view of the business model and make judgements about the future investment plans. The Amazon.com business model was deemed sufficiently robust to garner a high level of goodwill amongst its investor community.

The goodwill of investors is part of the evaluation process of organisations. Indeed, Amazon.com had their own investor-relations specialists to communicate with key lenders and investors. By 1999 the goodwill of investors was being tested to the limits by the $1.5 billion long-term debt that the company had built up. Like many other dot-com firms the market value of Amazon.com had also declined during this period to $16 billion compared to £23 billion only a few years earlier. In previous meetings with key investors Amazon.com had emphasised the number of unique visitors to their website on a monthly basis as the key growth indicator. Where once this proved sufficient evidence for investors to remain loyal, by 2000 they had become impatient and were only interested in when Amazon.com was going to start registering profits.

This case illustrates that even the most prominent and globally recognised companies cannot exist on goodwill alone. Sooner or later, every business needs to be profitable to be economically viable. Profits attract a greater number of investors and a greater volume of investment funds for the organisation to grow and achieve its objectives.

E-business strategy evaluation

The final part of evaluation should focus on the longer-term aspirations of the e-business. An evaluation of e-business strategy should determine whether or not the organisation is heading in the right direction to achieve stated objectives. However, there are a number of factors that make evaluating an e-business strategy distinct from evaluating the strategy of traditional firms. These distinctions include:

■ The need for a full understanding of the capabilities and attributes of the internet when applied to business functions;

■ The need to change the internet architecture in order to measure relevant criteria;

■ The need to clearly define business processes as a distinct e-business activity;

■ The need to recognise that workgroups do not operate in isolation, but have to recognise their impact on other groups within a network organisation;

■ The need to recognise that the impact of the internet extends beyond the internal environment.

If the e-business is nearing, or is at the final phase of a strategy cycle then analysis will focus on where the organisation is positioned relative to where they intended to be. The analysis should reveal:

■ Where the organisation is currently positioned;

■ Where the organisation can be positioned given current resources and capabilities;

■ The benefits of adopting different levels of e-business;

■ The position that the organisation should aspire to;

■ The practical steps for implementing a new strategy to achieve competitive advantage.

The evaluation of the performance of an e-business strategy will focus on the extent to which it achieves stated long-term objectives. Some examples of strategic objectives include:

■ Targets for increasing market share (either overall or in a market segment);

■ Becoming the technological leader in the industry sector (e.g. Apple's strategy for technological leadership in browser applications);

■ Acquiring the best skills (Microsoft maintain their competitive advantage partly through their ability to attract key workers with key skills);

■ Setting profit targets (the phase of existing on investor goodwill has passed and now more and more e-businesses set specific annual profit targets);

■ Developing a range of new products or services (Yahoo! build their business model around researching what customers want and delivering it);

■ Targets for customer satisfaction (US dot-coms have a benchmark of 80.8% set by the American Customer Satisfaction Index for e-commerce);

■ Targets for delivery times of products (Tesco.com guarantee delivery within set parameters).

The e-business strategy will be based on broad-based objectives that relate to where the organisation wants to be at some point in the future. The key elements to be evaluated help managers analyse the progress the organisation has made towards achieving long-term objectives. There are, of course, difficulties in measuring some of the key elements and managers have to use their experience, analytical skills and intuition in order to make value judgements about the performance of such elements. Nevertheless, managers have to address a number of key issues relating to the evaluation of strategy. These include:

■ The extent to which existing strategies achieve desired outcomes;

■ The effectiveness to which the strategies were executed;

■ The effectiveness to which the strategies were communicated to all parties;

■ The accuracy of the internal and external analysis;

■ The extent of managerial commitment to the chosen strategy;

■ The depth to which alternative strategies were analysed;

■ The extent to which results were monitored, recorded and analysed;

■ The level of proper diagnosis of trends;

■ The level of consistency between strategic choice and its implementation;

■ The extent to which the strategy was properly resourced.

Mini Case Study: Zen Internet

Evaluation of strategy is of vital importance in the learning process about the competitive environment and helps managers make the correct decisions at the correct time. In a rapidly changing business environment such as e-business this can very often make the difference between success and failure. The case of Zen Internet illustrates how important evaluation of current strategy is when it comes to making important decisions about the future.

Zen Internet is an Internet Service Provider (ISP) formed in the mid 1990s by Richard Tang. During this period, service provision to the internet was in its infancy and Tang believed that first-mover advantages would prove crucial in growing the business. The initial investment of £20 000 allowed Tang to set about building a network that would connect his customers to the internet. The original network held only six lines and could cope with a mere fifty customers. However, by 1996 demand was growing faster than the company's ability to invest in the necessary hardware.

The evaluation of the business model and strategy revealed a number of threats and opportunities for Zen Internet. The threats included running out of money and the looming free access to the internet offered by companies such as Dixons (through their Freeserve venture). The company needed to borrow more money to invest in the equipment to match supply with growing demand. This was achieved by borrowing from friends and family rather than through financial institutions where interest payments would prove costly. The evaluation of the business model also revealed that, although the company would lose some home customers, the business customers would remain loyal if the current support service was enhanced. This proved sufficient for the company to register year on year profits between 1996 and 1998.

The continual evaluation of the business environment meant Tang was able to pre-empt challenges that technological and market changes brought. By the end of the 1990s Tang realised that the industry was about to take another technological leap through the development of broadband. However, investment at that time was a high risk. Nevertheless, after evaluating the strategy of the company, Tang realised that future success depended on the same principles that brought initial success – being among the first-movers. The evaluation of strategy informed the decision to invest in broadband.

In 2005 Zen Internet had some 60 000 customers, 70% of whom have broadband. Sales have doubled every year since the company was established and is valued at £13 million. Much of this is down to the astuteness with which the business model and the e-business strategy were evaluated and the findings acted upon.

Summary

The evaluation stage of the strategy process is continuous and in-depth. Managers must undertake effective evaluation of performance to make better-informed judgements and decisions about future strategy. Evaluation is part of a control process and is based on setting performance standards and then comparing and contrasting these with actual performance over a set period of time. The information gained can be either quantitative or qualitative or, more likely, a mix of the two. Managers set the key criteria to be measured. Some criteria are generic to all industries, such as financial and human resources; however, website performance is a particular measure of effectiveness for those firms engaged in e-business and e-commerce.

E-business is a technologically-based activity and, therefore, evaluation of the performance of the technology is a high priority. Managers expect the technology to enable the firm to operate more efficiently and at lower cost. Technology should also facilitate communications across different functional areas and with partner organisations and customers. Evaluation of technology should comprise not only the effectiveness of the applications but also the choice and implementation of new technology. This latter element links in to evaluating the ability of the firm to attract key skills to operate systems effectively and to deliver training and staff development programmes to broaden skills and maximise the use of technology.

All firms need to evaluate the effectiveness of their business model. It is the business model that drives the strategy adopted for gaining a competitive advantage. Evaluation of the business model should reveal whether changes or modifications are required to realign performance with set standards. This may involve reassessing the mix of resources and capabilities possessed by the organisation and making changes that offer a better chance of gaining a competitive advantage. Organisations evaluate their business model through a process of learning. A learning organisation continually builds knowledge and experience that informs decisions about future strategy. The continuous evaluation of the performance of the business model is an important element in the learning process.

Finally, the overall long-term strategy of the organisation has to be evaluated. Here, managers need to look for signs that indicate that the firm is on course to achieve its long-term objectives. However, even where no signs of progress are evident, managers should have the courage of their convictions and stick with the chosen strategy.

Changing strategy is a major and significant manoeuvre and ought not to be undertaken at the first sign of trouble.

Questions and tasks

1. Summarise the main elements that comprise feedback control.
2. Find an annual report of an internet-based firm and undertake a financial analysis of the firm using financial ratios. Comment on the financial health of the firm.
3. What are the key criteria that firms must take account of when rolling out new technology?
4. Choose an example of an e-business website and critically assess its effectiveness using a range of evaluation criteria. Compile and use a ratings metric for measuring effectiveness.

References

Coulter, M. (2002). *Strategic Management in Action* (2nd edition). Prentice-Hall: Upper Saddle River, NJ.

Daft, R. L. (2003). *Management* (6th edition). Thomson: Mason, OH.

Daniel, E., Wilson, H. and Myers, A. (2002). Adoption of E-Commerce by SMEs in the UK, Towards a Stage Model. *International Small Business Journal*, Vol. 20, No. 3, pp. 253–70.

Dowling, R. J. (1999). Covering the world's e-Revolution. *Business Week*, 3640:1.

Fletcher, R., Bell, J. and Mcnaughton, R. (2004). *International E-Business Marketing*. Thomson: London.

Plant, R. (2000). *e-Commerce: formulation of strategy*. Prentice-Hall: Upper Saddle River, NJ.

Shu, S. T. and Wong, V. (2001). The use of online focus groups in marketing research: A feasibility study. In *Proceedings from the Academy of Marketing Conference*, University of Cardiff, Cardiff, 1–4 July, pp. 86–94.

Welbourne, T. (2000). New ASP Takes Workforce's 'Pulse'. *The New Corporate University Review*, July/August, pp. 20–1.

Further reading

Bamberger, P. and Meshoulam, I. (2000). *Human Resource Strategy: Formulation, Implementation and Impact*. Sage: London.

Dosi, G. (1982). Technological paradigms and technological trajectories. *Research Policy*, Vol. 11, pp. 147–62.

Treleaven, P. (2000). *E-Business Start-Up: The Complete Guide to Launching Your Internet and Digital Enterprise*. Kogan Page/The Sunday Times: London.

Wheelen, T. L. and Hunger, J. D. (2002). Strategic Management and Business Policy (8th edition). Prentice-Hall: Upper Saddle River, NJ.

Gaining and sustaining a competitive advantage

Key issues:

- Competing effectively;
- First-mover advantages;
- Generic strategies;
- Integrating generic strategies;
- Expanding product lines;
- Lock-in and switching costs;
- Bricks and clicks;
- Winner-takes-all;
- The problem of sustaining competitive advantage.

Introduction

Chapter 11 takes some of the concepts raised in previous chapters and analyses them in the context of gaining and sustaining competitive advantage in e-business. The chapter starts with an overview of what firms must do to compete effectively in the e-business and/or e-commerce environment. The issue of gaining and sustaining competitive advantage begins with first-mover advantages. This is followed by a discussion of how organisations can use generic strategies to gain and sustain competitive advantage. This section adds detail to how differentiation, cost leadership and focus can form the basis of determining the competitive position of firms in an industry and gives examples of how competitive advantage can be leveraged by organisations in the e-business environment. There then follows a discussion of modern management approaches to understanding generic strategies. In particular, the section outlines the key factors that determine an integrated generic strategy where low cost and differentiation work in tandem.

Although there are numerous factors that can determine competitive advantage, this chapter highlights some of the most prominent ones. These include expanding product lines to achieve growth quickly, the lock-in of customers and the mix of traditional business activities and e-business (bricks and clicks). The particularly advantageous position of 'winner-takes-all' in an e-business context also forms part of the discussion. The chapter concludes with analysis of some of the problems relating to sustaining competitive advantage in e-business.

Competing effectively

Although setting up business on the internet is relatively easy there are still some basic rules of engagement that have to be adhered to before firms can compete effectively. The rules are as pertinent to internet 'pure play' firms, who set up shop on the web or provide a service, as they are to traditional bricks-and-mortar firms who want to set up an e-commerce facility. To compete effectively in the internet economy requires managers to address the following criteria.

Draw up a business plan

Anyone seeking to start an online venture needs to draw up a plan of action. This includes determining the product or service to be delivered, the start-up costs, the website design, the identification of the target market, market research, and predicted returns on investment over a given timeframe.

Determine what is to be sold or what service is to be delivered

It is important to know exactly what is to be sold via the website. It may be one product or service or even a range of products or services. Managers must have a good knowledge of the characteristics and value of product(s) or service(s) offered.

Have a good quality website design

The quality and attractiveness of the website will determine how effective the business is in gaining and retaining website traffic. The website traffic that is converted into sales will, ultimately, determine the economic viability of the online venture. Consequently, the website has to be well designed, easily accessed and have a high level of usability. It cannot be assumed that every potential customer is computer literate, so the navigation of the website has to be simple and effective. Web page structure and layout is important when trying to attract online traffic. Customers should be able to easily view the products, make a choice and pay for goods with a few clicks of the mouse.

Ensure security

The security of the website, communications and payments systems is of vital importance when building customer confidence in the online venture. One bad experience usually means losing a customer permanently. Communications between customers regarding the website or online buying experience mean that bad publicity surrounding the quality of service, quality of products or security breaches is quickly disseminated around the buying community. It may be necessary to call in specialists to ensure a good level of security for communications and transactions. The security of the website may be underpinned by obtaining secure certificates from online organisations that can officially endorse the security of the website.

Set appropriate delivery times

The internet makes it easier for customers to buy products through electronic communications. However, customer expectations for delivery times have been ratcheted up because of the immediacy of the internet. This places pressure on businesses to deliver products quickly and efficiently to customers. There is great competition among firms to gain access to distribution specialists in order to meet the expectations of customers. A good business principle is never to promise more than can be delivered. That means setting realistic delivery times so that customers will not be disappointed. It should be possible to determine a series of delivery options based on combinations of cost-effectiveness and convenience that suit both the customer and the business.

Create a brand

It is important to create a brand identity so that customers can readily identify the products or services with the business. Branding means designing a logo and slogan that can be attached to all web pages and other forms of communication. The brand should be enhanced through advertising and promotional activities and be central to building a web presence so that customers make the link between the brand and the product.

Ensure good customer service

The website should have content that answers the vast majority of customers' questions relating to the products or services offered, or the trading practices of the firm. For answers not available to the 'frequently asked questions' page there should be a facility to contact a customer relations person operating either from the business or from a call centre. It is also important to provide an after-sales service. This enhances the relationship with customers and helps to build brand loyalty.

Promote the website

The website needs to be promoted to bring it to the attention of internet users. The online venture has to be nurtured so that customer awareness of what is being offered grows over time. This means using a variety of marketing techniques ranging from word-of-mouth to offline and online advertising. Accessing online advertising facilities, such as Google AdWords, can prove effective for spreading awareness of the site.

Pricing

The pricing strategy of an online venture has to help the firm compete effectively. There will be costs and overheads to consider as well as the desired profit margin. Pricing will depend on the level of demand for the product and whether or not it is possible to achieve sufficient volume sales to gain economies of scale. Economies of scale help to reduce costs and can be used to lower prices. In the initial start-up period it may be necessary for the firm to reduce prices below that of rivals in order to gain market share. This incurs a risk because the losses incurred in the short term will need to be quickly recovered. Undertaking competitor analysis may prove beneficial in understanding the level of competition that exists in the industry sector and helps to inform decisions on pricing.

Define terms and conditions of sale

It is necessary to have a set of clearly defined terms and conditions attached to the content of the website. These should be easily accessed and understood by customers. It is important to express terms and conditions in ways that help customers understand the terms of trade.

Ensure scalability of technology

If, or when, the online venture starts to gain ever-increasing amounts of traffic it is important to ensure that the technological systems in place can cope with the extra demands placed upon it. This is referred to as scalability. When investing in technology, either hardware or software, firms need to ensure that they have the capability to help extend the services provided.

Chapter 11

First-mover advantages

There are numerous benefits that firms can gain by being first-movers in a new industry. When e-business and e-commerce emerged as new means of communicating and transacting in the mid 1990s a few firms were able to gather resources together quickly and create a business model based on exploiting the benefits of trading electronically. Others quickly followed the leaders and became early-movers in the new and burgeoning industry of e-business. Some of the benefits associated with first- or early-movers are:

- The ability to amass a critical mass of customers;
- Developing distinct business models to exploit the advantages of the internet for trading;
- Gaining economies of scale through exploiting network externalities;
- Building customer loyalty through brand recognition;
- Building in switching costs to the website;
- Building relationships with customers electronically;
- Establishing partnerships with key industry players ahead of competitors;
- Influencing the industry infrastructure;
- Refining the value proposition and adding value to customers through innovation;
- Managing both physical and virtual value chain for competitive advantage;
- Build an understanding of customers and their buying habits via the internet;
- Become a learning organisation.

First-mover advantages are significant in creating competitive advantage as they enable firms to amass a huge market value. A crucial first-mover advantage is the development of network externalities. Timmers (1999) describes these as external benefits or costs of the presence of products in the market that are not reflected in the market price (as opposed to network effects which are reflected in price). There is no compensation through price and, therefore, externalities must be viewed as market inefficiencies (Choi et al., 1997).

First-mover advantages help to develop a large customer base that later entrants have to overcome in order to compete effectively. Branding and building customer loyalty are other important first-mover-related advantages. Building a reputation based on service is vital for effecting customer loyalty. This is especially the case for information driven e-businesses since their 'product' is essentially an experience good – that is, the quality is unknown until used.

Key to competitive advantage is building a business model around brand recognition and superior service such that customers are reluctant to switch to rivals even if the cost of doing so is zero. Indeed, the issue of switching costs are themselves a source of first-mover advantage. New entrants have to contend with the knowledge that customers are already familiar with the *modus operandi* of the first-mover's website.

However, in many cases, there are many more potential customers than actual ones and, therefore, the competitive advantage is likely to be diluted as new entrants vigorously pursue old and new customers alike. This makes competitive advantage unsustainable by first-mover advantages alone. Business models that help sustain competitive advantage must also have the attributes of robustness, innovation, adaptability and flexibility.

In e-commerce, firms need to compete effectively by offering lower prices because of the absence of significant search costs. This affects industry profitability and the level of competition. Firms need to adopt a range of strategies to counteract the shift in power to consumers. Differentiation, expanding the product range, and price discrimination are some options that firms may pursue to create competitive advantage.

Generic strategies

One of the most important tasks facing managers is to determine an appropriate competitive strategy to achieve stated aims. In his seminal work of 1980, Michael Porter asserts that competitive strategy should be based around achieving competitive advantage. In Porter's view, competitive advantage can be derived either by being the least cost producer in an industry or from possessing distinct differences from rivals that consumers value. A third element in Porter's generic strategy model is 'focus'. This refers to the scope of the product-market in which the organisation competes. Organisations may choose to focus on cost or differentiation in different markets. This may be the whole market (broad) or a small number of market segments (narrow).

These elements of differentiation, cost leadership and focus comprise Porter's generic strategy model. The defining characteristics of the generic strategy model were included in Chapter 8 (*E-business strategy: formulation*). In this section the attention turns to how organisations use generic strategies to gain competitive advantage in the context of e-business.

Differentiation

As noted in Chapter 8 (*E-business strategy: formulation*), value can be created by differentiation across each stage of the value chain. This is achieved by undertaking activities that lower buyers' costs or raise buyers' performance. Firms have to make policy choices regarding what activities to perform and how they are to perform them in order to implement a differentiation strategy. They must also effect linkages within the value chain or with suppliers and distribution channels. Other factors may also drive product differentiation such as timing, location, the sharing of activities among business units, learning, integration, scale and institutional factors (Porter, 1985). There are many ways to create a competitive advantage by differentiating products or services in the e-business environment. Some of the most prominent methods include:

- Creating a strong brand;
- Real world promotional programmes;
- Easy site navigation;
- Creating an online community;
- Offering personalisation of products or services;
- Offering customisation of products or services;
- Real-time merchandising;
- Offering valuable ordering applications;
- Quick order processing;
- Providing order status information;
- Developing incentives for repeat purchases;
- Offering excellent customer service;
- Creating loyalty programmes;
- One-to-one marketing techniques.

The internet has allowed customers to become more involved in the planning and design of products or services. This allows firms to differentiate their service through customisation or personalisation.

This may result in superior customer service and the creation of unique products. For example, some firms, such as Apple and Microsoft, can offer their customers personalised website summaries using software called Really Simple Syndication (RSS). This allows customers to access a summary of the information and entertainment available on a number of different websites of their choice without having to scan and download each of them individually.

For example, an internet user may habitually access websites for football scores, weather, latest music releases, news and an e-tailer.

Similarly, firms can differentiate their service by providing customers with one all-encompassing password to access a host of online activities including e-banking, e-mail or online shopping. Online financial firm First Direct launched their Internet Banking Plus initiative in 2004 giving customers access to all their online financial accounts using one set of security details. The company has now extended the service to include e-mail accounts, loyalty reward schemes, the e-Bay auction site and bill payments for utilities.

Firms can also differentiate through mass customisation strategies. Existing products can be customised in innovative ways such as providing CDs with a compilation of selected music or providing a service related to customers' specific interests. For example, online booksellers allow readers to read short extracts from books before they make a purchasing decision. Customer relationship management provides information about customers that forms the basis of differentiating the service according to each of their customer's tastes.

The innovation associated with developing small niche markets according to specific customer needs means firms can charge higher prices (Sinha, 2000) and create a competitive advantage. The threat of substitute products is diminished, as is the level of competition among incumbent firms in the industry. Also, established firms can develop customer relationship management to differentiate the service or product and create brand loyalty or 'lock-in' of customers. This reduces the threat of entry.

As part of the differentiation strategy, organisations must address how they deal with customers within the e-business environment. In the internet economy consumers have an enhanced role in the relationship between themselves and businesses. Prahalad and Ramaswamy (2000) assert that a product is no more than an artefact around which customers have experiences. Organisations can produce the product but they cannot determine the customer's experience. This 'ownership' of experience empowers consumers.

However, the internet can lessen this threat to organisations because it can be used to reach customers in new ways and offer new experiences. The new experiences include ways for customers to determine their own choices in terms of the types of products made available, product characteristics and design, and levels of additional service built into the transaction. Personalisation, customisation and the formation of communities of buyers are examples of how organisations can differentiate their offerings to include the customers in the process. Organisations can then tap into customers' feedback and suggestions for improvement to further add value and enhance the relationship. The differentiating factor is the collaborative relationship between the organisation and the customer.

Cost leadership

An organisation that adopts a cost leadership strategy strives to be the lowest cost producer in the industry. A cost leadership position can create a competitive advantage in e-business because it may allow an organisation to lower prices. In the internet economy, rivalry is intense and there is greater price competition. Those firms that compete effectively on price are the ones most likely to gain customers and competitive advantage.

As well as offering opportunities for lower prices, use of the internet can also lower costs, most notably, the transactions costs. Chapter 4 (*E-business economics*) discussed the various ways in which the internet helps reduce transaction costs. A cost leadership strategy based on reducing transaction costs is likely to include lower costs associated with the buy/sell transactions as well as those that accrue through interacting with each functional area of the firm's value chain, both internally and with partner organisations and customers.

There are many ways in which organisations can seek to reduce costs using the internet. Some of the ways e-businesses can achieve cost leadership include:

- Focusing on a broad market to gain economies of scale;
- Minimising customer acquisition costs;
- Creating a community of buyers to gain network economies;
- Minimising the risk of first-time purchasing by ensuring secure transactions;
- Minimising the cost of servicing customers;
- Imitating successful business models and web applications;

■ Limiting the product range;

■ Selling products with low distribution costs (e.g. information-based products and services);

■ Investing only in technology that further helps to reduce costs;

■ Minimising staff numbers;

■ Advertising solely through the internet.

Much of the cost saving activity relates to internal efficiency. In particular, the internet (and intranet) helps to improve the administration, monitoring and transactional processes within organisations. There are efficiencies to be gained in communications both internally and externally. Automating many routine and repetitive processes reduces the need for administration staff and reduces costs. There is less need for paper and printing services because much of the communications and data required can be produced and stored electronically. Extranets can help organisations collaborate with a range of partners electronically and in real-time. There are also opportunities for lowering the cost of reaching customers and marketing the products and services. The use of the internet can also reduce costs in internal processes such as production schedules, warehousing, logistics and distribution.

Outsourcing has become another important way of achieving competitive advantage through the cost savings it brings. This applies as much to small and medium sized enterprises (SMEs) as it does to large-scale companies. Outsourcing can make a considerable difference to companies where there are distinct cost differences between undertaking activities in-house as compared to hiring specialists. Increasingly, firms have been looking to overseas markets for hiving off a range of activities in order to achieve cost savings. Hence the rise in the number of call centres being located in countries such as India where labour costs are significantly lower.

Other IT or internet-related activities can also be easily outsourced to foreign countries. For example, a computer programmer in Sri Lanka can provide a service at one quarter the cost of a programmer in the UK. Many companies put work out to tender via the internet. IT specialists from around the world can bid for the work by submitting their costs and time schedule for completion. Firms then choose a particular service based on a combination of cost and completion times. When the work is carried out then the firm releases payment. The winning bid for IT and internet-related work can come from anywhere around the globe. For example, a freelance web designer can cost hundreds of pounds in the UK but bids for design work from India or Bangladesh range from only between twenty to thirty pounds. Such savings may enable UK-based firms to achieve a competitive advantage based on cost leadership.

Once competitive advantage has been gained through cost leadership, the next problem facing organisations is to determine how to sustain the advantage. Rivals may find ways of further lowering costs and eroding competitive advantage. However, one of the most imposing threats to sustaining competitive advantage is imitation by rivals. Ease of access to the internet means that many of the aspects of an organisation's activities that help towards creating a competitive advantage are visible to rivals. This may include the types and characteristics of the products or services offered, prices, quality, customer feedback, relationships with partner organisations, delivery times, discounts and other incentives, website design and navigation, and so on. The risk of imitation is ever-present and is especially prevalent among organisations that adopt a cost leadership strategy. It is cheaper to imitate new ideas, processes and products than to research, develop and implement them from scratch. There may not even be protection against imitation through law. Whilst there have been some attempts at copyrighting applications software, to date few have been successful.

Mini Case Study: Glasses Direct

Student entrepreneur James Murray Wells established online firm Glasses Direct (www.glassesdirect.com) in 2004 after a visit to the optician left him reeling at the price of new glasses. His plan was to become the cost leader in the industry for selling glasses online and using the transaction cost savings to offer low prices. After researching the pricing structure of traditional suppliers, Murray Wells realised that if he could find a laboratory that was prepared to supply him the glasses he could use the internet to sell them at a significantly lower price than mainstream suppliers, such as Boots. The response to the website and some traditional forms of marketing, such as handing out flyers, was positive. The low transaction costs and basic service provided has been the basis for gaining a competitive advantage for the company.

By early 2005 Glasses Direct had some 8000 customers and were selling around 300 pairs of glasses per day. The company is the industry cost leader because: its initial investment for entering the industry was low; using the internet as a communications channel meant that marketing costs were minimal; the service provided is confined to taking orders and delivering the product; and staff costs were minimised. In 2005 Murray Wells won the Shell Live Wire Entrepreneur of the Year award for his internet-based business idea.

Focus

A focus strategy is when an organisation seeks competitive advantage through cost leadership or differentiation in a broad market segment or narrow, well-defined market segment of customers. Organisations that adopt a focus strategy typically serve a specific niche market. The internet allows firms to target market segments more closely; they can then offer customised and personalised products and services to those customers. There is a great deal of competitive rivalry in small, well-defined niche markets that are characteristics of narrowly defined market segments. Firms can offer specialised products and services in a vast array of niche markets.

Those firms that gain a competitive advantage by adopting a focus strategy are the ones who are able to gain maximum returns from the resources they deploy across the value chain. These may involve focusing the marketing push towards specified customers (perhaps as a result of permission marketing), offering added services to the main product or service (chat-room facilities for a virtual community), or utilising e-procurement systems that specialise in matching buyers with specialist niche market suppliers. The key to success for firms adopting a focus strategy is to use their specialist knowledge and expertise to offer customers added value in the shape of better quality products or services, greater response times to customer requests and better customer service based on more personalised relationships.

There are some market segments that are particularly attractive to e-businesses because of the distinct characteristics they exhibit. Some market segments are more valuable than others in terms of their purchasing power and use of the internet. A 'winner-takes-all' market may develop in a market segment characterised by large numbers of affluent customers who want to shop online. There are different levels of internet use among different age groups. The age group most likely to shop online is the 25–35-year-olds. Online customers are most likely to be comfortable using computers and probably use them in their working environment. Professional people with higher education qualifications are also high internet users. All these characteristics may encourage e-businesses to target affluent professionals between 25 and 35 years old and tailor the marketing of their products and services to the needs, wants and aspirations of that particular group.

Using the internet means that organisations can undertake a continuous process of learning about their customers and their behaviour online. Understanding customers' needs and wants is an important aspect of gaining a competitive advantage and underpins a focus strategy by building a specialised knowledge of a niche market. An organisation that gains a superior knowledge of the market can respond quicker and more flexibly to changes in the market environment, better meet customer needs and create brand loyalty.

Integrating generic strategies

Porter (1980) suggests that firms should choose either a differentiation or cost leadership strategy and stick with it. According to Porter, having elements of both means organisations are 'stuck in the middle'. That is, they have no clear and consistent strategic direction. This can happen when an organisation's cost are higher than the industry cost leader's or if an organisation's products are not as differentiated as those of rivals.

Modern management thinking has challenged Porter's assertion that low cost and differentiation cannot be successfully pursued simultaneously. There are organisations that integrate low cost and differentiation as a generic strategy (sometimes referred to as a hybrid strategy). One of the reasons organisations adopt an integrated generic strategy is to make it more difficult for rivals to duplicate or imitate the activities that generate the competitive advantage. An integrated generic strategy bolsters the competitive position of an organisation by adding value to customers through differentiation (high quality, branding, reputation, etc.) and low prices (low costs means the organisation can translate the savings into lower prices).

The ultimate aim of an integrated generic strategy is to offer consumers a unique value proposition by providing high quality products in the most efficient manner. An example in e-business is the exclusive rights to certain high value financial information owned by the London Stock Exchange (LSE). The LSE can provide a range of differently packaged financial information services and distribute them in global markets at low cost. The service is differentiated through quality, branding and packaging, but it is also produced and distributed at low cost because additional copies can be made at almost zero marginal cost.

Expanding product lines

Porter (1987) notes that firms can achieve competitive advantage by expanding into related product lines and exploiting the transfer of skills or the benefits of sharing of activities such as promotion or distribution. Sharing can lead to economies of scale, cost reduction and the maximum utilisation of the firm's resources. Crucially, the ability to achieve competitive advantage is determined by how well firms combine activities as a basis for increasing differentiation. Porter (1996) argues that the level of 'fit' among activities reduces costs and increases differentiation.

An example of an organisation expanding product lines is Friends Reunited (www.FriendsReunited.com), the website that specialises in bringing together old school friends. Buoyed by the success of the initial web application, the organisation intends to expand into online recruitment. In 2005 the company bought online recruitment agents Topdogjob.com for around £2 million. The site has been rebranded as FriendsReunitedJobs.com and will retain the skills and expertise of the co-founders of Topdogjob.com. The acquisition is part of a strategy to expand and diversify the services provided. The company had already diversified into providing a genealogy site (www.GenesReunited.com) and an online dating agency. The expansion and diversification fits into the distinct web application that has proved so successful in the past – namely, bringing people together for different purposes. FriendsReunited has around 12 million members and gains around 5000 new registrations each day.

Lock-in and switching costs

A 'pure play' e-business needs to attract and retain browsers to its website, then transform them into customers. An e-business that has a customer base twice as big as its rivals has four times the economic value. The greater proportionate value attracts increasing numbers of customers, and again, disproportionately increases the value relative to rivals. As noted in Chapter 4 (*E-business economics*) this positive feedback is the basis of Metcalfe's Law where an e-business can lock-in its competitive advantage through network economies. This type of positive feedback process is similar to the scripture found in Matthew verses 13:12 of the Bible 'For whosoever hath, to him shall be given, and he shall have more abundance, but whosoever hath not, from him shall be taken away even that he hath'. Positive feedback systems give to those who have and take from those that have not. This goes a long way to explaining how competitive advantage is gained in the e-business environment.

Bricks and clicks

Some 'pure play' e-businesses have been spectacularly successful by using the internet effectively in marketing and selling their products and services. However, the majority of dot-com firms struggle to make any significant profits. The attraction of e-business is the potential it offers for lowering costs and expanding access to markets and customers. There is a compelling argument that favours a mix of 'bricks and clicks' as the most effective means of using the internet (Gulati and Garino, 2000). This means that the internet is used for e-business to support functions within the organisation, and for e-commerce as an additional service to customers alongside the core activities undertaken by traditional methods.

One of the advantages that 'pure play' internet firms have is the low cost associated with not having to own large premises or employ large numbers of employees. Although this advantage still plays an important role in determining the success of e-businesses there has been a growing trend towards traditional firms adopting e-business and e-commerce applications.

Traditional firms have a number of advantages over 'pure play' internet firms. First, they have an established brand name around which they can build their e-marketing strategy. Second, they have physical assets that can add value to and support the e-business venture. Third, they have long-standing and established relationships with distributors. This helps them to meet the high expectations of customers regarding delivery times. Perhaps the most significant advantage that traditional businesses have over internet 'pure plays' is that they are not wholly reliant on the success of the e-business venture for the continued existence of the firm. Invariably, traditional businesses use the internet as a means of offering customers an additional sales channel and medium of communication as well as providing an additional marketing channel for the firm.

Winner-takes-all

One of the key characteristics of the e-business competitive environment is the dominance of a few organisations that have been able to globalise their brands and achieve a critical mass of customers with repeat orders for economic viability. Although there are a great many internet-based firms that comprise the industry, relatively few achieve profitability and fewer still come to dominate the industry. The industry structure has a clear 'winner-takes-all' characteristic. There are a number of key factors that determine the development of 'winner-takes-all' markets. These include:

- Economies of scale in production;
- Network economies;
- Cumulative advantage;
- Familiarity;
- Status.

Economies of scale in production

Once the costs of developing and marketing a new product have been covered, further production can lower average costs and bring economies of scale. In e-business this is especially true for information-based products or services where the main cost is incurred in the initial production; thereafter it is easy and cheap to produce and distribute any number of copies.

Network economies

As noted in Chapter 4 (*E-business economics*), network economies are linked to first-mover advantages and the formation of network communities. Firms that are first to market with a product or service gain distinct advantages over followers. They can influence industry structure, create a widely recognised brand name, provide a differentiated service and create switching costs. Network economies derive from the creation of a critical mass of customers who remain loyal and use the website repeatedly. The community of buyers attracted to the website add value to that site by participating in the exchange process. This attracts other customers who further add value to the website and so on. Amazon.com and e-Bay are the two most prominent examples of organisations gaining a competitive advantage based partly on network economies.

Cumulative advantage

A cumulative advantage may be gained from organisational learning and the transformation of that learning into action. This is particularly the case among organisations that are at the forefront of developing cutting-edge technologies. The rate at which technology is improved is related to how dominant it is in the market. The leading technologies are improved faster than the followers (Frank and Cook, 1995). This leads to a cumulative advantage that can help gain and sustain a competitive advantage. Organisations that develop new technologies have to attain a certain level of market penetration before costs are recovered and cumulative advantage sets in. Microsoft Windows is an example of cumulative advantage based on organisational learning being transformed into highly valued products in the form of computer applications that rivals could not match. Microsoft has achieved the winner-takes-all market domination through cumulative advantage.

Familiarity

A 'winner-takes-all' market may be determined by the familiarity of a particular website in the consciousness of customers. Consumer behaviour is geared towards finding what is wanted in the most expedient manner possible and undertaking a transaction speedily and securely. Customers also want to access a wide range of information pertinent to their interests. The convenience factor extends to memorising website addresses. Few internet buyers can name more than half a dozen websites because they invariably stick to only the few that meets their needs, have recognised brand names and have built up a reputation for meeting customer needs.

Customers also become familiar with navigating their way around favoured websites and are generally reluctant to spend time and effort switching to other websites. Again, first-mover advantages can prove critical to achieving this type of convenience and familiarity-based loyalty of customers as a means of gaining a competitive advantage. The customers can be 'locked-in' by maintaining a relationship based on meeting their needs and continuing to add value so that they are not tempted to switch to rivals. Customers' familiarity with a known and trusted brand can be the basis for a firm achieving 'winner-takes-all' market dominance.

Status

Some organisations build a reputation and status that acts as a magnet to customers seeking association with a brand, a type of service or an application of a product. Customers place a value on the association they have with different products and services. Online communities are based on adding value to individuals who gain a positive feeling from being part of a group with similar interests. A firm that can attain high value status among a large customer group will be in a position to achieve 'winner-takes-all' since rivals will find it almost impossible to match their status.

The problem of sustaining competitive advantage

By definition a 'winner-takes-all' market is dominated by a single firm but in many e-business competitive environments the industry structure is characterised by numerous firms vying for competitive advantage. Whereas the beneficiaries of 'winner-takes-all' are well placed to sustain their competitive advantage through entry barriers, most firms in e-business find it difficult to gain a competitive advantage and even more difficult to sustain it once achieved. E-business and e-commerce are designed to edge competitive environments closer to that of perfect competition. However, it can be seen that this presents as much of a threat to sustaining competitive advantage as it does opportunities for entry and cost reduction (Besanko et al., 2000). Indeed, opportunities for achieving profitability in such an environment quickly disappear as new entrants are attracted and upward pressure is asserted on supply and prices fall.

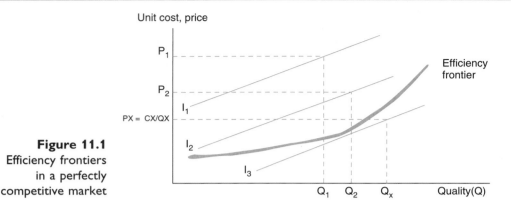

Figure 11.1
Efficiency frontiers
in a perfectly
competitive market

The above scenario can be illustrated using economic theory. Figure 11.1 illustrates efficiency frontiers in a perfectly competitive market (Rumelt, 1974).

Figure 11.1 represents a market in which consumers' benefits are based on a single attribute of quality (Q). The model assumes consumers have identical price/quality preferences. These are shown by the upward sloping indifference curves. The efficiency frontier represents the most efficient cost/quality positions that are possible for firms in the market. That is, no firm can extend efficiency beyond the frontier. In a market, such as online bookselling, entry is free and imitation incurs negligible costs. This allows any firm (incumbents or potential entrants) to attain any position along the efficiency frontier. Higher quality at lower cost becomes unattainable for individual firms in the market due to the ease of imitation of the business model that brought it about.

In Figure 11.1 price/quality preferences P_1Q_1 would not be sustainable because ease of entry would allow a new firm to offer higher quality (Q_2) and lower price P_2 and gain market share from incumbents. Opportunities for creating competitive advantage through price, cost or quality combinations end at point PX = CX/QX where the market is in equilibrium. By implication this model adds emphasis to the importance of 'lock-in' for customers whereby the switching costs are significant enough to maintain brand loyalty.

Imitation

High profile e-businesses such as e-Bay and Amazon.com have achieved exponential growth in sales and stock value through exploiting first-mover advantages and monopoly status between 1995 and 1997. However, their business models have attracted imitators. Even though most goods continue to be sold through traditional retail methods, the potential of the online market is sufficient to attract traditional 'bricks-and-mortar' firms. Many of the business models and website designs of new entrants closely resemble those developed by established incumbents. In response, incumbent firms can vertically differentiate to create competitive advantage. Amazon.com created a differentiated product based on service, design and brand image. However, as new entrants arrive price competition ensues.

The market illustrated in Figure 11.1 shows that all consumers have the same preferences. A firm offering a price/quality trade-off inferior to competitors would be unable to compete. Nevertheless, as the market heads towards one of monopolistic competition (many sellers), sellers differentiate horizontally in distinct market segments. This allows prices to be raised without incurring a dramatic fall in demand. For a firm facing a downward sloping demand curve the optimal price is above marginal cost. This though does not guarantee profits since total costs may not be covered. The industry structure will be determined by how long incumbent firms make profits that attract new entrants. Each successive new entrant chips away at industry profitability until it is no longer attractive.

Summary

E-commerce has radically altered the way many firms conduct business. It has presented a number of opportunities for developing business models and strategies to achieve competitive advantage in a wide range of business sectors. However, few 'pure play' internet organisations have achieved profitability let alone sustained a competitive advantage. Some reasons for this include intense price competition, price transparency that increases the power of customers, low entry barriers, and the high investment of expanding the range of products and services.

Meanwhile, there is increasing evidence to suggest that traditional businesses that use the internet for improving internal efficiency and adding an additional channel of communications and sales to customers are the ones that are gaining the greatest returns from e-business. The industry structure for internet 'pure plays' tends towards domination by the few firms who have gained and sustained competitive advantage through a combination of first-mover advantages, lock-in of customers, built-in switching costs, and network economies. The competitive environment of e-business tends towards a 'winner-takes-all' characteristic.

To compete effectively in e-business requires organisations to develop business models based on applications that bring unique value propositions to customers. The continued growth of shopping online witnessed since the dot-com crash of 2000 suggests that customers are ready, willing and able to participate in e-commerce. However, organisations wishing to tap into this stream of revenue have to match or exceed customer expectations. Organisations may adopt a generic strategy as a means of creating a competitive advantage, but it would have to be backed by a robust business model and include distinct characteristics that set it apart from the offerings from rivals. For organisations trying to challenge well-known and trusted industry leaders this can be a daunting prospect. Many take a pragmatic approach and focus on providing a specialist product or service for a well-defined niche market.

Questions and tasks

1. What are first-mover advantages? Choose a leading e-business and identify its first-mover advantages.
2. Outline some examples of how an e-business can differentiate its product or service.
3. What are the main advantages that 'bricks and clicks' organisations have over internet 'pure plays'?
4. What factors determine a 'winner-takes-all' market?
5. What barriers would a new e-business face when trying to gain a competitive advantage in the online auction industry?

References

Besanko, D., Dranove, D. and Shanley, M. (2000). *Economics of Strategy* (2nd edition). Wiley: Chichester.

Choi, S. Y., Stahl, D. O. and Whinston, A. B. (1997). *The Economics of Electronic Commerce*. Macmillan Technical Publishing: Indianapolis.

Frank, R. H. and Cook, P. J. (1995). *The Winner-Takes-All Society*. Penguin Books: New York, NY.

Gulati, R. and Garino, J. (2000). Get the Right Mix of Bricks and Clicks. *Harvard Business Review*, May/June, pp. 107–14.

Porter, M. E. (1980). *Competitive Strategy*. Free Press: New York.

Porter, M. E. (1985). *Competitive Advantage: Creating and Sustaining Superior Performance*. Free Press: New York.

Porter, M. E. (1987). From Competitive Advantage to Corporate Strategy. *Harvard Business Review*, May/June.

Porter, M. E. (1996). What is strategy? *Harvard Business Review*. November/December, pp. 61–78.

Prahalad, C. K. and Ramaswamy, V. (2000). Co-opting Customer Competence. *Harvard Business Review*, January/February, pp. 79–87.

Rumelt, R. P. (1974). *Strategy, Structure and Economic Performance*. Division of Research, Harvard Business School: Boston.

Sinha, I. (2000). Cost transparency: The Net's Real Threat to Prices and Brands. *Harvard Business Review*, March-April, pp. 43–50.

The Holy Bible (2004), HarperCollins: London.

Timmers, P. H. A. (1999). *Electronic Commerce: Strategies and Models for Business to Business Trading*. John Wiley: Chichester.

Further reading

Bakos, Y. (1998). The Emerging Role of Electronic Marketplaces on the Internet. *Communications of the ACM*, **41**(8), August, pp. 35–42.

Porter, M. E. (2001). Strategy and the Internet. *Harvard Business Review*, March, pp. 62–78.

Rumelt, R. P. (1984). Towards a Strategic Theory of the Firm. In *Competitive Strategic Management* (R. Lamb, ed.), pp. 556–70, Prentice-Hall: Englewood Cliffs, New Jersey.

Schiesel, S. (2001). Planning the Digital Smorgasbord: For this Media Conglomerate, the Future is All-You-Can-Eat. *The New York Times*, 11 June, p. 48.

Shin, N. (2001). Strategies for Competitive Advantage in Electronic Commerce. *Journal of Electronic Commerce Research*, Vol. 2, No. 11, pp. 164–71.

Turban, E., Lee, J., King, D. and Chung, H. (2000). *Electronic Commerce: A Managerial Perspective*. Prentice-Hall: New Jersey.

CHAPTER 17

E-business: the future

Key issues:

- The phases of e-business development;
- The performance of e-business;
- The future of e-business.

Introduction

This final chapter looks at the future prospects for e-business. First, though, the chapter outlines the characteristics of the three distinct phases that e-business has been through during the decade 1995 to 2005. Next, there follows a review of the performance of e-business and e-commerce during that period. The chapter concludes with a discussion on the likely future prospects for e-business from the perspective of organisations and customers.

The phases of e-business development

E-business and e-commerce have been through three distinct phases since the commercialisation of the internet. In many ways the e-business industry has evolved in much the same way as other technologically led industries have in the past, such as the building of the railroad system across the USA in the nineteenth century. In the initial phase there is a great deal of excitement and optimism that generates considerable investment funds and lends impetus to the early development of the new industry. The high value placed on the new industry attracts ever-increasing numbers of investors who fear missing out on a potential financial return. This scenario reflected the so-called 'dot-com era' between 1995 and 1999 when the numbers of internet-based firms rose dramatically each year. Eventually, the market value far outstrips the true value of the industry and new investment starts to slow. Meanwhile, the industry has attracted ever-increasing numbers of competitors who, similar to investors, do not want to miss out on potential profits. The industry cannot sustain inflated values and high numbers of competitors and this, eventually, ushers in phase two – the industry shake out.

Phase two is when the industry seeks to establish an equilibrium that better reflects the value of competitors and matches supply with demand. The dot-com crash of 2000 was an example of the market mechanism righting itself after a period of instability caused by the initial fervour associated with the business potential of the internet. Many dot-com firms disappeared as quickly as they had arrived and the new business reality meant that only firms with first-mover advantages or a robust business model based on adding real value to customers would survive.

Phase two was a chastening experience for entrepreneurs, investors and lenders in the internet economy. The two-year period following the dot-com crash was a period of reflection and learning for managers regarding the use of the internet for business and commerce. Organisations had to regroup and think through their e-business strategies more carefully before venturing back into the fray. Customers had also experienced a steep learning curve in relation to buying online. The first two phases were the learning period for customers as they determined how to use the new channel for browsing and transactions. By 2002, increasing rates of connectivity and interactivity meant that customers were beginning to warm to the idea of online shopping.

Post-2004 has witnessed the start of phase three of the development of e-business and e-commerce. This phase represents a new found confidence in the use of the internet for business purposes and trading with customers. However, the re-emergence of e-business as a viable means of transacting and communicating is very different from the initial phase of its development. Entrepreneurs, investors and customers are much wiser and more experienced when it comes to using the internet.

Managers have thought through their e-business strategies more carefully and have brought in the key skills to their organisations that can help them create a competitive advantage. Managers have also undertaken restructuring programmes to better align their organisations with the new working environment required to take advantage of the internet for communicating internally and externally. Entrepreneurs have re-entered e-business with better applications and more robust business models for gaining a competitive advantage. Many more customers have learned how to use the internet effectively and have had their confidence boosted by good experiences of transacting online. Although there are risks associated with privacy and security, the vast majority of online transactions are smooth, efficient and effective. This is underlined by the fact that internet-based organisations score some of the highest customer satisfaction rates of all commercial ventures.

The performance of e-business

After the dot-com crash of 2000 and in the wake of falling share values of technology firms during the same period, many analysts predicted the end of the internet as a viable means of transacting and undertaking business processes. However, in the intervening years the performance of the internet economy has been impressive with year on year growth, businesses reporting cost savings and increased efficiency, and an ever-increasing customer base driving e-commerce to unprecedented heights.

Connectivity rates have increased dramatically meaning that access to the internet has never been easier for a vast number of people. There are now around 200 million Americans with access to the internet. The US market for online transactions was $120 billion in 2004 with the American Department of Commerce reporting a 26% rise in online sales for the period (*The Economist*, 2004). Europe and the Far East are other areas where online transactions have increased markedly since 2002. The introduction of broadband internet access in key regions of the globe has given a boost to the internet economy both in terms of customers and the number of e-business start-ups. The start-up costs and potential for making profits has encouraged many thousands of small business entrepreneurs to move into the e-market space.

Larger organisations have also been won round by the potential of the internet. The vast majority of organisations now have some level of interest in the internet, whether it be simply a website offering information on the company or more sophisticated levels of engagement such as transactions with customers or collaboration with partners. The effect of the renewed confidence in e-business has been to move ever-increasing amounts of business from the old economy to the new internet-based economy. While the traditional forms of shopping still account for over 98% of all retail sales, the growth patterns for online sales suggest that by 2010 the internet economy will account for 10% of all sales. The performance of e-business and e-commerce can be analysed by focusing on the two most important markets – business-to-consumer (B2C) and business-to-business (B2B).

The performance of B2C e-commerce

United Kingdom

In the UK, consumer spending online reached almost £5 billion in 2004. In 2000 online spending represented just 0.8% of total retail spending but by 2004 this figure had risen to 2.4%. The growth rate of online shopping in the UK is six times faster than that of the overall retail sector. There are a number of reasons for the growth. One reason is that broadband has made it easier and quicker for people to shop online. Also, customers want to take advantage of what the internet has to offer them. One of the principle reasons for shopping online is the lower prices quoted. Around 58% of internet shoppers quote price as the main reason for opting for online shopping. Traditional retailers with an e-commerce website very often have offers that are available only online as part of their web marketing strategy.

As the discussion in Chapter 4 (*E-business economics*) revealed, there is much debate as to whether prices are significantly lower on the internet compared to traditional bricks-and-mortar retailers. Price comparison sites help to clarify the difference. Accessing price comparison site Pricerunner (www.pricerunner.com) revealed that in 2005 the price of a Sony PlayStation 2 was £9 cheaper online compared to traditional retail shops. A Toshiba 32WL48 television cost £1700 offline compared to £1250 online, and a Zanussi ZWF1640W washer cost £429 offline compared to £349 online (*The Sunday Times*).

The internet also allows comparisons to be made between different online retailers, and these can be based anywhere around the globe. Comparison sites will literally translate thousands of offers into English from thousands of retailers around the globe. In 2005 an iRiver PMP-120 20GB music player was £40 cheaper from Singapore-based website Team Digital (www.teamdigital.com) compared to the cheapest UK online price of £337.

One industry that has been revolutionised by the arrival of the internet is car retailing. Car prices in the UK were traditionally much higher compared to other parts of Europe. The internet has allowed customers to access foreign dealers more easily and gain significant savings. This has forced UK dealers to align their prices more in line with those of their European rivals. Between 1999 and 2002 the average price difference between UK and European car dealers had shrunk from 39% to 3%. Customers can also take advantage of differences in exchange rates when buying expensive items such as cars and many e-commerce sites facilitate this too. It is not just car sellers that have had to change because of the internet. The whole retail sector offline has had to reassess their strategies as a result of the challenge posed by the price transparency that is a feature of the internet.

United States

Although the UK gives a good indication of the revival of e-commerce since the crash of 2000, it is the American market that truly confirms the re-emergence of online shopping as a business phenomenon. The two months prior to Christmas is an ideal timeframe to record and analyse online shopping trends. Between November and December 2003 American shoppers spent £18.5 billion online (excluding travel). This represented a 35% increase from the same period in 2002 (*The Economist*, 2004). The corresponding timeframe for 2004 saw spending break through the $20 billion barrier. The most sought after items online were clothing, toys, videos and DVDs. Clothing alone registered sales worth £3.7 billion – a 40% increase in online demand in 2003 compared to the previous year. Just as in the UK and other parts of the world, e-commerce in the USA has benefited from the rollout of broadband internet access. Some 50 million Americans now have broadband at home making online shopping fast, efficient and more convenient.

Although the figures for online transactions in the USA are already impressive, they may be understated since they do not include travel.

Travel is another B2C market that has been revolutionised by the internet. Travel constitutes the largest percentage of online transactions. In 2003 around 35 million Americans bought travel products online, a 17% increase from 2002. Significantly, two-thirds of online consumers report that they are happy to continue to buy travel online (*The Economist*, 2004). Many travellers search for deals online and then book offline. Online travel agents are faced with the challenge of persuading those customers to take the next step to buying online as well as browsing for best deals.

The performance of B2B e-commerce

During the initial phase of e-business development it was the B2C market that gained the most prominence on the back of over-hyped and over-valued dot-com ventures. However, it was in the B2B market where organisations experienced real growth. In the period 1995 to 2000 the number of B2B e-marketplaces increased from zero to almost 2000. More and more firms were attracted to the B2B market as a means of making cost savings on procurement of the inputs they required. Simultaneously, many firms set up as B2B intermediaries providing a wealth of information on websites to smooth transactions between businesses. Online auctions for the B2B market were a particular feature of the growth of this sector. However, the optimism was not to last. Although the dot-com crash of 2000 did not help the cause of the B2B sector there were more fundamental issues that undermined its development.

The failure of B2B e-marketplaces to sustain their growth can be put down to two main factors. First, organisations preferred not to search through numerous tenders from the multitude of suppliers. Instead, most opted to maintain relationships with existing suppliers whom they knew and trusted. Second, organisations did not use B2B infomediaries as facilitators of transactions but opted instead to deal with partners directly using integrated applications systems such as EAI or the extranet.

Some organisations use general online exchanges for procuring supplies. One example of this is Tube Lines, the consortium responsible for maintenance on three London Underground lines. Engineers at the company use e-Bay and other virtual markets to search for parts no longer in production. The parts of the network that the company is responsible for are so old that there are no longer any replacement parts in stock. This has forced managers to think 'laterally' and use whatever means available to procure the parts they need to keep the lines running.

The future of e-business

The internet is now firmly established in the life of most people where connectivity is available. The business community and consumers have been through a learning experience in applying the internet to meet their specific needs. The ability of consumers to access and use the internet has been one of the main reasons for the revival of online shopping in recent years. Likewise, managers have been able to use their internet experiences to learn about the market characteristics in the internet economy, and to build effective business models to take advantage of the opportunities that the burgeoning online market presents.

Different organisations have different levels of use for the internet. Some are internet 'pure plays' who are totally reliant on the internet for their business. Others use the internet as an additional service for their customers. The vast majority of organisations use information technology as a means of improving internal efficiency and communicating with suppliers, partners and customers. The internet, extranet and intranet all play a key role in the internal and external processes of organisations.

In future, managers will continue to find internet applications that bring competitive advantage. To this end the internet helps to extend markets, create new products and broaden sources of revenue. Using past experience and current knowledge it is possible to make value judgements regarding the future impact of the internet on key parts of the economy including:

- The development of new technologies;
- The nature of industry changes;
- The development of new products and services and the demise of others;
- The extension of markets;
- The behaviour of buyers online;
- New business applications of the internet;
- Bridging the digital divide;
- Internal applications;
- Security.

The development of new technologies

The e-business and e-commerce industries are driven by the development and application of technology. The future of e-business will be characterised by competition among organisations centred on the ability to maximise efficiency through the integration of IT infrastructure. Organisations will seek to gain competitive advantage through reducing the complexity of communications whilst simultaneously broadening the range of communications technologies that facilitate business.

The future lies in the development of Internet Protocol (IP) that extends the application of the internet beyond text, e-mail and data to include voice and video communications in real-time. IP is set to transform e-business in the coming years since it takes the IT infrastructure, upon which all e-business depends, to a new level. For example, traditionally, organisations required separate network connections at each of their offices for data, fax, video and conventional phone calls. With IP all forms of communication are handled through one dedicated network and it is accessible from different locations using laptops or mobile phones. The complexity of the system is reduced because, unlike conventional systems, it only requires a contract with one supplier. This reduces costs because the single supplier deals with all access lines, equipment, cabling, installation, management and maintenance requirements.

Cost savings will play a key role in determining competitive advantage among e-businesses in future. To this end the development of high quality, low cost video-conferencing technology will form an increasingly important part of communications within and between businesses. With broadband internet access now widely available, organisations have an opportunity to add visual communications to their portfolio of media. Visual communications complement data and information in the decision-making process. Crucially, video-conferencing can save organisations significant amounts in travel costs as well as facilitating decisions more efficiently. For large organisations with multiple business units scattered around the globe the cost savings from video-conferencing are potentially considerable. Pharmaceutical giant GlaxoSmithKline is one organisation that is already rolling out video-conferencing software to its thousands of workers spread over forty-seven main sites around the globe. Others are sure to follow in the years ahead.

Industry changes

The internet is a disruptive technology that causes rapid change in industries. The impact on the car dealership industry in the UK and the travel industry generally, has already been noted, but other industries have been transformed because of the influence of the internet too. In particular, industries such as media and entertainment, retailing, manufacturing and telecommunications have been subject to radical change because of developments in information technology, digital technology and the internet.

These technological developments present opportunities as well as threats to businesses. In future, industry structures will cluster around those products and services that take advantage of new technologies to clearly add value to customers. Some industries will be in an advantageous position because of the nature of the products or services provided. For example, industries such as banking and games deal in information-based products and services where distribution costs are low and margins high. Other industries will struggle to absorb the challenges posed by new technology.

The music industry is one prime example where the internet, and the illegal downloading of music files, has sent shock waves through the industry. However, despite reeling from the effects of widespread piracy, the industry is staging something of a comeback. In 2004, sales of legally downloaded music reached 5.7 million in the UK compared to practically zero the year before. Globally, digital music sales increased tenfold. The change in fortunes can be put down to the popularity of mobile music players such as the Apple iPod. Over a million songs are now available on legal websites. In the USA legal downloads increased by twenty million in 2004 to 140 million. Where once the music industry was the victim of technological innovation, so technological innovation has been its saviour too.

Traditional industries have also been affected by the development of the internet. Bricks-and-mortar stores have had to deal with the impact of price transparency and the cheaper prices offered on the internet. Many have adapted their strategy to include an online service for customers. In future, it is likely that traditional retailers will find their market share of trade increasingly squeezed by online shoppers. Some retail managers believe that consumers take traditional retailers for granted and that they expect them to always be there. If the growth of online retailing continues at rates witnessed in the first five years of the new millennium then there is a distinct possibility that by 2010 more and more high street retailers will start to disappear. The economics of retailing will make this inevitable because offline shops need to invest in premises and larger numbers of staff.

The future for traditional retailers is most likely to be a mix of online/offline trading. Whilst their core business is likely to remain offline, increasingly, customers will expect an online service too. Some traditional stores have sought partnerships with established online businesses as a way of establishing a foothold in the internet economy.

In April 2005, Marks and Spencer (M&S) announced that they had agreed a deal that would allow Amazon.com to run their website. Amazon.com have the experience to increase the speed, functionality and capacity of the website. M&S are particularly keen to integrate the online service with its stores and telephone ordering system. Amazon.com, for their part, get to extend their technology service provision element of their business.

This case is an example of how industry structures are likely to form in future with many more partnerships, alliances and collaboration taking place between offline and online businesses. There are mutual benefits to be gained from such agreements. The traditional businesses are able to provide customers with an additional channel for communication and transaction using the expertise and experience of an established online business. Meanwhile, the online business gets to extend its activities to technology service provision and management of online services whilst simultaneously increasing the goodwill of their business by forming partnerships with established brand names.

The structure of e-business and e-commerce related industries will continue to be dominated by a few large companies. The winner-takes-all characteristics of the internet economy mean that dominant firms will be able to maintain their position through powerful entry barriers such as market share and access to superior technology and skills. Other, smaller sized firms, will seek competitive advantage in a huge array of niche markets characterised by a large number of competitors with an emphasis on differentiating the products or service.

Intense competition will ensue at the top end of the industry with companies such as Google, e-Bay and Amazon.com joining the likes of AOL as global multimedia enterprises rather than being interested in solely e-business related products and services. For example, in September 2005, e-Bay bought internet phone company Skype for £1.4 billion. Skype's software allows PC users to talk to each other for free and make cut-price calls to mobiles and landlines using voiceover internet protocol (voip). This follows the launch of a talk service offered by rivals Google. For e-Bay and others, investing in communications firms makes sense. E-business and e-commerce are communications-driven industries and e-Bay's acquisition of Skype (leaders in internet voice communications) and PayPal (the leaders in secure payments technology) makes for a powerful synergy of expertise.

Products and services

The internet and other technologies have helped firms create many new products and services and heralded the demise of others. Digital technology, in particular, has radically transformed the media and entertainment industries alongside many others. Organisations with exclusive rights to high value information-based products and services have been particular beneficiaries of the internet revolution. The games industry now challenges the Hollywood film industry in terms of sales and revenue. The convergence of technology means that consumers can buy into products and services via numerous forms of media including the internet, television and mobile phones. Soon, Internet Television will allow viewers to download any number of films or programmes of their choice and view through any digital media. This is likely to spell the end for video shops that rent out films on video-cassettes.

Whilst technology makes obsolete some products, it also heralds the arrival of many new ones. In future, competitive advantage is likely to be gained by organisations who are able to combine a differentiated application of technology that can be marketed on a global scale and delivered at low cost. The media and entertainment industries are well placed to achieve this. They thrive on creativity, knowledge and information, can attract key skills to help innovation, and already have a distribution network in place to sell products and services worldwide. The financial industry is also well placed to take advantage of new communications technologies to extend their markets and co-ordinate their activities around the globe.

The extension of markets

The vast majority of sales of products and services are still made through traditional retail shops. There remains considerable scope for e-business and e-commerce to penetrate into the consumer market. Even though the growth of online shopping has been impressive, there is still some way to go before it fully challenges offline shopping. Much will depend on the future growth patterns for connectivity and broadband access as well as educating consumers as to the benefits of using the internet. Organisations will continue to exploit existing markets as well as seeking new ones. Although use of the internet is increasing year by year there remains a significant number of people for whom the internet is an alien device. Organisations have to be innovative in the way they try to engage with people who are unable or unwilling to access and use the internet.

The future for many businesses will lie in their ability to extend markets. The example of the small business sector illustrates the way forward for e-business to bring previously excluded or marginalised sections of the community into the fold. Large parts of the service sector have traditionally shunned the internet as a means of doing business or even as a means of advertising. Small businesses in the carpentry, plumbing and electrical trades have shown little interest in using the internet for advertising their services, preferring instead traditional means of word-of-mouth or local free sheets or local directories. There are many thousands of similar small business services that remain untouched by what the internet can offer. However, in future Internet Service Providers (ISP's) such as Google and Yahoo!, will provide a form of internet advertising that will bring many thousands of such businesses into the internet community.

In future, ISPs will offer 'pay-per-call' as a development of the existing 'paid search' service. Using the paid search system advertisers bid for the search terms − whether it be life assurance or a travel deal or any other offer − that attract traffic to their website. They pay only for each potential customer who clicks through to their site. This makes the cost of generating sales easily measured. With pay-per-call, ISPs will compile their own searchable directories that list many thousands of telephone numbers of small businesses and charge advertisers only when customers call through to them. This extends the market for ISPs and gives small businesses greater exposure to potential customers without actually having to engage with the technology − a win/win situation for both parties.

E-businesses are not only looking to local and regional markets as a means of expanding their reach. The internet gives access to global markets. Some global markets are already firmly established, such as the USA, Europe and Japan. Others such as India and China represent great potential for those organisations that can adapt their business model to take account of differences in culture, incomes, language and demand conditions.

In China, for example, there were ninety-four million internet users in 2004 with almost half having broadband access. This figure is predicted to grow to 150 million by 2010. Google, the Internet Service Provider, has recognised the potential of the Chinese market by acquiring a licence to operate in the country. This will allow the company to add to the 20% market share in China that it already possesses. Previously, the company had no physical presence in China but with the new licence they were able to set up an office in 2005. The company has also acquired a Chinese web address (www.google.com.cn). Managers at Google expect the investment in China to help them compete more effectively against rivals Sina and Yahoo! and local providers Baidu (www.baidu.com.cn). There is, of course, heavy censorship of websites in China as the government is keen to protect Chinese culture and avoid general dissemination of politically sensitive information. Western companies such as Google and Microsoft have to tread carefully in the Chinese market to maintain the goodwill of the political establishment.

The behaviour of buyers online

Since the commercialisation of the internet in the mid 1990s both business and consumers have been on a steep learning curve. From the consumers' perspective the learning is focused on what the internet can do to bring them the added value. Online consumers can afford to adopt a purely selfish approach to buying online because there is great competition and they are under no pressure from shop assistants to buy. As consumers become ever more adept at using the internet, firms will in future have to pass some stringent tests if they are to compete effectively in the e-business environment.

Online buyers look for ease of access, ease of navigation of websites, low prices and excellent service and delivery. The internet has increased expectations of customers and firms will continue to be pressured into meeting those expectations. Traditional businesses are also affected by changes in consumer behaviour because of the internet. More and more consumers are tapping into price comparison sites to pressure traditional retailers to match the low prices they find online. Increasingly, shops are becoming showrooms where consumers inspect products before buying online where prices are generally lower. The sophistication of consumers in the way they use the internet is only likely to increase in future and both online and traditional businesses have to deal with the consequences of that.

The current trend of traditional businesses moving to develop an online service alongside their core activities will continue into the future and will pose an increasing threat to internet 'pure play' firms. As traditional businesses develop their capabilities and competences in the online trading environment so they will be in a position to leverage a sustained competitive advantage. The mix of 'bricks and clicks' is a model that is proving successful across a number of sectors, especially in food retailing, banking and car dealerships. At the very least, traditional businesses will have to develop a website as a means of re-enforcing their brand and marketing their products and services. Research reveals that consumers prefer to shop online with an established and trusted brand name to allay their fears relating to the security of transactions.

New business applications

Organisations will continue to seek the 'killer application' of the internet that brings them sustained competitive advantage. The number and type of applications of the internet for e-business grows each year but few have brought a defining and sustained competitive advantage. The applications developed by auction site e-Bay and first-movers in the travel industry lastminute.com (www.lastminute.com) stand out as exemplars of e-business. Leading organisations in e-business already know what their customers want and can concentrate on adding value to them by developing the current application of the internet. Most organisations in the internet economy do not enjoy market domination and will continue to seek new ways of applying the internet in their field of business to bring in more and more customers. The e-business environment is, and will remain, a highly competitive arena for the majority of organisations.

One of the problems facing organisations is the market dominance of a few firms who have sustained competitive advantage by being first-movers in applying the internet in a particular industry. The business models of Amazon.com, e-Bay, Tesco.com, lastminute.com and others have been copied by others but the first-mover advantages have ensured continued market dominance for these leading firms. The globalisation of these brands is likely to further consolidate their leading market position in future.

Bridging the digital divide

Although connectivity rates have increased year on year since the rollout of the internet in the mid 1990s, it is clear that a digital divide still persists in many areas. Although the internet is notionally a global phenomenon, there are large swathes of the globe that remain either untouched by or marginalised from the internet. This may be for numerous reasons including political (North Korea); geographical (remote or mountainous regions where infrastructure investment would not be cost-effective); demographics (low population density); or technological (some people do not engage with new technology).

One of the most important signposts for determining the extent of the digital divide has been the availability and take-up of broadband internet access. Taking England and Wales as an example, it is clear that a significant digital divide still exists. According to Point Topic, an internet consultancy, the digital divide in England and Wales has both geographical and social dimensions. In urban areas, such as London, Cardiff, Birmingham and Manchester, broadband is more likely to be available through existing BT phone lines or cable networks. In affluent urban areas around one-third of all households have broadband compared to less than 10% for those in poor urban areas.

The most noticeable divide is between urban and rural. Rural areas lag well behind urban in accessibility to broadband. Because it is not always economically viable to install land-based lines in rural areas, providers need to explore wireless solutions to bridge the digital divide in these areas. There is also a distinct digital divide by age group. Although increasing numbers of 55–65-year-olds are accessing the internet, beyond that age there is very little evidence of significant usage.

Internal applications

The most dynamic changes in the e-business environment centre on developments in technology. The internal efficiency of organisations will become an increasingly important aspect of competition in many industry sectors. The internet and other information technologies can be used to leverage a competitive advantage in many different ways. One of the most important is the ability of firms to communicate instantly with any other interested party. To this end, the future will be shaped by continuing integration of network systems using a range of communications media. Workers will be able to communicate with colleagues, suppliers, partners and customers in many different ways using technologies such as video-conferencing, e-mail, internet telephony, mobile phone and others.

Around a fifth of all workers in the UK spend some time working from locations other than the office (ESRC/Tomorrow Project, 2005). In future, there will be an increasing trend towards 'mobile' workers rather than office-based workers. This trend will have a number of implications. It is likely that the traditional office space occupied by individual workers will be replaced by the 'collective office' where workers 'hot desk' on a number of work stations. The time allocated to work will become more fluid as opposed to the traditional 9–5pm slot. Technology will facilitate greater flexibility in the time for and location of work activities.

However, the boundaries of work and leisure time are likely to become blurred, putting pressure on the work/life balance. The control aspect of working life will also become a topic of debate and will bring forward new rules for working relationships between workers and managers. Technology allows electronic surveillance of workers' activities and is sure to become an industrial relations issue in future.

Technology also helps managers carry out their duties more effectively. Modern data storage and retrieval technologies allow managers to be better informed when making key decisions. Crucially, technology will be able to deliver the types of information required to make decisions quickly so that firms can respond to changes in their competitive environment and meet the needs of customers more effectively. In future, competitive advantage will be determined by the ability of firms to be agile and flexible enough to respond quickly to changing conditions. Successful organisations will be the ones that are able to unify their computer and IT infrastructure to reduce the complexity of communications and create links between offices around the globe using a common system.

The internet will continue to play a pivotal role in the process of integrating systems. Internet Protocol (IP) extends internet capabilities to include mobility, voice and video alongside existing data and text capabilities. This will offer greater opportunities for organisations to improve efficiency in communications and decision-making and enhance their ability to share knowledge. IP will facilitate the transformation of many businesses by increasing the productivity of knowledge workers, increasing the flexibility and agility of organisations, encouraging creativity and innovation, and reducing the costs of doing business. These factors will be key to creating a competitive advantage in many industry sectors.

Security

The issue of security will determine whether or not increasing growth rates for internet use will continue into the future. The infrastructure and market is already in place for organisations or individuals to enter the e-business competitive arena. Customers have shown a willingness to shop online in great numbers, broadband has facilitated quick and efficient access to internet sites, and firms offer every service conceivable to smooth transactions from search engines through to payment systems and delivery services.

Organisations operating in the e-business environment need to apply a value-added service or product and achieve a critical mass of customers to have a viable online venture. Consumer confidence in the internet as a sales channel has increased as consumers learn more about shopping online. However, confidence is ephemeral and any security breach has the effect of damaging hard-won reputations for secure transactions.

Even though, statistically speaking, there is more chance of being mugged on the street than being defrauded over the internet, perceptions count for everything. The big difference is psychological. Victims of internet fraud are highly likely to abandon it as a means of transacting. They may continue to use it for communications, browsing, entertainment and as a source of information, but it is actual transactions that drive the internet economy. Consequently, organisations place a great deal of emphasis on ensuring security. Indeed, some of the modern business applications of the internet require high levels of consumer confidence in security. For example, in future, personalisation services will become more sophisticated allowing e-tailers to recommend particular items based on the depth of knowledge acquired from individual customers.

From 2006 software will be available that facilitates highly personalised services. For example, by offering access to a business diary the software will remind the individual of important dates, what to prepare for meetings, and summaries of previous meetings with the same group or individual. The same type of highly personalised service can be extended to numerous sectors including retailing, banking, health and recreational activities. Of course, the success of these applications of the internet is dependent on a high level of confidence in the ability of the organisation to protect the privacy of the user and guarantee security of information and transactions. Organisations will continue to have to work very hard to stay one step ahead of criminals to maintain sufficiently high levels of consumer confidence that ensure growth for the internet economy.

Predicting the future

Futurologists are people hired by companies to predict the future. This can involve looking at long-term trends in markets, demography, economics, social conditions, technology, education and much more. Futurology requires a very different perspective from normal analytical techniques for determining how the environment is likely to change. Futurology typically has a longer timeframe for prediction. Also, it requires imagination as much as analytical skills.

BT is one of many large-scale companies that has invested in futurology to help the company understand how technology will impact all areas of life well into the twenty-first century. Key areas of investigation include the internet, artificial intelligence, robotics, health, education, business, space exploration, demographics, transport and, of course, telecommunications. The timeline set by BT is to 2051; it is designed to enable organisations to design technology and products with future customers in mind and is reliant on understanding the nature of the environment in which those future customers live.

Previous timeline predictions from the BT futurology lab have been around 90% correct. For example, the futurologists predicted the emergence of spam, text messaging and search engines as early as 1992. The business opportunities stemming from the development of the internet were similarly predicted by BT futurologists well before the commercialisation of the World Wide Web. Figure 12.1 highlights some of the technology-based predictions made by the futurology department at BT.

Conclusion

The internet is now firmly established as a part of most people's lives and this is set to continue as connectivity and interactivity increases year on year. The commercialisation of the internet in the

2006–10	Electronic prescriptions Virtual farming co-operatives Internet attendance at theatres Supercomputer as fast as a human brain Totally automated factories No more movies sold on VHS format Vibration on cellphones to convey emotion
2008–12	Personalised advertising on television Virtual windows Holographic animated advertisements Robots in hospitals Immersive virtual reality shopping booths
2012–15	Full voice interaction with PC Robot gardeners Automatic dialling from smart business cards Computer enhanced dreaming
2016–20	50% of the world's population has internet access Nanotechnology toys Holographic displays for continuous video Robots guide blind people Hotels in space Emotion control devices

Figure 12.1
Predictions of the
BT futurology
department
(2006–20)

mid 1990s unleashed a new and powerful channel of communications, the effects of which have been felt around the globe. The ease of access and lack of regulation surrounding the internet has had profound impacts on many countries, industries, governments and people. While governments wrestle with the social and political implications, the use of the internet has increased greatly each year. New technology, such as broadband, will add to the demand for internet access in the years ahead.

The internet has provided opportunities and challenges to the business community. Some firms that have been first-movers in adopting internet-based business models have enjoyed market domination. For the vast majority of internet 'pure play' organisations, making a profit remains a struggle. This is likely to continue into the future. The dot-com crash of 2000 brought a new realism to the industry and consequently investors are much more cautious when considering e-business plans. Organisations will continue to seek the 'killer application' that brings a distinct added value to customers that rivals cannot match. In many ways it is the traditional businesses that have gained the most from using the internet.

In the first rush of excitement surrounding the commercialisation of the internet the industry was saturated with new entrants as entrepreneurs sought to make quick gains by using the new technology for business and transactions. However, most traditional organisations waited to see how the internet economy was going to develop before committing resources to it. Subsequently, this has proved a wise move, as the traditional businesses gain second-mover advantages by learning from the mistakes of earlier movers. The mix of 'bricks and clicks' is proving to be a successful model for many traditional businesses as they incorporate the best of what the internet can offer with their existing capabilities and core competences.

There are, however, some threats posed to traditional businesses from the development of the internet. As consumers become increasingly sophisticated in their use of the internet so they will use their increasing market knowledge to pressure traditional businesses to match prices offered online. Although not an immediate danger, there may come a point when traditional retailers become merely showrooms for consumers to inspect products before buying online. There is already some evidence of this happening.

Finally, the internet will continue to play a key role in the internal processes of organisations. Competition will feature the ability of firms to respond quickly and efficiently to changes in their internal and external environments. Much will depend on the ability of managers to determine what technology is appropriate to help them achieve their aims. Successful organisations are likely to be the ones that can acquire key workers who harness the capabilities of new technologies effectively. This means using the internet and related technologies to share knowledge, create new products and services, add value to customers and improve internal efficiency.

References

ESRC/Tomorrow Project (2005). *Working in the Twenty-First Century*. ESRC.
Kinnes, S. (2005). Net effect slashes the cost of living. *The Sunday Times*, 23 January, p. 14.
The Economist (2004). A survey of e-commerce, 15 May, p. 17.

Amazon.com

Introduction

In the early 1990s Jeff Bezos was a young computer programmer on Wall Street, the financial district of New York. Intrigued by the development and potential of the internet, Bezos decided to give up his career to explore the business opportunities that this new medium of communication could offer. Setting up in business from his garage in Seattle he decided to set up an online book-selling business. The rationale for this choice was his belief that most people would be prepared to take the risk of online buying for a product such as a book. If the experience proved unfulfilling then they could exit the market and return to traditional forms of buying without too much of a financial loss. Of course, Bezos was determined that the experience of buying online would become a compelling alternative to traditional shopping and he set about developing a service that could offer real added value to customers.

The benefits of using the internet for buying books and other products were identified as:

- Greater selection;
- Convenience;
- Ease of use;
- Information search and retrieval capability;
- Ease of access from multiple locations;
- Competitive pricing;
- Price comparison capability;
- Personalisation.

The key components of Amazon.com's offerings include:

- Browsing;
- Searching;
- Reviews and content;
- Recommendations and personalisation;
- 1-Click technology for fast checkout service;
- Secure credit card payment;
- Availability and fulfilment;
- Interactivity with other customers;
- High level of customer service.

There are a number of web-based activities and services available to customers on Amazon.com's website. Customers can:

- Order books;
- Conduct targeted searches from the database of around five million titles;
- Browse highlighted selections;
- View bestseller lists and other features;
- Read and post reviews;
- Register for personalised services;
- Participate in promotions and check order status;
- Purchase gift certificates.

Bezos was able to use his contacts from the financial world to help attract sufficient investment funds to initiate the business plan and he decided to call his new venture Amazon.com. In the initial phase, Bezos handled customer orders himself but this soon changed as the volume of orders increased. Specialist distributors were hired to deliver books to customers in quick-time. The quality of the delivery service was crucial to the Amazon.com concept of making online buying quick, convenient and cheaper than traditional methods.

Importantly, Amazon.com became the first-mover in the e-tailing sector and was able to build a brand name that quickly became recognised in key markets where connectivity and inter-activity rates were soaring. In 1997 Amazon.com was floated on Nasdaq, the US market for trading shares in high-tech companies. By 1998 the net sales of the company were $540 million compared to $148 million the previous year. However, actual profits remained elusive.

The Amazon.com business model for online bookselling

The initial concept of Amazon.com was to create a virtual bookshop on its website. Bezos believed that this would create a competitive advantage from a number of sources including offering a greater range of titles; greater convenience for customers; 24-hour access; quick and efficient search capability; and a competitive price based on lower transaction costs. One of the key advantages the bookselling industry enjoys is the fact that it is mostly information driven.

Information is the raw material with which publishers produce products in the form of books and booksellers depend on data regarding book genres, design, price, print-run and delivery times. Booksellers use the internet for book search services, ordering and payment, after-sales services and for delivery systems. Information is collected through feedback from authors, customers and a host of book reviewers.

This ever-expanding bank of information creates a network between all the interested parties in the book buying and selling arena. This is in contrast to the linear relationship that has traditionally characterised interaction between the main players in the book publishing industry. Figure CS1.1 illustrates the linear value chain relationship in book publishing. Figure CS1.2 illustrates a publishing and bookselling value network.

Amazon.com is the leading proponent of utilising e-commerce applications in the bookselling arena. The model outlined in Figure CS1.2 forms the basis of the Amazon.com business strategy. A key asset is the ability of the firm to build and enhance relationships across the value chain. Customers, authors, publishers and distributors all contribute to the increasing bank of in-house and market information required to respond to requests from customers.

Customers include those who purchase books, publishers who request market information and book resellers who also rely on

Author → Publisher → Distributor → Bookshop → Reader

Figure CS1.1   Linear value chain in traditional book publishing. Adapted from *Electronic Commerce: Strategies and Models for Business-to-Business Trading* by Paul Timmers (1999) with permission from John Wiley & Sons

Amazon.com services. The former constitutes business-to-consumer (B2C) e-commerce whereas the latter two are business-to-business (B2B) e-commerce. Amazon.com created two groups to specialise in B2B e-commerce: Amazon.com Advantage offers services for publishers and Amazon.com Associates deal with book resellers. The value network permits each party to offer different roles depending on the value functionality offered. Thus, crucially, all functionality is vested with Amazon.com.

Timmers (1999) identified a business configuration emphasising value networks. Four main elements comprise the model and include community building, sales interface, core information management, and core handling and processing. Figure CS1.3 illustrates the functions comprising the business configuration.

Information to authors and customers forms the basis for building up the community within the bookselling process. The sales interface relies on building up a bank of knowledge from each and

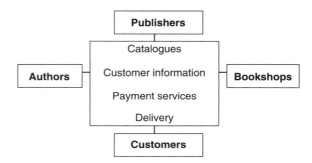

Figure CS1.2   Publishing and bookselling value network. Adapted from *Electronic Commerce: Strategies and Models for Business-to-Business Trading* by Paul Timmers (1999) with permission from John Wiley & Sons

STRATEGY	FUNCTIONALITY
Community building	Author/customer supplied information related to specific books.
Sales interface	Direct customer order intake and the registration of individual shoppers. Indirect via Associates.
Core information management	Building and providing access to book catalogue; building customer database and the value-adding information.
Core handling and processing	Payment processing, shipping and delivery services.

Figure CS1.3 Business configuration strategies and functionality of Amazon.com every sale whether from readers (through Amazon.com) or resellers (through Amazon.com Associates). Core information management builds and provides access to the Amazon.com catalogue of books and is linked to Amazon.com Advantage. The customer database also provides value-adding information. Finally, core handling and processing maintains payment services between the company and its customers whether they be readers, publishers, resellers or authors. This function also covers shipping and delivery administration. From this configuration it is clear that the process of bookselling is much more dynamic than the traditional linear model with each party in the process interacting with greater intensity.

It can be seen that bookselling is only part of the Amazon.com operational strategy. Readers form the core customers in terms of business-to-consumer (B2C) operations but another important strategy is to develop services based on information for publishers and bookstores – business-to-business (B2B). By providing access to information covering a huge range of books worldwide Amazon.com have built a catalogue which publishers and bookstores value.

The low cost and ease of access make it an attractive online system for practitioners across the industry. With each click on the system Amazon.com increases its bank of knowledge and extends its customer reach. Also, with each successive 'click of interest' the brand name of Amazon.com becomes ever more ubiquitous. Each site has local characteristics, including language, thereby allowing Amazon.com to claim to be a truly global phenomenon, not just in terms of customer reach, but also culturally.

The growth of the Associates aspect of the business has been without precedent in the publishing world. In September 1997 Amazon.com had 15 000 bookselling associates (Timmers, 1999). By September 1998 this figure had risen to 150 000. Indeed, most of the figures relating to Amazon.com. are spectacular, such as the 135.2% revenue growth rate in the year to the end of 1999 and the $720 million loss registered over the same period. The market value of the company saw a decline to $12 billion in 2000 from a $23 billion peak in 1998. Results in the first quarter of 2000 showed signs of improvement as losses declined to $308 million. This was as a result of the company increasing its focus on efficiency and financial prudence in order to allay the worst fears of investors and to counteract the increasing competitive forces in the market for online bookselling.

First-mover advantages

Amazon.com's first-mover advantages have enabled the company to amass a huge market value. Barnes and Hunt (2001) assign much of the value to perceptions of Amazon.com being not just a bookseller but also a mechanism for selling a variety of goods. One of the most valuable assets possessed by Amazon.com is the computer software developed to enhance customer benefits through database management. The core competence of the firm lies in the added-value service to customers that the software provides and that the highly skilled Amazon.com workforce exploit. A crucial first-mover advantage enjoyed by Amazon.com is the development of network externalities.

The internet is an ideal medium for creating increasing benefits for increasing numbers of customers joining the network. As customers are not charged for these benefits they are termed 'network externalities'. Amazon.com is among many e-commerce firms who have developed business models around the concept of creating virtual communities, internet auctions, value chain integrators and a host of other applications. The more the community grows the greater the attraction of joining because information service continues to rise but the cost to users is static.

Amazon.com, through its monopoly status between 1995 and 1997, was able to develop a large and loyal customer base that later entrants had to overcome in order to compete effectively. The computer software technology was (and remains) the key to sustaining competitive advantage in the face of increasing rivalry in the online bookselling industry. Amazon.com has gone to great lengths, including litigation, to protect the firm's development of software technology against imitators.

Branding and building customer loyalty are other important first-mover related advantages for Amazon.com. Their reputation based on service is vital for effecting customer loyalty. This is especially cogent to Amazon.com since their 'product' is essentially an experience good − that is, the quality is unknown until used (technically, Amazon.com could be deemed a logistics company under the Hypertext Markup Language (HTML) code rather than a bookseller).

The company has based its strategy around brand recognition and superior service such that customers are reluctant to switch to rivals even if the cost of doing so is zero. Indeed, the issue of switching costs are themselves a source of first-mover advantage.

New entrants have to contend with the knowledge that customers are already familiar with the *modus operandi* of the first-mover's website. However, in the case of online book buying there are many more potential customers than actual ones and, therefore, the competitive advantage enjoyed by Amazon.com is likely to be diluted as new entrants vigorously pursue old and new customers alike. Again, this makes competitive advantage through being the first-mover difficult to sustain.

Amazon.com experienced exponential growth in sales and stock value through exploiting first-mover advantages and monopoly status between 1995 and 1997. However, as noted, the Amazon.com business model attracted imitators. Even though most books continue to be sold through traditional retail methods, the potential of the online market was sufficient to attract big name booksellers such as Barnes & Noble, Borders and, latterly, Waterstones. Many of the business models and website designs of new entrants closely resemble those developed by Amazon.com.

Partnerships

Corporate partnerships are an important element of the Amazon.com strategy. The company has formed alliances with portals (internet search engines) and Internet Service Providers (ISPs). These offer access to heavily trafficked websites that play a crucial role in directing customers to the Amazon.com website, thereby increasing the company's brand awareness and market share. These alliances form critical elements of the company's strategy for achieving growth quickly.

There are mutual benefits that derive from such alliances. The high profile of Amazon.com offers 'corporate' sponsors such as the *Star Wars* franchise, the opportunity to gain exposure from the website. A sample list of some of Amazon.com's partners illustrates the breadth of interests the company has:

> AOL (Internet Service Provider)
> Adobe (Internet graphics)
> Back to basics (toy catalogue)
> Della.com (online wedding registry)
> drugstore.com (health, beauty and prescription drugs)
> exchange.com (rare products)

eZiba.com (world crafts)

Gear.com (designer sportswear)

Greenlight.com (online car sales)

HomeGrocer.com (home delivery service for groceries)

Internet Movie Database (movie and entertainment information)

Kozmo.com (one-hour delivery service for entertainment and convenience products)

Motley Fool (online brokerage of financial products)

Magellan Internet Guide

Netfind (Internet search)

Pets.com (pet supply shop)

sothebys.Amazon.com (auctions).

Expansion of services

Throughout the history of Amazon.com the strategy has been consistent – to grow quickly. This has entailed expanding the types of services offered to customers either through innovation of existing capabilities or through acquisitions. The expansion of the product portfolio was a natural progression from online bookselling and included videos, CDs, gifts, toys, healthcare products, gardening tools, electronics and digital products among many others.

Amazon.com have also acquired internet companies that brought specific capabilities that Bezos felt could not be developed internally. Exchange.com (www.exchange.com) ran a bibliographical database of around ten million hard-to-find and rare books. It also had lists of thousands of independent dealers and retailers. Amazon.com also acquired Alexa Internet (www.alexainternet.com), a company that specialised in compiling Web navigation software. A third acquisition was of Accept.com (www.Accept.com) an Internet start-up company run by former Netscape employees that specialised in developing technology for online transactions.

A further acquisition was of the Internet Movie Database (a partner company of Amazon.com) which emphasised the synergies that Bezos was looking for in his acquisition strategy. The Internet Movie Database had a very popular website featuring movie and entertainment information and had links to Amazon.com for every related book, movie or CD. Amazon.com also opened a shopping site called 'Shop the Web' that is designed to link shoppers with websites of products that Amazon.com do not sell, such as clothing.

Another venture involved entering into competition with e-Bay by setting up the auction site Amazon.comAuctions.

The expansion was not all about acquiring other internet-based firms though. Amazon.com ventured into the 'bricks-and-mortar' world by investing in warehouses to stock their books and other products ready for delivery. This added greatly to overhead costs but was deemed necessary in order to have some controlling hand on the distribution element of the business and to meet its promises in terms of order fulfilment. The company has also expanded geographically with the launch of several international websites sporting the Amazon.com brand including in the United Kingdom (www.amazon.uk) and Germany (www.amazon.de). These sites share the customer database of the parent company but are located in their respective countries and sell mostly titles indigenous to those countries.

Amazon.com has also extended its service to providing a platform for other firms who seek to exploit the popularity of the Amazon.com website. For a fee, Amazon.com allows other companies to use their website as a channel for selling their products to customers. Many traditional bricks-and-mortar retailers, such as Toys R Us, use the Amazon.com site for this purpose, as do many thousands of small-scale businesses.

This development has marked a shift in the business model of Amazon.com from one entirely geared towards products and services within the company's portfolio to one that incorporates a service for helping customers find what they want. This shift can be viewed as a strategy for competing with e-Bay in the market for bringing buyers and sellers together. To this end, Amazon.com have rolled out a Yellow Pages service that offers enhanced business listings, including digitally enhanced maps for locating businesses. The service also offers a call-up capability where customers can phone a business simply by clicking a button on the screen.

Expanding sources of income

Apart from the revenue gained from providing an e-tailing service to customers, Amazon.com also receives income in other ways. One method involves providing online advertising space on the website. Amazon.com provides space for banner advertisements that other organisations wish to place to promote their products or services. Amazon.com also acts as an affiliate site for other web-based organisations. This is where traffic can be diverted to other sites via the Amazon.com web pages.

Amazon.com also gains additional income from so-called 'co-op money'. Publishers have traditionally given 'co-op money' to retail bookshops for prominent display sites in the shop or for advertising titles. In print advertising this is deemed a 'co-operative' venture since the bookshop and the publisher share the cost of the advertisement since both are being advertised simultaneously. Amazon.com, as a virtual bookshop, receives 'co-op money' from publishers for high visibility on the website. Publishers also have their titles placed in prominent book reviews on the website. Some critics have argued that this practice is unethical because it blurs the line between the editorial function and advertising. Nevertheless, these 'paid for placement' titles provide a lucrative extra source of income for Amazon.com.

The crisis years 2000–2

The growth of e-commerce has been one of the great business stories of the late twentieth century. At the forefront of this phenomenon has been Amazon.com. With its leader Jeff Bezos at the helm providing energy and vision the company built it's e-tailing around bookselling and then other areas such as music and video. Key to its initial success was the ability to win customers and maintain their loyalty. Investors rushed to pump money into the venture and Amazon.com's share price rocketed in 1998. With a clear strategy and business plan formulated it appeared that the prospects for Amazon.com could only get brighter. However, three years on from its stock market flotation Amazon.com was in crisis. On June 23, 2000 analysts Lehman Brothers reported that Amazon.com would run out of money within a year. Debts had built up significantly since 1997 and yet there remained no sign of profit.

Alongside many other dot-com firms, Amazon.com found investors bailing out in early 2000, thereby cutting the share price by some 20%. By 2001 the Amazon.com share price had fallen to $11 from a peak of $110 two years previously. New internet companies had soaked up investment capital like a sponge based on little more than potential future profits.

The success of Amazon.com was built on its knowledge and expertise in online bookselling. Essentially, this was the core business – both B2B and B2C. The initial business strategy did not include ventures into other areas of retailing. After a series of acquisitions and partnerships Amazon.com entered other markets. Fuelled by deficit spending Amazon.com drifted from the core activity of bookselling where they had garnered much goodwill. By diversifying into other areas of e-tailing the company diluted the effect customer loyalty played in attaining investment credibility. The expectation that the company would be self-sustaining by the time the market corrected proved to be erroneous.

During the late 1990s e-commerce was still an evolving way of doing business and the savings it could bring to organisations had yet to translate into profits. For instance, the delivery of goods after an internet sale remained sluggish in the first few years after the rollout of the internet for commercial purposes. Also, maintaining inventory and warehousing meant Amazon.com incurred high costs in order to guarantee availability of goods. This problem was exacerbated by spreading the portfolio of goods ever more widely. The business model formulated by Amazon.com was heavily dependent on the e-commerce aspect of operations and the benefits that lower transactions costs would bring. The dynamic value network incorporating authors, publishers, bookshops and customers relied on the internet for the dissemination of information between the various players.

To compound the problems facing Amazon.com during this period the company faced increasing competition from rivals, particularly in the B2B element of their service as other leading booksellers built online systems for customers within the book trade. In October 2000, Amazon.com suffered the demise of the alliance with Internet Service Provider (ISP) Yahoo! To make matters worse Yahoo! then formed an alliance with Amazon.com's biggest rival, Barnes & Noble. More worryingly Amazon.com also briefly lost their market share leadership to Borders Bookshops (who later became a partner of Amazon.com) in 2001.

The competitive advantage that Amazon.com had built up since 1995 was being eroded by its main competitors Barnes & Noble and Borders Bookshops. One of the important features of competitors' strategies was the convergence of the retailing and online businesses. Barnes & Noble and Borders set up strategic links between the traditional methods of bookselling and the new one in the form of the internet. Barnes & Noble set up hundreds of internet counters in their retail shops, broadening the choice for customers in terms of purchase arrangements, delivery and collection. Borders fared well principally because of its focus on the sort of detail that customers want. Order totals were posted to customers before any credit card details were requested and they had a comprehensive and up-to-date list of book stocks.

Other competitive pressures came from publishers and booksellers who maintained and built upon their own in-house catalogues. In terms of distribution Amazon.com had to operate in a highly competitive world market for shipping and transportation of products. During the first five years of Amazon.com's existence distribution was not one of the company's core strengths.

There were also human resource issues that Amazon.com had to contend with that threatened to undermine the company's reputation. Despite the fact that the company was at the leading edge of 'new economy' business, the majority of the jobs performed by workers were distinctly 'old economy' in nature. Most work involved handling customer service calls and packing in warehouses. Many Amazon.com workers were part-time or temporary staff working long shifts. There was no recognised trade union in Amazon.com as Jeff Bezos argued that every worker had some part ownership of Amazon.com. The rationale for this position stemmed from the fact that Amazon.com workers were given the option of buying stocks in the company after completing a set period of working tenure. However, since the share values of dot-com firms had collapsed in 2000, this option became less attractive and the demands for trade union recognition grew among the workforce.

The key human resource issue facing Amazon.com is one that affects many firms in the new economy – the gulf between workers and management in the transformed business environment. Workers generally want job security and stability, whereas managers need to embrace change and establish a flexible organisation that can change quickly according to the vagaries of the market. Maintaining worker satisfaction in this environment is a challenge that few new economy firms have succeeded in meeting.

Turnaround 2003–5

The Amazon.com strategy for creating competitive advantage is now well established and has remained consistent since its inception in 1995. Jeff Bezos had a guiding principle that the internet was all about swapping real estate for technology and that the former almost always gets more expensive as time goes by whereas the latter gets cheaper (remember Moore's Law).

To leverage the greatest competitive advantage from utilising new technology in the form of the internet, Bezos always maintained that Amazon.com had to grow as big as possible as quickly as possible. The way he achieved this is based on: the first-mover advantages that built brand loyalty and captured the major slice of market share; the strengthening of the Amazon.com brand name to become a globally recognised business; and the development of new products and services through innovation and partnerships with other organisations.

The competitive advantage has been sustained through repeat purchases by customers who are loyal to the Amazon.com brand either through perceived added value or 'lock-in'. This has provided a formidable barrier to entry in favour of Amazon.com. Another source of competitive advantage for the company has been through developing proprietary technologies that facilitate a range of activities and functions such as website management, search capabilities, interactivity with customers, transaction-processing, distribution logistics and payments.

After the dot-com crash of 2000 Amazon.com had to ensure maximum efficiency to prevent debt spiralling out of control, whilst continuing the expansion of products, services and markets. Key aims were identified as reducing the burden of debt, lowering costs and increasing efficiency whilst continuing to expand the product line and entry into international markets.

Reduce debt, lower costs and increase efficiency

By 2001 Amazon.com had amassed debts of over $2 billion. To address this burden the company bosses embarked on a relentless cost-cutting exercise right across the business. This was designed to link into improving efficiency as well as helping to reduce costs. The main focus for increasing efficiency lay in the warehousing and distribution functions within Amazon.com. The company had invested in a sophisticated distribution system that ensured targets for delivery times were met. However, the system was complex and expensive to run. Amazon.com's senior vice president, Jeff Wilkie, set about the task of reducing Amazon.com's fulfilment costs. One method adopted was the use of Six Sigma DMAIC (define, measure, analyse, improve and control) reviews to identify sources of inefficiency. This led to Amazon.com's operations team being able to effect improvements in the accuracy of inventory records. The reputation of Amazon.com depends on meeting its delivery promises and this means knowing exactly what there is on the shelves of every warehouse and distribution centre at any given time.

Another efficiency improvement featured changes to the way the work of temporary employees was checked. Traditionally, when temporary workers were hired to stock items in the distribution centres there was no additional layer of verification to ensure that each item was placed in the proper place. This was the catalyst for introducing a new fulfilment auditing process to reduce the number of mistakes by temporary workers.

Continued expansion

Amazon.com has expanded into product and market sectors other than books. Product development is a key strategic direction for the company as it seeks to use innovation and technology to maintain its position as market leader in online trading. The company now has online websites for products as diverse as health products and garden implements. Amazon.com has also undertaken expansion geographically with investment in new ventures in Europe and Japan. The company seeks growth through acquisition of, and alliances with, internet and entertainment related firms.

Amazon.com has had to face a number of difficulties as a result of adopting strategies of low cost, growth, and expanding the product and service range. There have been labour relations problems relating to long hours and low pay that have resulted in the increasing desire for unionisation among the Amazon.com workforce around the world. There have also been some cultural problems associated with the Amazon.com expansion into other markets, most notably in France where Jeff Bezos made the *faux pas* of criticising the 'art' of comic writing not realising that this art form is afforded high cultural status in France. However, in terms of expanding the Amazon.com e-tailing concept it is clear that the new range of products sold on the internet has become as successful as bookselling. The Amazon.com brand is primarily recognised as an online bookseller but the expansion into products such as toys, health products and garden tools has gained in prominence and now represents important elements of the company's product portfolio.

The generic strategy of Amazon.com

The generic strategy of Amazon.com can be identified as 'differentiation'. This is a deliberate strategy and not 'stuck in the middle' as Porter would caution. Internet firms have to differentiate in order to raise the profile of their website against the myriad rivals in an over-crowded market. As first-movers in the e-commerce bookselling market, Amazon.com created a distinct brand image. Since 1995 their main rivals have been playing catch up in this regard. Amazon.com also differentiates the service provided to customers by using market share to create online communities whose members can share information and ideas on shared interests.

The software that Amazon.com applies to its operations is another important differentiator. This facilitates quicker and more efficient services for customers; makes navigation of the website easier; smoothes the process of ordering, transactions and distribution; and helps build knowledge on customers through database management and customer relationship management (CRM). The relationship that Amazon.com has with its millions of customers is the key differentiator that sustains the company's competitive advantage. The Amazon.com site extends beyond business-to-consumer information on purchasing but also includes a well-established consumer-to-business aspect including hundreds of millions of customer ratings and product reviews that form the basis of its all-important recommendations to buy.

Amazon.com has also pursued opportunities for reducing costs by taking advantage of low transaction costs. Low transaction costs are a feature of trading on the internet and Amazon.com have been able to pursue the possibilities that this presents in terms of providing the most competitive service at minimal cost. Cost reductions and efficiency savings have also been gained using software applications to automate and control functions such as order processing, warehousing, logistics and distribution.

The guiding principle: Get Big Quick!

The guiding principle behind the Amazon.com strategy has consistently been to 'get big quick'. During the crisis years Jeff Bezos came under pressure to slow the rate of expansion the company had embarked upon. Investors were nervous of the spiralling costs of adding ever more product ranges to the portfolio, the costs of warehousing, and the expansion into new markets such as Canada and Japan. However, by 2005 Amazon.com was reporting a strong financial turnaround that vindicated the Bezos approach.

Since 2002 Amazon.com has been able to reduce debt, improve cash flow and report small profits. The improved cash flow is important because it means that Amazon.com can more easily manage its debts. This is likely to ensure long-term survival for the company. Perhaps the most important figures are the ones that highlight the increasing popularity of Amazon.com year on year. Amazon.com had 14 million customers in 1999, 20 million customers in 2000, 25 million in 2001, and so on. By 2005 the company had almost 50 million active online customers worldwide. Sales have grown from $148 in 1997 to £8 billion in 2005.

The main assets of Amazon.com

As first-movers in bookselling e-commerce Amazon.com have built a world-class brand name, differentiated and highly recognised across a number of important territories including the USA, Europe and Japan. This creates competitive advantage because of the customer loyalty it brings. Once engaged in the Amazon.com virtual community few customers switch to rival online booksellers.

Information is the product that Amazon.com sells. It has more data on books, authors, reviews and prices than any other online bookseller. It has a customer base of 10 million worldwide all of whom add to the bank of knowledge for Amazon.com. The information acts as a magnet to those in the book trade who rely on it for gaining valuable insights into what customers want and what they are buying. This creates competitive advantage in business-to-business (B2B) trade and provides Amazon.com with the opportunity for cost leadership in the market for services to other sectors of the book trade.

The high profile of Amazon.com attracts specialist internet firms who seek to form partnerships and bring expertise and economies of scale through marketing, management and technology. Each area of expertise creates its own sphere of influence in creating competitive advantage. Partnerships are mutually beneficial for the companies involved and form an important aspect of the Amazon.com strategy. Finally, the drive, energy and vision of founder Jeff Bezos is a key asset to Amazon.com. The brand name is synonymous with the management ethos, particularly in the USA. This creates competitive advantage for Amazon.com through the positive association in the minds of customers.

The future

The future aims of Amazon.com are to continue expansion of products and services through innovation and applying new technology; to continue to expand into new markets and become a truly global competitor; to reduce the burden of debt in the medium term (next five years); and to continue to be market leaders in online bookselling as well as consolidating their position in the range of new online products. Amazon.com intend to maintain growth levels through acquisitions and alliances, continue to add value for customers, and achieve the status of price leaders in the market whilst maintaining high quality.

A number of strategic options are available to Amazon.com to achieve their objectives in terms of products, markets and finance.

- Products/services – maintain existing services and develop new ones through innovation and use of technology;
- Markets – Amazon.com have the strategic option of pursuing globalisation through their world-class brand name. They can also target specialist markets where the use of the internet is of clear added value to customers. This stems from the added value for customers and the cost reductions for Amazon.com. To remain as market leader the company must continue to differentiate its services in its target markets and take a pro-active approach to developing applications through the use of technology. As the company expands its operations around the globe it is an increasing imperative that decentralisation of management takes place. To maintain customer loyalty the Amazon.com service has to be culturally specific and relevant to the needs of each market.
- Finance – it is of great importance that Amazon.com continues to reduce debt. This may entail increasing share issues to raise finance or seeking further investment funds. The company must balance the cost

savings in terms of offering competitive prices for customers with the need to effect expansion within a controlled budget whilst reducing debt.

References

Barnes, S. and Hunt, B. (2001). *E-commerce and V-business: Business Models for Global Success*. Butterworth-Heinemann: Oxford.

Timmers, P. H. A. (1999). *Electronic Commerce: Strategies and Models for Business-to-Business Trading*. John Wiley: Chichester.

Further reading

Bayer, C. (2002). The Last Laugh: His Plan for Amazon.com is Really Working. *Business 2.0*. Business 2.0 Media: San Francisco, CA., September, pp. 86–96.

Choi, S. Y., Stahl, D. O. and Whinston, A. B. (1997). *The Economics of Electronic Commerce*. Macmillan Technical Publishing: Indianapolis.

Hof, R. D. (1998). A new chapter for Amazon.com. *Business Week*, Vol. 3591, pp. 39–41.

Saunders, R. (1999). *Business the Amazon.com way: secrets of the world's most astonishing Web business*. Capstone: Washington.

Stockport, G. J. and Street, D. (2000). *Amazon.com: from start-up to the new millennium*. European Case Clearing House, No. 300–014–1.

e-Bay

Introduction

Pierre Omidyar is the son of French-Iranian parents who arrived in America in the early 1970s to pursue academic careers. Omidyar was a student at Tufts University near Boston where he spent much of his time exercising his passion for Apple programming. A move to Silicon Valley, the nerve centre for US technology development, was a natural progression for the self-confessed computer nerd. In 1991, Omidyar founded his first business called 'Ink Development Corporation' specialising in producing software for pen-based computers. Although the market was not ready for the pen-based computing idea a spin off from the Ink Development venture showed more promise.

The software tools that Omidyar and partners developed facilitated online commerce. The company was turned into a retailer of electronics called 'e-Shop'. Although retaining his share of the business, by 1994 he had left to work in developer-relations for General Magic, a mobile-communications start-up company. In 1996 Microsoft bought out e-Shop making Omidyar a millionaire before he turned thirty.

It was during his stay at General Magic that Omidyar created 'AuctionWeb', the first tentative steps towards creating an online marketplace. He had an ambition to create the perfect market and believed the internet was the ideal mechanism for making this happen. His timing coincided with the first wave of excitement created by the commercialisation of the internet in the mid 1990s. Many academics, entrepreneurs and technologists spent a great deal of time and energy thinking up the 'killer application' that would harness the power of the new medium for communication to create an entirely new and lucrative business. This period saw the emergence of Amazon.com (online bookselling) and Webvan (groceries) as early-movers in the e-commerce environment. Many others quickly followed, some survived, many did not.

Omidyar decided that his application would be based on the auction model where people could come together electronically to reach an agreed price for a transaction. Since the venture remained a hobby rather than his livelihood he decided to offer the service free. The initial program that Omidyar wrote allowed users to do only three things – list items, view items and place bids. It was during this period that he gained proprietorship for his web-based consultancy and freelance technology work and called it 'Echo Bay Technology Group'. However, when it came to registering the name he discovered that EchoBay.com was a domain name owned by a Canadian mining company. He decided on the abridged version called e-Bay.com and an internet legend was born (Cohen, 2002).

The AuctionWeb site was one of several that ran on the e-Bay home page but it took some time for it to register even a few clicks of interest due to the lack of publicity afforded it. The only advertising it received was on Usenet newsgroups that listed new websites. However, by the end of the summer of 1995 the first trickle of interest emerged with an eclectic mix of goods appearing for auction on the site. These included computers, posters, toys, underwear and a host of items that could generically be called 'bric-a-brac'. The trickle grew into a steady flow and the value of items began to widen in range from a few cents through to thousands of dollars.

Importantly, AuctionWeb was gaining in prominence through that tried and tested marketing technique – word-of-mouth. By the end of 1995 the site had attracted more than 10 000 bids. What turned AuctionWeb from a hobby into a business was the site's Internet Service Provider deciding to charge a fee for access based on commercial rates. The approach Omidyar took to covering the charge was to introduce final-value fees. This would be a percentage of the agreed sale price. The charging of fees did not seriously harm the business as Omidyar had feared and soon the cheques started to arrive on his doorstep. In the first month of charging fees the website earned more than the ISP charge, thereby making it almost unique in internet start-up history by registering a profit right from the first month of trading.

From early 1996 onwards the popularity of the AuctionWeb site continued to grow. Omidyar knew he had a viable business but believed that the auction-based model would eventually be imitated by larger companies, such as AOL. His long-term view was that the core business would swing more towards the licensing of software. However, the auction site continued to grow.

Previously, Omidyar had recruited entrepreneur Jeff Skoll to manage the strategy, but as the business grew out of all proportion to expectations they decided to seek advice and funding from Benchmark, a venture capital company run by Bruce Dunlevie and Bob Kagle. Initially, the two prevaricated on backing Omidyar but two factors brought them round.

First, the idea of bringing people together to haggle over a transaction was the purest form of entrepreneurship. Second, and more importantly, though, was the sheer numbers of people that were being attracted to the site. In the first few months of 1997, traffic on AuctionWeb was so heavy that it gained the nickname the Great e-Bay Flood. From gaining a quarter of a million hits in the whole of 1996, AuctionWeb was attracting over one million hits in a single two-week period in January 1997. The Benchmark team were persuaded to invest $5 million for a 21.5% share of the business. The investment is now worth over $4 billion.

One of the measures taken by Omidyar after seeking the advice of Dunlevie and Kagle was to maintain the consistency of the brand by dropping AuctionWeb in favour of the now world-recognised name of 'e-Bay'. The company is now the most widely recognised and most successful internet business in the world. E-Bay operates in thirty-two international markets, has 135 million registered members who buy or sell goods worth $1050 every second from over 34 million items listed. The company has a turnover of $34 billion per annum, 95% of which is generated from small businesses or individuals. Although the site attracts some notable big money transactions and is used by leading corporations, such as Vodaphone and IBM as a way of disposing of excess stock, the majority of transactions are for less than $50 thereby making e-Bay a classic example of a long-tail business (see Chapter 4).

The mission of e-Bay

The mission of e-Bay is a statement of intent that reflects the philosophy of founder Pierre Omidyar in creating the perfect market. Trust lies at the heart of the e-Bay concept and much depends on the goodwill and honesty of the 'community' of buyers and sellers. Omidyar believes that creating a transparent, open and free market will drive away the relatively few traders who exploit the system dishonestly. One means of doing so is the creation of the feedback forum where users can offer opinions on all aspects of the e-Bay trading experience. Using the forum, users can rate the experience of buying or selling with another trader. Ratings are simply defined as positive, negative or neutral with a space for additional comments. The feedback is available to all who access the website. Essentially, the traders self police the website by bestowing credibility on honest traders and exposing the dishonest ones.

How it works

The e-Bay system of online auctions is simple, effective and capable of generating huge sums of money for the company. It also provides a cheap and easy way for users to make money on items they no longer want or to access products they seek. The e-Bay site also provides a facility for many different kinds of businesses to sell their products. The e-Bay auction site works by bringing buyers and sellers together electronically to effect transactions. Sellers place an item on the e-Bay list and set a reserve or fixed price for the product. Interested buyers then bid for the product and the highest bid is accepted. Buyers pay the price of the item as well as delivery charges.

Traditionally, sellers provide credit card details so that e-Bay can charge a fee for listing their product. However, since 2005 e-Bay has made participation easier by allowing conventional banking arrangements. Nevertheless, the majority of fees are gathered via credit cards. In the UK, fees range from 15p for items under £1, to £2 for items over £100.

There are extra charges for sellers who wish to update or upgrade their product listing. For example, a listing on the home page costs £49.95 (2005 rates). Setting a reserve price is a further 2% of the price chosen. Extra fees are then payable when the item sells. Sellers determine the length of their auction and the postage costs. Reserve prices are given to ensure that the seller makes at least enough to cover the listing costs. Some sellers will place an item on a fixed cost basis to secure a quick sale.

The electronic payment system used by e-Bay is PayPal (a company specialising in secure payments encryption acquired by e-Bay) and there is a further charge of up to 3.5% for that. If an item fails to sell it can be listed again for free. When it finally sells, e-Bay charges a final value fee of 5.25% of the first £30, plus 3.25% for products up to the value of £600 and 1.75% of any remaining value.

Very often it makes economic sense for sellers to set high postage costs. From the total income gained from the sale of an item a seller pays for overheads, the cost of the item and fees to e-Bay. By setting a high postal charge sellers can set a *de facto* reserve price. It also helps sellers avoid e-Bay charges since these relate to the start price, the sale price and on the reserve price (if the seller sets one). No charge is set on postal costs. For example, if an item is sold for £10 but the postage is set at £100 the seller only incurs charges for the £10. As for buyers, they need to ensure that they are paying a realistic price for any item they intend to purchase regardless of how the costs pan out. The principle of *caveat emptor* is as valid in cyberspace as it is in the real world.

e-Bay in the USA

There are some staggering statistics relating to the phenomenon that is e-Bay. In 2005, the company had 150 million registered users worldwide, 60 million of whom are termed 'active users' in that they have bid for an item within the previous twelve months. Wherever there is internet connectivity there is sure to be buying and selling activity taking place using the e-Bay website.

However, it is the US market that is the powerhouse driving the 'e-Bay economy'. The company accounts for around 25% of all e-commerce sales in the US and around half a million Americans make their living by trading on the company's website (*The Economist*, 2005). There is a vast array of goods traded on the e-Bay site, but the US market is distinctive for a number of reasons. For example, no other country has used cars as the most valuable category, or has as many fixed prices as a proportion of all items listed (30%). Fixed prices have given a boost to several markets including sales of clothes and accessories.

Perhaps the most striking feature of e-Bay in the USA is the relationship the company has with the thousands of traders that rely on the site for their livelihood. For professional traders the e-Bay website is not simply a platform for having fun trying to sell an unwanted toy or family heirloom, but is the trading floor for their business. When e-Bay increased fees in 2005 there was a great deal of protest from professional traders. The rationale for the increase was to balance the market and introduce clearer differentiation between standard listings and optional features that users pay extra for.

The disquiet over fees and the lack of effective dialogue between traders and e-Bay management has seen some disgruntled sellers seeking other sites. Although this represents a trickle not a haemorrhage, the company is sensitive to users' changes in trading habits. This is especially true when monitoring the share price and the operating profits. Whilst e-Bay broke through the $1 billion profit barrier in 2005, the rate of growth of the business showed the first signs of slowing by the third quarter of 2004.

Figure CS2.1 illustrates the share price of e-Bay since 1998 and Figure CS2.2 illustrates the profits made by the company over the same period.

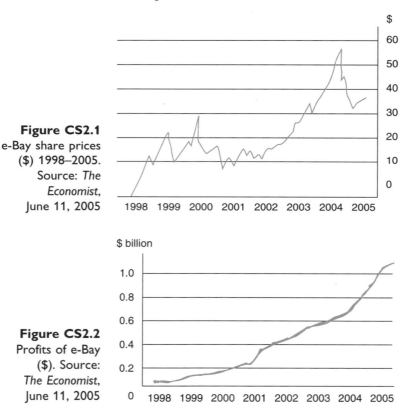

Figure CS2.1 e-Bay share prices ($) 1998–2005. Source: *The Economist*, June 11, 2005

Figure CS2.2 Profits of e-Bay ($). Source: *The Economist*, June 11, 2005

e-Bay in the UK

The phenomenal growth of e-Bay in the United States has been mirrored in the UK. The website has around 10 million registered members in the UK and is achieving growth rates of 160% per annum.

The site continues to attract thousands of new users every month. The UK now represents the third biggest market for e-Bay behind the US and Germany.

Perhaps the most striking statistic is that about a third of all UK internet users access the e-Bay website each month (Rowan, 2005). Most are either buyers or sellers and a significant number access the e-Bay chat room to discuss their experience of using the site or to swap stories relating to particular transactions and other related issues. However, for around 10 000 people in the UK the e-Bay website is their livelihood. Most use e-Bay as their 'shop window' to sell products, others advertise their services and a growing number have transformed their hobby into a business by providing advice or selling products and services relating to their particular interest.

Managers at e-Bay in the UK believe that there is much more growth to come in future. There is, for example, a huge market for second-hand cars, office equipment and industrial components. To leverage maximum advantage from these and other markets e-Bay has made it easier for businesses to use its site by facilitating conventional banking arrangements and personalising customer service.

Expansion of markets and services

The popularity of e-Bay has grown steadily around the globe since its inception in 1995. However, in the face of increasing competition from Yahoo! and Amazon.com, both of whom have set up auction sites to rival e-Bay, the company has had to expand globally to maintain its level of growth and to broaden the customer base.

The website is well established in Europe, with Germans leading the way with 12% of all time spent on the internet being dedicated to browsing or using the e-Bay website. Expanding into the German market was achieved by acquiring Alando.de, a German version of e-Bay that had been building an impressive customer base since its inception in 1999. In the first two months of trading the company achieved around a quarter of a million items sold and registered 50 000 users. The growth of the business attracted e-Bay executives and in 2000 Alando.de was absorbed into e-Bay, albeit with a distinctly German culture remaining in tact.

Other areas of expansion include Australia, where e-Bay launched in 1999 and leads the market, Canada and South Korea. However, the internationalisation of e-Bay has not been all plain sailing.

The venture into the Japanese market proved painful as rivals Yahoo! stole a march on them by setting up an auction site five months earlier than e-Bay and attracting around two million listings compared to a paltry two thousand for e-Bay. The company failed to understand the distinct cultural factors that characterise the Japanese market. For example, sticking to company policy by charging fees was a mistake since the Yahoo! site was free. Also, customers could only pay by credit card on e-Bay, but few Japanese own a credit card. The combination of these factors led e-Bay to withdraw from Japan in 2002.

In future, e-Bay is set to expand into the lucrative Chinese market. Chief Executive, Meg Whitman, sees China as becoming e-Bay's biggest market by 2015. The company has committed $100 million to promote the business in China for five years from 2005. Although rates of growth have eased in the USA, the company expects new markets in Asia to make up the difference with some to spare.

The company is already investing in the skills and expertise required to make the e-Bay experience culturally and socially relevant to users in different parts of the globe. This means thinking through service provision more carefully. The old adage of 'think global, act local' still has a resonance with companies seeking a foothold in countries such as China, Malaysia and Japan.

The expansion of services has been one of the key elements of the e-Bay strategy. The company has developed new services such as business listings and 'pay-per-click' advertising services as well as acquiring other companies that can add to the service portfolio. Acquisitions of companies such as payments specialists 'PayPal' and shopping comparison site 'Shopping.com' have extended the services to users, and brought benefits from the synergy of specialist activities and the core activity of e-Bay that is bringing people together for trading purposes.

Security

Security is often viewed as the achilles heel of the internet. In the United States in 2003/4, reported consumer losses due to fraud amounted to $200 million, half of which involved online auctions (*The Economist*, 2005). Companies are also victims of fraud and other types of security breaches, although the true cost is unknown due to the reluctance of organisations to reveal the extent of the problem. As noted earlier, the e-Bay concept is based on a high degree of trust between buyers and sellers. Whilst the vast majority of transactions are legitimate and generate high satisfaction ratings, the system is open to abuse by criminals and others with malicious intent. The company employs nearly 1000 people around the globe whose job is to police the website and identify any suspicious or damaging activity by users.

Incidents of fraudulent behaviour on the website are bad news for e-Bay since they inevitably undermine consumers' confidence in the system. The ease of access and use of the internet has attracted rogue elements. A judge in the UK criticised the e-Bay website for being an 'open shop for fraud' after presiding in a case that involved a woman selling non-existent tickets for the Glastonbury music festival to unsuspecting buyers. Sellers too can be victims of fraud. Computer hackers can steal someone else's identity, put in a winning bid and receive goods before the scam is detected. In such instances, e-Bay, through their payments arm PayPal, will only compensate losses up to £105.

One of the most common forms of fraud is so-called 'phishing' where victims are duped into visiting bogus sites and divulging private information (passwords, credit card details, etc.) after receiving fake e-mails. To combat 'phishing' e-Bay has launched 'My Messages', a private messaging service. 'My Messages' is a read-only inbox for subscribers logged into the e-Bay website. This ensures that any messages subscribers receive in their own inboxes purporting to be from e-Bay are fakes.

Critics point out that if such private e-mail services proliferate then the convenience of using e-mail will be diminished as users have to access messages via numerous commercial sites (Young, 2005). Others suggest that it may attract 'phishers' to the e-Bay site. The use of 'Tojans', software that tracks keystrokes, is increasingly used for 'phishing' expeditions by fraudsters and the private inboxes provided by e-Bay could be a target.

In some instances buyers can be duped into paying more for items than they retail in shops. Although this does not constitute fraud, it is against the spirit and ethos of the unwritten rules of trading on e-Bay. The items that feature mostly in this sort of unscrupulous activity are CDs, computers and mobile phones. Often dealers will put in spurious bids to initiate a price hike for an item.

To protect the reputation of the business, e-Bay has had to take measures to minimise the number of items listed that are either illegal (guns and other deadly weapons, controlled drugs, terrorist manuals) or immoral (certain types of pornography). In 1999, a seller listed one of his kidneys as an item for sale with a reserve price of $25 000. The bidding reached $5.7 million before e-Bay removed the listing and declared it a hoax. It also violated both company policy and federal law relating to the sale of body parts in the US.

In the UK, the e-Bay UK site has taken action to end the auction of a semi-automatic CZ75 pistol. However, the Association of Chief Police Officers (ACPO) has issued warnings that increasing numbers of weapons are appearing on the e-Bay site in the UK. The problem facing e-Bay is the sheer volume of listed items that appear at any given time. Items such as guns are likely to only appear for a 24-hour period before being snapped up by criminals. This makes detection and eradication difficult for e-Bay.

There are measures that users of e-Bay can take to protect themselves from being victims of fraudulent activity. These include:

- Check out the seller or buyer through feedback from other users;
- Do not bid too high since sellers can get agents to bid on items to artificially raise the price;
- Establish whether or not the item bid for is insured;
- Find out where the trader is based;
- Do not pay by money transfer services, pay by credit card or via PayPal accounts.

Occasionally, e-Bay is confronted by ethical questions relating to trading practices. One such example was the auctioning of Live8 tickets on the website by people who were lucky enough to have obtained a ticket through the lottery system operated by the organisers of the highly popular musical event. Although the sellers were doing nothing illegal, the practice called into question the ethical issue of gaining monetary reward for a cause intended to highlight poverty in Africa. Managers at e-bay came under pressure from the event organisers, most notably Sir Bob Geldof, to ban the auctioning of Live8 tickets on the website.

Although most people would agree that such a practice is morally reprehensible, it does highlight the dilemma facing e-Bay. Their mission is to bring people together for trading purposes in a spirit of free market enterprise. As noted previously, illegal or immoral trading is actively discouraged by e-Bay. The dilemma is where to draw the line between trading items for monetary gain where there is an ethical dimension to the transaction. Some would argue that in a truly free market environment it should be left to the conscience of the trading partners to determine whether or not the transaction takes place. However, in the case of the Live8 tickets, e-Bay stepped in to ban their auction on the website. Critics argued that the company had compromised their free market ethos to escape the negative publicity surrounding the issue.

Tax

The high profile of internet firms such as Google, Yahoo! and e-Bay has attracted the attention of the tax authorities. Online auctions are of particular interest because of the large amount of undeclared income that the websites generate for sellers. In the UK the tax authority is the Inland Revenue (IR). Although a strategy for dealing with tax evasion from goods sold online has yet to be established, the authority is looking at ways of tightening the gap in the law pertaining to online sales.

In the first instance, the IR has been engaged in discussions with e-Bay to develop educational programmes for users of their website so that they become aware of their tax obligations. Agreement has been reached regarding the placement of links on e-Bay to relevant pages dealing with tax on goods sold online on the web pages of the IR. The UK government is also seeking ways of making the tax system fairer and is committed to tackling tax evasion both offline and online.

The thousands of people who use e-Bay as a trading platform have tax obligations since anyone who buys goods with the intention of selling them on (trading) will be liable to pay tax on any profits made. However, users of e-Bay or any other auction website who sell unwanted items online are not liable to pay tax unless the profits generated exceed £6000.

The future

While it is difficult to predict the future shape of the industry that e-Bay inhabits with any certainty it seems clear that the big players in the internet arena, such as Amazon.com, Yahoo!, Google and AOL, will follow a similar strategy to e-Bay by expanding internationally (especially in China) and in the number of differentiated services they provide. It is likely that sometime in the next decade e-Bay will evolve into a portal for servicing a wide range of demands from a huge and diverse customer base. Being first to market with new, innovative and differentiated services that clearly add value to customers will determine who the winners and losers are in the fiercely competitive internet environment.

Each of the internet heavyweights has its own strengths and weaknesses but e-Bay has the sheer numbers of loyal users who generate vast sums in repeat business as their main competitive advantage. The company is a truly global business phenomenon and continues to rack up more and more users as each month passes. Although the rate of growth may slow, the economies of scale in servicing such a huge customer base mean the company is well placed to dominate for years to come.

Key issues:

Main strengths of e-Bay:

- First-mover advantages in online auction market;
- Global brand awareness;
- Network externalities created by developing a community of buyers and sellers;
- Brand loyalty of buyers and sellers because of quality of service;
- Economies of scale from huge customer base;
- Profitable from first month of trading;
- Acquisition of specialist firms to create synergy and provide value-adding and differentiated services;
- Conservative management style.

Main weaknesses:

- Managing expansion into key markets such as Japan;
- Communications with professional traders who are reliant on the e-Bay website;
- Understanding cultural differences in foreign markets.

Main opportunities:

- Expanding services;

▨ Expanding internationally, especially in the growth markets of China and India;

▨ Forming alliances with other firms to manage expansion.

Main threats:

▨ Security breaches and fraud;

▨ Intensity of competition;

▨ Pressure to meet expectations of shareholders, stakeholders and customers;

▨ Pressure to maintain growth rates;

▨ Pressure to maintain profit levels;

▨ Retaining key management personnel.

References

Cohen, A. (2002). *The Perfect Store: Inside e-Bay*. Piatkus: London.

Rowan, D. (2005). The Cult of e-Bay. *The Sunday Times Magazine*, 20 February, pp. 42–9.

The Economist (2005). Special report: e-Bay. 11 June, pp. 71–4.

Young, D. (2005). Protect your achilles heel. *The Guardian: Inside IT*, 13 January, p. 15.

Tesco.com

Supermarket giant Tesco was founded in the aftermath of the First World War in 1918. Jack Cohen used his army discharge money to set up a grocery stall in the East End of London. The first Tesco store opened in 1929 and a UK retailing institution was born. Throughout the rest of the twentieth century Tesco continued to grow, with the number of stores opening increasing year on year.

The philosophy of Tesco was to sell a wide range of quality products at reasonable prices. There was an added convenience factor for consumers by ensuring that a Tesco store was located within easy reach of the majority of customers. Stores were opened in many urban and suburban areas throughout the UK. The company proved profitable because of the economies of scale associated with buying in bulk and selling at high volume. This also meant that costs were kept low. By the early 1970s Tesco was a major presence on the UK retailing landscape and maintained the philosophy of selling basic groceries at low prices. Indeed, the knighted Sir Jack Cohen recognised this overriding philosophy by naming his autobiography *Pile It High, Sell It Cheap.*

The 1980s saw Tesco continue to grow and expand its products and services. Greater emphasis was placed on the physical environment of the stores and the management of Tesco sought out knowledge on the psychology of shopping from experts around the globe. The non-food element of the business took on more importance as the company sought to bolster the brand image and build on the already significant brand loyalty it enjoyed. The strategy of becoming as strong in the non-food sector as it was in the food sector was one of the key aims of the company into the 1990s. Alongside expansion internationally, the way Tesco sought to improve services to customers was identified as providing financial services and information and delivery services via the internet.

Tesco benefited from having a customer-focus to its operations. This was evident in a number of different ways. The 'One in Front' initiative was designed to ensure that queues of customers did not exceed two at any checkout. Although it cost the company many millions of pounds to implement, the plan worked since customers appreciated the quick and efficient service provided. Tesco was also a first-mover in providing loyalty cards in the UK. Launched in 1995, the loyalty cards rewarded customers for shopping with Tesco. By 2000 there were nearly ten million Tesco Clubcard members throughout the UK. The company has built on its success and has been Britain's biggest retailer since the mid 1990s.

In 2005 Tesco broke through the 30% market share in the grocery market for the first time. The company was also the first UK retailer to register profits of more than £2 billion. This is hardly surprising given that for every £8 spent by UK consumers, £1 will be spent in Tesco. Part of the reason for the success of Tesco has been the ability of the managers at the company to determine exactly what their customers want and provide it quickly, efficiently, conveniently and at low cost. The company has been able to draw customers away from rivals whilst consolidating their grip on the loyalty of their existing customers.

Tesco has been able to use the value of the brand to enter the financial services market successfully. Where rivals have struggled to make much impression against traditional financial services retailers, Tesco has used the brand effectively to offer a range of services such as savings accounts, travel and motor insurance, and loan facilities. There has also been an internet mortgage-finder service. A partnership agreement with the Royal Bank of Scotland ensured that customers received a quality service that they could trust. However, one of the most risk-bearing and adventurous initiatives adopted by Tesco was to be first-movers in the online grocery delivery sector in the UK.

Tesco online services

In 1995 Tesco began offering online services based on customers making orders from their local Tesco store using the internet. The company also launched their own Internet Service Provider (ISP), Tesco.net, as a means of linking the online delivery service with internet access facilities. This provided customers with a greater choice of ISP. Since the existing stores, warehouses and distribution networks were already in place, the initial investment for the online service was relatively small. The company spent around £25 million getting the online service up and running throughout the UK.

The Tesco.com online service is simple and convenient for consumers who are willing to pay extra for having their groceries collected and delivered to their door. Orders are taken and processed online and the information sent to the nearest store to the consumer. Tesco stores have a number of staff known as 'pickers' who gather together the items on each list sent online. The groceries are then assembled at a delivery point and distributed to households within a given area during a given timeslot. Tesco gives approximate times within the timeframe for delivery so that consumers can ensure that someone is home to collect the goods when they arrive. Most payments are undertaken online too. Crucially, each Tesco store could update information on prices, what items were available and their sell-by date. Where items are unavailable the 'pickers' will include a close substitute.

Everyday grocery items such as bread, fruit, vegetables and milk are the most popular items bought online, but Tesco.com also report a healthy online demand for non-food items such as CDs, videos, electrical goods and books. The convenience factor is the biggest driving force behind the demand for online delivery. The company has developed sophisticated software to help manage the collection and delivery of the goods to customers.

There are also a number of marketing benefits associated with developing the online service. The information derived from the database of customers helps Tesco determine what products are in high demand; what products require specific types of marketing and promotion; and when, and for how long, customers interact online and what they want. The information derived from this database also provides Tesco with feedback on satisfaction rates and responses of customers to new offers or products. The bank of information helps Tesco to hone their online strategy and deliver an added-value service to customers by responding to what they want.

The online service helps the company to form more intense relationships with customers through offering a more personalised service. For example, the company has collaborated with software developers to tailor web promotions of products that individual customers habitually buy. It also advertises complementary products or related products to those habitually bought by individual customers. Customers perceive an added value to the personalised characteristics of the advertising campaign. This is much more effective than generic advertising because customers are more responsive to promotions that interest them.

By 2001 Tesco.com had one million registered customers making it the biggest online grocery service in the world. Although profits from the venture remained elusive for the first few years of its operation there were a number of other advantages the service brought that would serve Tesco well in future. The marketing benefits were already becoming clear by the late 1990s.

The online service helped to broaden the appeal of the brand to new customers, especially younger customers. The first-mover advantages meant that Tesco had a head start in the learning process of operating an online service compared to its rivals. There were links between the online and offline service provided by the company, such as the extension of the Clubcard loyalty scheme and access to discounts. The Clubcard loyalty scheme was relaunched to reflect different levels of spending by customers. Customers were allocated either gold, silver or bronze status according to their spending habits. This is available to online as well as offline shoppers.

By 2005, Tesco.com was available to 98% of the UK population through the distribution network working from over 350 stores. No other UK supermarket could compete with the service provided by Tesco. Indeed, such is the company's dominance of the UK supermarket sector that there have been some calls for government to step in and limit their continued expansion. In particular, small-scale grocery retailers have complained that Tesco have squeezed them out of the marketplace.

Competition

Tesco were the first-movers into the online grocery services in the UK. The company has built up a significant lead over other supermarkets and retailers and used the brand effectively to attract new customers. The company claim that around a third of their online customers have never shopped at Tesco before (MyWebGrocer.com). If this is the case, then the online service has been able to attract a new kind of shopper – one that is more likely to use the internet for many of life's transactions and services.

Among the closest rivals to Tesco, both ASDA and Sainsbury's have online services. Initially, ASDA rolled out a service based on giving

CD-ROMs to customers that could be used to order from a select number of items. ASDA would update the CD-ROM periodically with changes to prices and products available, as well as information on special offers and promotional campaigns. However, the system proved cumbersome and unpopular with customers.

In 2001 the company rolled out their internet-based order system called ASDA@home. Although the online service proved more flexible and effective than the CD-ROM initiative, the service was only available in a very limited number of locations. ASDA did not have anything like the number of stores around the country that Tesco had and this limited their ability to distribute groceries in key locations. However, where the service was available ASDA offered a free delivery for orders exceeding £99, something Tesco had not considered.

Sainsbury's is the nearest rivals to Tesco but was slow to develop an online service. It was only after former Prudential boss Sir Peter Davis took over that the company took the online service seriously and backed it with significant investment. Sir Peter saw the benefits of the internet after successfully implementing an online strategy for delivery of financial products in the insurance industry.

Although the company is still playing catch up with Tesco for market share of online services, giant strides have been made. The company can now service over 70% of the UK for online delivery services. Also, like Tesco, the company has been able to extend the reach of the brand using the internet. In particular, the 2004 marketing campaign focusing on price cuts across a range of products was a central feature of the promotional campaigns used on the website. The online service is likely to become an increasingly important channel for Sainsbury's in its pursuit of market share in the highly competitive supermarket industry.

Pricing policy of Tesco.com

The pricing policies of firms selling products and services via the internet has attracted the interest of various bodies including, in the UK, the Office of Fair Trading (OFT) and, in the EU, the European Commission. The OFT has been active in investigating some of the UK's biggest supermarkets following allegations of overcharging. Both Tesco and Sainsbury's have been accused of charging higher prices than are advertised on their websites; charging for a premium product and supplying a regular product; charging more for online products than those in-store; and using websites to offload food close to its sell-by date (Winnett and Leppard, 2004). The OFT is also investigating the high number of customers who have reported deliveries falling short of those ordered.

Many of the problems stem from the website content of supermarkets. Consumers believe that the information on websites relating to prices and availability of goods is a definitive account. Although Tesco could benefit from introducing dynamic pricing for its products sold online the company has yet to adopt this strategy. The websites offer only a 'guide' to prices and availability. The websites are not 'real-time' and very often do not provide up-to-date information on prices and availability. Where ordered products are unavailable, the supermarkets will deliver 'an appropriate substitute'. Just how 'appropriate' is often a bone of contention between supermarkets and customers.

Another regular complaint centres on the delivery slots available. Typically, Tesco makes twelve deliveries per van during each 4-hour shift (Finch, 2001). There are particular slots during the day when demand for deliveries is high. It is not always possible for Tesco to deliver to everyone in the slots they want. Customers may have to wait until later slots, even into the night, before receiving their deliveries.

Tesco has to weigh up the difference between investment in more vans and distribution costs with the prices charged and the level of demand. Nevertheless, if customers are unable to gain deliveries of their groceries when they want then, from their perspective, the convenience and speed of the online service has failed. This may have a detrimental effect on customer loyalty, although Tesco reports high levels of customer satisfaction overall. Online shopping is becoming an increasingly important aspect of the company's activities. However, there is a gap between consumers' expectations and fulfilment that needs to be addressed.

Effective use of the internet by Tesco

Tesco uses Information and Communications Technology (ICT) to help manage its operations. In particular, its extranet has been an invaluable tool in managing relationships and operations with its suppliers. Traditionally, supermarkets have restricted the type of information they give out to manufacturers and suppliers for operational reasons. Since the development of the extranet, however, the benefits of sharing knowledge have become apparent to companies such as Tesco. Crucially, the extranet allows Tesco control over who has access to the information.

Efficient Consumer Response (ECR) is a technique that encourages information exchange between retailers and manufacturers and is the basis for co-operation between the two parties for mutual benefit. The key areas of operations that ECR is designed to improve include store assortment, re-stocking, marketing and promotion, and new product introductions.

In 1998, Tesco developed their own system called 'Tesco Information Exchange' (TIE) and linked it with half a dozen of their suppliers. TIE allows the sharing of information on Electronic Point of Sale (EPOS) data, stock movements, the introduction of new products and the latest marketing campaigns. The system also features directory services of stores, key personnel and general in-house news. However, the system for information sharing incurs a cost that has to be covered. The system is run by a third-party company and suppliers have to pay a fee for access to the information. The fee is dependent on the volume of business the supplier has with Tesco.

Tesco has built up a huge database of information on the socio-economic profile of customers and their spending habits. The company employs data analysts to search for trends or pinpoint opportunities that underpin supply chain management and the marketing effort.

So-called 'data mining' is a technique geared towards searching for correlations that offer valuable insights into customer behaviour. This, in turn, helps inform the buying and marketing strategies of Tesco. Each market segment will be subjected to data mining and analysis to determine the trends in buying behaviour. For example, through analysis of data, Tesco discovered that those people who shop online are more likely to buy financial products from the company than offline shoppers. This led to an increase in the marketing effort for their portfolio of financial services offered to online customers.

Tesco has also been actively engaged in developing artificial neural networks. This technology is designed to let computers solve problems by recognising trends in data. The technology takes over some of the roles previously played by humans in identifying trends. Artificial neural networks are programmed to recognise previously recognised trends and to adapt responses according to those trends.

The 'learning' from previous problems and solutions is an in-built capability of the computer and allows it to offer new solutions to new problems. The capability of the computers to detect trends from a vast amount of data far outstrips human capability. This not only increases the bank of relevant knowledge that the company has, but also provides that knowledge much more quickly and efficiently.

Furthermore, the system can be tailored to focus on all buyers, groups of buyers or even individual buyers. Tesco has used artificial neural networks to discern patterns of buying behaviour across a wide range of different products in different regions by different socio-economic groups. For example, the system was able to highlight differences in tastes of crisp buyers across different regions of the UK. This helped inform managers of stock requirements for particular flavours of crisps and led to reductions in excess capacity and better use of shelf space for those particular products.

Information technology and the internet also help Tesco develop pricing strategies. The data gathered on customers helps the company to understand buying habits and tailor supply accordingly. The information is crucial for linking pricing to particular target markets and helps to underpin the competitive position the company seeks to adopt in the marketplace.

The information gathered also extends to distribution and manufacturing costs. These costs are linked to levels of consumers' demand for particular products to determine a pricing strategy that creates a suitable margin of profit for the business. Analysts are also employed to track responses to price changes. Again, technology can help in identifying changes in demand in response to changes in price. An elasticity curve for price changes graphically represents the responses of customers to changes in price and managers can respond appropriately to the changes in buying behaviour. Importantly, the information allows the company to set optimal prices for each individual product sold to maximise margins and profits.

The data gathered by Tesco on consumers' buying habits not only informs them of past consumer behaviour but also provides the basis for making accurate forecasts of future buying behaviour. Most humans are creatures of habit and it is possible to identify fairly accurately what people will buy on each visit to the shop. Shopping habits rarely change and can be identified accurately over a period of time. This again helps Tesco in supply chain management, marketing and promotion, shelf-space capacity, the store layout and a host of other factors that determine efficient store management.

Tesco also operates an effective intranet for employees and management. The intranet provides a communications channel for any Tesco staff member to access to put forward suggestions or comments regarding any aspect of work within the company. The intranet provides an ideal channel for management to communicate ideas and directives to staff and to explain the rationale for changes in the management of stores. The intranet supplements face-to-face communication between management and staff and reinforces important messages. The intranet also hosts a wide range of in-house news featuring job vacancies, performance reviews, promotional campaigns, customer feedback, management changes, work regulations, health and hygiene issues and many others.

The internet has played a role in determining where Tesco locates its stores. Geographic Information Systems (GIS) provide 'intelligent maps' of locations including information on road networks and the location of rival stores (O'Connor and Galvin, 2001). From this information Tesco has been able to make decisions on the precise location of their stores. Factors that are taken into account include the drive time from the main residential areas surrounding the proposed site, the population density and the performance profile of the local economy.

Tesco has an agreement with Ordnance Survey for the provision of digital maps of areas designated as possible sites for locating stores. Information on road driving conditions and times on particular routes are provided by the Department of Transport. The census is a useful source of information on population density and socio-economic profiles in particular regions. Research by Tesco has revealed that most people do not want to drive for more than fifteen minutes to a supermarket. The company has also determined the minimum population density required to justify investing in a new site location.

Summary

Tesco was one of the first supermarkets in the world to take advantage of the internet to add another channel of communication and trade with customers. The first-mover advantages gained by the company in providing online services have enabled Tesco to gain and sustain a competitive advantage in online services. The initial costs of setting up the online service were relatively low because Tesco already had the network infrastructure in place to help them meet stringent distribution and delivery targets.

The internet and related technologies have also been used effectively in helping the company better understand its customers. The huge amount of information on the shopping habits of customers has proved invaluable to Tesco when managing their supply chain and designing marketing and promotional campaigns. Analysis of buying trends reveals likely demand conditions for each product, which helps save costs by maximising use of shelf space and optimising capacity in stores. Meanwhile, the use of the company extranet helps to manage relationships with a wide range of different suppliers. Internally, the company intranet provides a useful means of communication between all employees and management at Tesco stores.

Technology has played a key role in helping Tesco become the UK's biggest and most successful supermarket. The company enjoys a significant lead in market share and this is reflected in the year on year increases in profits reported by the company. ICT and the internet have enabled Tesco to:

- Better understand its customers;
- Manage demand and supply conditions effectively;
- Save on costs;
- Create better target marketing and promotion campaigns;
- Deliver quality service;
- Underpin overall strategy, including the location of stores throughout the country.

The combination of all these advantages has enabled Tesco to build a huge brand loyalty among large numbers of customers and this has been translated into a sustained competitive advantage over rivals.

References

Finch, J. (2001). Tesco's share of UK market rises above 30%. *The Guardian*, 14 July, p. 21.

O'Connor, J. and Galvin, E. (2001). *Marketing in the Digital Age*. Prentice-Hall: Harlow.

Winnett, R. and Leppart, D. (2004). Sold out by the online stores, *The Sunday Times*, 12 December, p. 14.

Yahoo!

One of the common characteristics of internet pioneers is the high level of intelligence they possess. Pierre Omidyar of e-Bay, Marc Andreeson and Jim Clark who developed Mosaic and Tim Berners Lee, the developer of the World Wide Web, are all academic achievers. The internet has attracted some of the best intellectual minds across the globe, with the epicentre of the technological revolution being Silicon Valley in California.

The inventors of search engine Yahoo! fitted into this profile perfectly. Jerry Yang and David Filo were two Stanford University PhD students who amused themselves by building lists of web addresses in-between writing their theses. Their hobby grew into a multi-billion dollar global business. However, like their counterpart Pierre Omidyar of e-Bay, Yang and Filo did not develop their internet idea for entrepreneurial purposes. Each had an obsessive interest in computers and was motivated solely by what the technology could achieve. It was only when their ideas took form and phenomenal growth in demand followed that they considered the business opportunities.

Yang and Filo were very different personalities but complemented each other perfectly. The outgoing gregarious Yang was the human face of Yahoo! while Filo was the technology guru. Between them they organised their database of websites into 19 different categories including business, arts, computing, economics, education, and so on. There was a hierarchy of websites afforded to each category to ease the process of searching. This was significant because it would later form the basis of delivering advertising revenue from firms seeking exposure on the list, but also because it provided the basis for the brand name.

Yahoo! is an acronym for Yet Another Hierarchical Officious Oracle. The exclamation mark was added to further distinguish the brand. The Yahoo! site offers users quick and easy access to many millions of websites by creating links to different categories. Keyword software provides the first link and then each click on a heading leads to pages of related links around the subject matter. Crucially, the search behaviour of users could be logged and used as a basis for income generation. Information on where users had come from across different links and where they wanted to go was the basis for building an advertising revenue model. The information also allows the company to determine what is popular and most used. This acts as a guide to creating content.

The Yahoo! search engine was launched in 1993 and generated a few clicks of interest. However, by early the following year the clicks could be measured in thousands. By the end of 1994 Yahoo! had created thousands of web links and gained some 80 000 hits per day. It was during this initial growth period that Yahoo! received an important endorsement from industry pioneers Netscape. Netscape introduced a beta browser and decided to link the directory facility on its corporate website to Yahoo! This had the immediate effect of hugely increasing demand for the Yahoo! search engine. The company was registering around one million hits a day, enough to convince Yang and Filo that they had the makings of a significant business. The acquisitive overtures made by industry giants AOL among others merely served to confirm this.

The rise of Yahoo!

By 1995 Yahoo! was the search directory of choice for millions of internet users. The numbers all added up to a significant sized business. Yang and Filo sought venture capital to take the company to a level where they could compete effectively with established media companies such as Walt Disney and AOL. Ex-Motorola CEO Tim Koogle was appointed Chief Executive Officer and, after successful flotations by rivals such as Lycos and Excite, Yahoo! had an Initial Public Offering (IPO) on the NASDAQ (US technologies stock exchange) in April 1996. Demand for stocks immediately soared and the first day's trading saw their value increase by 150%. This meant that Yahoo! was valued at a staggering $850 million with Yang and Filo each worth $150 million.

The principle that access to the Yahoo! directory would be free survived the new management regime. However, this put added pressure on the need to gain revenue by other means, most notably through online advertising. In the frenzied atmosphere of the late 1990s few investors, entrepreneurs or internet pioneers gave much thought to the long-term implications of relying on the vagaries of the traditional advertising market, let alone the untested and untried online advertising market.

The high valuations placed on internet companies was partly due to the marketing effort put in to persuade investors of the benefits of online advertising. These included being able to better target specific groups of buyers through monitoring website traffic, personalisation of the marketing effort, cheap dissemination of messages, and building relationships with customers. The business model would be built around the number of internet users who 'click through' to access information on products and services after seeing a banner advertisement on a web page. The initial success of many internet companies including Yahoo! was based on the confidence of investors that increasing amounts of revenue could be generated through this business model.

The value and reputation of Yahoo! rose throughout the late 1990s as more and more investment funds poured into the internet economy. The company sought to expand its services and signed deals with key partners to facilitate this. The most important ones included a deal with Hewlett Packard for MyYahoo! to feature as the start page on all new HP Pavillion PCs from January 1999. This was quickly followed by a similar deal with IBM.

With revenues high, earnings per share rising and investor confidence booming, Yahoo! was one of the world's most successful internet firms. Buoyed by the success of the business, CEO Tim Koogle set about expanding the Yahoo! business through acquisition. The first target was GeoCities, a provider of personal homepages. The site was the third most trafficked site on the internet in 1998 and attracted around 20 million unique visitors. Koogle believed that the combined power of the GeoCities and Yahoo! would give access to around 60% of American homes and attract advertisers like no other in the internet economy. The acquisition of Broadcast.com, an online audio and visual service provider, underlined the company's determination to be seen as a global media company and not just a portal.

Although there were some signs that the internet economy was over-inflating and that some investors were expressing concerns (Japanese company, Softbank, the largest backer of Yahoo! sold three million shares to stave off losses for 1999), the management of Yahoo! remained confident in their advertising business model. By 1999 the company had amassed over 3000 regular advertisers. Many firms saw value in having their brand related to a globally recognised portal. Drugstore.com, for example, became partners with Yahoo! in order to guarantee advertising banner space for their healthcare products. Other firms followed this line of reasoning too and Yahoo! did not need to try too hard to attract advertisers during this golden period of the internet economy.

The new millennium started with the stock valuation of Yahoo! reaching a new peak of $237.50 giving a market capitalisation of $128 billion. Yahoo! was firmly established as one of the world's foremost media companies and one that had made a profit of almost $50 million for 1999. The firm was continuing to attract more and more unique monthly users (120 000 by December 1999 – double that of the previous year) and attracted around 3500 advertisers. Yahoo! was also beginning to penetrate international markets with around 13% of users being from outside the USA. However, despite the promising figures, all was not well in the internet economy and some of the deficiencies in the business models that underpinned the existence of dot-coms were beginning to unravel by early 2000.

The fall of Yahoo!

The online advertising model described above had some merits but the reality was very different from its potential. The 'click through' rates recorded never reached anywhere near expectations and there was growing evidence that internet users found banner advertising obtrusive and off-putting. The low level of interest in online advertising expressed by internet users made this form of advertising more expensive than traditional media such as newspaper advertisements and radio and television commercials. Nevertheless, confidence in this new media remained buoyant throughout the late 1990s. There was simply too much investment pumped into the industry to let it all deflate, so investors stayed true to a failing business model.

Everyone connected to the internet industry had a vested interest in its success and this economic fact served to prolong the mood of confidence even in the face of indisputable evidence that pointed to the industry being grossly overvalued and overhyped. For example, online publishing company EarthWeb had registered a loss of over $5 million in the first quarter of 1998. However, that economic fact did not deter investors from snapping up the company's stock when its IPO was announced. The stock valuation of the company rose by 250% in the first day of trading.

The IPO of online community TheGlobe.com was even more spectacular in its meteoric rise. Despite registering losses of $11.5 million by the third quarter of 1998, the company's share price rocketed from $9 to a peak of $97 before closing the first day at $63.50 – a rise of 600%. The market for internet stocks had spiralled out of control and was ripe for a 'South Sea Bubble' collapse.

The portents of doom were evident early in 2000. In February, many of the most trafficked websites, including Yahoo! and Amazon.com, were shut down for hours due to a series of 'denial-of-service' attacks. Surprisingly, Yahoo! had no back-up system to cope with what was a well-documented threat. Although the immediate effects of the attacks were manageable, the episode served to highlight the vulnerability of websites to determined attack. A fifteen-year-old Canadian boy was eventually convicted of the attack.

By early summer 2000 investors had clearly lost patience with the promises of profits from the internet economy. The figures relating to Yahoo! illustrate the change in mood. Even though the company continued to register increasing revenues, added more users to its portfolio and became the internet's number one portal, the stock price continued to slide. Investors were now only interested in the bottom line. Most worryingly, not only had the number of new advertisers slowed, but in the first quarter of 2000 the number had actually dropped by around two hundred. The first cracks in the design of the business model were beginning to emerge. The demise of prominent dot-coms such as boo.com, Pets.com and Living.com added to the sense of unease in the industry.

To bolster investor confidence and re-invigorate the business, Yahoo! undertook a management transformation and with it a fundamental change in philosophy. Henceforth, it was decided that Yahoo! would charge a fee for services. This was a high-risk strategy for the company because internet users were used to gaining access to content for free and with switching costs low the company risked losing brand loyalty. However, the move to charging fees was deemed necessary because the decline in banner advertisement 'click-through' rates by users was beginning to turn advertisers away from the internet.

The first sign that the internet economy was in serious trouble came in the form of a damaging articles appearing in weekly investment newspapers (Angel, 2002). For the first time financial journalists were writing about when the internet bubble would burst rather than if it would burst. This had the effect of concentrating minds on an issue that had been avoided – that the internet economy could not sustain the large number of firms that populated it and that very soon an industry shake-out would occur. The only way firms could survive was to be bought out by a larger more secure organisation, merge with a partner or find additional funding.

By mid April 2000 the selling of technology stocks on the NASDAQ was gaining momentum and no company was immune. Yahoo!, Amazon.com, Cisco, Microsoft and other technology and internet standard bearers were all subject to successive falls in share values. There followed a prolonged decline in stock market values of technology and internet firms culminating in the loss of some $2 trillion worth of wealth. The value of stocks for Yahoo! in the five-week period between March 10 and April 14, 2000, fell by almost 35%. It was not alone. Amazon.com registered a 30% decline in their stock value, TheGlobe.com 62.5% and e-Bay 27.9%. Throughout the rest of 2000 dot-coms disappeared from the scene as quickly as they had arrived.

The meltdown of the internet economy had serious consequences for Yahoo! and heralded a period of great turmoil for the company. The reliance on online advertising for the bulk of its revenue was the main weakness of the company. By 2000 it had become clear that this business model was not going to be sustainable and that a new strategy was required that focused on Yahoo! as a provider of multi-media services to a broad range of consumer and business clients. The moves that Yahoo! had already made towards being a media company rather than a pure dot-com probably saved the company from sliding into oblivion.

From mid 2000 onwards the emphasis of the company was to provide quality services and concentrate on non-advertising revenue streams. As well as charging fees for access to the search engine, the company also started charging for a range of other services, such as on auction listings. Yahoo! also changed their approach to advertising by building relationships with traditional advertisers that focused on more traditional forms of advertising such as linking portal users to the products they use and offering rewards for feedback or information given. The Corporate Yahoo! initiative underpinned the relationships the company sought with global companies such as Pepsi, McDonald's and Quaker Oats.

Despite all the changes that Yahoo! put in place to restructure and re-energise the company, the financial sector remained unimpressed. Most analysts and investors believed that only a major partnership or merger with another media giant could drag Yahoo! out of its malaise. Several companies were touted as potential suitors for Yahoo!, including Disney, Viacom and Vivendi Universal. However, the management at Yahoo!, and David Yang in particular, steadfastly resisted the merger option.

By 2001 it had become painfully clear that the presence of Koogle and Yang, alongside Chief Operating Officer Jeff Mallett, had become as much a liability as a driving force for Yahoo!. Confidence in their ability to take the company forward had diminished where it mattered most – in the hearts and minds of financiers and investors. Several major management changes followed including resignations from key posts in international markets, such as Savio Chow in China and Mark Rubinstein in Canada. The most significant, however, was when Tim Koogle vacated the CEO position to become vice-chairman of the company in March 2001. By April, a new era at Yahoo! began with the appointment of former Warner Brothers co-chairman Terry Semel as CEO.

The new regime at Yahoo!

When Terry Semel took over as CEO at Yahoo! the first thing that he realised was that the company did not operate much differently from when it first trailblazed its way into the consciousness of net users in the mid 1990s. The company still relied on the power of the brand and the loyalty of users that the brand bought. The management structure was still very centralised just as it had been from the company's inception. Although the number of business units had increased, all budgetary decisions were made by only a few people at the apex of the organisation.

One of the first moves Semel made was to reduce the number of business units to make the firm more manageable, flexible and focused. It also served to reduce costs. He also set about surrounding himself with managers he knew and trusted. Two important approaches to achieving growth were identified. Firstly, to make the existing businesses work better and generate improved revenues, and, secondly, to expand services into new markets where first-mover advantages were still up for grabs. Managers were appointed to oversee the mergers, acquisitions and partnerships that would facilitate these growth strategies.

In many ways the new regime breathed new life into Yahoo! by reinventing the organisation along a clearly defined pathway that featured broad-based media services at its core. Semel ensured that his Hollywood contacts would serve Yahoo! well by tying up deals with a wide range of firms in the creative industries. There was also a move into the music industry with the acquisition of Launch Media, a producer of CD-ROM music magazines and web-based streaming music and video content. Other big deals followed including a lucrative tie-in with Sony where mutual promotional benefits were derived. Importantly, the deals with Sony, Disney and other big media players gave Yahoo! the credibility to pitch for the position of online marketing partner of choice for the giants that ran Hollywood.

The Semel era at Yahoo! heralded some significant changes but the centralised nature of management remained. This was deemed necessary to push through deals quickly. The high number of new initiatives and the rollout of new services required a great deal of speed and flexibility and it was determined early on that this could only be achieved by a streamlined management structure.

Despite the frenzied activity in expanding markets and services, investors remained sceptical. Between 2000 and 2003 the market capitalisation of Yahoo! had declined from $130 billion to just over $5 billion. To turnaround the company's fortunes both metaphorically and literally, Semel undertook to reinvigorate the company not just in the USA, but across the globe. Key markets were identified and resources poured into making them work.

Yahoo! in Europe

Since 2000 Yahoo! has increased operations around the globe, most notably in Europe and the Far East. However, it is only in the USA that the company has reached a critical mass of customers. The European market is seen as crucial to the growth of Yahoo! and has been the focus of much investment by the company. To effect competitive advantage the company has operated a strategy of differentiation in local markets. The acquisition of key firms with specialist knowledge has been a feature of the marketing effort by the company in the European arena. In particular, the 2004 acquisition of e-shopping site Kelkoo for £319 million allowed Yahoo! to expand services into e-tailing and price comparisons. This is in line with the company's aim of expanding the range of services to customers.

Yahoo! Europe vice president Dominique Vidal believes that online customers have come through the learning phase of interacting with companies online and are now highly sophisticated in their choice of website and the value propositions. Competitive advantage is deemed to stem from continuous innovation and the supply of new products and services to customers. Consequently, Yahoo! has been engaged in broadening its portfolio of interactive services including video content, photographic services, music sharing and games consoles.

These services are designed to complement its core offerings of search, e-mail, short message services, news, weather, travel and financial information. To differentiate these offerings Yahoo! has focused on personalisation. This relates the service to the type of information each individual wants to receive, what games they want to play, what music they want to hear and the main search sites they habitually want to access. For example, the firm has a service called Y360 that builds on the personalised MyYahoo! home page. To achieve the aim of personalising services the company has acquired a number of specialist firms in each of the service provision areas. Acquisitions include Flickr (online photo storage), Musicmatch (music sharing) and Inktomi (search technology).

Europe is one of the key battlegrounds for internet heavyweights such as Yahoo!, Amazon.com, Google and e-Bay. All of these companies have expanded their products and services and now compete on what was previously deemed the preserve of one of them. For example, Amazon.com now competes directly with Yahoo! and Google by providing search facilities, e-mail and news services. Yahoo! offers an auction site that competes directly with e-Bay.

In Europe the challenge is to build market share and reach a critical mass of loyal customers. Another strategy for achieving this is to build partnerships with key industry players, especially telecommunications firms. In the USA Yahoo! has a partnership agreement with SBC. This arrangement allows Yahoo! to supply content for the co-branded internet service providers they share with SBC. A similar agreement exists with BT in the UK and others will follow in mainland Europe. All of these ventures in Europe are funded by the growth in advertising revenues, and the rollout of new services is likely to continue so long as that sector remains buoyant.

There is scope for even more growth in online advertising in the European market. In 2005 online advertising spend in Europe was between 1–4% compared to overall internet usage of 15%. Yahoo! intends to exploit the opportunities for gaining more advertising revenue as a means of financing their expansion plans in Europe.

Expansion into China

In 1999 Yahoo! entered the Chinese market trading under the domain name of cn.yahoo.com. The competitive environment in China presented some formidable challenges for the company as it sought to take advantage of the growing market for internet use in the country. These challenges included dealing with one of the most stringent regulatory regimes in the internet economy; the low volume advertising market in China; high market share of domestic internet providers such as Sina and Sohu; and the distinct cultural characteristics of the Chinese market. There were also concerns relating to where effective demand would stem from given that the domestic economy is characterised by low average incomes. Few people have credit cards in China, making payments slow and cumbersome. There are also infrastructure problems to overcome, especially in the area of distribution where delivery times lag significantly behind those seen in the West.

The main factor behind Yahoo! expanding into the Chinese market is the rate of growth of internet users in the country. Figures from the state sponsored China Internet Network Information Center (CNNIC) reveal that there were around 650 000 internet users in China in 1997 (CNNIC, 2003). By 2001 this figure had risen to 22.5 million. In 2005 the estimated number of internet users in the country reached over 100 million. If internet penetration of homes in China reflects growth rates similar to those seen in the West, by 2010 there will be a quarter of a billion internet users. The Chinese Government has recognised the economic potential of the internet and invested heavily in the restructuring of the country's telecommunications infrastructure to facilitate demand for internet services.

As well as the search facilities, Yahoo! offered e-mail, news services, instant messaging, and financial and weather information on the Chinese website. However, the response from Chinese consumers was one of indifference. The service provided by Yahoo! was the same as that provided in other local markets, except for the Chinese language provision. This generic strategy for service provision did not take account of the distinct characteristics of the Chinese market and made no attempt to gain knowledge of exactly what different types of services Chinese consumers wanted from a portal. Since 2001, Yahoo! has been engaged in market research with the aim of gaining a further understanding of the Chinese market and has enlisted the help of local managers to aid the learning process.

The regulatory regime under which Yahoo! had to build a market share also proved problematic. The Chinese Government has recognised the importance of the internet in driving forward the economy, but they have been wary of western companies who seek to influence the dissemination of information throughout the country. Companies such as Yahoo! are at the forefront of testing the boundaries of commercial freedom permitted by the Chinese Government.

In 2002, Yahoo! received criticism from human rights groups by signing a pledge called the 'Public Pledge on Self-discipline for the China Internet Industry' (Maldar, 2004). Although the main part of the pledge focused on promoting healthy competition in the internet industry there was also a clause that required companies to 'abstain from producing, posting or disseminating pernicious information that may jeopardize state security and disrupt social stability'. Whilst critics pointed to the restriction this placed on freedom of expression, managers at Yahoo! took the pragmatic view by accepting that there had to be a compromise on the differences between the business environment in western style democracies and the one that exists in China. The company also took the view that the pledge did not pose any restrictions beyond those already in place under Chinese law.

A more important reason for the initial failure of Yahoo! to penetrate the Chinese market was the reliance of the business model on advertising revenue. Demand for advertising on websites and portals was of such a low level in China that no effective strategy for growth could be built around it. The domestic portals in China had a better knowledge of the trading environment and built business models based around a series of services such as mobile phone ring tones, short message services and online games provision. Crucially, these services proved popular with the affluent and well-educated segment of the Chinese market.

Organisational restructuring at Yahoo! in the wake of the dot-com crash of 2000 also slowed the company's growth in China. One of the casualties was Savio Chow, managing director of Yahoo! Asia and the man responsible for the company's Chinese operations. After the bloodletting, Yahoo! decided to reinvigorate the Chinese operations and in 2003 set about adding to the services the company provided. The core activity of internet search was added to by introducing new functions such as Yellow Pages and geographical search facilities. The company also sought to steal a march on e-Bay by being the first foreign company to enter the growing online auction market.

In response, e-Bay acquired Eachnet, the Chinese auction site that had captured 80% of the market.

A series of acquisitions of key internet businesses in Hong Kong and the USA, alongside collaborations with Chinese firms, enabled Yahoo! to gain the capabilities and market insights to make an impression on the trading environment that was proving much more difficult to crack than anyone at the company had previously envisioned. An important breakthrough came in the form of Hong Kong-based internet firm 3721 Network Software that could provide search facilities using Chinese characters. Yahoo! acquired 3721 for $120 million in 2003 and the synergies provided a compelling proposition for Chinese customers. Yahoo! provided the brand and search technology and 3721 provided the expertise and understanding of the Chinese online market.

Other acquisitions of technology specialists, such as Inktomi and Overture, further enabled Yahoo! to develop its sophisticated search site. These investments ensured that Yahoo! went head-to-head with main rivals Google for market dominance in China among foreign providers. However, both Yahoo! and Google still faced formidable competition from domestic internet service providers.

The venture into the Chinese market has been a steep learning curve for Yahoo!. The company has had to rely on local expertise to gain an understanding of the distinct characteristics of the market. Through a series of acquisitions and partnerships Yahoo! has been able to combine its technical capabilities with the market expertise of others to provide a means of competing effectively in China. Nevertheless, the challenges that face Yahoo! remain strident. The company has to compete within the restrictions imposed by the Chinese Government whilst trying to make an impression against the brand loyalty that local firms had acquired through first-mover advantages. Meanwhile, other foreign companies such as AOL, Microsoft and Amazon.com have also made moves into the Chinese market, thereby further increasing competitive pressures.

Summary

Yahoo! is one of the most recognised brands in the world and certainly a leading force in the internet economy. The combined efforts of internet pioneers Jerry Yang and David Filo ensured that Yahoo! was a first-mover in the development of search facilities for internet users. The growth of Yahoo! from the mid to late 1990s was one of the most remarkable business phenomena of the late twentieth century. That the company survived the dot-com crash of 2000 was testimony to the resilience of the management team that had been assembled and the ability of the company to respond rapidly to changes in a dynamic business environment.

One of the key characteristics of Yahoo! has been the ability of management to continually seek improvement, develop and deliver new and innovative services, form partnerships, share knowledge and reinvent the organisation to take advantage of opportunities in the marketplace. These are the attributes of a modern, technology- and learning-based organisation seeking competitive advantage. Innovation has been at the heart of what Yahoo! is all about. The company has expanded services greatly and is now engaged in e-commerce, e-business, marketing, music and a host of other customer-centred activities. The evolution of Yahoo! has seen the business transformed from a dot-com providing search facilities to a truly global multimedia organisation.

References

Angel, K. (2002). *Inside Yahoo!: reinvention and the road ahead.* John Wiley & Sons, New York, NY.

CNNIC Internet Information (2003). China Internet Update, July 22.

Maldar, F. (2004). Yahoo! in China, The ECCH Collection, Cranfield.

boo.com

Boo.com was an ambitious, but ultimately doomed, venture into the online retailing of designer fashion. The case of boo.com represents one of the most high profile new economy failures and illustrates the need for good old-fashioned business acumen even in a modern, new economy environment. The founders of boo.com were two young Swedish entrepreneurs who had experience of the cultural industries having previously worked variously as models, book publishers and poet festival organisers.

Ernst Malmsten and Kajsa Leander grew up in the southern Swedish town of Lund in the 1970s. Their paths diverged in their late teens as they sought excitement and glamour in the more cosmopolitan and exotic settings of New York, Paris and Milan. Leander found success as a glamour model featuring in top fashion magazines such as Vogue and Elle. Meanwhile, Malmsten discovered a talent for organising cultural festivals and even made a success of introducing Scandinavian poetry to the cultural elite of New York society. A chance meeting in Paris was the beginning of a relationship that was both personal and business orientated.

In 1994, the newly formed company, LeanderMalmsten, ventured into the book publishing industry. Malmsten was confident that the creative input of Leander, combined with his business and organisational skills, would prove a compelling formula for success. Both partners had built up a reputation in the cultural and literary society and could call on a considerable number of contacts for help and advice. The partners were determined to publish books that were not only of literary merit but also of high design quality. Much emphasis was placed on the style of the books including the typography, paper quality, photographic quality, and so on. The emphasis on style and glamour was a feature of the mindset of the partners and was to become a major factor in undermining their later internet venture.

Nevertheless, in the mid 1990s, with most western economies experiencing a boom, the partners spared no cost in marketing and promoting their book publishing venture. At book fairs the company would spend lavishly on hospitality and display design and would treat their authors as superstars. Although the company registered some successes, a few failed book launches was enough to plunge the partners into a financial crisis. The pressure affected their personal relationship and it was decided that henceforth they would be strictly business partners. Much of 1996 was spent trying to fend off the demands of creditors such as printers and photographers.

The first venture into the internet economy for Leander and Malmsten came in 1997 when they expanded their book publishing business to incorporate an online service. The internet bookselling service was called 'bokus' and it achieved around 60 000 customers in the first four months of operations. If the growth of the online business in Sweden was an indicator of what could happen across Europe then it was clear that the potential of the business was huge.

However, the online service was always struggling to raise enough cash to grow the business and eventually the partners sold their shares to Swedish supermarket and publishing giants, KF. Although the partners were disappointed at having to bail out of the venture before its potential was realised, they did have the compensation of becoming millionaires on the back of the sale. Also, the success of the 'bokus' venture gave the partners the business credibility to seek investment backing for their next venture, that of online fashion retailing.

The value proposition of boo.com

In March 1998 the headquarters of LeanderMalmsten was moved to Stockholm and a new era for the company started. The finance from the sale of 'bokus' allowed the partners a greater degree of freedom to explore new ideas. The two entrepreneurs decided on a fashion website that would e-tail designer wear around the globe. The rationale behind the idea was that designer labels were culturally homogeneous, making them as relevant in Tokyo and Taiwan as Los Angeles and Madrid.

The global reach of the internet would facilitate communications with customers no matter where they were located. Having worked in the fashion industry, Kasja Leander was aware that top designer labels were not easily available in many locations, particularly rural or remote regions. She saw the internet as a way of bringing such products to a truly global market. When financial expert Patrik Hedelin joined the company the partnership was complete and the new venture was called boo.com.

Malmsten was convinced that the company had to achieve first-mover advantages to make a success of the venture. Speed to market was, therefore, deemed of crucial importance. The partners saw Europe and the USA as the two principal markets for the online service. The US market was already of sufficient size to merit investment and the European market had a great deal of potential. The target market was 18–24-year-olds. This age group was seen as the trendsetters, would be comfortable using computers, be in employment and have a reasonable level of affluence. In essence, boo.com would bring together both famous brand names and niche brands in fashion and sportswear, such as Lacoste, Tommy Hilfiger, Adidas, Versace, DKNY, Calvin Klein, Nike, etc., and offer customers an online shopping experience that could not be derived elsewhere on the net. As a truly global enterprise, it was decided to relocate the business from Stockholm to London, one of the most fashion-conscious capitals in the world.

Maintaining a relationship between boo.com and the designer labels depended crucially on upholding the value of the brands. To boost confidence, boo.com guaranteed not to discount any of the products. There was also the possibility of extending the reach of brands. The website would facilitate international access to products that were previously only available in the USA or Europe. This global reach would, in turn, extend the value of the brands and draw in more customers. There were also benefits to be derived from using the internet. These include 24-hour access, high level of customer service, more intense relationship with customers, more targeted marketing campaigns and better communications with suppliers, distributors, retailers and customers.

The partners believed that these attributes would attract high numbers of customers from the target market segment. The success of the venture depended on attracting around half a million customers in the first six months from its launch in May 1999. With the help of consultants from J.P. Morgan the company estimated that each customer would spend around $85. After subtracting the costs the margin was estimated to be $30 per customer. The plan was to gain bigger and bigger discounts from suppliers as the customer base grew, and to achieve economies of scale and, therefore, ever-higher margins and profits.

Problems with the boo.com concept

During numerous failed fund raising visits to the USA, the partners were made aware of some concerns regarding the whole boo.com venture. Firstly, in the late 1990s, the European market for online services was in its infancy and there was no sign that e-commerce would mirror the growth seen in the USA. One reason was the reluctance of many Europeans to own and use a credit card, which was, and remains, the most used method of payment for online products and services.

There was also the question of actually convincing people to buy clothes online without trying them on for size. The partners believed that customers would be prepared to pay for clothes that they had only viewed on a screen. Subsequent data suggests that this is indeed the case since clothes are one of the most popular items bought online. However, in the fledgling internet economy of the late 1990s, this was a huge assumption and not one that had any market research to back it up. New technology, such as body scanning to determine 'best fit' was one way round the problem of not actually being able to try clothes on. However, there was no evidence that customers would be prepared to use such technology. Nevertheless, the partners sought out companies that could deliver 3D imaging of sufficient quality and in time for the proposed launch date.

In the first instance the company chose Eriksson to develop and deliver the technology. Although principally a telecommunications company, Eriksson wanted to expand into new growth areas such as the internet. Eriksson was a well-known and respected Swedish company and the partners felt they could trust them to deliver. However, the relationship did not survive beyond the first consultancy fee and the partners had to look elsewhere. The search for a suitable imaging company led them to eVox, specialists in imaging software. Although eVox was able to deliver a workable solution, the whole concept required the co-operation and understanding of the suppliers. It was the suppliers who had to send eVox photographs of each and every item for sale along with the correct size and colour. Very often this proved beyond the capability of the suppliers and left the website bereft of a key differentiating component that would attract and retain customers.

There were a number of other technical challenges that the partners had to overcome if their vision for boo.com was to be realised. What the partners proposed was for boo.com to become a global brand in itself, a gateway to buying designer goods online. The proposal required a sophisticated back-end fulfilment system that guaranteed delivery of goods within set parameters. The fulfilment guarantees had to contend with multiple languages, currencies, methods of payment, tax regulations and links with partner organisations.

There were also numerous different forms of business etiquette to learn and understand, different local customs and a myriad of trade bodies and government departments to deal with. There are also great differences in advertising regulations around the world that meant greater thought had to be given to marketing and promotional campaigns targeted at different countries.

The free access to the internet by users based anywhere in the world posed problems for the company when trying to remain within the regulations set by individual governments in different countries. For example, and ironically, Sweden has one of the most stringent advertising regulatory regimes in the world when it comes to promoting goods for sale to children. Any advertising of children's designer fashion goods online would have to adhere to those regulations set by the Swedish government.

Language can also pose problems. Although English is widely spoken around the world, in France it is prohibited to advertise products or services in the English language. Likewise, vast cultural differences need to be taken into account when accessing global markets.

Perhaps the most intractable problem facing boo.com was to overcome the stranglehold that suppliers had on the fashion industry. In the late 1990s fashion retailers were suspicious of the internet. Retailers believed that the internet was all about reducing costs and prices. For them this meant reducing the value of the brand. Part of that value was the exclusivity of the product. To gain easy access at lower prices, they believed, would simply undermine the brand. Hence, the cold-shoulder treatment meted out to the partners whenever they contacted major fashion retailers.

Designer label and sportswear manufacturers who had global reach already had well-established relationships across the supply chain. These included wholly-owned subsidiaries, licensees, joint ventures or distribution partnerships. Regardless of the type of agreement, each partner invariably enjoys exclusive rights to supplying the products in their particular region. This was a formidable barrier for boo.com to overcome since it would require manufacturers to change their relationships with the suppliers that had served them well for so long in the past. For this reason the majority of companies actively opposed the introduction of third parties entering the supply chain.

Also, internet-based firms generally proposed selling goods at similar prices across the globe, whereas fashion retailers traditionally sold their wares at prices dictated by economic and social conditions prevailing in different countries. To circumvent this boo.com would have to have a different website for each country they sold to, and with prices that reflected conditions in each country.

Finally, there were concerns over keeping costs down. This was especially relevant in dealing with returned goods. Malmsten proposed a scheme where customers could return goods free of charge but it was quickly pointed out that the costs of organising this would prove prohibitive. Established firms in catalogue retailing traditionally had to deal with around a 35% return rate. Customers would often order several sizes of clothes and return the ones that did not fit. The costs of returning items on a global scale would be too much for boo.com to absorb. The investment poured into gaining a 3D photographic imaging capability that would allow customers to 'test for fit' in a virtual environment was seen as a way of largely circumventing the problem of returns.

The launch of boo.com

The lure of the internet in the late 1990s had enticed many entrepreneurs, investors and venture capitalists to support a vast array of different business plans. The value proposition of boo.com was compelling enough for one of Wall Street's most prestigious finance institutions to back the idea. J.P. Morgan had a London office from where the partners discussed the nature of the relationship with the investment bankers. J.P. Morgan were confident that the internet economy would eventually take off in Europe and were keen to steal a march on their rivals by being first to tap into the potential of the new medium.

The running of the business would be left entirely up to the three partners. The proposal from the bank was to raise $100 million in funding from investors over the following 18 months from the launch date of May 1999. It was also estimated that the Initial Public Offering (IPO) would be announced some six months after the launch.

After securing the backing of J.P. Morgan the partners set about the task of persuading the fashion and sportswear industry that the internet was going to revolutionise the industry for the better. This process proved to be laborious, time-consuming, frustrating but, ultimately, necessary for the whole venture to succeed. Slowly but surely more and more companies started to be won over to the potential of the internet. Crucially, the partners had emphasised that the brands would be protected from any discounting.

The partners worked ceaselessly with potential partners on a range of different issues including taxation, advertising, business consultancy, technology provision and logistics. However, the biggest achievement was to bring on board the suppliers. Sportswear suppliers were the first to be persuaded of the benefits of the internet for extending their market reach. New Balance, Converse and North Face had made agreements with boo.com and others quickly followed. The industry was beginning to break away from the very rigid associations that had characterised the supply chain for decades.

By September 1999 Malmsten was boasting to business journalists of the progress the partners had made since the inception of boo.com. The company had six offices around the world; twenty-two suppliers had signed up to the venture; there was an inventory of 11 000 products; the customer service centres had been built; and the website was already attracting significant numbers even before the official launch. The mood of optimism continued throughout the autumn and reached a peak on Wednesday 3rd November 1999 when boo.com was officially launched.

Expectations surrounding the performance of the boo.com website proved to be too high. Although the site attracted reasonable hits, there was no tidal wave of customers logging on to buy into the boo.com experience. The partners had forecast a million visitors to the site on the first day but only 25 000 hits were registered. These generated only eight orders. Worse still was the negative response from the once enthusiastic business press. The most damaging article was written by respected new economy commentator, James Ledbetter (1999). He wrote about the 81 minutes it took him to order a product on boo.com and his struggle to contact customer services. There were a number of technical problems that the company had to overcome quickly. These included very slow download times, computer viruses, a fraud detection system that rejected orders and the fact that Mac users were unable to use the site for ordering products.

The partners knew that funding the venture was going to be an on-going problem unless they were able to solve the technical problems and leverage their marketing effort to reach a critical mass of customers. By Christmas 1999 it was not only the business press that was expressing doubts about the boo.com venture. An indication of the fall from grace that the company had experienced was the cool response to their search for further investment.

Federated Department Stores in the USA was an established bricks-and-mortar company who had desires on entering the internet economy. Initially they were attracted to the trendy and fashionable website that boo.com had built. However, after scrutinising the sales figures, the number of hits the website attracted and the amount of money that the company was soaking up just to stay in business, the would-be investors backed off. Of particular concern was the poor level of sales in the USA. The partners had expected 40% of sales to come from their American site but it only contributed 20%. It was predicted that boo.com would incur losses of just over $100 million for 2000/1. It was clear that the company would need an injection of at least $20 million to keep it in business to February 2000.

Relations with bankers J.P. Morgan had suffered because of the lack of investors being brought to boo.com. However, they were chosen as the bank to lead the company towards their proposed IPO. The bank insisted on some major restructuring of boo.com and a stringent cost-cutting exercise.

By January 2000 the first effects of these measures started to filter through. Whilst job losses would affect most parts of the organisation some parts had to be radically overhauled, or in the case of the online magazine *Boom*, a complete closure of operations ensued. In all, around 50% of staff at the company had lost their jobs by the end of March 2000. The closure of *Boom* was particularly galling for Leander since she was responsible for both developing the magazine and, ultimately, closing it down. *Boom* was generally regarded as the voice of the boo.com concept, the vehicle through which the spirit and vision of the organisation could be communicated to suppliers, customers and employees.

Further humiliation followed when the company offered an end-of-season sale with up to 40% discounts. Although this is normal practice in traditional fashion retailers, boo.com had made promises never to undermine the value of brands through discounting. The fact that all fashion retailers seek to shift excess capacity by doing so cut no ice with business journalists who viewed the moved by boo.com as indicative of the increasing desperation of the partners to get the finances of the company under control.

The end game for boo.com

By early 2000 doubts about the viability of boo.com were growing among investors and business journalists and analysts. To head off the welter of negative publicity surrounding the plight of the company, Malmsten undertook a series of presentations to assure interested parties that there were grounds for optimism regarding the firm's future. He pointed out that conversion rates were running at almost 3% compared to a mere 0.5% pre-Christmas 1999. Speed and accuracy of orders were out-performing the likes of Amazon.com and the gross value of goods sold was on an upward trajectory.

Whilst no one would dispute the figures, the key issue was the financial 'burn rate' of the company. Boo.com had built up significant debts and was spending investment funds at a rate that could not be sustained without further injections of capital from an already sceptical investor community. Even the company's core investors were beginning to harbour fears for the survivability of the company by early 2000.

A contributory factor in the build up of debt was undoubtedly the rather extravagant spending on luxuries by Malmsten and Leander. Whilst other successful dot.coms, such as Amazon.com and e-Bay, located in low cost, out-of-town office space and furnished their premises with cast-off desks and chairs, boo.com spared no expense in location and accommodation. Highly expensive offices in some of the world's most glamorous cities helped to rack up debts.

The partners believed that image was important to the company and set about creating an organisational culture that reflected the up-market and trendy character that they wanted to create for boo.com. The expenses included bills for fresh fruit and flowers delivered to each office on a daily basis, first-class air travel for executives, high quality office furnishing, and lavish hospitality and promotional activities. Malmsten had always been reluctant to divulge the financial position of the company, but when he had no option but to be entirely candid with the company's Chief Financial Officer, Dean Hawkings, the true scale of the financial crisis emerged.

A number of coinciding factors determined the end of the line for boo.com. Firstly, the resignation of Hawkings underlined the lack of confidence in the business by senior executives and precipitated the loss of other key personnel. This, in turn, affected investor confidence at a time when the partners were desperate to find further capital to keep the venture afloat.

Another blow to boo.com was the decision by the much sought after sportswear suppliers, Nike, to agree a deal with a rival online fashion e-tailer. The final nail in the coffin of boo.com was the collapse of the Nasdaq technology index that valued hi-tech firms and dot-coms. On Friday, April 14, 2000 the Nasdaq plummeted by 355 points meaning a devaluation of 10% – the worst fall in its 30-year history. The internet bubble had finally burst.

Summary

The boo.com story provided a salutary lesson for investors and entrepreneurs in the internet economy. In 18 months of trading the company had created offices in five countries, employed 350 staff, and had used up $135 million of investment funding. The partners behind the boo.com venture possessed all the drive, energy, creativity and ambition necessary to be successful in business.

However, there were fundamental errors of judgement and a lack of strict business discipline behind the collapse of the fashion e-tailer. The challenges of having the website fully operational in quick-time to achieve first-mover advantages proved too onerous. The technical difficulties experienced in the initial rollout of the website under-mined the company's ability to achieve a critical mass of customers quickly enough to cover the rising costs. It also took a long time for enough suppliers to agree to support the venture. Big name operators such as Nike proved elusive and created a gap in the portfolio of products available to customers.

The company lacked discipline in terms of financial management and control over spending. The emphasis placed on spending to enhance the company's image was misguided and costly. Although continuous progress was made in conversion rates and turnover, the spiralling costs served to undermine the ability of the company to grow. The aim of the company as stated by co-founder, Ernst Malmsten, was to grow as big as possible as quickly as possible. This was the aim of other internet companies such as Amazon.com. However, the business model of Amazon.com was much less complicated than that proposed by boo.com.

A great deal of time and money was expended fire-fighting problems from day one. The problems manifested themselves throughout the organisation and included technical glitches, personnel losses, legal disputes, government regulations, supplier contracts, distribution networks, and so on.

Finally, the relationship with the key backer J.P. Morgan proved to be less than satisfactory for the company. The investment bank was an organisation that had built its reputation in the old economy, whereas boo.com represented the cutting edge of the new economy; that is, high risk, entrepreneurial, fast paced and technology driven.

The collapse of boo.com and many other dot-coms during the internet crash of 2000 heralded the beginning of a new era for the internet economy. The initial rush to invest in new internet businesses has been replaced by a more cautious approach by investors. Internet entrepreneurs have their business plans scrutinised much more closely by potential backers before funding commitments are made.

The legacy of boo.com and other failed ventures has been to introduce a greater sense of realism in the internet economy. There are significant advantages to be gained by trading online that benefit companies and customers. However, for businesses to gain advantage from trading online requires the same business acumen and discipline as traditional forms of doing business. Perhaps this has been the biggest lesson learned from the experience of failed dot-coms such as boo.com.

Reference

Ledbetter, J. (1999). Driving Miss Boo. *The Industry Standard*, 4 November, pp. 24–5. IDG Publications: San Francisco, CA.

Glossary

Affiliate A business model based on e-tailers paying commission on sales referred by other sites.

Auction A business model based on bids for products.

Bandwidth Speed at which data is transferred (measured in bits/second).

Bluetooth System for enabling unification of communications across different electronic systems.

Brand Characteristics of a product as perceived by the consumer.

Branding Creation of a brand.

Bricks-and-mortar Traditional organisation with physical premises.

Broadband Digital data transfer mechanism.

Bundling Linking complementary products or services.

Burn rate Speed at which an organisation uses up investment funds.

Business model Framework for developing a business proposition.

Business process improvement (BPI) Process of maximising current capabilities with the aid of information, communications technologies.

Business process re-engineering (BPR) Radical alteration to the process of doing business, usually involving new technologies.

Buy-side e-commerce Online transactions between a trading organisation and its customers and suppliers.

Certificate authorities Trusted third party that makes public-keys available to organisations to ensure security.

Change management Managing change in an organisation by altering processes, organisational structure, human resources, technical resources and organisational culture.

Clicks and mortar Mix of online and offline capabilities.

Click-through Process of navigating from website to web pages.

Client-server An architecture that includes client computers sharing resources that are stored on server computers.

Competitor analysis The process of gaining and building knowledge on competitors.

Connectivity Participation in an electronic network.

Content The design of a web page – graphical and text.

Convergence The merging of communications media hardware such as television, telephone, and computers.

Conversion rate The rate at which website 'hits' are transformed into sales.

Cookies Small text files stored on an end-user's computer to enable websites to identify them.

Core competencies Resources employed by an organisation that provide distinct advantages to consumers.

Culture Shared values, beliefs and norms of behaviour that characterise the internal environment of organisations.

Customer acquisition Techniques for acquiring new customers.

Customer extension Techniques for encouraging existing customers to increase their involvement with an organisation.

Customer profile Characteristics that help to segment a customer.

Customer relationship management (CRM) Building long-term and intensive relationships with customers, usually with the aid of information and communications technologies.

Customer retention Techniques for retaining existing customers.

Database A collection of related information organised and stored together for easy search and retrieval.

Data mining Searching databases to discern patterns and trends.

Data protection Privacy of consumers' data underpinned by law.

Data warehouses Large database system for storing large amounts of information.

Denial-of-service Security breach leading to failure to access internet sites.

Digital authorities Designated organisations for issuing digital certificates authenticating e-businesses.

Digital certificates Issued by Digital authorities to authenticate an e-business.

Digital divide The gap between those who have access to ICTs and the internet and those who do not.

Digital economy Economic wealth created through development and sale of digital products and services.

Digital signature A public-key encryption method of identifying an individual.

Disintermediation Process of removing an intermediary from the supply chain.

Disruptive technologies New technologies that require firms to review their current business practices.

Domain name The name given to a web server, usually the same as the company name or a derivation thereof.

Dot-coms Businesses who trade using the internet.

Downstream supply chain Transactions that take place between an organisation and its customers and its intermediaries.

Dynamic pricing Up-dating prices in real-time in response to changing trading conditions.

E-business Information exchanges for business purposes using electronic media.

E-business strategy A formal approach to utilising the internet to achieve stated aims.

E-commerce Exchange of products and services via electronic media.

Economies of scale Benefits gained when increasing volume results in lower costs.

Economies of scope Rate at which relationships are leveraged to add value to customers.

E-government Use of the internet to provide government services for the public.

E-mail Use of the internet for sending and receiving messages or documents.

E-marketing Use of the internet to achieve marketing objectives.

E-marketplace A virtual marketplace where buyers and sellers can meet to effect transactions.

E-marketspace The scope for undertaking electronic trading in virtual markets.

Encryption Coding information for protection against unauthorised access and reading.

e-procurement Use of the internet to manage procurement including purchases, authorisation, ordering, delivery and payment between buyer and supplier.

e-tailers Organisations who retail products and services using the internet.

Explicit knowledge Knowledge that can be expressed and recorded within information systems.

Externalities Costs or benefits gained for which there is no compensation or extra charge.

Extranet Communications channel for exclusive use of customers, suppliers and partners.

Firewall A system component that sits between an organisation's network and the external world to prevent unauthorised access.

Fulfilment The delivery of a customer's order.

Globalisation Increasing levels of international trade.

Hackers Individuals who break into systems illegally.

Hardware Physical components of a computer system.

Hits Recorded request for graphic or text from a web server.

Home page Main page of a website.

Host Server that is hooked up to the internet.

Hub Large-scale computing facility for feeding local services.

Hyperlink A method of moving between one web page and another.

Infomediary A company that specialises in the collection and analysis of information that is of value to other companies.

Information infrastructure The hardware that supports ICTs and the internet, such as telecommunications systems.

Intellectual property Ownership of property created by intellectual, creative or innovative means.

Interactive television Electronic communication between television viewer and content on television screen.

Interactivity Communications, dialogue or other form of contact between customers and a company via the internet.

Intermediary An organisation or individual who brings together buyers and sellers.

Internet Global network of computer networks using a common protocol.

Internet economy Economy activity related to trading on the internet.

Internet diffusion Extent of internet access.

Internet protocol Agreed set of rules and routines for sending data through the internet.

Internet pureplay A company that trades solely using the internet.

Interoperability The capability of making dissimilar systems work together.

Intranet A network within an organisation for exclusive use by people within the organisation.

Java A program language standard for writing complex and graphical customer applications.

Jini Program language that allows communication.

Just-in-time Logistics management system for maximising efficiency.

Killer application An application of the internet that creates and sustains a competitive advantage.

Knowledge management Techniques and tools for disseminating knowledge within an organisation.

Localisation Customising products or services to meet local demand characteristics.

Logistics Planning and organisation of movements in resources.

M-commerce Commerce using mobile technology such as cellphones, PDAs or laptops.

Metcalfe's Law Law that states that the utility or satisfaction gained from a network or website increases exponentially with the number of users.

Middleware Software used to facilitate communication between business applications.

Moore's Law Law that states that the density of microprocessors doubles every two years while costs decrease.

Navigation Ability to move between pages on a website.

Network infrastructure Activities that maintain and support e-business such as IT specialists, computer programmers and Internet Service Providers.

Network organisation An organisation that acts as a hub bringing together geographically dispersed workers for specific tasks.

New economy Economic activity created by exploiting Information and Communications Technologies (ICTs) such as the internet.

Non-repudiation System that prevents denial of trade by any party to a transaction.

Old economy Economic activity in traditional and non-ICT activities, sometimes referred to as bricks-and-mortar.

One-to-one marketing Marketing communication between a company and an individual.

Online Actively engaged in using the internet.

Online community A community of people who access an internet website for similar reasons.

Opt-in Choose to receive information via the internet.

Opt-out Choose not to receive information via the internet.

Outbound logistics Part of the value chain dealing with the movement of products or information to customers.

Outsourcing Contracting of functional tasks to a third party.

Payment systems Methods of transferring funds electronically.

Permission marketing Customer agrees to receive marketing information through electronic means.

Personalisation Customised content delivered direct to an individual.

Portal A website that is a gateway to information on the internet, usually in the form of search engines, directories or other services.

Pricing strategies Approaches to pricing models' policies by firms.

Privacy The right of an individual to control the dissemination of information about them held by third parties.

Privacy statements A web page that explains how a company intends to protect the privacy of its customers.

Public-key A unique identifier of a buyer or seller that is available to other parties to enable secure e-commerce using encryption based on digital certificates.

Public key encryption An asymmetric form of encryption in which keys or digital certificates used by the sender and receiver of information are different. The pair of keys have to be used together to encrypt and decrypt information.

Reintermediation The creation of new intermediaries between customers and suppliers.

Risk management Evaluation and management of strategies to reduce risk.

Scalability Capability of a system to adapt to increasing levels of demand placed upon it.

Search engines Automated tools using keywords to search for web pages.

Sell-side e-commerce E-commerce transactions between a supplier and its customers.

Software Instructions in programs that control the operations of a computer system.

Spam Unsolicited e-mail, sometimes referred to as junk e-mail.

Strategic analysis Collection and review of information pertaining to an organisation's internal processes and resources, and external environmental factors that highlight strategic performance.

Strategy Formal course of action designed to achieve stated aims.

Strategy evaluation Process of evaluating performance of key strategic indicators in an organisation.

Strategy formulation Process of undertaking internal and external analysis to form strategic options and help managers choose appropriate course of action to achieve stated aims.

Strategy implementation Formal process of implementing a chosen course of action to achieve stated aims.

System A collection of interrelated components that combine to achieve a stated objective.

Upstream supply chain Transactions between an organisation and its suppliers and intermediaries (buy-side e-commerce).

Usenet newsgroups Electronic bulletin board.

Value chain Model for analysing how supply chain activities add value to products and services.

Value network Links between an organisation and its partners that form an external value chain.

Viral marketing E-mail used for communicating promotional messages.

Virtual organisation An organisation that uses information and communications technologies to operate and carry out functions without clearly defined physical or geographical boundaries.

Virtual reality A graphical representation of real environments.

Web browser Method of accessing and viewing information on websites.

Web page Visual information in graphical or text form on a website.

Websites Pages of information stored on the internet.

Acronyms

3G Third generation mobile telephone technology.

4G Fourth generation mobile telephone technology.

4GL Fourth generation languages.

ADSL Assymetric Digital Subscriber Line – a means of increasing bandwidth of existing copper cables by using a greater range of frequencies than traditional telephony.

AI Artificial intelligence.

B2B Business-to-business online trading.

B2B marketplace Virtual markets for businesses who trade with other businesses.

B2C Business-to-consumer online trading.

B2G Business-to-government online trading.

C2C Consumer-to-consumer online communications and trading.

CGI Common Gateway Interface – facilitates online interactivity.

EAI Enterprise Applications Integration – software that integrates front- and back-office applications.

EDGE Enhanced Data Rates for Global Evolution – transmission speed for mobile phones.

EDI Electronic Data Interchange – the exchange of structured business information using electronic or digital media.

ERP Enterprise Resource Planning – software that allows the integration of all the processes in an organisation by storing all the transactional data in a central database.

Gbps One gigabyte per second.

GPRS General Packet Radio Service – transmission speed for mobile phones.

GSM Global System for Mobile Communication – transmission speed for mobile phones.

HTML Hypertext Markup Language – a standard that defines the text and layout of web pages.

HTTP Hypertext Transfer Protocol – a standard that defines the way information is transmitted across the internet between web browsers and web servers.

ICTs Information and communications technologies.

IP Internet protocol – a system that facilitates the convergence of voice and video with existing forms of internet communication such as e-mail.

IPO Initial Public Offering – the first offering of shares in a company that is made available to the public.

IPTV Television programmes delivered over the internet.

ISP Internet Service Provider – company that provides homes and businesses with access to the internet.

LAN Local area network.

MP3 A file format for storing and sharing music.

OBI Open Buying on the Internet – an architecture for business-to-business procurement systems.

OOP Object-orientated programming – languages that bind together the data elements and procedures to be performed upon them to create objects.

P2P Peer-to-peer – where each party has the same capabilities for initiating communications over a network.

PDA A hand-held electronic device with a range of capabilities such as notebook, calendar, addresses, etc.

Perl Practical Execution and Report language – used for server-side scripting and producing Common Gateway Interface scripts.

PKI Public-key infrastructure – infrastructure of organisations and technology that allows public-key encryption to be used.

SCM Supply Chain Management – the planning, control and co-ordination of all supply activities in an organisation.

SET Secure Electronic Transaction – a standard public-key encryption for securing e-commerce transaction developed by Mastercard and Visa.

SGML Standard Generalized Markup Language – a way of describing the treatment of any kind of document in a processing system.

SMS Short Message Service – text messaging.

SSL Secure Sockets Layer – an encryption technique for scrambling data sent over the internet between a customer's web browser and a seller's web browser.

TCO Total Cost of Ownership – the sum of all costs associated with managing information systems.

TCP Transmission Control Protocol – set of rules for disassembling and reassembling a file for transmission.

UMTS Universal Mobile Telecommunications System – third generation transmission speed for mobile phones.

URL Universal Resource Locators – a web address used to locate a web page on a web server.

VAN Value added network – a secure wide-area network that uses proprietary technology.

Voip Voiceover internet protocol – a means of making telephone calls over the internet.

WAP Wireless Applications Protocol – a technical standard for transferring information to wireless devices such as mobile phones and PDAs.

Wi-fi Wireless-fidelity – a high-speed local area network enabling wireless access to the internet.

Wimax High-speed, wide-reach broadband service for mobile internet.

WWW World Wide Web – most used technique for publishing information on the internet.

XML Extensible Markup Language – a standard for transferring structured data.

List of Companies

account4.com
aeroflight.co.uk
Alfred McAlpine
AltaVista
Amazon.com
Ananova
AOL
Apple
Ariba
AskJeeves.com
Baidu.com
Barnes & Noble
BBC
befree.com
birdguides.com
Bloomingdales
boo.com
Boots
BPB
British Telecommunications (BT)
BSkyB
Cahoot
Charles Schwab
ChemConnect.com
Chemdex
Chrysler Daimler
Cisco
CommerceNet

CommerceOne
Costco
covia.com
Covisint
dealtime.co.uk
Dell
DHL
Disney
Dow Chemical
easyJet
e-Bay
EchoBay.com
empiredirect.com
e-Steel
eutilia.com
Fedex
Ford
Forrester
Freeserve
FriendsReunited.com
General Motors
Glasses Direct
GlaxoSmithKline
Google
Hewlett Packard
Hilton Group
homewinemaking.co.uk
Hotmail

IBM
imdb.com
Intel
IQNC
kelkoo.co.uk
K-mart
lastminute.com
letsbuyit.com
Levi Strauss
Lycos.com
Marks and Spencer
matrixone.com
Mercata.com
Microsoft
Mondex
Motley Fool
Napster
Nokia
nurserygoods.com
oag.com
OneSwoop.com
onevillage.com
onsale.com
Open Buying on the Internet
Oracle
orchid.org.uk
ParadisePoker.com
PartyPoker.com
Pilkington
Post Office

Priceline.com
pricerunner.co.uk
ratemyteachers.co.uk
Reed Elsevier
reviewcentre.co.uk
Ryanair
Saga
Sainsbury's
SAP
Sina.com
Sony
spec2000.com
spoilt4choice.com
Sportingbet
stamp.co.uk
steampics.com
Sun Microsystems
teamdigital.com
Tesco.com
Toshiba
UPS
Verdict
Verisign.com
verticalnet.com
Wanadoo.com
wipro.com
YouGov
Zanussi
Zen Internet

Index